ORDER AND HISTORY

VOLUMES IN THE SERIES

I. Israel and Revelation

II. The World of the Polis

III. Plato and Aristotle

IV. The Ecumenic Age

V. In Search of Order

Volume Four – The Ecumenic Age

ERIC VOEGELIN

ORDER AND HISTORY

VOLUME FOUR

The Ecumenic Age

LOUISIANA STATE UNIVERSITY PRESS
BATON ROUGE AND LONDON

ISBN 0–8071–0081–1
Library of Congress Catalog Card Number 56–11670
Copyright © 1974 by Louisiana State University Press
Manufactured in the United States of America
Set in Linotype Granjon
by Typoservice, Indianapolis, Indiana

1990 printing

Coniugi Dilectissimae

In consideratione creaturarum non est vana et peritura curiositas exercenda; sed gradus ad immortalia et semper manentia faciendus.

(In the study of creature one should not exercise a vain and perishing curiosity, but ascend toward what is immortal and everlasting.)

ST. AUGUSTINE, *De Vera Religione*

Acknowledgment

The study on Historiogenesis has previously been published in a German version in the *Festschrift fuer Alois Dempf* (Munich, 1960) and again as a chapter in my *Anamnesis* (Munich, 1966). The present English version has been increased in size by about one half.

The completion of *Order and History* has been unduly delayed during the years when I had to organize and direct the new Institute for Political Science in Munich. The administrative duties seriously impaired the time left for scholarly work. After my retirement from Munich I was awarded the Henry Salvatori Distinguished Scholarship of the Hoover Institution. The leisure this Scholarship permitted made the completion of the work possible. I want to express my thanks to Mr. Henry Salvatori as well as to Dr. Glenn Campbell, Director of the Hoover Institution.

Table of Contents

	Introduction	1
Chapter 1	Historiogenesis	59
Chapter 2	The Ecumenic Age	114
Chapter 3	The Process of History	171
Chapter 4	Conquest and Exodus	212
Chapter 5	The Pauline Vision of the Resurrected	239
Chapter 6	The Chinese Ecumene	272
Chapter 7	Universal Humanity	300
	Index	337

Analytical Table of Contents

Introduction   1

Linear Time and Axis Time: Cultural Diffusion. Linear Speculation. Jaspers and Toynbee. Mankind and Mystery (2). *The Beginning and the Beyond:* Historiogenesis. Stratification of Consciousness. The Presence of Divine Reality. Two Modes of Experience. Cosmological Myth and Cosmogonic Myth. The Secondary Field of Differentiations (7). *The Tension of Consciousness—Plato, Aristotle, Israel:* The Philosopher's Myth. The Infinite Cosmos. The Creative Beginning (11). *The Tension in the Gospel of John:* The Word of the Beginning and the World of the Beyond. The Presence of the "I am." The *ego eimi* Sayings. The Death of the Beginning and the Life of the Beyond. The language of Revelation and the Myth of Creation. The Gnostic Influences in John (13). *The Balance Lost–Gnosticism:* Essential Core and Variable Parts. The Impact of Empire. The Contraction of Divine Order. Multicivilizational Piety. Syncretistic Spiritualism. The Hymn of the Pearl. The Israelite-Judaic Exodus. Magic Pneumatism. The Loss of Balance (20). *The Balance Regained—Philo:* The Mystery of the Cosmos Recovered. Philo's Allegoresis. His Cosmopolites. Philo's Pattern of Inadequate Analysis (27). *Allegoresis:* Origin of the Symbolism. Literal and Underlying Meaning. The Encounter of Philosophy with the Torah (33). *The Deformation of Philosophy into Doctrine:* The Classic Rejection, the Stoic Acceptance, of Allegoresis. The Stoic "Dreams." Spiritual Insecurity. The Literalization of Mythopoetic Symbols. The Stoic Materialism. Propositional Metaphysics (36). *Religion:* Cicero's Introduction of the Symbolism. Doctrinal Theology. Ecumenic Spiritualism. Cicero's Confession of Faith. Tertullian on the Plurality of Religions. Stoic Doctrine as a Millennial Constant (43). *Scripture:* The Torah as a Protective Device. The Cosmogony of Genesis. *Creatio ex nihilo.* Wisdom, in Proverbs, in Sirach. The "Fear of the Lord." Wisdom and Torah. The Word of Creation. The Torah as Scripture. The Deformation of the Word of God and of History (48). *Conclusion* (57).

Chapter 1   Historiogenesis   59

§ 1. MYTHO-SPECULATION   60

The Quest of the Ground. Theogony, Anthropogony, Cosmogony, Historiogenesis, Equivalence to Philosophy of Being. Pragmatic Historiography, Mythopoesis, Noetic Speculation. The Roman Case.

§ 2. HISTORIOGENETIC SPECULATION   64

Motives. Sumerian King List. The Timeless Line of Time. Hegel. Its Ubiquity. Millennial Constant.

§ 3. EXISTENCE AND NON-EXISTENCE   67

1. *The Primary Experience of the Cosmos*   68
Intra-Cosmic Divinity. The Ruler under God. Hatshepsut. Crisis of Empire and Noetic Advance. Existence out of Non-Existence. Eliade's *statisation du devenir.* Leibniz' Questions. Between Something and Nothing.

2. *The Cosmological Style of Truth*   75
Instability of the Style. The In-Between Reality of the Cosmos. The Dynamics of Disruption. Kant.

3. *The Modes of Time*   78
The Lasting of Reality. The Multiple Modes of Lasting. Cyclical Time. Eternal Recurrence. Celestial Cycles. The Great Year. The Hierarchy of Times.

§ 4. NUMBERS AND AGES   82

Projection of History into Past and Future. Numerical Speculation. The Sumerian King List. Berossus. Israelite Speculations. Declining Ages and the Fall.

§ 5. IMPERIAL MEDIATION OF HUMANITY

The Survival of Historiogenesis. Empire and the Truth of Humanity. The Turin Papyrus and the Palermo Stone. Antiochus Soter. The Israelite Case.

§ 6. THE HELLENIC CASE–EUHEMERUS' *Historia Sacra*   101

The Non-Imperial Civilization. Hesiod. Herodotus. The Hellenistic Sequel. Egyptian Influences. *Hiera Anagraphe*.

§ 7. HISTORIOMACHY   109

Berossus and Manetho. Dionysius of Halicarnassus and Josephus Flavius. Clement of Alexandria. Eusebius.

Chapter 2   The Ecumenic Age   114

§ 1. THE SPECTRUM OF ORDER   115
Temporal and Spiritual Order. Ethnic Societies and Ecumenic-Imperial Society.

§ 2. THE PRAGMATIC ECUMENE—POLYBIUS   117

Imperial Expansion. Persia-Macedon-Rome. Polybius on Empire: The Course of Pragmatic Events; the Spectacle of Conquest; the Ecumene; General History. Ecumene: Cultural, Pragmatic, Jurisdictional, Messianic. The Telos of Pragmatic History. Rome and the Cycle of Constitutions. Fortune. Ecumenic Empire and Ecumenic Age.

§ 3. THE SPIRITUAL ECUMENE   134

1. *Paul*   134
The Salvational Telos of the Ecumene. The Temptation of Christ. Missionary Fervor. The Ecumene to Come. The Delay of the Parousia. Ecumenicity and Universality.

2. *Mani*   138
The Sequence of Messengers. Regional Limitations and Ecumenicity. Unwritten and Written Wisdom. The Ecumenic Paraclete. Succession of Empires and Succession of Religions.

3. *Mohammed*   142
The Convergence of Empire and Church. The Byzantine and Sassanian Models. The Seal of the Prophets. The War of Ecumenic Truth.

§ 4. THE KING OF ASIA   145

1. *Achaemenian Prologue*   146
The Dissociation of Cosmological Order into Power and Spirit. Literalist Derailment. *De facto* Ecumenism. Ecumenic Literalism from Cyrus to Xerxes. The Truth of Ahuramazda. The Autolouange of Darius. The Persepolis daiva Inscription of Xerxes.

2. *Alexander*   153
Motives of the Campaign. Alexander's Letter to Darius. Plutarch on Alexander. Opis. Homonoia. The Marriage Feast of Susa. Proskynesis. The Divine Fire. Alexander's Divinity. Aristotle. The Oracle of Ammon. Pothos.

3. *Graeco-Indian Epilogue*   165
The Maurya Empire. The Kingdom of Bactria. Demetrius. The Title Soter. Eucratides.
Menander's Kingdom.

Chapter 3   The Process of History   171

§ 1. THE PROCESS OF REALITY   171

1. *The Subject of History*   172
The In-Between Reality of History. The Identification of Subjects—Augustine, Hegel.
The Two Histories. Toynbee.
2. *Anaximander's Truth of the Process*   174
Apeiron and Time. Mortals, Immortals. The Metaxy of Existence. Tragical Meditation.
3. *The Field of Noetic Consciousness*   176
Truth and Things. The Discovery of Consciousness. Psyche-Depth-Nous-Philosophy. The
Truth of the Search.

§ 2. THE DIALOGUE OF MANKIND   178

1. *Herodotus*   178
The Wheel of Human Affairs. The Imperial Entrepreneurs. Success and Envy of the
Gods. The Divided Self. Concupiscential Exodus.
2. *Thucydides*   181
The Melian Dialogue. Tragic Consciousness and Untragic Vileness. The Succession of
Empire and the Senselessness of History.
3. *Plato*   183
The Revelatory Character of Symbols. The One and the Unlimited. Noetic Conscious-
ness. Diotima. The Dialogue of the Soul. The Continuity of the Dialogue in Society and
History.
4. *Aristotle*   187
Constitution of Meaning in History. Before-and-After. The Irreversibility of Meaning.
Equivalences of Symbolic Forms. From Apeiron to Nous. The Noetic Movement.
Metaleptic Reality. Myth and Philosophy. The Modern Revolt against the Dialogue.

§ 3. JACOB BURCKHARDT ON THE PROCESS OF HISTORY   192

Selfishness of Evaluation. Egoism and Infantilism. Ethics and the Plethos. The Moralist
Apocalypse. Metaleptic Consciousness and the Unconscious.

§ 4. EXPANSION AND RETRACTION   197

1. *The Pseudo-Aristotelian* De Mundo   198
Concupiscential and Spiritual Exodus. Truth and Power. Cosmos and Empire.
2. Oikoumene *and* Okeanos—*The Horizon in Reality*   201
Homeric and Imperial Ecumene. Ecumenes in the Plural. The Habitat of Man. The
Horizon. Okeanos: The Divine Border of the Ecumene. The Horizon from Homer to
Alexander. Knowledge and Conquest. The Plurality of Ecumenic Empires.
3. *The Polybian Symbolism Resumed*   207
The Roman Perspective. The Meaning of the Telos. Ecumenic Consciousness in the Re-
stricted Empires. Ecumenic Society and Civilization. The Global Ecumene. Thomas More.
Cusanus.

Chapter 4   Conquest and Exodus   212

§ 1. EXODUS WITHIN REALITY   214

The Non-Finality of Ecumenic Finality. The Receding Horizon. Reality Moving toward
Eminent Reality. Participation in the Directional Flux of Reality. Plato and Aristotle on
the Factors beyond Human Control. The Paradigms.

§ 2. PLATO ON HISTORY 218

Cosmic Rhythm and Uniqueness of Meaning. The *Laws* on History. The Hellenic Federation. Ethnos and Multicivilizational Empire. Civilizational Progress. The Plurality of Civilizations. The Lasting of the Cosmos and the Limits of Memory. The Cosmic Cataclysms. The Ages of Cronos, Zeus, and Nous.

§ 3. THE BALANCE OF CONSCIOUSNESS 227

Lasting and Transfiguration. The Postulate of Balance. Reason and Revelation. The Theophanic Event. Messengers—Old Gods—Father God. The Hyperouranion. The Platonic Uncertainties. The Beyond. The Danger of Gnosticism. The Exodus into Ecumenic Death. The Intelligibility of Reality Revealed.

Chapter 5 The Pauline Vision of the Resurrected 239

§ 1. THE PAULINE THEOPHANY 240

1. *Noetic and Pneumatic Theophany* 241
From Anaximander's *phthora* to Paul's *aphtharsia*. Plato and Paul on the Structure of Reality. Vision, not Dogma.
2. *Vision and Reason* 244
Pneumatic Center and Noetic Periphery. The Code for Tongue-Speakers. Pauline-Aristotelian Equivalents. Participation and Anticipation.
3. *Death and Transfiguration* 247
Vision and Hope. Vision, the Beginning of Transfiguration. The Tale of Death.
4. *The Truth of the Pauline Myth* 249
Compact Types of Myth. The Pauline Differentiation. The Dynamics of Theophany.
5. *Truth and History* 251
The Classic Consciousness of History. The Theophanic Turbulence in Reality. Theophanic Turbulence and Man-Made Revolution. *Aphtharsia* through Revolution. The New Christs. Transfiguration as an Historical Constant.
6. *The Truth of Transfiguration* 256
The Vision of the Resurrected and the Presence of God. The Apostle. The Self-Analysis of Romans 7. Abraham and Paul. History of Faith. The Distribution of Revelation over Israel and Hellas. The Open Field of Theophany and Dogmatic Construction.

§ 2. THE EGOPHANIC REVOLT 260

1. *The Egophanic Deformation of History* 260
The Construction of Egophanic History. The Ancient Gigantomachia and the Modern Christs. Hegel's Forcing the Parousia into History. The Definition of Chalcedon Inverted. Egophany Dogmatized. Participation and Identification. Modern Deculturation. Revelation Delivered Speculatively.
2. *The Constancy of Transfiguration* 266
Paul's Metastatic Interpretation of his Vision. The Non-Occurrence of the Parousia. Augustine's *saeculum senescens*. Otto of Freising and Joachim of Flora. Petrarca's Dark Age. The Degradation of Symbols into Systems. The Mystery of Transfiguration in Reality. The Bias in Reality toward More Reality.

Chapter 6 The Chinese Ecumene 272

§ 1. THE HISTORIOGRAPHIC FORM 274

Historiogenetic Speculation. Chinese Traditional and Modern Critical History. Genealogical Construction. The *té*. The Shang Dynasty. The Five-Hundred-Year Periods. The Thinkers as Successors to the Kings.

§ 2. THE SELF-DESIGNATION OF THE ECUMENE 282

Chung-kuo, chung-hua, t'ien-hsia. The Near Eastern Cosmological Form. The Identity of China and Mankind.

§ 3. THE INCOMPLETE BREAKTHROUGH   285

Max Weber on China. The Conflicting Opinions on Chinese Philosophy, Science, and Religion. The Muted Differentiation.

§ 4. SYMBOLS OF POLITICAL ORDER   287

The Western Rise and Fall of Empire and the Chinese Internal Periods. The *wang* and the *t'ien-hsia.* The *Po-hu-t'ung* on Pre-imperial Kingship.

§ 5. T'IEN-HSIA AND KUO   291

The Pre-established Harmony between *t'ien-hsia* and *kuo.* Expansion by Cultural Attraction. The Sets of Symbols. Power Organization and Cultural Substance. Mencius on *t'ien-hsia* and *kuo.* The Historical Course.

§ 6. CYCLES   296

The Dynastic Cycle. The Five-Hundred-Year Cycle. The Cycle of Sages. From Clan Society to the Ecumene of Civilized Mankind.

Chapter 7   Universal Humanity   300

§ 1. THE WESTERN ECUMENIC AGE   300

Characteristics of the Western Configuration. The Field of Disorder and the Realm to Come. The Phantasy of Two Realities. The Truth of Order Emerging. The Insights Gained.

§ 2. ESCHATOLOGY AND EARTHLY EXISTENCE   304

The Plurality of Ecumenic Ages. Universal Mankind, an Eschatological Index. Participation in the Divine Flux of Presence. Material Civilization and Differentiation of Consciousness. Plato, Feng Hu Tzu, Lucretius. History as the Ecumenic Horizon. The Triad of Ecumenic Empire, Spiritual Outburst, and Historiography.

§ 3. ABSOLUTE EPOCH AND AXIS-TIME   308

Hegel's Absolute Epoch in Christ, Jaspers' Axis-Time. The Jaspers-Bultmann Debate on Demythization. The State of Experiential Analysis.

§ 4. THE EPOCH AND THE STRUCTURE OF CONSCIOUSNESS   313

The Horizon of Divine Mystery. The Events of Consciousness and the Consciousness of the Events. Eschatology. The Modes of Universal Participation.

§ 5. QUESTION AND MYSTERY   316

The Question as a Symbolism *sui generis.* The Question in the Primary Experience of the Cosmos. Cosmological Construction from the Ground. The Ascending Question of the Upanishadic Type. *The Apocalypse of Abraham.* The Divine Beyond and the Divine Within. The Consciousness of Epoch. Apocalyptic Brutality. The Question as a Constant Structure in the Experience of Reality. Trust in Cosmic Order and the Differentiating Question. The Response of the Buddha. The Question and Epoch. The Mystery of Reality.

§ 6. THE PROCESS OF HISTORY AND THE PROCESS OF THE WHOLE   330

The Question in the Metaxy. Openness to Reality and Contraction of the Self. The Long Breath of History. What is Worth Remembering about the Present. The Length of Time. The Stop-History Movements. The Interdict on the Question. The Process of the Whole. The Fallacies of Time. The Eschatological Direction.

Index   337

The Ecumenic Age

Introduction

The present volume, *The Ecumenic Age,* breaks with the program I have developed for *Order and History* in the Preface to Volume I of the series. I shall, therefore, recall the program and indicate both the nature and the cause of the break.

The opening sentence of the Preface formulated the principle that was to govern the projected six volumes of the study: "The order of history emerges from the history of order." History was conceived as a process of increasingly differentiated insight into the order of being in which man participates by his existence. Such order as can be discerned in the process, including digressions and regressions from the increasing differentiation, would emerge, if the principal types of man's existence in society, as well as the corresponding symbolisms of order, were presented in their historical succession.

Following the statement of the principle then, I enumerated the types of order to be covered by the study. They were:

(1) The imperial organizations of the Ancient Near East and their existence in the form of the cosmological myth;

(2) The revelatory form of existence in history, developed by Moses and the prophets of the Chosen People;

(3) The polis and the Hellenic myth, and the development of philosophy as the symbolism of order;

(4) The multicivilizational empires since Alexander, and the emergence of Christianity;

(5) The modern national state, and the emergence of modern Gnosticism as the symbolic form of order.

In carrying out the program, the volumes on I. *Israel and Revelation,* II. *The World of the Polis,* and III. *Plato and Aristotle* treated the first three of the types enumerated; the remaining two types were to be treated in the subsequent volumes: IV. *Empire and Christianity,* V. *The Protestant Centuries,* and VI. *The Crisis of Western Civilization.*

The study could not be brought to the projected conclusion. As the work on the second sequence of volumes progressed, the structures that emerged from the historical orders and their symbolization proved more complicated than I had anticipated. They were so refractory indeed that the projected volumes could not accommodate the results of analysis as they accumulated. Not that anything was wrong with the principle of the study; on the contrary, the difficulties arose from the side of the materials when the principle was conscientiously applied. In the first place, as my knowledge of materials increased, the original list of five types of order and symbolization turned out to be regrettably limited; and when the empirical basis on which the study had to rest was broadened so as to conform to the state of the historical sciences, the manuscript swelled to a size that easily would have filled six more volumes in print. That situation was awkward enough. What ultimately broke the project, however, was the impossibility of aligning the empirical types in any time sequence at all that would permit the structures actually found to emerge from a history conceived as a "course." The program as originally conceived, it is true, was not all wrong. There were indeed the epochal, differentiating events, the "leaps in being," which engendered the consciousness of a Before and After and, in their respective societies, motivated the symbolism of a historical "course" that was meaningfully structured by the event of the leap. The experiences of a new insight into the truth of existence, accompanied by the consciousness of the event as constituting an epoch in history, were real enough. There was really an advance in time from compact to differentiated experiences of reality and, correspondingly, an advance from compact to differentiated symbolizations of the order of being. As far as this line of meaning, drawn by the differentiating events in the time of history, was concerned, the program had a solid core; and by the same token, the analyses contained in the first three volumes were still valid as far as they went. Still, the conception was untenable because it had not taken proper account of the important lines of meaning in history that did not run along lines of time.

LINEAR TIME AND AXIS TIME

There was, for instance, the crosscut pattern of the spiritual outbursts which, in the first millennium B.C., occurred parallel in time in several otherwise unconnected societies from Hellas to China. The pattern had been observed ever since the 1820s and, more recently, Jaspers had elevated it to the dignity of the "axis-time" in the history of mankind. I was very much aware of the problem when I wrote the earlier volumes, since the Israelite and Hellenic differentiations of consciousness, running parallel in time as they did, could definitely not be brought on a single line of differentiating, meaningful advance in history. As a matter of fact, I reflected at length on the issue in the Introduction to *The World of the Polis,* presenting on that occasion both the theory of Jaspers and the objections of Toynbee. Later analysis, however, proved these reflections wanting on several counts: They did not penetrate to the core of the issue, to the brute fact of meaningful structures which resist arrangement on a time-line, nor did they penetrate to the experiential force which motivates the construction of such lines even though they are incompatible with the empirical evidence; nor were they sufficiently conversant with the ingenious devices for straightening out obstreperous facts on a fictitious line, so that they will carry the eschatological meaning of that other line that runs from time into eternity. I had not yet realized, for instance, that the theory of cultural diffusion, used by Abel-Remusat in his *Mémoire* of 1824 to explain the contemporaneity of Hellenic and Chinese philosophers, was such a device to reduce a disturbingly diversified field of spiritual centers to the oneness of an event in history. Nor had I discerned the same function in Jaspers' symbolism of an axis-time in the history of mankind.

The devices just mentioned revealed their nature under more careful analysis. In the case of Abel-Remusat, it was not necessary to disprove his assumption on empirical grounds; today nobody would maintain anyway that comparable experiences and symbolizations in Heraclitus and Lao-tse are due to cultural diffusion. However, since there were no empirical reasons for making the assumption in the first place, not even in the 1820s, the function of cultural diffusion as a device for obliterating the plurality of centers of meaning in the field of history came into focus. A *horror,* not *vacui* but *pleni,* seems at work, a shudder at the richness of the spirit as it reveals itself all over the earth in a multitude of hierophanies, a monomaniacal desire to force the operations of the spirit in history on the one line that will unequivocally lead into the speculator's present. No independent lines must be left dangling that conceivably could lead into somebody else's present and future. Undeterred by the obsolescence of earlier constructions, ever-new ones will be undertaken as soon as new finds of materials seem to offer the opportunity. When the Hermetical writings, erroneously supposed to be ancient Egyptian texts, became better known in the West, toward the end of the fifteenth century, a movement of humanist thinkers placed Moses and the Bible farther down on a line of spiritual evolution that starts from the wisdom of Egyptian priests. The movement lasted for centuries, and was still strongly alive in Schiller's lectures on *Universal History* in 1789. When Chinese sources became known in the West, Hegel forced the spirit to start its march through history from China, while Egypt and Israel tumbled down the time-line into the Persia that conquered them. When ethnographic materials accumulated and became fashionable, the "primitives" moved to the head of the line and originated the Communism that would ultimately issue into the dream of Marx and Engels. And when the Mesopotamian excavations struck the West with their great discoveries, pan-Babylonian historians were ready to construct a new history of cultural diffusion from the origin of culture in Babylon. But the nature of the enterprise reveals itself in its purity, when the historical materials that offer the opportunity for a new construction do not exist at all but have to be produced by speculative fancy for the specific purpose—as in the recent wave of speculations on the origin of human culture on earth through astronauts landing from another star. The fancy seems still to be gaining momentum, as it is supported by so-called scientists in the employ of various institutions richly endowed with public funds. As a result, if you are not happy with the progress of history from the enlightened priests of Egypt to the enlightened intellectuals of the eighteenth century, or with its progress from primitive to final Communism, take your choice and have a history advancing from stellar to earthly astronauts.

The speculators juggle facts and chronology with such insouciance, if not impertinence, that sometimes there seems to be no limit to the game. Nevertheless, the facts have a way of asserting themselves. It is difficult to ignore the parallelism of spiritual outbursts observed by Abel-Remusat and his successors. The chronologically parallel events simply cannot be brought on a time-line. How then can a philosopher cope with the phenomenon if, on the one hand, the dissolvent of cultural diffusion does not work and if, on the other hand, he is loath to admit that the spirit listeth where it will, unconcerned about the difficulties its divinely mysterious movements will cause to a humanly conscientious observer? Jaspers, I suspect, intended his conception of the axis-time to be an answer to this question.

The device was exposed to Toynbee's objections: In order to elevate the period from 800 to 200 B.C., in which the parallel outbursts occur, to the rank of the great epoch in history, Jaspers had to deny to the earlier and later spiritual outbursts the epochal character which in their own consciousness they certainly had. In particular, he had to throw out Moses and Christ.[1] The construction did not seem to make sense. If spiritual outbursts were to be recognized as the constituents of meaning in history, the epiphanies of Moses and Christ, or of Mani and Mohammed, could hardly be excluded from the list; and if they were included, the axis-time expanded into an open field of spiritual eruptions extending over millennia. The objections appeared to have disposed of the axis-time for good. On closer examination, however, the argument proved less conclusive than it had seemed at first. For Jaspers had supported the exclusiveness of his period with the argument that the earlier and later outbursts had only regional importance, while a universal consciousness of humanity, pervading all the major civilizations from Rome to China, had indeed been created by the outbursts of the axis-time. Moreover, when all the pointing to earlier and later outbursts had been done, the phenomenon of the parallel outbursts was still there, waiting to be dealt with.

The problem became manageable only when I realized that both Jaspers and Toynbee treated hierophanic events on the level of phenomena in time, not letting their argument reach into the structure of experiencing consciousness. The construction of an axis-time dissolved when I applied the principle of the study more carefully to the types of order and symbolization actually to be found in the period in question. The analysis of the order concretely experienced in the spiritual outbursts had the negative result: There was no "axis-time" in the first millennium B.C., because the Western and Far Eastern thinkers did not know of each others' existence and, consequently, had no consciousness of thinking on any axis of history. The "axis-time," I had to conclude, was the symbolism by which a modern thinker tried to cope with the disturbing problem of meaningful structures in history, such as the field of parallel spiritual movements, of which the actors in the field were quite unaware.

The conclusion then led on to the questions concerning the validity of the modern symbolism: Could one really interpret the pluralistic field of outbursts, though it had no consciousness of itself, as a meaningful structure in

---

[1] Incidentally, Moses is a somewhat ubiquitous figure as a disturber of the constructivist peace. In the preceding paragraph I had to note how he slides down on the time scale of meaning, from the Hermeticists, through Hegel and Marx, to the pan-Babylonians. Now it should be noted that Toynbee himself, though he criticizes Jaspers for his exclusion of Moses, excludes Judaism from the sacred precinct of universal religions. And something of the same tendency can be discerned in Freud's attempt to make Moses an Egyptian. Vico's admirably perceptive caution to exempt the Mosaic-Christian line of meaning in history from his law of the *corso* is apparently not considered a warning to be heeded.

the history of mankind? or did the field not rather suggest the existence of a plurality of mankinds, each having a history of its own? If then one opted for the first interpretation, the further question concerning the subject of history arose: Which was the society concretely existing in time in whose history this curious structure appeared? Certainly not the Hellenic, Hindu, or Chinese societies of the first millennium B.C.; and certainly not any concrete societies of the nineteenth and twentieth centuries A.D. Who then was the subject hidden behind the bland symbolism of "mankind"? who was this *humanitas abscondita?*

Mankind is no concrete society at all. In the pursuit of this question, the analysis had to acknowledge the spiritual outbursts, not as phenomena in a history of mankind, but as the sources of meaning in history and of such knowledge as man has of it. By letting man become conscious of his humanity as existence in tension toward divine reality, the hierophanic events engender the knowledge of man's existence in the divine-human In-Between, in Plato's Metaxy, as well as the language symbols articulating the knowledge. Moreover, they are experienced as meaningful inasmuch as they constitute a Before and After within time that points toward a fulfillment, toward an Eschaton, out of time. History is not a stream of human beings and their actions in time, but the process of man's participation in a flux of divine presence that has eschatological direction. The enigmatic symbolism of a "history of mankind," thus, expresses man's understanding that these insights, though they arise from concrete events in the consciousness of concrete human beings are valid for all men.

If the puzzle of the symbolism is solved, however, the mystery of the process itself becomes even more awesome. For the spiritual outbursts are widely scattered in time and space over concrete human beings in concrete societies. The events, though they constitute structures of meaning in history, do not themselves fall readily into a pattern that could be understood as meaningful. Some of the structures constituted, such as the advances from compact to differentiated consciousness, bring the time-dimension in the flux of divine presence to attention; others, such as the cluster of events in the crosscut under discussion, appear to accentuate the process in its broadness, as it affects mankind in the spatial-dimension of existence. But in either case, the emergent meanings remain open toward the future of the process in time, as well as toward its eschatological fulfillment. I had to conclude: The process of history, and such order as can be discerned in it, is not a story to be told from the beginning to its happy, or unhappy, end; it is a mystery in process of revelation. *j*

THE BEGINNING AND THE BEYOND

When I devised the program I was still laboring under the conventional belief that the conception of history as a meaningful course of events on a straight line of time was the great achievement of Israelites and Christians who were favored in its creation by the revelatory events, while the pagans, deprived as they were of revelation, could never rise above the conception of a cyclical time. This conventional belief had to be abandoned when I discovered the unilinear construction of history, from a divine-cosmic origin of order to the author's present, to be a symbolic form developed by the end of the third millennium B.C. in the empires of the Ancient Near East. To this form I gave the name *historiogenesis*.

The discovery disturbed the program seriously. There was more at stake than a conventional assumption now disproved. For the very unilinear history which I had supposed to be engendered, together with the punctuations of meaning on it, by the differentiating events, turned out to be a cosmological symbolism. Moreover, the symbolism had remained a millennial constant in continuity from its origins in the Sumerian and Egyptian societies, through its cultivation by Israelites and Christians, right into the "philosophies of history" of the nineteenth century A.D.

These facts raised a number of hitherto unsuspected questions. For instance, if the symbolism of a unilinear history with its climax in the present could be engendered by the experience of a cosmological empire being threatened and preserved, was there perhaps something of a "leap in being" in the foundation of empire? and inversely, was there perhaps something imperial about spiritual outbursts? Such questions became even more poignant when, on further analysis, the later variants appeared to continue the symbolism not only in its general conception but in certain details of construction. The techniques of selecting and omitting materials, as well as of rearranging their time sequence, so as to let one line of meaning emerge from a field that in fact contains several such lines, in brief: the previously mentioned impertinent distortions and falsifications of history which today are called interpretations, were for instance in Hegel's *Philosophy of History* the same as in the Sumerian King List. And if that was the case, did there not impose itself the question: What exactly was modern about modernity, if the great struggle among the historiogenetic constructions, among Enlightened Progressivism, Comtism, Hegelianism, Marxism, had to be understood as a dogmatomachy among imperialist speculators in the best cosmological style? But such special questions could be answered only when the general structure of history that formed their background was sufficiently clarified; and this contextual structure was indicated by the observation that the meaningful advances of differentiating consciousness were throughout history accompanied by the equally meaningful persistence of a "cosmological" symbolism.

This peculiar structure in history originates in the stratification of man's consciousness through the process of differentiation. The truth of existence discovered by the prophets of Israel and the philosophers of Hellas, though it appears later in time than the truth of the cosmos, cannot simply replace it, because the new insights, while indirectly affecting the image of reality as a whole, pertain directly only to man's consciousness of his existential tension. When in the revelatory process the hidden god behind the intracosmic gods lets himself become manifest in visionary and auditory experiences, or in the "sound of gentle stillness," or in the meditative probing of the seeker, and thus be known against the background of his unknowability, the man who responds to the presence becomes conscious of his response as an act of participation in divine reality. He discovers the something in his humanity that is the site and sensorium of divine presence; and he finds such words as *psyche,* or *pneuma,* or *nous,* to symbolize the something. When he participates in a theophanic event, his consciousness becomes cognitively luminous for his own humanity as constituted by his relation to the unknown god whose moving presence in his soul evokes the movement of response. I have circumscribed the structure of the event as strictly as possible, in order to make it clear how narrowly confined the area of the resulting insights actually is: The new truth pertains to man's consciousness of his humanity in participatory tension toward the divine ground, and to no reality beyond this restricted area.

The human carriers of the spiritual outbursts do not always realize the narrow limits of the area directly affected by the differentiating process. For the differentiation of consciousness indirectly affects the image of reality as a whole; and the enthusiastic discoverers of the truth are sometimes inclined to treat such secondary effects as they believe themselves to perceive, and not always correctly, as direct insights. Historically, this secondary impact of the events has been impressive indeed: The truth of revelation and philosophy has become fatal to the intracosmic gods; and the removal of the gods from the cosmos has set a dedivinized nature free to be explored by science. Still, while these consequences testify to the centrality of consciousness in man's experience and symbolization of reality, they must not obscure the fact that the differentiation of existential truth does not abolish the cosmos in which the event occurs. Regarding its existence and structure, however, the cosmos is experienced as divinely created and ordered. The new truth can affect the belief in intra-cosmic divinities as the most adequate symbolization of cosmic-divine reality, but it cannot affect the experience of divine reality as the creative and ordering force in the cosmos. Hence, as the truth of existence embarks on the long process of developing the adequate symbols for its expression, one can observe the various attempts at coming to terms with the problem of cosmic-divine presence. The Hidden or Unknown God who reveals himself in the movements of the soul will be identified with the creator-god, while all other gods become false gods, as in Israel; or he will be identified with the creator-high-god, as a *summus deus* in relation to all other gods, as in the Egyptian Amon Hymns; or he will be permitted to coexist with the intracosmic divinities, as in Hinduism; or he will be discerned as the truly highest god above the Olympians, and even above the divinities of the philosopher's myths, as with Plato or Plotinus. But he also can become the good god to whom the spark of the divine pneuma returns when man has escaped in death from the prison of the cosmos, created by an evil god for the purpose of entrapping the spark, as in certain Gnostic movements. The field thus has considerable amplitude; but whatever the choice will be, the aggregate symbolism must provide for the experience of divine presence, not only in the soul but in the cosmos in its spatio-temporal existence and order.

As the examples show, the issue does not arise in retrospect from the superior historical knowledge of the twentieth century; it is part of the consciousness as it differentiates in the hierophanic events. Moreover, going beyond their concrete solutions, the participants in the events developed the fundamental symbols which articulate the structure of the issue. Drawing on Israelite, Christian, and Hellenic sources, this symbolization of the structure can be concentrated in the formula:

> The divine reality, the *theotes* of Colossians 2:9—
> that moves man's consciousness from the Beyond of all cosmic contents,
>   from the *epekeina* in Plato's sense—
> also creates and sustains the cosmos from its Beginning, from the
>   *bereshit* in the sense of Genesis 1:1.

The Beyond and the Beginning, articulating the directions in which divine reality is experienced, have remained the unsurpassably exact expression of the issue to this day.

Though the transfiguration of the cosmos into a dematerialized reality under God is the dream of such apocalypses as that of John, the cosmos in fact does not disappear when the spiritual outbursts occur. On the contrary, when consciousness has become luminous through the hierophanic events, its symbolization of reality now must accommodate both the Beyond and the Beginning. The divine-cosmic beginning, however, requires for its expression a story of genesis, a cosmogonic tale. No more than the cosmos, I had to conclude therefore, will the cosmogonic myth disappear. Any attempt to overcome, or to dispose of, the myth is suspect as a magic operation, motivated by an apocalyptic desire to destroy the cosmos itself.

The issue is central to a theory of the myth, but I realized its centrality only slowly as the work progressed. Using the symbolism of the Mesopotamian and Egyptian empires as a model, I had originally conceived the myth as "cosmological." This conception proved too narrow even in the earlier volumes of *Order and History,* as the richly diversified phenomena of the myth came into view one after the other. Besides the cosmological myth of the Near Eastern empires there had to be considered the differently structured, non-imperial myth of Homer and Hesiod; there was furthermore an Hellenic people's myth to be distinguished from the myth of the tragic poets; then there followed Plato's creation of the philosopher's myth, culminating in the *Timaeus* in a myth of the cosmos that was not a cosmological myth; and there was the great block of the Israelite Genesis, with a type of cosmogony that arose from the epochal break with the cosmological form of the empire. When this long list now was further lengthened by the historiogenetic symbolism, as well as by the problems of its origin, persistence, and deformation, it seemed advisable to abandon the method of *ad hoc* qualifications and to attempt conceptual distinctions that would bring at least some theoretical order to a badly neglected field of structures in history.

The task is less formidable than it may sound. In accordance with the principle of the study, one only has to permit the lines of theory to emerge from the history of order without disturbing the process by idiosyncratic ideas. I have mentioned the historical data which determine the structure of the issue; they are (a) the Beyond and the Beginning which ever since antiquity have symbolized the directions in which the presence of divine reality is experienced and (b) the cosmogony as the symbolism which expresses the experience of the divine-cosmic Beginning. If the data are accepted, it will be necessary, short of neologisms, to use the term *cosmogony* or *cosmogonic myth* as the general concept that will apply to all symbolisms engendered by the experience of divine initiative in the existence of the cosmos. The concept then will apply not only to the mytho-speculative forms developed in the imperial societies of the Ancient Near East, but also to the more compact symbolisms in the pre-imperial, tribal societies; and not only to cosmogonies in strictly cosmological form in which divine presence is symbolized by the intra-cosmic gods, but also to the cosmogonies in which these gods have been affected, to a lesser or greater degree, by the spiritual outbursts which locate divine reality in the Beyond of all intramundane content.

which was also realized by the people of myth (?)

The concept will make the dynamics of the issue intelligible. While cosmogony is a constant, the manner of its symbolization is affected by the increasing luminosity of existential consciousness. By their impact on the symbolization of the Beginning, the hierophanic events which illuminate consciousness in the direction of the Beyond thus create historically a secondary field of differentiations. A remark or two on representative manifestations of this tension between the two areas of experience and symbolization will intimate the proportions of the problem.

THE TENSION OF CONSCIOUSNESS—PLATO, ARISTOTLE, ISRAEL

The classic manifestation of the tension is Plato's creation of the philosopher's myth. On the one hand, Plato senses the gods of the tradition in so severe a conflict with the divine reality experienced by the erotically conscious soul that he demands harsh educational measures, in order to prevent the disordering effects of the older myth. On the other hand, he is aware of the limits set to the philosopher's exploration of reality by the divine mystery of the noetic height and the apeirontic depth. Since the philosopher cannot transcend these limits but has to move in the In-Between, the Metaxy, delimited by them, the meaning of his work depends on an ambiance of insight concerning the divine presence and operation in the cosmos that only the myth can provide. Plato's answer to the predicament is the creation of the *alethinos logos,* the story of the gods that can claim to be true if it fits the cognitive consciousness of order created in the soul of man by the erotic tension toward the divine Beyond.

Plato's perception of the conflict, with the memory of Socrates alive, is brimming with its seriousness to the point of deadliness. A generation later, when Plato's elucidation of the conflict and its nature had become a fact in history, the heat of the struggle is much less intense. The accents shift toward the transition from myth to philosophy as an event in history to be described and analyzed. An Aristotle can acknowledge the lover of myth, the *philomythos,* to be engaged in the same quest of the ground as the lover of wisdom, the *philosophos;* and in the divine creative force symbolized by the gods of an Hesiodic cosmogony he can recognize the same eternal ground of being that the philosopher experiences as the noetic mover of his soul. The problem of cosmogony proper, thus, begins to emerge from the observation of its historically successive symbolizations by the intracosmic gods and the unknown god of the Beyond.

No more in Aristotle than in Plato, however, does it fully emerge. The primary experience of the cosmos prevails so strongly that the experience of the Beginning itself still remains immersed in its compactness. A re-symbolization of cosmogony becomes necessary, when the truth of existence invalidates the intracosmic gods; but the differentiation of consciousness in the direction of the Beyond has degrees and the philosophers' differentiation of the Nous is apparently not sufficient to compel a radical break with the primary experience; only the experience of the absolutely creative Beyond, it seems, can dissolve the compactness so far that the absolutely creative Beginning will become visible. In the Platonic-Aristotelian case, a cosmogony in cosmological form is no longer tolerable, but the noetic luminosity of existence does not impose the alternative of an absolutely creative Beginning. As a result, the symbols which intend to cope with the problems are oddly ambiguous. The Aristotelian cosmos is not in need of a Beginning at all; the ineluctable expression of its divinely sustained existence and lasting can be satisfied with the ambiguous symbolism of infinite duration. For the same reasons the Platonic Demiurge cannot become absolutely creative. The Demiurge of the *Timaeus* is bound by the Ananke of the cosmos; he does not create it, but is restricted to the action of imposing form on pre-existent matter. Nevertheless, while the symbols are still in bondage to the primary experience, their ambiguity reflects the impact of differentiating consciousness on the cosmogonic dimension of reality and its symbolization.

The more elaborate articulation of at least certain aspects of the problem, then, finds favorable conditions in the Judaeo-Christian environment with its millennial Israelite background of differentiating consciousness. In this environment, the hold of the primary experience of the cosmos has been decisively shaken at an early date by Moses' experience and symbolization of divine reality as the "I am" of the Thornbush Episode. The experience brings the deeper stratum of divine reality, its absolute Being, into immediate view, bypassing the Hellenic philosopher's concern with its manifestation as the source of order in the cosmos. The creative act, furthermore, is forcefully symbolized as a divine course of action that continues down to the historian's own present, even though the language still betrays an aura of intracosmic divinities surrounding the one god who creates the heavens and the earth. And finally, the substance of the creative action is the "word." From the Beginning, reality is the divine word speaking in succession the evolution of being from matter through plant to animal life, until it speaks man who, in the persons of patriarchs and prophets, responds by his word to the word spoken by god in history. The reality of the cosmos, thus, becomes a story to be told by the man who participates responsively in the story told by the god. In the Hellenic context, the sense of a close relationship between reality and the word that renders it truly engenders the meaning of *aletheia* as both reality and truth; in the Israelite context, the relationship is traced back to its source in the divinely creative word-reality. The word of man when he articulates his consciousness of reality emerges from the reality that is the word of god. It would be incautious to do more than point to this assembly of symbols. In their Israelite context, they do not mark the steps in a philosopher's analysis of structures in reality; they are indeed no more than an assemblage of insights, depending for their coherence on a sure pre-analytical grasp on the truth of reality. Still, they are the potent precondition for certain differentiations of the cosmogonic problem that would be unintelligible without this background.

THE TENSION IN THE GOSPEL OF JOHN

The event that lets the assembled elements crystallize into a coherent symbolism is the epiphany of Christ; and the thinker who articulates the cosmogonic Beginning in its relation to the presence of the divine Beyond in man's consciousness is the author of the Gospel of John. The Gospel opens with the "In the Beginning" of Genesis 1:1, but John retains nothing of the story of creation but the *praeteritum* of the storyteller. In this *praeteritum*, instead of telling the story, he reflects on the divine-creative substance and its internal structure: "In the beginning was the word; and the word was with god; and the word was god." The creative tension in the Beginning is understood in terms of the paradox that the word and god are related by both difference and identity simultaneously. Carefully stressing the difference then by its iteration (1:2), the author lets the creative tension become creative action. The god who has the word that he is makes all things by speaking it:

"All things were made by it; and without it nothing was made that was made." For the creative word was "life," and its life was "the light of man." At this point, the creative word of the cosmogony blends into the presence of "the light that shines in the darkness" of man's existence with such intensity that the darkness cannot overcome it. The word of the Beginning is present in the epiphany of Christ, as experienced and witnessed by John the Baptist, and further attested by the author of the Gospel.

The reflection on the relationship between the word of the Beginning and the word from the Beyond is resumed in the great debate between Jesus and the Pharisees (8), this time however not moving from the word of the Beginning to its life in the epiphany, but from its presence in Christ, back through history, toward its being again with god in the tension before creation. The debate intends to clarify the meaning of divine presence in a man. When the disbelieving interlocutors ask of Christ "Who are you?" he identifies the divine reality present in him as the Mosaic "I am" (8:24). When the divine reality experienced as present in man's consciousness is to be ascertained, thus, the symbolic language sensibly appeals to the precedent of the word revealing itself in the consciousness of Moses rather than to the word of the Beginning. Still, the recourse to precedent must not obscure the novelty of what is happening now. For the god who spoke to Moses from the Thornbush, now speaks through the mouth of man to other men; the god of a revelatory event in the past has become "the true light that illumines every man who comes into this world" (1:9). The revelation of the "I am" to Moses is still so deeply embedded in the primary experience of the cosmos that it must surround itself with such cosmological symbols as the voice of an intracosmic god of the fathers who speaks from a prodigial thornbush; and it constitutes, not everyman's humanity, but the qualities in Moses that enable him to lead Israel collectively from bondage in a cosmological empire to its freedom under God in history. The "I am" in Jesus, on the other hand, reveals itself as the living presence of the word in a man; it does not intend to establish a people in history but will, for every man who responds to its appeal, dissolve the darkness and absurdity of existence into the luminous consciousness of participating in the divine word. Inexorably the author lets the debate between Jesus and the Pharisees advance toward the point where the conflict between the earlier, more compact revelations to Israel and the luminous presence of the "I am" in Jesus breaks into the open. How can the deathless, immortalizing presence of the "I am" in the man Jesus be reconciled with the death of man bound to history, be he so venerable a figure as Abraham? This crucial question provokes the climactic declaration, with its magnificent break in the sequence of tense: "Before Abraham was, I am" (8:58). After this declaration, the infuriated audience wants to stone him; but Jesus makes his escape (8:59).

The great events of spiritual insight becoming articulate do not necessarily please everybody; the poor in spirit are numbered. There are also the spiritual pragmatists, be they the Pharisees of the debate or their modern Christian and ideological counterparts, who will listen to a voice that speaks into history as long as it does not become too clear that the movement from the Beyond demands the countermovement toward the Beyond, out of history, into eschatological fulfillment. They want to eat their cake of revelation and keep it in history. The declaration infuriates because its linguistic miracle suddenly makes the ahistorical, anti-apocalyptic, eschatological intent of the "I am" visible beyond a doubt. The Johannine language can indeed surprise as the discourse proceeds, because the author does not develop new language symbols to express new meanings but uses the same symbol continuously to cover the several meanings as they emerge from the compact "I am" in the process of differentiation. I have distinguished already two components of the complex. There is, first, the self-revelation of the hidden god to Moses in Exodus 3. This is the stratum in the complex that moves an Etienne Gilson to understand all Christian metaphysics of Being as the metaphysics of Exodus. There is, second, the "I am" that becomes luminous, through its presence in Christ, for its participatory presence in every human being, even in the pre-Christian men of faith: "Your father Abraham rejoiced that he was to see my day; he saw it and was glad" (8:56). This is the stratum that moves Thomas to say that Christ is the head, not of an historically limited *corpus mysticum*, but of all men from the creation of the world to its end. And there is, third, the eschatological meaning, terminologically not separate from the others, which dominates the Gospel through the famous "I am (*ego eimi*) . . ." pronouncements.

The divine voice from the Thornbush identifies itself as the "I-am-who-I-am," and then continues to Moses: "Say this to the people of Israel, 'I-am has sent me to you'" (3:14). In the Beginning, the word of the hidden god creates the cosmos; when the word moves from the Beyond into man's consciousness, it reveals itself through language. And in this revelatory language, the I-am becomes a subject that acquires predicates. On the side of the subject, the god who reveals himself is absolute Being; on the side of the predicate, he is what he lets be seen of himself concretely in the revelatory event. In the Thornbush Episode, he is the I-am who sends Moses to his people. In the

Gospel of John, the I-am is the presence of the divine word in Jesus and sends him as the Christ to everyman with the offer and demand of redemptive return from the darkness to the light. In the Johannine context, thus, the I-am-who-I-am becomes something like a blank form to be filled in by the *ego eimi* ... sayings:

> I am—the bread of life (6:35);
> I am—the light of the world; he who follows me will not walk in
>   darkness, but will have the light of life (8:12);
> I am—the good shepherd (10:11);
> I am—the resurrection and the life; he who believes in me,
>   though he die, yet shall he live; and whoever lives and
>   believes in me, shall never die (11:25-26);
> I am—the way, and the truth, and the life (14:6);
> I am—the vine, you are the branches (15:5).

The sayings are clear: the predicates express the movement of the word from the Beyond into everyman's existence and demand the countermovement toward the word that speaks through Christ.

Still, when John lets Jesus elaborate on the sayings, as for instance in 6:38-40, some important implications become articulate: "For I have come down from heaven, not to do my own will, but the will of him who sent me; and this is the will of him who sent me, that I should lose nothing of all that he has given me, but raise it up at the last day. For this is the will of my Father, that every one who sees the Son and believes in him should have eternal life; and I will raise him up at the last day." The human carrier of the word has no will of his own; it is the will of the hidden god that speaks the word and its demand through the mouth of Jesus. As a consequence, the personal pronoun in the passage becomes ambiguous. Who is the "I" that should lose nothing of all that he has given me? Is it Jesus, or the word that he speaks? And again, who is the "Son" who bestows eternal life on everyone who sees him and believes in him? The man Jesus, or the word? And finally, who is the "I" that raises man up at the last day?

These ambiguities will become intelligible, if they are understood as engendered by the experience of the eschatological movement and its history. The movement toward the Beyond of the cosmos can become fully articulate only when the Beyond itself has revealed itself. Only when man has become conscious of divine reality as moving his humanity, not through its presence in the cosmos, but through a presence reaching into his soul from the Beyond, can his response become luminous as the immortalizing countermovement toward the Beyond. John is as much aware of this advance from compactness to differentiation in the process of pneumatic revelation, as Aristotle is aware of it in the process of noetic revelation. The "I am" that speaks in Jesus, as the debate with the Pharisees has shown, is the same "I am" that has formed the humanity of man in the past by evoking the response of faith. But the faith of Jesus does not have the compact mode of Abraham's faith. In the epiphany of Christ, the formation of humanity in history has become transparent for its meaning as the process of transformation. In Jesus, the participation of his humanity in the divine word has reached the intensity of his absorption into the word. The ambiguous personal pronoun in the Gospel expresses this transfiguring absorption as it was experienced by the men who had seen the Christ.

But the cosmos continues to exist from the Beginning; and the Christ transfigured from the Beyond has to die the death of man. What then is the meaning of transfiguration? In the critical hour of truth before the Passion, the evangelist lets Jesus speak to his disciples: "The hour is coming, indeed it has come, when you will be scattered, every man to his home, and will leave me alone; yet I am not alone, for the Father is with me. I am telling you this, that in me you may have peace. Though in the cosmos you have affliction, be confident, for I have been victorious over the cosmos" (16:32–33). That is all. But that is all that matters. In the following prayer, Jesus prays for the men who have kept his word: "I do not pray that you take them out of the cosmos, but that you preserve them from evil. They are no more of the cosmos than I am. Sanctify them in the truth that is your word." "This is eternal life: That they know you as the only true god, as the one who has sent Jesus Christ" (17:15–17; 17:3). For himself he prays: "And now, Father, glorify me into the glory I had with you before there was a cosmos" (17:5).

Though the divine reality is one, its presence is experienced in the two modes of the Beyond and the Beginning. The Beyond is present in the immediate experience of movements in the psyche; while the presence of the divine Beginning is mediated through the experience of the existence and intelligible structure of things in the cosmos. The two models require two different types of language for their adequate expression. The immediate presence in the movements of the soul requires the revelatory language of consciousness. This is the language of seeking, searching, and questioning, of ignorance and knowledge concerning the divine ground, of futility, absurdity, anxiety, and alienation of existence, of being moved to seek and question, of being drawn toward the ground, of turning around, of return, illumination, and rebirth. The presence mediated by the existence and order of things in the cosmos requires the mythical language of a creator-god or Demiurge, of a divine force that creates, sustains, and preserves the order of things. If however the oneness of divine reality and its presence in man is experienced with such intensity as it is by the author of the gospel in Christ, even an extraordinary linguistic sensitivity may not guard him against using the two languages indiscriminately in his articulation of the two modes of presence. And that is what happens in the Gospel of John when the author lets the cosmogonic "word" of creation blend into the revelatory "word" spoken to man from the Beyond by the "I am." In the symbolisms available in the culture of the time, the mythical word of creation that goes back to the Egyptian cosmogonies is copresent with the revelatory word that goes back to Moses and the prophets. The two "words" are liable to blend into one language of divine presence, corresponding to the one divine reality, in a thinker who is so strongly formed, and transformed, by the epiphany of Christ that the future problems of language analysis do not occupy his attention.

Inevitably difficulties will arise. The word that reveals itself in Jesus does not return to the subject "I am" whose predicate it is, not to the god of the Beyond, but to the god who speaks the word of creation in the Beginning. However, since the Christ who in his death is victorious over the cosmos does not care to be glorified into the word that creates it, he must return, beyond creation, to the status of the word in the creative tension "before there was a cosmos" (17:5). But what does the author mean by this language? Does he understand creation to be an evil, perhaps caused by a fall in the divinity, and now to be undone by the redeeming act of Christ? In brief: Is he a Gnostic? Hardly. For the Christ sends his disciples into the cosmos, as he has been sent into it, to convert still others to the truth of the word, so that the divine love can become manifest in them. The believers will be a community in the cosmos while not being of it (17:14–26). Still, the clarity of the last passage does not disperse the shadow cast on the cosmos by the earlier one. New Testament scholars acknowledge the conflict by speaking of Gnostic "influences" or "tendencies" in the gospel.

The diagnosis of Gnosticism is correct, but an observation on historical influences does not resolve the problem. The question is rather what causes Gnosticism to appear, and to become influential, precisely at the time when the consciousness of a pneumatic Beyond becomes intensely luminous in the various movements radiating from the epiphany of Christ, as well as in such manifestations of a pagan Gnosis as the *Poimandres*. If the question is formulated in this manner, it implies its answer: The intensely experienced presence of the Beyond brings the problem of the Beginning to intense attention. When the formerly unknown god of the Beyond reveals himself as the goal of the eschatological movement in the soul, the existence of the cosmos becomes an ever more disturbing mystery. Why should a cosmos exist at all, if man can do no better than live in it as if he were not of it, in order to make his escape from the prison through death? This is the critical question that brings the mystery of reality into full view: There is a cosmos in which man participates by his existence; man is endowed with cognitive consciousness of the reality in which he is a partner; consciousness differentiates in a process called history; and in the process of history man discovers reality to be engaged in a movement toward the Beyond of its present structure. A cosmos that moves from its divine Beginning toward a divine Beyond of itself is mysterious indeed; and there is nothing wrong with the question as such.

Nevertheless, it is also the specifically Gnostic question inasmuch as it moves on the edge where the divine mystery can turn into a human absurdity, if the consciousness of the movement toward the Beyond is torn out of the context of reality in which it arises and made the autonomous basis for human action that will abolish the mystery. The fallacy at the core of the Gnostic answers to the question is the expansion of consciousness from the Beyond to the Beginning. In the construction of Gnostic systems, the immediate experience of divine presence in the mode of the Beyond is speculatively expanded to comprehend a knowledge of the Beginning that is accessible only in the mode of mediated experience. In the imagery of the expansive speculation, the process of reality becomes an intelligible psychodrama, beginning with a fall in the pneumatic divinity, continuing with the imprisonment of parts of the pneumatic substance in a cosmos created by an evil Demiurge, and ending with the liberation of the imprisoned substance through its return to the pneumatic divinity. The knowledge, the Gnosis, of the psychodrama is the precondition for engaging successfully in the operation of liberating the pneuma in man from its cosmic prison. The imaginative game of liberation derives its momentum from an intensely experienced alienation and an equally intense revolt against it; Gnostic thinkers, both ancient and modern, are the great psychologists of alienation, carriers of the Promethean revolt.

The futility of existence in a time of imperial expansion, however, can find less-complicated ways to vent itself, as the history of zealotism and apocalyptic movements shows. Alienation and revolt, though they provide the momentum, do not alone produce a Gnostic system that, with considerable speculative effort, tries to comprehend the whole of reality and its process. The additional factor required is a consciousness of the movement toward the Beyond of such strength and clarity that it becomes an obsessive illumination, blinding a man for the contextual structure of reality. For a Gnostic thinker must be able to forget that the cosmos does not emerge from consciousness, but that man's consciousness emerges from the cosmos. He must, furthermore, be able to invert the relation of the Beginning and the Beyond without becoming aware that he destroys the mystery of reality by his speculative inversion. And finally, when his imagination invents the drama of the divine fall, in order to bring it to its redemptive end by his speculative action, he must be insensitive to the fact that he is indulging his *libido dominandi*. I am stressing the magnitude of insensitivity required in the construction of a Gnostic system, in order to stress the strength and luminosity of eschatological consciousness necessary to make the Gnostic deformation intelligible. Considering the history of Gnosticism, with the great bulk of its manifestations belonging to, or deriving from, the Christian orbit, I am inclined to recognize in the epiphany of Christ the great catalyst that made eschatological consciousness an historical force, both in forming and deforming humanity.

The Balance Lost—Gnosticism

The Gnostic deformation of eschatological consciousness accompanies its differentiation from antiquity to the present. This parallel process, however, is still obscure in many respects, so obscure in fact that sometimes even its reality is doubted. The difficulties are caused by the variability of the concrete imagery employed in the construction of the systems. It is difficult indeed to recognize Gnostic speculations which present such widely differing phenotypical surfaces as the *Evangelium Veritatis,* attributed to the Valentinian circle if not to Valentinus himself, and the Hegelian system as individuals of the same species. I shall distinguish, therefore, between the essential core and the variable part of a Gnostic system. The essential core is the enterprise of returning the pneuma in man from its state of alienation in the cosmos to the divine pneuma of the Beyond through action based on knowledge. Moreover, the god of the Beyond to whom the Gnostic speculator wants to return must be identical, not with the creator-god but with the god of the creative tension "before there was a cosmos." This essential core, then, can be imaginatively expanded by a variety of symbolisms, as for instance by the precreational psychodrama in the Valentinian speculations. The psychodrama relates the fall in the divinity, employing for the purpose a formidable apparatus of figures: the divine Pleroma and the Syzygies, the Ogdoads, Decads, and Dodecads of Aeons, a higher and a lower Sophia, a Demiurge, a Cosmocrator, and a pleromatic Savior. If these richly varied expansions and their colorful personnel are considered the characteristically Gnostic symbolism, as they frequently are, misgivings about the Gnostic character of the modern systems will understandably arise. However, in order to let the matter rest at this point of confrontation, one must ignore the fact that the modern Gnostics do not appeal to Valentinus or Basilides as their ancestors but to the Gospel of John. One must ignore, for instance, that Schelling has developed a law of three phases for Christian history: The Petrine Christianity was followed by the Pauline of the Reformation; and the Pauline will now be followed by the Johannine Christianity of the German speculative systems. In the prototypical case of modern Gnosticism, in Hegel's system, the essential core is the same as in the Valentinian speculations, but the concrete imagery is definitely Johannine. The obscurities in the history of Gnosticism, thus, are not caused by the actual differences between ancient and modern systems, but by a conception of ancient Gnosticism which too narrowly concentrates on the instances of psychodramatic expansion. Hence, if the "Gnostic influences" in the New Testament writings are to become intelligible as a Gnostic manifestation in its own right by the side of the more spectacular Egyptian, Syrian, and Anatolian varieties, the phenotypically oriented conception must be replaced by a genetic conception. For this purpose, the Gnostic deformation of consciousness must be put into the pragmatic and spiritual context of the Ecumenic Age which is the subject-matter of the present volume.

The genetic context to which I refer is the interaction between expansion of empire and differentiation of consciousness. In pragmatic history, Gnosticism arises from six centuries of imperial expansion and civilizational destruction. The ecumenic expansion of the Persians, of Alexander and his successors, and ultimately of the Romans destroys the cosmological empires of the Ancient Near East; and the ecumenic empires destroy each other down to the Roman victory. Nor do Israel and Hellas, the societies in which the pneumatic and noetic illuminations occur, escape victimization by the process. This pragmatic impact of conquest on the traditional forms of existence in society is abrupt; and its abruptness is not matched by an equally sudden spiritual response to the situation. The divine authority of the older symbols is impaired when the societies whose reality of order they express lose their political independence, while the new imperial order has, at least initially, no more than the authority of power. Hence, the spiritual and intellectual lives of the peoples exposed to the events are in danger of separating from the reality of socially ordered existence. Society and the cosmos of which society is a part tend to be experienced as a sphere of disorder, so that the sphere of order in reality contracts to personal existence in tension toward the divine Beyond. The area of reality that can be experienced as divinely ordered thus suffers a severe diminution.

This contraction of divine order to personal existence, however, must not be misunderstood as a differentiation of consciousness. On the contrary, the image of order in reality becomes deformed, because the intracosmic gods of the ethnic cultures prove inadequate to the task of symbolizing the supra-ethnic humanity of an imperial society, while the differentiation that would supply the pragmatic ecumenicity imposed by the empires with the spiritual consciousness of universal humanity does not occur. Not that the populations of the intercivilizational area engulfed by the empires are completely helpless in their encounter with the events, but their response has to find forms inter-mediate between the truth of the cosmos and the truth of existence. In Babylon and Egypt, cosmological piety and the cult of the old gods survive the im-pact of the Persian and Greek conquests, as in the Greek city-states the cult of the polis gods survives the Roman conquest; and the conquerors in their turn do what they can to support their ecumenic conquest by the sanction of high-gods judiciously selected from the old gods or newly created for the purpose. In the vacuum of personal order left by this equitable distribution of social pieties, then, the Greek mystery religions spread interculturally as the new form of soteriological order in personal existence. Nevertheless, these adaptations of spirituality in cosmological form to the ecumenic situation did not satisfy everybody. As the Gnostic outburst proves, there must have ex-isted thinkers and groups in the multicivilizational empires who sensed the makeshift character of the adaptations. Behind the facade of Hellenistic syncre-tism, profounder changes in man's understanding of his humanity were in the making.

The causes and structure of the outburst of Gnosticism will remain a puzzle as long as one does not clearly discern the variety of genetic factors adumbrated: the disordering effect of imperial expansion; the contraction of divine order in reality to the sphere of personal existence; the difficulties of expressing, in the absence of an adequate pneumatic differentiation, an anti-cosmic contraction with the pro-cosmic means of the cosmological gods; the gradual articulation of anti-cosmism in Israelite-Judaic history; the catalytic effect of the epiphany of Christ; and the paradoxical desire, stemming from the noetic differentiation of philosophy, to bring the disorder of reality, as well as the salvation from it, into the form of a well-ordered, intelligible system. There remain enough open questions even if these factors are taken into account, but at least it will be possible to avoid certain errors.

Above all, the anti-cosmism of the Gnostic movement is not a deformation of Christianity, for the Gnostic distortion of reality through the contraction of divine order into the Beyond of consciousness precedes the Christian pneumatic differentiation. The error of exaggerating the catalytic function of Christianity into a dependence of Gnosticism on Christianity has been induced by the struggle of the Patres against Gnosticism as a Christian heresy. Regarding the pre-Christian growth of anti-cosmic consciousness, then, the prehistory of the essential core in Gnosticism can be more clearly discerned in the Israelite-Judaic than in any other area of the multicivilizational empires. The fact should not be surprising, for the Mosaic and prophetic break with the cosmological form of empire had created a language of pneumatic consciousness that could be used, and further elaborated, in the encounter with the ecumenic empires. Though the fact must be acknowledged in order to give the "Gnostic influences" in Christianity their due weight, it must not be exaggerated into a specifically Judaic origin of Gnosticism. The exaggeration would break down in face of the psychodramatic speculations whose symbolism draws on the cultures of Persia, Babylon, Syria, and Egypt that had been overrun by the ecumenic conquerors.

As far as these expansions of the essential core are concerned, their prehistory is obscure. The symbols used in the psychodrama, it is true, can be traced to their sources in the pre-ecumenic cultures; and there is no lack of theories concerning the Iranian, Babylonian, or generally "Oriental" origin of Gnosticism. But none of the theories is quite convincing, not because there could be any doubt about the origin of the symbols but because the changes on the experiential level which must have occurred between the earlier cosmological and the later anti-cosmic use of the symbols cannot be adequately documented. Though it is possible, of course, that the literary manifestations of the transition are lost or have not yet been found, I rather suspect that sources comparable to the Israelite-Judaic documentation of the process have never existed, because no comparable language of pneumatic consciousness had developed in the "Oriental" areas of the empire. This suspicion is further based on an observation concerning the syncretistic character of the great

Gnostic systems. When the psychodrama becomes tangible in the speculations of the Valentinian type, its symbolism does not derive from one particular culture but indiscriminately employs Egyptian Ogdoads and Pythagorean Tetrads, Iranian, Babylonian, Israelite, and Christian symbols. If this syncretism is taken as much for granted as it is in the phenotypical convention, important experiential implications may be overlooked. For in the concrete case of the precreational psychodrama, the symbols have separated from the function they had in the cultural context of their origin; the imagination of the Gnostic thinkers moves them freely in the game of liberating the pneuma from the cosmos. The divine figures are no longer the intracosmic gods of a society in cosmological form; though they still carry the same names, they are a new type of symbols created by the spiritual response of the experience of existential alienation in a society in ecumenic-imperial form.

Syncretistic spiritualism, I venture to suggest, must be recognized as a symbolic form *sui generis*. In the multicivilizational empire it arises from the cultural area of less-differentiated consciousness as the means of coping with the problem of universal humanity in resistance to an unsatisfactory ecumenic order. Under this aspect, therefore, syncretistic spiritualism must be placed as a symbolism of resistance by the side of the apocalyptic development in Judaism—though only under this aspect, for syncretism knows no frontier within the empire. Israelite symbols are taken over by the Gnostic psychodrama, as are "Oriental" symbols by the apocalypses. A comparatively harmless case is the appearance of angels with names, probably an Iranian import, in Judaic writings, such as the angel Gabriel in the Book of Daniel. Before *ca.* 165 B.C., the date of Daniel, the angels have no names. But matters become rapidly complicated, as the controversy about the famous Hymn of the Pearl shows, if one tries to trace and date major manifestations of syncretistic spiritualism.

The Hymn is contained in the apocryphal Acts of Thomas but is so thinly related to the story of the apostle that it can reasonably be argued to be a poem of extraneous origin inserted into the Acts. The authorities, then, split over the question whether this poem of an undoubtedly acosmic, pneumatic, soteriological content is a document that proves the existence of a pre-Christian, Iranian Gnosticism, or whether it represents the spirit of Encratistic Christianity in the Syrian area and must be dated in the second century A.D. The disagreement, with scholars of the rank of Hans Jonas on the Gnostic-Iranian and Gilles Quispel on the Christian-Encratistic side, cannot be expected to dissolve quickly, if at all, as it is caused by yet insufficiently explored problems in the process of syncretistic spiritualism. For the precreational psychodrama, though it is one of the forms into which the process can issue, is not the only one possible. The spiritualist who experiences the contraction of divine order to personal existence is not obligated to expand the acosmism of his experience into an anti-cosmic construction of reality as a whole; he can restrict himself, as does the author of the Hymn, to the tension of existential order and symbolize it as the struggle to wrest the Pearl of Salvation from the Dragon of this world. In such a case it is difficult indeed to decide whether the literary document should be understood as a pre-Christian step in the direction of Gnosticism, or as a Gnostic manifestation in the context of early Christianity, or as a non-Gnostic poem representative of Syriac Christianity. The spiritualist's search for the Unknown God with syncretistic means would fit into any one of these contexts.[2]

The contraction of divine order into personal existence, as well as its

[2] For the acquisition of proper names by angels in the context of Judaic apocalyptic see D. S. Russell, *The Method and Message of Jewish Apocalyptic* (Philadelphia, 1964), 243ff.

The Acts of Thomas, with the Hymn of the Pearl, is in *The Apocryphal New Testament*, transl. by M. R. James (Oxford, 1960). See also the translation in Hans Jonas, *The Gnostic Religion* (2nd ed.; Boston, 1963), 113ff. In the prevalent opinion, the Hymn is considered Gnostic and therefore included in the anthologies of Gnostic texts. See Robert Haardt, *Die Gnosis* (Salzburg, 1967), 138ff., and *Die Gnosis*, ed. Werner Foerster (Zurich, 1969), I, 455ff. For the Encratistic interpretation see Gilles Quispel, *Makarius, das Thomasevangelium und das Lied von der Perle* (Leiden, 1967), 39–64.

The study of Gnosticism and its Iranian derivation still suffers from the application of the doxographic category of "dualism," which originates in the eighteenth century A.D., to both Zoroastrianism and Gnosticism. The term *dualism* was applied, as a neologism, to the Zoroastrian symbolism of Ormuzd and Ahriman for the first time by Thomas Hyde in his *Historia religionis veterum Persarum* in 1700. (Lalande, *Vocabulaire*, Paris, 1962, *s.v. Dualisme*). Hyde's dualistic interpretation was resumed and given wide circulation by Pierre Bayle's *Dictionnaire Historique et Critique* (5th ed.; Amsterdam, 1734, *s.v. Zoroastre*). Hyde was aware, however, that a Zoroastrian "dualism" is controversial and related the alternative opinion that the good and evil divinities are not primordial but entities created by a higher god. Bayle in his turn discussed the issue at length and decided for the uncreated character of the divinities as "deux causes coëternelles." In support of his decision he referred to Plutarch's opinion in *Isis and Osiris*, 369D ff. This passage is of considerable importance for the present issue of syncretistic spiritualism, because Plutarch indeed relates the gods of good and evil as Zoroastrian doctrine but is also aware that the doctrine in this form is a piece of nonsense. If there are two opposed principles in the cosmos, they cannot be primordial; in the background there is Nature (*physis*) which is the source (*arche*) of both good and evil (*ibid.*, 369D). As far as Plutarch is concerned, Ormuzd and Ahriman are intracosmic gods who have drifted into syncretistic usage; in a spiritualist's reflection they make sense only with Nature as the Unknown God in the background. That the *Gathas* of Zoroaster are not "dualistic" has by now been established by the studies of R. C. Zaehner, *The Dawn and Twilight of Zoroastrianism* (New York, 1961), and Walter Hinz, *Zarathustra* (Stuttgart, 1961). I am inclined, therefore, to see in the Zoroastrianism of the imperial period, which indeed has "dualistic" characteristics, the result of an existential contraction under the pressure of ecumenism. This view would support the search for the origins of Gnosticism in the Iranian "dualism" inasmuch as the "dualism" is not originally Zoroastrian but already a syncretistic contraction in the process that can end in Gnosticism.—The immense ramifications of the problems here indicated can be gathered from the volume U. Bianchi (ed.), *The Origins of Gnosticism. Colloquium of Messina* (Leiden, 1967).

motivations, has become most clearly articulate in the Israelite-Judaic case. The process can be characterized as a series of even more radical variations on the theme of Exodus. There is, first, the pragmatic escape from Egypt which is, at the same time, a spiritual exodus from the cosmological form of imperial rule. The sonship of god is transferred from the pharaoh to the people of Israel in immediate existence under Yahweh. In order to survive pragmatically, however, the tribal federation under the Kingship of God has to give itself a ruling son of god, a king like the other nations. This establishment of a second son of god by the side of the people injects an ambiguity into the political symbolism that is never quite resolved intellectually as long as the Davidic-Solomonic empire and the successor kingdoms last. In the eighth century, the conflict between pragmatic kingship and prophetic theopolitism culminates in the Isaianic demand that in a war the king should not rely on fortifications and the army, but on his faith in Yahweh who would miraculously divert the danger from his people. This metastatic faith of the prophet, expecting from a royal act of faith a miraculous change in the vicissitudes of war, marks an exodus not from the cosmological form only but from the pragmatic structure of existence in society and history. In the sixth century, then, when Cyrus conquers Babylon, Deutero-Isaiah develops the symbolism of Israel as the Suffering Servant who now will come into his own as the "light of the nations" and "the prince and commander to the peoples." After the creation of the world and the covenant with Israel, history now enters its third phase as the Kingdom of God, comprehending all nations, with Jerusalem as the spiritual center. Israel is no longer a nation among others but the transformer of all nations into herself; in a second exodus she has to go forth from herself to carry the news of salvation to the ends of the earth. The creator-god (*bore*) has been transformed into the Redeemer (*goel*) for all mankind. In the second century, finally, during the clash with the Seleucid Empire, the symbolism assumes its apocalyptic form in the Book of Daniel. The succession of empires is senseless; there is no hope of pragmatic victory over the imperial enemy or of a spiritual transformation of mankind. Since the present structure of reality is without meaning, a divine intervention has to change the structure itself, if divine order is to be reintroduced. The consciousness of divine ordering reality has contracted into the visions of an apocalyptic thinker. The stage is set for the divine messengers who abandon created reality altogether and concentrate on the Gnosis of the redemptive exodus from the cosmos.

The Israelite case leaves no doubt about the nature of the issue. The process of contraction is a disturbance of consciousness through the loss of balance between the Beginning and the Beyond. Moreover, since the disturbance reaches farther back than the ecumenic empires, the revelatory experience of the Israelite type becomes visible as an independent cause of imbalance, for the metastatic expectations of Isaiah arise from his sense of contradiction between the order of faith in Yahweh and the order of power in political existence. The component of eschatological direction in the experience is so strong that the prophet can confront cosmos and society with an anticipatory demand of spiritual fulfillment and declare the reality which does not conform to be devoid of meaning. This peculiar twist in prophetic spiritualism can be historically understood as the consequence of pneumatic differentiation in a tribal society, wanting in noetic differentiation and conceptual distinctions. The Exodus from Egypt symbolizes compactly the exodus from both cosmological form and from political organization beyond that of a tribal federation. The effects of this archaic compactness will become clearer through a comparison of the Isaianic with the Platonic attitude toward the problem of realizing the truth of existence in the order of society. When Plato lets his analysis of right order in society culminate in the symbols of the Philosopher-King and the Royal Ruler, he is fully aware of the obstacles presented by human nature and the course of pragmatic history to the event of a paradigmatic polis ever becoming the institution of a society; he stresses both the improbability of its establishment and the inevitability of its decline if it ever should be established. When Isaiah lets his faith culminate in the vision of the Prince of Peace who will set the act of faith which the pragmatic king rejects, he believes in the magic power of an act that will transmute the structure of reality, as well as in his own advice as a Gnosis of transmutation. If to this component of archaic magic in prophetic pneumatism is added the series of political catastrophes, which appears to support the thesis of a pragmatic reality devoid of meaning, the pneumatic process seems to be bound to issue into Gnosticism by its internal logic. Though Gnosticism is not a Jewish but a multicivilizational movement in an ecumenic empire, its peculiar fervor and secular momentum are hardly intelligible without the prophetic and apocalyptic prehistory, culminating in the epiphany of Christ, as an important genetic factor.

The Balance Regained—Philo

Gnosticism, whether ancient or modern, is a dead end. That of course is its attraction. Magic pneumatism gives its addicts a sense of superiority over the reality which does not conform. Whether the addiction assumes the forms of libertarianism and asceticism preferred in antiquity, or the modern forms of constructing systems which contain the ultimate truth and must be imposed on recalcitrant reality by means of violence, concentration camps, and mass murder, the addict is dispensed from the responsibilities of existence in the cosmos. Since Gnosticism surrounds the *libido dominandi* in man with a halo of spiritualism or idealism, and can always nourish its righteousness by pointing to the evil in the world, no historical end to the attraction is predictable once magic pneumatism has entered history as a mode of existence. Nevertheless, it is a dead end inasmuch as it rejects the life of spirit and reason under the conditions of the cosmos in which reality becomes luminous in pneumatic and noetic consciousness. There is no alternative to an eschatological extravaganza but to accept the mystery of the cosmos. Man's existence is participation in reality. It imposes the duty of noetically exploring the structure of reality as far as it is intelligible and spiritually coping with the insight into its movement from the divine Beginning to the divine Beyond of its structure.

Under the intellectual and spiritual conditions of the multicivilizational empire, with its diaspora of both Jews and Greeks, the recovery of balance was as complicated a process as its loss. In a viable balance, the movement of spiritual contraction had to come to terms with existence in the ecumenic-imperial society; the intracosmic gods of syncretistic spiritualism had to give way to the monotheistic tendencies in both the Israelite pneumatic and Hellenic noetic differentiations of consciousness; the Israelite-Judaic pneumatism, if it was to hold its own in the intellectually superior environment of Hellenistic culture, had to assimilate the philosophers' noetic thinking; and the philosophers in their turn, whose noetic differentiation had never quite broken with the symbolization of divine presence through intracosmic gods, had to live with the more radical differentiation of the one god of the Beyond in Judaic and Christian pneumatism. This process belongs no more to any of the former ethnic cultures—Roman, Greek, Persian, Egyptian, Babylonian, Israelite—than the genesis of Gnosticism; it is a process in which the multicivilizational society finds itself as an ecumenic society. The movements and symbolisms emerging, whether major ones like Talmudic Judaism, Christianity, Gnosticism, Stoicism, Skepticism, and Neoplatonism, or minor ones like Hermetism, Alchemy, and Astrology—they all represent pressures and tensions in the mobile and fluid culture of a new society in the making. Still, though the process creates a widely diversified, open field of phenomena, it has direction because its dynamics is governed by the standards of consciousness radiating from the pneumatic and noetic differentiations, as well as by the pragmatic exigencies of imperial power. The superior strength of these historical forces, as well as the direction they impose, becomes tangible when Justinian symbolizes the result in his conception of the Emperor as the representative of the three sources of authority in the new society: The Emperor is the *religiosissimus juris,* the most conscientious administrator of the law based on philosophy; he is the defender of the faith in the form established by the Councils; and he is the *imperator,* the chief magistrate of imperial power based on the army.

A critical episode in the struggle for finding the balance of consciousness in the ecumenic society was the encounter of Judaism with philosophy in Alexandria, culminating in the work of Philo, the older contemporary of Christ. The Philonic fusion of pneumatic and noetic insights through the literary device of a philosophical commentary on Scripture set the pattern of methods and problems later to be followed by the Patres in their fusion of Christianity and philosophy. The method of interpretation developed by Philo is called Allegoresis; the pattern of problems presupposed and engendered by the method comprehends the conception of Scripture as the Word of God, the issues of reason and revelation, as well as of faith and reason, and the conception of philosophy as the handmaid of Scripture. As Wolfson stresses, Philo has laid the foundations for seventeen centuries of religious philosophy in Judaism, Christianity, and Islam, until Spinoza broke with the pattern in his *Tractatus Theologico-Politicus.* In the course of this long history, the stratification of this complex symbolism has become obscured. The problems mentioned have separated from the allegoric method from which they arose and acquired an authority of their own as the unquestioned premises of intellectual debate. And the Philonic Allegoresis has separated from the problems of the multicivilizational society in the ecumenic empire which caused it to be developed. The experiential origins of the symbolism are barely discernible under the wealth of data on these millennial issues of Western intellectual history.

Moreover, I must go one step further than Wolfson in estimating the historical consequences of Philo's work. The pattern set by Philo does not remain restricted to the religious philosophy of Judaism, Christianity, and Islam. It continues in the creation of the ideological systems as new types of Scripture, in the use of philosophy as the handmaid to the new Scriptures, and in the conflict of reason with the newly revealed truth. The Philonic

symbolism is still a major obstacle to the life of reason in the twentieth century
A.D. Since this obstacle relies for its effectiveness largely on the fact that it has
become an unconscious structure in Western thought, I have to bring to
consciousness its origins in the problems of the Ecumenic Age, as well as the
inadequacies connected with this origin.

Before entering into these inadequacies in detail, however, I must recall
the comprehensive issue in which they become important, *i.e.,* the rebalancing
of consciousness through the return to cosmogony.

Within the Judaic tradition, pneumatic extremes can be countered by
asserting the authority of the Torah against the prophets; and within the
Torah, a cosmogony practically free of intracosmic remnants lends itself to the
recognition of man as a citizen of the god-created cosmos. Philo makes full
use of these possibilities in his commentary *On the Creation of the World
According to Moses.* As far as Philo is concerned, the Torah is a body of laws
given by Moses, and the code proper is prefaced by the story of creation. By
this arrangement Moses wants recipients of the code to understand that the
law is attuned to the cosmos and the cosmos to the law. The man who obeys
this law is a citizen of the cosmos, because he regulates his conduct by the will
of nature (*physis*) which pervades the whole cosmos. By the end of the first
page of commentary, man is established as the *cosmopolites* under the law of
nature and of nature's god. The feat of transforming the members of the
Chosen People into cosmopolitans is remarkable. Moreover, it should be noted
that the word *cosmopolites* is possibly a Philonic neologism. It does not occur
in the Stoics to whom it is still frequently ascribed; and the attribution to a
dictum by Diogenes the Cynic stems from Diogenes Laertius in the third
century A.D. In the extant literature the term appears for the first time in this
passage of Philo's *De opificio, 3.*[3]

In the commentary on the cosmogonic preface to the Torah, then, the
status of the creation story as a symbolism becomes thematic. Though Philo's

---

[3] On Philo cf. Harry Austryn Wolfson, *Philo: Foundations of Religious Philosophy in Judaism,
Christianity, and Islam* (Cambridge, Mass., 1947). On Philo's Allegoresis and on "The Handmaid
of Scripture," cf. Wolfson, *ibid.,* I, 2. On the corresponding problems in the Patres cf. Wolfson,
The Philosophy of the Church Fathers (2nd ed.; Cambridge, Mass., 1964), I, 2–4. For Wolfson's
elaboration of the Philonic problems in later history cf. his *Religious Philosophy: A Group of
Essays* (Cambridge, Mass., 1961). On the pre-Philonic encounter of Judaism and Hellenism cf.
Martin Hengel, *Judentum und Hellenismus* (Tuebingen, 1969). On the Christian Allegoresis, in
particular its development through Origen, cf. the pertinent chapters in Jean Daniélou, *Origène*
(Paris, 1948); Henri De Lubac, *Histoire et Esprit. L'Intelligence del l'Ecriture d'après Origène*
(Paris, 1950); Henri Crouzel, *Origène et la "Connaissance Mystique"* (Paris, 1961).

analysis of the issue is inadequate, I shall present both its structure and its motivations with some care, because this analysis has set the pattern of inadequacy that was taken over by the Christian thinkers and transmitted by them, through the Middle Ages, into the modern period. The inadequacy is the millennial constant that must be dissolved by raising it into consciousness.

The cosmogony of Genesis breaks with the compact symbolism of the intracosmic gods, characteristic of its Egyptian predecessors, and identifies the creator-god of the Beginning with the Unknown God of the Beyond whose presence is experienced in the theophanies of Moses and the prophets. It is a cosmogonic myth, affected in its structure by the pneumatic differentiations of consciousness. Philo is aware of the issue but nevertheless declares the creation story to be a body of philosophical "thoughts" (*noemata*). Since Philo knew the *Timaeus* well, as the text of *De opificio* shows, and could have followed Plato's procedure in dealing with the issue, the decision is somewhat surprising. If Plato could create the philosopher's myth as the symbolism that would satisfy the criteria of noetic truth while expressing the problems of divine reality beyond the range of dialectics in the Metaxy, and if he specifically created the noetic myth of the Demiurge in the *Timaeus*, it should have been possible for his successor to recognize in the cosmogony of Genesis a pneumatic myth of the Beginning. If the idea never crossed Philo's mind, as far as we know, the reasons should be sought less in a personal failing than in the decline of analytical standards during the imperial period since Alexander. Plato's conceptual distinctions between dialectics and the philosopher's myth had been lost; and the likely myth of the *Timaeus* had become a nondescript "philosophy of nature." In Philo's language, the term *myth* strictly denotes a myth of the polytheistic type, while the term *philosophy* indiscriminately denotes anybody's thoughts about god and the world. Since he intended to make the creation story acceptable in the Alexandrian intellectual milieu in which this usage was current, the cosmogony could under no circumstances be a "myth," but had to be a "philosophy" like the Platonic, only better.

As a consequence Moses himself has to be transformed into a philosopher. Philo works the miracle in his interpretation of the Thornbush Episode in *De fuga,* 161ff: Moses did not see a thornbush burning at all. Being a lover of knowledge, in search of the causes of things, he wondered why things waste away and come to birth, why in all this perishing there is a remaining, and he expressed his wondering about the Anaximandrian becoming and perishing by the metaphoric question, "Why is that bush burning and yet not being consumed?" By this question, however, Moses was trespassing on the divine mystery of creation. Were he to engage in further pursuit, his labor would be futile, for man is not able to penetrate the causal structure of the cosmos. Hence, the voice of the savior-god comes from the holy ground of aetiology and orders the intellectual adventurer to restrain his curiosity. The warning "Do not come near" means that the subject-matter of causation, the question why things are as they are, is inaccessible to man's understanding. Moses minds the divine warning, but his desire to know (*pothos epistemes*) now urges him on to lift his eyes higher and to ask the question concerning the essence (*ousia*) of the creator-god. Again, however, his search is frustrated by the divine information that no man can see the face of Him-Who-Is and live. For the sage (*sophos*) it will be enough to know what follows after god and in his wake.

The *De fuga* passage reveals the structural core of what I have called the Philonic pattern of inadequacy. Philo ignores the experience expressed by the Thornbush Episode, fragmentizes its symbolism, and interprets the fragments as allegories of a different experience. In the context of *De fuga,* this other experience is only briefly intimated as the search of the *philomathes*, the lover of knowledge, for the causes of things. In *De opificio,* 69–71, it becomes more fully articulate as the philosopher's *via negativa,* as the ascent of the Nous in man from the contemplation of things on earth through the sciences, to the ether and the revolutions of the heaven, and further on to the intelligible world of the paradigms of the things of sense perception. When the ascent has reached the world of intelligible forms, the surpassing beauty of the spectacle fills the mind with a sober intoxication, something like a Corybantic enthusiasm; it is gripped with a desire (*pothos*) to see the Great King himself. Though it presses on in its longing, however, it cannot reach its goal, for a stream of purest light breaks forth from the divine source and darkens the sight of understanding.

This account of the experience is not a piece of secondary information. Philo has really an articulate conception of the existential tension toward the divine ground. In *De migratione,* 34–35, he describes it with circumstantial detail as his own experience (*pathos*) of the divine-human encounter in its modes of frustration and elation. At times, when he sits down to write on a philosophical subject he has clear in his mind, the ideas will not come, for experiential analysis is not a matter of human effort alone; he recognizes the self-conceit of his attempt; and he gives up, filled with amazement at the power of Him-Who-Is, who can open or close the womb of the psyche. At other times, he approaches his work empty, and suddenly the ideas shower from above; he finds himself in a state of divine possession (*katoche entheos*); he becomes unconscious of himself and his surroundings, of what is spoken or written; in a joy of light, with clearest vision, he distinguishes the object and obtains the language to express it.

I have presented certain aspects of the Philonic experience and analysis at some length, in order to bring the oddity of the situation to attention. Philo is a spiritually and intellectually sensitive thinker. He knows about the experience of existential tension in the search of the ground, about the ascent of the *via negativa,* about the movement of thought in the In-Between reality, about the limits set to this movement by the apeirontic depth of becoming and perishing and by the noetic height of the light that darkens understanding as it hides the divine essence. He is furthermore familiar with the self-conceit (*oiesis*) of self-reliant effort, with Corybantic enthusiasm and divine possession, with sober intoxication, and with something like automatic talking and writing in a state of unconsciousness (*panta agnoein*) which at the same time is a state of pellucid distinction and symbolization. And in spite of the ample exposition of the problem by Plato, this knowledgeable thinker is unable to recognize the cosmogony of the *Timaeus* as a noetic myth; he is consequently unable to recognize in the creation story of Genesis a pneumatic cosmogony, dependent for its creational symbolism on the Mosaic and prophetic differentiations of consciousness; and finally he fragmentizes the Thornbush Episode by an allegorical interpretation which makes nonsense of the text, transforms Moses into a philosopher, and misses the point of the pneumatic experience in the revelation of divine reality as the I-am-who-I-am.

ALLEGORESIS

The various oddities of Philo's analysis have their common source in his development and use of Allegoresis for the purpose of interpreting the Torah. To Philo, the Torah is a work written by Moses, a man beloved of God. As it goes back, through Moses, to God himself, it presents in ultimate form the truth about God, the cosmos, and the order of man's existence in society and history. This work is not easy of access, because its meaning is stratified into a surface or literal meaning and an underlying meaning that must be extracted by interpretation. Its language has the character of a sacred oracle whose mysterious formulae must be made intelligible, and the underlying, hidden meaning can be extracted by translating the oracle into the language of what Philo considers to be philosophy. In his interpretation of the Garden of Eden, in *De plantatione,* 36, he formulates the issue succinctly: "Now we must turn to allegory (*allegoria*), dear to men who are able to see; and the oracles (*chresmoi*) offer us indeed definite signs (*aphormai*) from where to begin; for they say that in paradise there are trees not similar to any we know, but trees of life, of immortality, of knowledge, of apprehension, of understanding, and of the conception of good and evil." Since a garden of this kind does not grow in the soil of the earth, only its growth in the rational soul (*logike psyche*) of man can be meant. Philo can continue, therefore, with a description of the "garden of virtues" intended by the oracle.

Though in the extant literature Philo is the first thinker to let the term *allegoria* denote the extraction of an underlying meaning, of an *hyponoia,* from a literary text, it probably had already some currency for this purpose in his time. In a letter possibly written still within the lifetime of Philo, in Galatians 4:24, for instance, Paul speaks of the story of Hagar and Sarah as an allegory (*allegoroumena*) for the old convenant from Sinai and the new one through Christ, and he uses the term as if it did not require an explanation. Moreover, in the Alexandrian milieu there was a long-standing need for such a term, for already Aristobulos had recognized, in the tract he addressed to the young Ptolemy VI Philometor in *ca.* 175–170 B.C., the necessity of making the mythical and anthropomorphic language of the Torah intelligible for its underlying philosophical meaning through adequate interpretation. And the same need was felt in the Hellenic milieu proper for denoting the philosophers' interpretation of Homeric and Hesiodic gods, as attested by Plutarch's (*ca.* A.D. 46–120) use of the verb *allegorein* in the sense of "interpreting allegorically" (*Moralia,* 363d).

The vocabulary of Allegoresis, as the account of its origin shows, emerges casually in the first century A.D. from a need to refer topically to a widespread hermeneutic phenomenon of considerable ancestry which by this time apparently has entered an acute phase. The vocabulary does not arise from analysis; it does not have the character of analytical concepts but remains strictly topical. As a consequence, nothing can be extracted from it but the fact of its reference to the phenomenon and its obvious characteristics: Important bodies of literature, belonging to the cultural heritage of Israel and Hellas, have suffered a severe atrophy of meaning; the hermeneutic enterprise has clearly the purpose of saving the cultural heritage and preserving the continuity of history in an existentially new situation; since philosophy, Judaism, and Christianity are actively engaged in the enterprise, the noetic and pneumatic illuminations of consciousness are important factors in establishing the new historical situation as well as in causing, by their differentiated insights into the truth of existence, the meaning of an older, more compactly experienced and symbolized literature to atrophy. In this new situation, the problem of preserving the continuity of meaning in history is resolved by superimposing on the original meaning of literary texts an interlocking set of two new meanings: First, the older symbolic language, separated from its compact engendering experience, is declared to have a surface or literal meaning of its own; and second, this literal meaning is transmogrified into an underlying meaning, an *hyponoia,* by relating the compact symbols imaginatively to the differentiated experiences of the interpreter. Even this restrained description of the phenomenon, however, already modifies the topical reference by an injection of analysis. If the users of the allegoric method were analytically conscious of the structure just described, they probably would not engage in their enterprise but would prefer analysis to Allegoresis themselves. The phenomenon will become intelligible only if a state of noetic semiconsciousness is recognized as an important factor in allegoric thinking.

An inquiry into Allegoresis in terms of experiential motivations must go beyond the modest analytical expansion of the topical reference just given. Above all, it must take cognizance of the concrete issues. The Philonic Allegoresis is not a random interpretation of a random text, but the great encounter of Hellenic philosophy with the Israelite-Judaic Torah in Alexandria; it is an attempt at cultural integration in an ecumenic-imperial society. Moreover, the philosophy and Torah which enter into Philo's integrative act are not quite so Hellenic and Israelite as they are made to sound by the conventional language I have just used. For neither is Philo's philosophy the noetic analysis which Plato and Aristotle developed under this name, nor is the divine word of the canonical Torah the word of God revealed through the mouths of the prophets. What Philo means by philosophy is the modification, or rather deformation, which classic philosophy has suffered under the impact of Alexander's imperial expansion; and the canonical Torah is the deformation of the prophets' pneumatic word by the post-exilic creation and imposition of a sacred Scripture, motivated by the political catastrophes which Israel had suffered from the imperial conquests. The peculiar inadequacies of Philo's analysis, the state of noetic semiconsciousness as I have called it, would be unintelligible without the imperial deformation of its components. The method of allegoric interpretation itself, finally, has a long history of ecumenic range, well explored on the phenotypical level. The allegoric interpretation of Homer and Hesiod can be traced back in continuity to Theagenes of Rhegium in the late sixth century B.C., while the Philonic interpretation of the Torah is preceded by centuries of Midrashic allegory. Tracing the phenotype establishes Allegoresis as an ecumenic phenomenon, but the data will render their full meaning only if the experiential dimension is added. For the pre-Stoic Allegoresis of the epic poets is not philosophical; the philosophers, Plato and Aristotle, treat it with amused irony, if not contempt. And the experientially important point about Midrashic exegesis is not the allegoric method, but its application to a sacred Scripture to which there is no equivalent in Hellenic history. In the Hellenic case, philosophy must be deformed before it can become a suitable instrument of allegoric interpretation; in the Israelite case, the immediate pneumatic experiences are deformed by Scriptural mediation before they become the object of allegoric interpretation. These structural differences between noetic and pneumatic history in the common ecumenic-imperial society require some further reflections.

THE DEFORMATION OF PHILOSOPHY INTO DOCTRINE

The deformation of philosophic analysis becomes tangible in the transition from the Platonic-Aristotelian aloofness from Allegoresis to the Stoic acceptance of the method. As a philosopher Plato has no use for an allegoric interpretation of Homer and Hesiod. He experiences divine reality as the ordering force in the cosmos and in personal existence; he recognizes his dialectical exploration of structures in reality as a movement of thought in the Metaxy; and he knows that divine reality beyond the Metaxy, if it is to be symbolized at all, can be symbolized only by the myth. The truth of the myth then is to be measured by the truth of noetically illuminated existence. Since the myth of the epic poets falls short of the standard, Plato roundly disposes of it as *pseudos*, as falsehood, and solves the problem of the true myth by creating it in the *alethinos logos*, the true story of his own mythopoesis. In both respects he follows the precedent of Hesiod who opposes the truth of his theogony to the *pseudos* of the still more compact myths which he absorbs and transforms in his mytho-speculative work. The same method of relating later phases in the process of differentiation to the earlier ones as truth to falsehood, it should be noted, is used by the prophets when they oppose their pneumatically true god to the false gods of the cosmological myth. When the differentiated truth of reality is intensely experienced and adequately symbolized, the more compact symbols of the older truth become false. And that would be the end of the matter, if a discovery concerning man's humanity in relation to God were no more than a personal affair, if it did not have also a social and historical dimension.

Though Plato knew that the old myth had been true before it had become false through the rise of philosophy, he sometimes could assume the personal stance of the true-false decision quite intensely, because as an educator he had to contend with the social influence of the epic myth. The young men whom he wanted to educate had received their previous education through the study of the epic poets under instructors who, at their discretion, used various allegorical interpretations in their exposition of the subject-matter; and Plato was no happier about the results than a scholar is today, when the pitiful, ideologically confused products of previous education are handed over to him for further treatment. It is the educator's compassion for the victims of education that moves him to reject for his model society the Homeric and Hesiodic tales of the gods in the education of the young. "For the young are not able to distinguish what is underlying meaning (*hyponoia*) and what is not, and whatever enters into opinion at that age has a way of proving indelible and unalterable" (*Republic,* 378D). As the passage in context shows, allegoric interpretation has become a social necessity, because in the centuries of the rise of the polis and its social conflicts, of the Persian Wars, the Athenian Empire and the Peloponnesian War, of philosophy, tragedy, comedy, and sophistic, the epic myth of the gods has lost its meaning together with the experiences that have engendered it. The myth has been literalized into stories about gods who engage in such immoral actions as adultery, incest, war, and infliction of war upon men. This literalism as a social force endangers the humanity of the young, because it converts the real truth which the symbols of the myth have as the real expression of a real experience of real divine presence into the fictitious truth of human propositions about gods who are objects of cognition. Literalism splits the symbol from the experience by hypostatizing the symbol as a proposition on objects. Literalizing the old myth carries with it the danger of literalizing every myth and, as the myth is the only symbolism man has to express his experience of divine reality, the further danger of deadening the formation of man's humanity through man's opening to divine presence. Since derailment into literalism and the loss of faith are always possible as a response when a man is confronted with a plurality of more and less differentiated symbolisms, Plato cautions, in the *Epinomis,* against molesting the faith of the true believer with philosophy, because once his faith is shaken he quite possibly will not become a philosopher but will be-

lieve nothing at all. If the loss of faith, however, has occurred already, the philosopher can try to induce the turning around, the *periagoge*, by his educational
effort. But the means to that end is philosophy, not an allegoric interpretation
of Homer which does not reach down to the experiences from which true
insights, whether old or new ones, arise. What concrete allegoric efforts Plato
had in mind cannot be said with certainty, but if they looked anything like
the etymologizing allegories of the gods enumerated in the *Cratylus* his irony
was well justified. Aristotle has only an occasional remark about "these old
Homerics" who see minor similarities but cannot see the important ones
(*Metaphysics,* 1093a28ss).

The problem presented by the transition from classic to Stoic philosophy,
as well as the perplexity it causes in contemporary science, has been well
formulated by Carl Schneider in his standard treatise on Hellenistic culture:
"The turn of Hellenism from science to religion is certainly in part due to
Platonism, but to the larger part it must be attributed to the Stoa. The real
reason for this turn we shall probably never fully penetrate."[4] Though I do
not share Schneider's resignation, I can sympathize with the perplexity caused
by the Stoic experiences and their symbolization. Deformations of symbols
already differentiated are indeed more difficult to understand than the original
symbols themselves, because as a rule the deformers neither analyze their
method of deformation themselves, nor are they informative about their
motives. And yet, the work of penetration must be done because deformation
of differentiations achieved is a force in world-history of the same magnitude
as differentiation itself. The issue at hand is all the more important because
the technique of deformation developed by the Stoic thinkers has been continued through Philo into Christianity, and through Christianity into the
modern deformation of philosophy by the ideological thinkers.
    What Schneider calls the turn from science to religion in Stoicism implies,
though the issue is never formulated, the abolition of Plato's critical distinction between the dialectical movement of thought in the Metaxy and the mythopoetic symbolization of the divine ambiance. Though the Stoics engage in
mythopoesis, adding new symbols to the Platonic ones, they no longer acknowledge mythopoetic creation as such, but treat the symbols as if they were
concepts referring to objects on which the philosopher has to advance proposi-

---

[4] Carl Schneider, *Kulturgeschichte des Hellenismus* (Munich, 1969), II, 581.

tions. The literalism that formerly had affected the epic myth is now expanded
to philosophy itself. Only the critical distinction, however, is abandoned. The
Stoics neither reject the noetic differentiation of consciousness which caused
the distinction to be made, nor do they deny the reality of the cognitive
tension toward the divine ground in man's psyche which Plato and Aristotle
made noetically articulate. On the contrary, they are so much aware of its
importance that they introduce the abstract term *tension* into the philosophical
vocabulary. While Plato and Aristotle still speak the concrete language of the
tension, of wondering and turning around, of searching and finding, of love,
hope, and faith, the Stoics develop the abstract *tasis* to denote the tension in
matter toward its form, and the abstract *tonos* to denote the tension toward
divine order in man's psyche and in the cosmos as a whole. And yet, precisely
with the development of these abstracts that confirm the tension as the center
of philosophizing, begins the deformation of reality which perplexes the historians and interpreters. For the more abstract the language of the tension
becomes, the more liable is its user to forget that the language is part of the
divine-human encounter in which man's tension toward the ground becomes
luminous to itself. There is no language in the abstract, as some modern
linguists appear to assume, by which man can refer to the hierophantic events
of the noetic and pneumatic differentiations, but only the concrete language
created in the articulation of the event. The emergence of a language of truth
is part of the mystery of a truth that constitutes history by revealing itself.
However, the hierophantic event that engenders the language passes with the
man who has been graced by it, while the language remains in the world.
When it enters history, truth has to carry the burden of death and time; and
in the hands of lesser thinkers, who are sensitive to the truth in a measure
but are not able to reactivate the engendering experience fully, the surviving
truth of the language can acquire a status independent of the originating
reality. The truth of reality living in the symbols can be deformed into a
doctrinal truth about reality; and since the object to which the doctrinal truth
refers propositionally does not exist, it must be invented. This is what happens
in the Stoic case. The divine-human encounter, carefully analyzed by Plato
as the immaterial In-Between of divine and human reality, and by Aristotle
as the metaleptic reality, becomes for the Stoics under the name of tension the
property of a material object called the psyche. The materialization of the
psyche and its tension is then extended to divine reality and the cosmos at
large. And the materialized divine entities of Nous, Logos, Aether, Nature,

Cosmos, finally, become the basis for establishing the cultural continuity with the Hellenic past by finding Stoic philosophy, through allegoric interpretation, the underlying meaning of the Homeric and Hesiodic myth.

The Stoic procedure was noted and criticized by contemporary thinkers. A good deal of the information on the issue we owe to its critical presentation by the Epicurean speaker, Velleius, in Cicero's *De natura deorum*. The critical complaint is directed against the hypostases of a variety of symbols into gods. Zeno is reported as according the status of gods to the law of nature, the aether, reason, the stars, the years, months, and seasons; and as depriving, in his interpretation of Hesiod's *Theogony,* Jupiter, Juno, and Vesta of their divinity by insisting that their names allegorically signify divine entities of a material nature. Cleanthes assigns divine status to the cosmos, to the mind and soul of the world, and to the aether. Chrysippus has a similar list, adding fate and necessity, water, earth, air, the sun, moon, and stars, and the embracing whole of the cosmos; in his interpretation of the myths of Orpheus, Musaeus, Hesiod, and Homer he assimilates their gods to his own gods so skillfully that "even these oldest poets, who never suspected it, are made out to be Stoics" (I, 36–41). In the opinion of the reporter, these doctrines must be characterized as "dreams of deliriously raving men rather than opinions of philosophers," as little less absurd than the poet's stories about lustful and licentious gods, the similarly "demented" fables of the Magians and Egyptians, and generally the beliefs of the ignorant people (I, 42–43). As far as the rationale of this judgment is concerned, finally, it becomes apparent from the historical survey of Greek philosophy. The "Stoic dreams" come at the end of a long history of phantasies about the gods, from the water of Thales and the air of Anaximenes, to the infinite mind of Anaxagoras and the world-soul of Pythagoras, down to such "vain inventions" as the architecture of the universe in the *Timaeus* and especially Plato's conception of the Demiurge. In accordance with the practice established by the Stoics, the reporter reduces the rich variety of symbols, developed from the Ionian philosophers to Plato and Aristotle in the process of noetic differentiation, to the level of doctrines about the gods to which also the Stoic doctrines belong. All of them are fanciful, because they do not fit the notion of the gods that is shared by all tribes of men without the benefit of doctrine (*sine doctrina,* 43).

Though that is not Cicero's intention, his account of the "Stoic dreams" describes with clinical exactness a state of profound spiritual disturbance as well as the syndrome of the tactics employed to escape from it. The spiritual insecurity is caused by the two events of Platonic-Aristotelian philosophy and

Alexander's imperial expansion, both of which close old horizons by opening new ones; the diagnostically decisive symptoms of escape are the doctrinal deformation of Plato's mythopoesis and the preoccupation with allegory. The devices of deformation and allegory have the purpose of minimizing the magnitude of the epochal break in history by pretending that not too much has happened after all and veiling, by this pretense, the unwillingness or inability to face the spiritual problems of universal humanity that had been created by the break. The problems were formidable indeed. From the noetic differentiations of Plato and Aristotle one could not return to the intracosmic gods, one could only pursue the truth of existence further, in the pneumatic direction, through experiential response to the soteriological and eschatological implications of a revelation from the Beyond. Plato, though he was aware of the pneumatic direction in which philosophy had to move, had set in his published work the philosopher's myth as the limit to his exploration; if the Stoics were to follow his intimations, they would have had to set aside the Platonic mythopoesis, especially the *Timaeus*, as an interim solution and indeed to pursue the Unknown God further into the pneumatic depth of his Beyond of the cosmos. Moreover, an advance of this kind, required by the internal logic of philosophizing, would also have met the parallel problems created by Alexander's imperial expansion. As in the case of philosophy, one could not return from the conquest to the cultures of the ethnic units conquered and to their gods; one could only advance toward the culture of an ecumenic society under the universal god of all men. Nevertheless, though Alexander had already recognized the problem and attempted a solution, the Stoics did not take the course of pneumatic differentiation. They rather compromised on literalizing Plato's intermediate symbolism and letting the deformed symbols absorb as much of the pneumatic component, compactly present in the symbolization of divine reality by the intracosmic gods, as was possible.

The compromise was not quite without merit in coping with the new situation. The Hellenic polis had been conquered, but the Stoics developed the myth of the cosmos as the common habitat and polis of gods and men, a symbolism that satisfied the needs of an ecumenic society after a fashion. In fact it was so good that Philo, who had no use for the gods, could refine it into the myth of the cosmos as the *megalopolis* which comprises all nations.[5] The cultivation of intracosmic pneumatism, furthermore, was intense enough to

[5] Philo, *De Iosepho*, 29.

find expression in one of the most famous Stoic documents, the Hymn to the pancratic Zeus by Cleanthes. What this Hymn means as a manifestation of the pneumatic compromise will perhaps be better understood if one tries to imagine the unimaginable, that Plato should have written such a hymn to the Demiurge of the *Timaeus*. And finally, the personal tension of existence was strong enough to preserve the dignity of man under the conditions of empire by developing the conceptions of apathy as the comprehensive virtue and of ataraxy as the *summum bonum*. Nevertheless, a heavy price had to be paid for these compromise achievements.

The application of the allegoric method to the epic myth will appear at first sight as a comparatively harmless pastime, perhaps no more than an ano-dyne for the shock caused by the epochal events. If Homer and Hesiod could be made over into Stoics, the Stoic thinkers in their turn would still be living in the same faith in the same gods as the poets. The events notwithstanding, no real break in man's existential consciousness, or in Hellenic political cul-ture, had occurred; the ecumenic-imperial society was still Hellas. Moreover, this vivid concern with cultural continuity possibly had something to do with the fact that, with the exception of Cleanthes, the principal Stoic thinkers were not Greeks but came from the eastern part of the empire. The problem had not worried the philosophers whose work consummated the noetic differentiation of consciousness that had been long in the making; Plato and Aristotle were Hellenic enough to be sure that Hellas was where they were. Whatever the incidental motives may have been, the construction of an imaginary continuity went far beyond the allegoric interpretation of the poets; it radically deformed the history of Greek philosophy and philosophic analysis itself. The notorious symptom of the deformation is the so-called Stoic materialism that still baffles historians today inasmuch as the "religious" inclinations of the Stoics seem to be incompatible with a "materialism" that is supposed to be the privilege of atheist reprobates. In fact, there is no such conflict or contradiction, for the Stoic "matter" is not the matter of physics but an imaginary medium that will permit the literalized gods of Stoicism to move in continuity with an older Hellenic tradition. What appears to be materialism is actually a return, back of Plato and Aristotle, to the symbolism created by the Ionian philosophers when in their noetic-mythical vision they let the divine cause of being blend with one of the principal elements, with water, air, or fire. It would be difficult indeed to distinguish between the pneuma which the Stoics let pervade and order the cosmos, and the pneuma, identical with air and the soul of man, to which Anaximenes assigns the same functions. And yet, the return is not

genuine, for the noetic component in the Ionian symbols has unfolded into
the noetic differentiation of consciousness, and the Stoics do not intend to
reverse this differentiation. It is an imaginary return, made possible by the
creation of an imaginary medium of thought in which the differences between
cosmological myth and philosophy, between dialectics in the Metaxy and
mythopoesis, dissolve. The divine elements of the Ionian symbolism can be
deformed into a "matter," and this imaginary "matter" then can become the
underlying substance by which the symbols, engendered by the noetic experience of the philosophers, are deformed into the divine entities which
aroused the contempt of the Epicurean critic in *De natura deorum*. A new
intellectual game with imaginary realities in an imaginary realm of thought,
the game of propositional metaphysics, has been opened with world-historic
consequences that reach into our own present. One of the immediate effects
of this deformation of symbols into doctrines was the damage to the exploration of structures in reality through science. Aristarchus of Samos had suggested, *ca.* 250 B.C., that the movements of celestial bodies could be described
more simply if the earth were assumed to rotate around its axis and to move
on an elliptical orbit through the heavens. Cleanthes, the successor to Zeno in
the Stoic school, was shocked to the bottom of his pneumatic piety and de-
manded that the Hellenes should prosecute Aristarchus for impiety because
he had dared to move the earth, the hearth of the cosmos, from its place. The
ban remained effective for seventeen centuries.[6]

RELIGION

When the Stoics literalize mythopoetic symbols, they deform philosophy
into concepts and propositions concerning imaginary objects; when they further apply the deformed philosophy to literary documents of the Hellenic
past, they deform history by replacing the experiential meaning of symbols
with a new literal-allegoric meaning; and these deformations still affect the
state of philosophy and historiography in the twentieth century A.D. Nevertheless, despite its analytical defects the Stoic enterprise of doctrinizing philosophy
must not be valued merely negatively. For the Stoic dogmatism, like the later
Christian theology, has the civilizational purpose and effect of protecting an
historically achieved state of insight against the disintegrative pressures to
which the differentiated truth of existence is exposed in the spiritual and in-

[6] Hans von Arnim, *Stoicorum Veterum Fragmenta*, I. 500.

tellectual turmoil of the ecumenic situation. It was the genius of Cicero to discern the forces of disintegration as well as the necessity of protecting the truth through language symbols, through a "word" that incarnates the truth of divine presence in reality. In the pursuit of this problem, Cicero developed the older Latin term *religio* into the symbol that comprehends protectively both the truth of existence and its expression through cultic observance and doctrine.

As the symbol Religion has to function on the level of doctrine, it can be no more an analytical concept than Allegoresis, but as it is devised to protect a *status quo* of insight achieved by philosophy, it makes the doctrine transparent for the truth it means to stabilize. Not surprisingly, therefore, the principal topics comprehended by Religion are closely related to the Platonic-Aristotelian problems. There is, first of all, the tension between the philosopher's mythopoesis and the *pseudos* of the older myth. In Cicero's language, the philosopher's understanding of divine reality becomes *religion*, while the older myth is depreciated as *superstition* (*De natura deorum*, II, 70–72). There is, second, the Platonic problem of the *typoi peri theologias*, of the Platonic theology as opposed to the Sophistic type: The Sophists claim that the gods, if they exist at all, do not care what men do, and if they care they can be bribed by sacrifices; Plato insists that the gods do care and cannot be bribed. In the introduction to *De natura deorum*, Cicero makes this conflict the motivating issue of his work: "Whether the gods do not act at all, and move nothing, and refrain from any direction and administration of things; or whether on the contrary all things were made and ordered by them in the beginning, and are controlled and moved by them for the infinity of time; that is the great issue, and as long as it is not decided, man must necessarily labor under profound uncertainty and ignorance concerning the most important matter" (I, 2). The matter is for Cicero important indeed, for if it were true that the gods exercise no control over human affairs, how then could piety, reverence, and religion exist? If piety toward the gods is senseless, then reverence and religion (*sanctitas et religio*) will disappear; and when they are gone, loyalty and the social bond among men will in all probability disappear too, and with them justice, and life will become disorder and confusion (I, 3–4). Though the types of theology are the issue at stake, and the Platonic decision is accepted, thus, the Ciceronian ratiocination shifts the problem from experiential to doctrinal truth. The false theology is not invalidated by the philosopher's noetic experience; rather it is false because if it were true it would psychologically destroy the piety and religion on which the order of man's existence in society depends. The philosopher's noetic illumination of consciousness is accepted, but converted into a doctrinal absolute to be symbolized by the older Roman virtues of *pietas, sanctitas,* and *religio;* and the types of theology have become doctrines, floating around in the ecumenic society, whose acceptability is to be measured by the effect they would have on the experiential absolute. This doctrinal inversion of the issue, finally, becomes explicit when the hierarchy of doctrinal symbols is enumerated in *De legibus,* I, 42–43: The supreme symbol is the Justice (*ius*) which can be only one, and is therefore not a matter of dictatorial or tyrannical arbitrariness; this one Justice is based on the one Law (*lex*) which is Right Reason (*recta ratio*); and Right Reason is Nature (*natura*). If this hierarchy of symbols were not the truth of doctrine, there would be no room for the natural propensity of man to love his fellow men, nor for the religious observances in honor of the gods which are maintained, not from fear, but as a manifestation of the close relationship (*coniunctio*) between man and god. The original issue is still recognizable in this construction of Religion, but it has been transposed from the fervor of experiential analysis to the muted mode of an argument about true doctrine.

The Ciceronian topos *religion* has had an historical success of the first magnitude. It was taken over by the Latin Patres for reference to their own doctrine, transmitted by the Latin Church to the modern West, and has become in such modern contexts as "philosophy of religion," "history of religion," and "comparative religion" a topos of such generality that it can refer to the experiences and symbolizations of man's relation to divine reality at all stages of compactness, differentiation, and deformation. The awareness that *religion* is not an analytical concept of anything, but a topical response to certain problems in the Roman subsection of an ecumenic-imperial society is practically lost. At the present state of the historical sciences, however, the topos is developing cracks. A good example of the difficulties is the previously quoted statement by Carl Schneider that the Stoics are chiefly responsible for the Hellenistic turn from science to religion. As a matter of fact, the Stoics could not turn to religion because religions did not yet exist; they rather created the phenomenon of a doctrinally deformed mythopoesis to which Cicero applied the term *religio;* and they were motivated in their creation by the desire to endow the noetic truth of existence with a pneumatic authority, which they could do only by hypostatizing the symbols of the philosopher's mythopoesis to the rank of the older compact divinities. Short of a spiritually universal humanity that became possible only through the epiphany of Christ, they could create a spiritually ecumenic humanity within a cosmos that was providentially ordered and supervised by its creator-god.

Ecumenic spiritualism deserves some attention, because it has remained an effective component in the meaning of Religion to the present. In *De republica*, III, 33, Cicero gives his confession of faith: "True law is right reason in agreement with nature. . . . It is a sin (*nec fas*) to alter this law. . . . We cannot be absolved from the law by either the senate or the people, and we need not look for an interpreter of it outside of ourselves. There will be no different law in Rome and Athens, no different law now or in the future; there will be the one everlasting and immutable law that applies to all nations at all times; and the common master and ruler will be the one god of all men, the author, arbiter, and maker of this law. Whoever does not obey this law, is fleeing from his own self and rejecting his human nature and, as a consequence, will incur the severest penalties, even when he escapes what conventionally is considered punishment." The ecumenic spiritualism of the Stoic *religio,* crystallized in this Ciceronic confession, is so close to Christianity that the Latin Patres not only could take over the symbol Religion for their own doctrinal efforts but could clarify them by relating them to the Stoic symbolism. Tertullian, for instance, uses in his *Apology* the terms *religion* and philosophical *sect* or school indiscriminately for Jews, Christians, and Stoics. The Christian *secta* which arose only recently in the reign of Tiberius is superior to the older, famous *religio* of the Jews, because the Christians have accepted the ecumenic command of God which the Jews have rejected, though they had been warned by "holy voices" that "at the end of time God would from every race and people and place gather for himself worshippers far more faithful, to whom he would transfer his favor." To this ecumenic end the Son of God has come as the illuminator and guide of mankind. Tertullian, then, places the ecumenic Son of God of the Christians on the level of the literal-allegoric meaning of the older myth, praising him for his superior ancestry compared with the sons of god produced by Zeus under various guises with mortal women, because the Christian god is Spirit (*spiritus*). From this doctrinal superiority of the Spirit over a bull, or a cloud, or gold-rain, finally, Tertullian turns his sarcasm against the Stoics. He agrees with Zeno that god is "Logos, that is Word and Reason" and that the Logos has created the universe; and he agrees with Cleanthes who gathers these divine aspects into Spirit. But this Spirit which is the substance (*substantia*) of god, the Christians believe, can go forth as the Word, as the Reason, and as the Power to realize itself in the world; and this realization, proceeding from the divine substance without separating from it, is the Son of God, it is the Christ.[7] While Tertullian's apologetic gusto has its appeal, and it is quite instructive to watch the son of god proceeding from the cosmic divinity of Zeno and Cleanthes into Mary, the tone of the debate among the contending religions has become distinctly vulgar. And what is worse, the experiential and analytical issues, while still recognizable, are badly obscured by the fracas of doctrinal debate. The first of these submerged issues is the question of the experiential criterion by which the truth of the various religions in the ecumenic society must be judged. The second issue, intimately connected with the first one, is the recognition of the critical experiences as epochal events constituting history. For Tertullian's Son of God cannot proceed from the God of Cicero's confession; he has even, as the analysis of the Gospel of John has shown, some reservations about proceeding from the creator-god of Genesis; he can only proceed from the god who is experienced as the Unknown God in the immediate experience of the divine Beyond. But it required a subtler mind than Tertullian's to discern the reflective ascent of the soul to the super-reflective truth which illuminates the reflection as the event in which divine reality becomes present in history. These problems became articulate only in Augustine's *De vera religione,* to be further elaborated in the *Civitas Dei.*[8]

The various sub-phenomena of doctrinal deformation have survived into the modern West. The Stoic deformation of philosophy, and especially its Ciceronian form, has remained a constant in history, because it is the only elaborate doctrine of law produced by the ecumenic-imperial society. It has become the formative force in Roman Law, and the Latin Patres had to adopt it, because the Christian concentration on salvational pneumatism did not favor an independent philosophy of law. The background of Roman Law in the formation of the European lawyers' guilds, and the neo-Stoic movements since the Renaissance, have left us the heritage of a "higher law" and of "natural law." The "Laws of Nature and of Nature's God" have even been incorporated into the *Declaration of Independence* as the foundation of the American Republic. In the contemporary situation, however, this doctrinal "rule of law" is encountering difficulties, because the spiritual sub-

---

[7] Tertullian, *Apologeticus,* XXI.

[8] Augustine, *De vera religione.* On the internal reflections see especially XXXIX, 72. On religion and history in *De vera religione,* see the "Notes Complémentaires" in *Oeuvres de Saint Augustin* (Paris, 1951), VIII, 483ff.

stance that had been furnished as the major premise for the interpretation of
nature's law by Christianity is disintegrating under the impact of the apocalyptic and Gnostic movements.[9] Moreover, the Stoic deformation had a
decisive influence on Christian theology in fostering the dichotomy of
reason-revelation. There is nothing "natural" in the noetic illumination of
consciousness of Plato and Aristotle; both thinkers were clear on the theophanic character of the event. That the insights of the classic philosophers
have something to do with "natural reason" as distinguished from "revelation"
is a conceit developed by the Patres when they accepted the Stoic symbols of
Nature and Reason uncritically as "philosophy." The conceit is still forcefully present in the contemporary theological literature. Most important,
finally, is the survival of the general deformation of experiential symbols into
doctrines. Within theology, the prestige of the deformation is the source of
the constant tension between dogmatic and mystic theology; and beyond the
Christian orbit proper, doctrine has been accepted as the proper symbolic
form for the egophanic ideologies. The attack on doctrinal "theology" and
"metaphysics" has not yet resulted in a socially effective return to the experience of reality, but only in the creation of doctrinal ideologies. This predominance of the doctrinal form has caused the modern phenomenon of the
great dogmatomachies, that is of the theological dogmatomachy, and the so-
called wars of religion, in the sixteenth and seventeenth centuries A.D., and of
the ideological dogmatomachy, and the corresponding revolutionary wars,
from the eighteenth to the twentieth centuries A.D.

SCRIPTURE

Doctrinal philosophy is a secondary symbolism, as it derives part of its
claim to truth from the literal acceptance of primary symbols engendered by
the noetic theophany. The deformation, however, protects the noetic truth
of existence against disintegration in the ecumenic-imperial situation by letting
the compact spiritualism of the older myth flow into the new hybrid symbolism. The language of Cosmos, Reason, Nature, Law, Creation from the
Beginning and Providence for the Infinity of Time acquires the sacrality
which formerly attached to the names of the Olympians. This archaizing
pneumatism breaks with the pneumatic dynamics of Plato's mythopoesis, but

[9] On the Aristotelian *physei dikaion* as distinguished from the Stoic *lex naturalis,* as well as
on the related problems of nature and experience, cf. the chapters on *"Das Rechte von Natur"* and
"Was ist Natur?" in my *Anamnesis* (Munich, 1966), 117–52.

it stabilizes philosophy as the Religion of ecumenic mankind in the cosmos.

The same desire to protect a treasure of insight against loss in adverse political circumstances appears to have moved the priestly and scribal circles of Israel when they superimposed the word of Scripture over the word of god, heard and spoken by the prophets. Unfortunately, very little is known about the process in which the *Book of the Torah, the Prophets, and the Writings* was organized, and that is especially true for the Pentateuchal Torah which contains the cosmogonic myth of Genesis. Even concerning the date at which the canonical Torah assumed the form that we know, no more than educated guesses are possible. The Torah is certainly post-exilic, probably connected for its beginnings with the resettlement of Babylonian exiles in Jerusalem and the building of the Second Temple after 520 B.C.; it probably exists in some form a century later, by the time of Nehemia and Ezra; it certainly exists in its practically final form by the time of the so-called Samaritan Schism, to be dated probably by the middle of the fourth century; and this last date brings us within a generation of Alexander, and within a century of the translation into the Greek of the Septuagint. Still, the one thing that can be inferred with certainty from these dates is the creation of canonical Scripture as a response to the disasters of the Ecumenic Age.[10]

Regarding the date of the cosmogony in Genesis 1:1-2:4a, again one cannot go beyond probabilities, because the materials that have gone into the construction of the Torah are not extant independent of their present context. In his analysis of the problem Gerhard von Rad hesitates to accept a date as late as the sixth century B.C., though his conscientious presentation of the materials appears to permit hardly another conclusion. For, compared with the wealth of cosmogonies in the Near Eastern environment, references to a creator-god are quite rare in the older parts of the *Book*. In the Abraham story of Genesis 14, there are traces of the Canaanite El-Elyon; in the Royal Psalms, traces of the Babylonian Marduk who wrests the land from the waters of the deep; and in the very cosmogony of Genesis, traces of the Babylonian Tiamath and of the Egyptian god of the Memphite Theology who creates the world by his word; but there is no indication that a specifically Israelite cosmogonic myth existed at all. That should perhaps be not too

[10] For the probability of the dates and especially for the date of the Samaritan Schism, cf. W. O. E. Oesterley, *From the Fall of Jerusalem, 586 B.C. to the Bar-Kokhba Revolt, A.D. 135* (Oxford, 1932), Vol. II of his *A History of Israel,* as well as the respective chapters in John Bright, *A History of Israel* (Philadelphia, 1952). For careful analysis of the probable dates and a survey of the controversy see S. H. Hooke, *Introduction to the Pentateuch* in *Peake's Commentary on the Bible* (New York, 1962), 168-74.

surprising, since the Yahweh who led Israel from cosmological bondage into the freedom under god in history was certainly not the god of the Beginning but the god who revealed himself to Moses as the I-am-who-I-am from the Beyond. The absence of cosmogonic speculations would only mean that the priests and prophets of Israel were sufficiently occupied with the new problem of the people's existence in the presence of the god who constitutes history; the force and importance of the pneumatic revelation would block the concern with an adequate symbolization of the Beginning. This situation appears to have changed with the sixth century. The first datable extrapolation of Israelite history to the Beginning, as von Rad stresses, is the construction of Deutero-Isaiah by which creation becomes the first act in the salvation work of Yahweh that culminates in the present delivery through the Persian conquest of Babylon in 538. It is the situation indeed in which the elaboration of the cosmogony, extrapolating the historiogenetic speculation to the Beginning, would make good sense. Moreover, this date suggests itself by the summarizing self-interpretation of the cosmogony as "the generations (*toldoth*) of the heavens and the earth when they were created," in Genesis 2:4a. The author applies the language of the "generations" in the tribal history to the phases of creation; it sounds as if this cosmogony had been specifically devised to serve as the opening chapter of the Torah and the history of Israel.[11]

An important factor in the scholarly controversies surrounding the cosmogony, as well as in the hesitations to accept a date as late as the sixth century B.C., is the unsatisfactory state of experiential analysis. It should be acknowledged that the cosmogony itself and the anthropogony of the so-called second creation story in Genesis 2:4b–25 are intermediate symbolisms. If the experience of divine reality in the direction of the Beyond were to be brought to bear on a myth of the Beginning, the result would have to be a *creatio ex nihilo*. Such a consistent mythopoetic expansion, however, would have required a more radical differentiation of pneumatic consciousness than, as far as we know, has ever occurred in the history of Israel. The cosmogony of Genesis, it is true, has pneumatic character inasmuch as it breaks with the myth of the intracosmic gods, but it makes Israel's god of the exodus no more than the magnificently dominant figure in a mythopoem which otherwise retains a good deal of the Babylonian and Egyptian demiurgic background. In this respect, the pneumatic cosmogony of Genesis is structurally related to Plato's noetic mythopoem of the Demiurge in the *Timaeus*. An analytical

---

[11] Gerhard von Rad, *Theologie des Alten Testaments* (Munich, 1950), I, 140–44.

[handwritten marginalia: "In the Beginning = The Time of the Tale not time of the Cosmos Wisdom Sophia Chr Lady"]

awareness that the god of the Beginning, if he is to be identical with the god experienced in the tension toward the Beyond, must be a creator *ex nihilo,* is to be found for the first time in the formulation that god did not make heaven and earth out of the things that existed, in II Maccabees 7:28. But with Jason of Cyrene, who wrote the historiographic work epitomized in II Maccabees probably in the 150s B.C., we are already deep in the struggles of Judaism with the Hellenistic environment in the ecumenic empire. The further analytical insight that the "In the Beginning" of the cosmogony is not a beginning in the time of the cosmos, but belongs to the Time of the Tale which symbolizes the originating divine reality, had to wait for the application of Platonic and Stoic insights concerning this point by Philo in *De opificio,* 26.[12]

A further differentiation of pneumatic consciousness actually did occur in the Jewish-Hellenistic society of the third century B.C. It engendered, in Proverbs 1–9, the remarkable and charming appearance of a Judaic female divinity, of the *hokhmah* or, in the Greek versions, *sophia,* conventionally translated as Wisdom. The new divine lady has a truly ecumenic personality, for historical scholarship can discover in her elements of the older Egyptian *ma'at,* of the Isis of contemporary hymns, of the Canaanite Ishtar, as well as numerous Greek parallels. Moreover, she is a polymorphic divine force. She is the Wisdom of God that was with him from the beginning: "Yahweh created me at the beginning . . . at the first, before the beginning of the earth. . . . When he established the heavens, I was there. . . . I was beside him like a little child; and I was daily his delight, rejoicing before him always" (8:22–31). But the little child can also be the planning wisdom of divine creation: "Yahweh has by Wisdom founded the earth; and the heavens established by Insight (*tebunah*)" (3:19). The companion of god in creation, then, is sent to man. She can appear as the queenly mediatrix of divine truth, who sets up her palace with the Seven Pillars, lays out the table, and sends out her maids to call in all who are "simple": "Come, eat of my bread, and drink of the wine I have mixed; leave folly, and live" (9:1–6). Or she can appear in the role of a temple girl at the gate, soliciting the potential customers: "O men! I am calling to you; my cry goes out to the sons of men" (8:1–5). Or she can be the Wisdom by which rule the princes (8:15–16). Still, Wisdom is not a

---

[12] Concerning the problem of the Time of the Tale and the time of the cosmos see also Philo, *Quod Deus immutabilis sit,* 31; Plato, *Timaeus,* 37–38; Chrysippus, *In Stoicorum Veterum Fragmenta,* 509. For the problem of God as the creator of time in the Christian context see Augustine, *Confessiones,* XI, 13.

gift to be simply possessed; like the pull of the Golden Cord, of Plato's god, her call requires response: "I love those who love me, and those who seek me will find me" (8:17). And behind Wisdom there is her creator, the god to whom man must respond if he wants to be man: "The fear of Yahweh is the beginning of Wisdom, and the knowledge of the Holy One is Insight" (9:10).[13]

Though the goddess assumes many forms, reflecting the presence of divine reality from the Beginning to the Beyond, the wide range has its experiential center in the "fear of Yahweh." By this phrase, the pneumatic tension toward the Beyond becomes articulate as the consciousness which dominates the symbolization of truth experienced. In the early second century B.C., Jesus-ben-Sirach praises the "fear of the Lord" as the beginning and the fulfillment, as the crown and the root of Wisdom; and he describes the seeker of truth as the man who meditates on wisdom, reflects in his mind on her ways, pursues her like a hunter, encamps near her house, and dwells in the midst of her glory (Sirach, 1:14–20; 14:20–27). As the meditative practice of the Wisdom-thinker becomes self-reflective, it develops the pneumatic equivalents to the philosophers' differentiation of noetic consciousness. The *hokhma* with its double meaning of divine and human wisdom corresponds to the divine and human *nous;* the search and the love of wisdom, to *eros* and *philia;* the call and attraction of divine wisdom, to the philosopher's being drawn and moved from the divine Beyond. Even the symbolism of the *via negativa,* with its searching ascent through the realms of being to the Wisdom of God, is fully developed in the hymn of Job 28: There is man engaged in mining operations, disemboweling the earth in search of treasure, and bringing to light secrets that were hidden. But Wisdom, where does it come from? It cannot be bought with the priceless goods of a prosperous merchant civilization; it is not to be found in the land of the living, nor do death and the depth know where it is hidden. "God alone has traced its path and found out where she lives"; and he said to man: "The fear of the Lord is Wisdom." This god beyond the world who alone knows Wisdom, and reveals to man the secret of access to her through the fear of the Lord, is the pneumatic equivalent to the Platonic distinction between divine *sophia* and human *philosophia.*

However, the parallels in the articulation of pneumatic and noetic con-

---

[13] On the Wisdom literature in the Hellenistic age, and for all dates concerning the documents, cf. Martin Hengel, *Judentum und Hellenismus* (Tuebingen, 1969). For the wide range of problems presented by the Wisdom literature see Gerhard von Rad, *Weisheit in Israel* (Neukirchen-Vleuyn, 1970).

sciousness are equivalences in the respective media of experience; they do not make the Wisdom thinker into a philosopher. The "fear of the Lord" rather recalls Cicero's archaizing recourse to "religion" as the source and criterion of truth in the turmoil of conflicting doctrines; and these archaisms in the process of the ecumenic society are more than a manner of speech. When Cicero replaces the philosophers' analysis of man's existence in the divine-human In-Between, in the reality of the Metaxy, with the more compact symbol "religion," he activates the more compact pneumatism of the older symbol for the purpose of protecting noetic insights gained, but at the same time he blocks the further advance of experiential analysis; he puts his seal on the Stoic deformation of philosophy into doctrine. When the Wisdom thinkers symbolize the In-Between of man's existence as the "fear of Yahweh," they impose on the universalist tendency of their pneumatic differentiation a limiting relationship to the Yahweh of the Covenant. The problem becomes thematic in Sirach 24. The author lets Wisdom praise herself before the Most High and his host: She came forth from the mouth of the Most High and covered the earth like a mist; she dwelt in the heights and the depths; made the circuit of heaven, earth, and sea; and held her sway over every people and nation. "From eternity, in the beginning, he created me, and for eternity I shall not cease to exist" (24:9). But then something happened to the universal dominion of the Wisdom who was spoken by the god of the Beginning, for the creator of all things commanded her to establish her dwelling in Zion (24:8-12). Summarizing the intent of the praise, the author concludes therefore that Wisdom is "the Book of the Covenant of the Most High God, the Torah which Moses commanded us, as an inheritance for the congregations of Jacob" (24:23). In the beginning was the Torah, and the Torah was with god, and the Torah was god. From this identification of Wisdom with the Torah there could evolve the later Jewish mysticism of the deified Torah and the Word of the Gospel of John.

While the archaizing identification of Wisdom and Torah protects the pneumatic insights against the pressure of competing wisdom in the multi-civilizational society, it is inevitably in conflict with the process of differentiation that manifests itself in the Wisdom literature and the consciousness of the scribe as its carrier (Sirach, 38:24-34). The conflict becomes tangible when Wisdom and Torah change places as subject and predicate in the identification. In Deuteronomy 4:5-6, the statutes and ordinances of the Torah are recommended to Israel for observation, because they are "your wisdom (*hokhma*) and your insight (*binah*)" before the eyes of the other nations.

In Sirach 24:23, the Wisdom that was with god from the beginning is the subject that has the Torah as its identifying predicate. If the Deuteronomy passage, as S. H. Hooke suggests, is not one of the older sources digested in the Torah but belongs to its very construction, to be dated in the first half of the fourth century B.C., it would document the spirit of self-assertion in the community of the Second Temple under the conditions of the Persian Empire and perhaps reveal one of the motives for the mytho-speculative extrapolation of Israel's history under the god of the Beyond to the god of the Beginning. At the time of Sirach's writing, the mythopoetic feat of creating the cosmogony as the suitable beginning for a history that culminates in the Covenant is a fact of the past; the construction of the Torah lies about two centuries back; and the great symbolism can now be literalized into a "history" in which the divine Wisdom speaks, first, the cosmos and man (Sirach, 42:15–43:33) and, second, the "famous men" of Israel and the Torah (Sirach, 44:1–50:21). In his Wisdom speculation, the meditating scribe has assimilated the process of creation to the process in which history is constituted by the word of god spoken through man. Both the word of the Beginning and the word from the Beyond are manifestations of the one divine Wisdom that speaks the one reality. As the mythopoetic symbols of classic philosophy are transformed into philosophical doctrine, so the mytho-speculative symbolism of the Torah is now transformed into a story of reality that can be told from the creation to the author's present. Moreover, one should note the formulation of Sirach 42:15: "By the words of the Lord his works are done." Whether this is the first time that the symbol *word* is used to denote the divine agency of creation is uncertain, but certainly it is one of the earliest instances. The appearance of the abstract *word* in the Wisdom literature parallels the appearance of the abstract *tension* in post-classic philosophy.

The Torah, in the sense of the Five Books of Moses, is the first part of Scripture in both the Judaic and Christian tradition. According to the traditional interpretation as Scripture, the Torah is not the monumental mythopoem created by post-exilic Judaism, but a literary document of divine-human origin, transmitted from the time of Moses through an unbroken line of intermediaries to the thinkers of the Ecumenic Age. The opening section of the *Pirke Aboth* promulgates this line of authorship and transmission: "Moses received the Torah from Sinai and committed it to Joshua, and Joshua to the elders, and the elders to the Prophets; and the Prophets committed it to the men of the Great Synagogue." The line of transmitters is then continued from Simeon the Just, one of the "remnants of the Great Synagogue," to Hillel and

Shammai, *ca.* 30 B.C.–A.D. 10 (Aboth, 1:2–12). Simeon the Just is possibly the same Simeon that is praised as the last of the "famous men" in Sirach 50; the comparatively loose sequence of the "famous men" thus hardens into the Rabbinical strict line of transmitters around 200 B.C.[14]

From the data and dates presented I conclude that "Scripture" is a layer of meaning, superimposed on a body of oral traditions and literary documents for the purpose of preserving it under the adverse conditions of the ecumenic-imperial society. One has to speak of superimposition, because the Torah is not simply a collection of older documents but a mythopoetic construction in its own right. Important pieces manifesting the intent of the construction appear to be the cosmogony of Genesis and certain parts of Deuteronomy. Moreover, the mythopoem is not created by one author, but is a collective work extending over centuries. The beginning of the process can hardly be dated earlier than the sixth century B.C.; and, though the Pentateuch itself appears to have reached its final form in the first half of the fourth century, the meaning of Scripture continued to radiate over other documents, so that the canonical *Book* contains not only the Torah but also the Prophets and instances of the Wisdom and apocalyptic literature of the second century B.C. By 200 B.C., there becomes noticeable the stricter line of transmission that leads to the compilers of the *Mishnah;* and this stricter line has also the effect of narrowing the range of problems open to discussion and differentiation. The tractate *Hagigah* says: "Whosoever gives his mind to four things it were better for him if he had not come into the world—what is above? what is beneath? what was beforetime? and what will be hereafter?" And the same passage enjoins specifically that the Story of Creation must not be expounded before two persons, and Ezekiel's vision of the Chariot not even before one alone, unless he is a Sage that understands of his own knowledge (*Hagigah,* 2:1). The enjoinder impressively documents the protective function of Scripture for the society that wants to exist under the Law, as it draws the line against areas of reality which, if explored, could lead beyond the Law in the direction of apocalyptic and Gnostic speculation, of Christian pneumatism and eschatology, of pagan mysteries and philosophy.

In the protective stratum of Scripture, the original symbols suffer the same kind of deformation into doctrine as the Platonic mythopoesis through the Stoic hypostases. The symbols primarily affected concern the interrelated prob-

---

[14] In this and the following paragraph I am quoting from the translation of the *Mishnah* by Herbert Danby (Oxford, 1950).

lems of the Word of God and of History. Since the structure of the issue has been amply clarified by the preceding reflections, for the present instance a brief statement will be sufficient.

The language of truth concerning man's existence in the divine-human In-Between is engendered in, and by, the theophanic events of differentiating consciousness. The language symbols belong, as to their meanings, to the Metaxy of the experiences from which they arise as their truth. As long as the process of experience and symbolization is not deformed by doctrinal reflection, there is no doubt about the metaleptic status of the symbols. In the prophetic literature, the word of truth can be indiscriminately said to be spoken by the god or by the prophet. Moreover, the original experience need not be auditory; the word need not be "heard"; it can also be "seen" as in Amos 1:1 or in Isaiah 2:1 and 13:1; or vision and word can blend into the tale of a dialogue between god and the prophet, as in the visions of Amos 7; or the "word" can emerge from the great divine-human dialogue in Jeremiah. The In-Between of experience has a dead point from which the symbols emerge as the exegesis of its truth, but which cannot become itself an object of propositional knowledge. If the metaleptic symbol which is the word of both god and man is hypostatized into a doctrinal Word of God, the device can protect the insight gained against disintegration in society, but it also can impair the sensitivity for the source of truth in the flux of divine presence in time which constitutes history. Unless precautions of meditative practice are taken, the doctrinization of symbols is liable to interrupt the process of experiential re-activation and linguistic renewal. When the symbol separates from its source in the experiential Metaxy, the Word of God can degenerate into a word of man that one can believe or not.

Closely related to the doctrinization of the Word is the doctrinization of History through the expansion of the Word from the immediate experience of the Beyond to the mediated experience of the Beginning. The cosmogonic myth of the Beginning will be affected, as I have said, by the degree of differentiation in the consciousness of the Beyond. Hence, there is nothing wrong with the cosmogony of Genesis, as long as it is understood as a mythopoem which reflects the state of pneumatic differentiation in its author, probably in the sixth century B.C. Nor is there anything wrong when the mytho-speculative creators of the Torah place the cosmogony at the beginning of their history of a mankind represented by Israel; nor when the cosmogony is refined into a *creatio ex nihilo;* nor when the Word that reveals the truth of reality in history is projected back into the cosmogonic myth of the Beginning.

The relation between the symbolization of the Beyond and the Beginning becomes existentially dangerous only if the centrality of man's consciousness in the process of symbolization, and man's imaginative ability to symbolize the Beginning, is misunderstood as a power to bring the Beginning under the control of consciousness. The danger became visible in the Gnosticism of the Ecumenic Age, and I have stressed in the analysis of the problem that the modern Gnostic movements derive rather from the Gnostic "influences" in the gospel of John than from the more colorful psychodramatic varieties. In support of this statement I shall quote the representative modern document of this deformation, to be found in the self-presentation of Hegel in his *Wissenschaft der Logik*:[15] "The *Logik* is to be understood as the System of pure reason, as the Realm of pure thought. *This Realm is the Truth as it is without veil and for itself.* It is possible therefore to say that its contents is the *presentation of God as He is in His eternal being, before the creation of nature and any finite being.*"

In the beginning was Wisdom; in the beginning was the Torah; in the beginning was the Word; in the beginning was Hegel with his *Logik*. With the egophanic deformation of the Symbol into the System, and the self-presentation of the thinker's consciousness as the divine Word of the Beginning, we are at the center of the ideological dogmatomachy which occupies the public scene with its murderous grotesque.

Conclusion

The introductory reflections just concluded are meant to give the reasons that the project of *Order and History* as originally conceived had to be abandoned. But the most convincing reason is the range of interrelated problems that had to be covered and the size to which the analysis has grown. The Introduction has introduced itself as the form which a philosophy of history has to assume in the present historical situation. And this form is definitely not a story of meaningful events to be arranged on a time line.

In this new form, the analysis had to move backward and forward and sideways, in order to follow empirically the patterns of meaning as they revealed themselves in the self-interpretation of persons and societies in history. It was a movement through a web of meaning with a plurality of nodal points. Still, certain dominant lines of meaning became visible while moving through

---

[15] Hegel, *Wissenschaft der Logik*, ed. Lasson (Hamburg, 1963) 31.

the web. There was the fundamental advance from compact to differentiated consciousness and its distribution over a plurality of ethnic cultures. There were the lines of pneumatic and noetic differentiation, distributed over Israel and Hellas. There was the outburst of ecumenic-imperial conquest which forced the former ethnic cultures into a new ecumenic society. There were the reactions of the ethnic cultures to the imperial conquest, with the lines of differentiation developing lines of protective deformation. And there was the imperial conquest itself as the carrier of a meaning of humanity beyond the tribal and ethnic level. From the Ecumenic Age, there emerges a new type of ecumenic humanity, which, with all its complications of meaning, reaches as a millennial constant into the modern Western civilization.

In our time, the inherited symbolisms of ecumenic humanity are disintegrating, because the deforming doctrinalization has become socially stronger than the experiential insights it was originally meant to protect. The return from symbols which have lost their meaning to the experiences which constitute meaning is so generally recognizable as the problem of the present that specific references are unnecessary. The great obstacle to this return is the massive block of accumulated symbols, secondary and tertiary, which eclipses the reality of man's existence in the Metaxy. To raise this obstacle and its structure into consciousness, and by its removal to help in the return to the truth of reality as it reveals itself in history, has become the purpose of *Order and History*.

This purpose has determined the organization of Volumes IV and V of the study. The present volume, *The Ecumenic Age,* presents the genesis of the ecumenic problem and its complications. The next and last volume, entitled *In Search of Order,* will study the contemporary problems which have motivated the search for order in history.

CHAPTER 1

Historiogenesis

In the civilizations of the Ancient Orient, the student will encounter a peculiar type of speculation on the order of society, its origin, and its course in time.

The symbolists who develop the type let governance spring into existence at an absolute point of origin, as part of the cosmic order itself, and from that point down they let the history of their society descend to the present in which they live. On closer inspection, however, the story of the events between the origin and the present is not the homogeneous tale it pretends to be; rather, it proves to consist of two parts of widely different character. For only the later part of the story, the part that issues into the author's present, can claim to relate *res gestae* in the pragmatic sense; the earlier part, covering an immense time-span of thousands and sometimes hundred thousands of years, is filled with legendary and mythical events. Though they had a certain amount of historical materials at their disposition, the symbolists were clearly not satisfied with merely relating them; they wanted to link them, through an act of mythopoesis, with the emergence of order in the cosmos, so that the events would have a meaning that made them worthy of transmission to posterity. By this method of mythopoetic extrapolation which does not break the form of the myth, they achieved a speculation on the origin of a specific realm of being, not differing on principle from the noetic speculation on the *arche*, on the ground and beginning of all being, in which the Ionian philosophers engaged. Historiography, mythopoesis, and noetic speculation thus can be distinguished as components in this rather complex symbolism.

The close resemblance between the several instances of the type as they occur in Mesopotamia, Egypt, and Israel has not escaped attention. Moreover, since they are a treasure-house for historians who want to extract from them the rich admixture of pragmatic events, the various cases have been well explored for the purpose of reconstructing the history of ancient societies. Nevertheless, no attempt has ever been made to identify the type as a symbolic form *sui generis,* or to inquire into the motives of its development, or to analyze its nature. The symbolism has indeed remained so far below the horizon of theoretical interest that it has not even received a name. Hence, as a first step toward its identification I propose the name *historiogenesis*. The name has been chosen in consideration of the Israelite instance of the symbolism, in which pragmatic history is extrapolated back to Genesis in the Biblical sense.

§ 1. MYTHO-SPECULATION

Once the type is recognized as such, it raises certain questions for a philosophy of experience and symbolization.

If historiogenesis is a speculation on the origin and cause of social order, it must be considered a member of the class to which also belong theogony, anthropogony, and cosmogony. All the varieties of the class have in common the quest of the ground. As from the experiences of participation in the divine, human, and cosmic areas of reality there arise questions concerning the origin of the gods, man, and the cosmos, so from the experience of the social realm there arise questions concerning the origin of society and its order; beside symbolisms expressing the mystery of existence that puzzles the explorer of divine, human, and cosmic reality, there develops a symbolism that expresses the same mystery with regard to the existence of society.

There is more to this classification than the possibility of defining historiogenesis by the rule of genus and specific difference. The recognition of the class discloses its full importance, if one remembers that gods and men, society and the cosmos exhaust the principal complexes of reality distinguished by cosmological societies as the partners in the community of being. The four complexes in their aggregate comprehend the whole field of being, and the four symbolisms enumerated form a corresponding aggregate covering this field. Through the addition of historiogenesis to the other three varieties, the aggregate becomes the symbolism that is, in the language of the cosmological myth, equivalent to a speculation on the ground of being in the language of noetic consciousness. The aggregate, it is true, expresses the experience of the ground of being on the level of the compact primary experience of the cosmos; it has by far not yet achieved the differentiated noetic level that we find in the Parmenidean vision of being. Moreover, it is still bound to the experiences within the various realms of being and, thus, has pluralistic character; it does not yet rise to the One Being that is the ground of all being things. Nevertheless, though the single speculations do not transcend the areas of reality from which they arise in the direction of the common ground, their aggregate, as it covers the whole of reality, equivalently expresses the philosopher's tension toward the Being that is One.

Even more: This character of equivalence pertains not only to the aggregate, but seeps into the component symbolisms severally, inasmuch as the respective speculations do not confine themselves to the area of reality in which they originate but draw into the orbit of their construction materials from the other realms of being. Within the framework of a genealogy of the gods, the Hesiodic theogony informs us, through its climax in the Titanomachia, about the civilizational victory of Jovian Dike over more primitive phases of human and social order. The Hesiodic *logos* of the Ages of the World, then, is primarily an anthropogony, but it also reflects on phases of political and civilizational history, such as the ages of the Homeric heroes and of their deplorable successors, or on the Mycenaean bronze and Doric iron ages. The cosmogony of the Mesopotamian *Enuma elish,* furthermore, is as much a theogony and an anthropogony, and quite probably contains allusions to such civilizational achievements as the regulation of rivers and the gaining of arable land. Finally, then, the historiogenetic speculations that are our present concern extend to theogonic, anthropogonic, and cosmogonic subject matters as well. Hence the ground of all being becomes visible as ultimately intended, not only through the aggregate of the four speculations but even within the single forms, through their mutual penetration.

In order to make the complicated network of experience and symbolization comprehensible at a glance, we shall introduce abstract signs for the elements and construct a formula representing the relations between them:

(1) The speculation is motivated by an experience in one of the sectors of reality. The speculative forms corresponding to the sectors are called theogony, anthropogony, cosmogony, and historiogenesis. We shall use the initials of these four nouns for designating the four sectors of reality as t, a, c, and h.

(2) The four varieties of speculation corresponding to the four sectors we shall designate as S_t, S_a, S_c, S_h.

(3) As far as subject matter is concerned, the four varieties do not confine themselves to their respective sectors of reality, but absorb into their symbolism materials from the other sectors, divesting them in the process of their autonomous meaning and sometimes transforming them thoroughly. Hence, we must distinguish between primary and secondary materials organized by the several symbolisms. This relation we shall express by enumerating the various ma-

terials, classified by their sector of origin, placing the primary materials first. The resulting sign will be: $S_t(t\text{–}a,c,h)$, $S_a(a\text{–}t,c,h)$, $S_c(c\text{–}t,a,h,)$, and $S_h(h\text{–}t,a,c)$.

(4) The four varieties correspond to the four sectors of reality. In their pluralistic manner they exhaust the possibility of speculation on the origin of being. This character of the aggregate, which makes it equivalent to a philosophy of being, shall be expressed by placing the varieties in order, held together by vertical lines:

$$\begin{vmatrix} S_t(t\text{–}a,c,h) \\ S_a(a\text{–}t,c,h) \\ S_c(c\text{–}t,a,h) \\ S_h(h\text{–}t,a,c) \end{vmatrix}$$

(5) The aggregate, though equivalent to a philosophy of being, is not itself a philosophical symbolism, but remains a speculation within the sphere of the cosmological myth. This subordination of mytho-speculations to the myth of the cosmos shall be denoted by prefixing a C to the sign for the aggregate:

$$C \begin{vmatrix} S_t(t\text{–}a,c,h) \\ S_a(a\text{–}t,c,h) \\ S_c(c\text{–}t,a,h) \\ S_h(h\text{–}t,a,c) \end{vmatrix}$$

The formula will convey, more effectively than discourse can do, what is meant by the language of a cosmological equivalent to philosophical speculation on the *arche* of things.

The equivalence of the aggregate to a noetic quest of the ground is recognizable in retrospect from the philosopher's position. In the context of cosmological civilizations, however, this differentiated meaning is yet dispersed over the four types of speculation. On the one hand, each of the types binds the noetic component compactly to the experience of the particular realm in which the speculation originates; on the other hand, each of them has its autonomy as a rational construction because the noetic component endows it with a dimension of speculative reason beyond the exploration of a particular area of reality. Historiogenesis must now be considered as an autonomous symbolism emerging from the cooperation of pragmatic historiography with mythopoesis and noetic speculation.

Regarding the pragmatic content, I have intimated that modern scholars use the symbolism as a quarry from which they break the materials for reconstructing ancient history. The procedure is quite legitimate in itself, since the pragmatic facts and events have to be fitted into the different symbolism of modern historiography; but if the exploration of historiogenesis stops at this point, it certainly destroys the meaning of the ancient symbolism. One cannot help feeling dismayed when one sees the remainder of the dilapidated structure discarded as so much dross not deserving further attention. In the comprehensive *Roemische Geschichte* (1960) by Andreas Heuss, for instance, the learned author examines the traditional history of Rome, which has historiogenetic character, dismisses its mythical part as "unhistoric fabulation," and displays no interest at all in the question why anybody should have gone to the trouble of fabulating the fabulation, and why the product was officially accepted as the history of Rome. With similar disdain Jean Bayet expresses himself in his *Histoire politique et psychologique de la religion romaine* (2nd rev. ed., 1969) about the Romans who have desacralized their myth and transformed it into a "national pseudo-history." The moderns take the ancients to task for not writing history in the manner approved by positivist historians. In the face of such superiority, one must remind our contemporaries that the ancient authors did not develop their symbolisms in order to please modern positivists; and one must, furthermore, raise the questions whether the creation of the myth and its acceptance were not also facts of history? and perhaps facts of considerable importance for the self-interpretation and cohesion of Roman society? and therefore of some interest to historians?[1] If one does not indulge in the vice of ideological intolerance toward reality, the matter will present itself in a different light: The mythical part of historiogenetic speculation is not a piece of unhistorical fabulation, but an attempt to present the reasons that will raise the *res gestae* of the pragmatic part to the rank of history; the symbolism as a whole has the status of an historical work whose authors are conscious of their principle of relevance. Phenotypical differences notwithstanding, historiogenesis is in substance, on the level of the cosmological myth, the equivalent to the later types of historiography—perhaps with the difference that the early symbolists were more subtly aware of the intricacies of relevance than their more recent *confrères*. The question of equivalence thus arises not

---

[1] In the recent work of Jacques Heugon, *The Rise of Rome to 264 B.C.* (Berkeley, 1973), trans. by James Willis from *Rome et le Mediterrané Occidental* (1969), however, appropriate attention is given to "The Growth of the Tradition" (128ff), though there is still no development of the type of historiogenesis.

only in regard to the aggregate but also regarding the historiogenetic variety.

The dimension of reason in the symbolism, however, does not reflect the light of a fully differentiated noetic consciousness; as far as their relevance is concerned, the pragmatic materials are illuminated rather by a speculation that remains subordinate to the cosmological myth. Mythopoesis and noesis combine into a formative unit that holds an intermediate position between cosmological compactness and noetic differentiation. It will suitably be called mytho-speculation, *i.e.,* a speculation within the medium of the myth. This is the formative unit than can be discerned as operative in historiogenesis as well as in theogony, anthropogony, and cosmogony.

§ 2. Historiogenetic Speculation

The motives for applying this mode of symbolization to pragmatic events arise from the experience of history. In the first place, wherever an historiogenetic speculation can be dated, it proves to develop later than the speculations on the other realms of being. That is not surprising, as a society must have existed for some time before it has acquired a course of history long enough to lend itself to extrapolation toward an absolute point of origin. However, while acknowledging a certain length of the course as the ineluctable substratum of the speculation, one must beware of the fallacy, current among modern historiogenetic thinkers, of hypostatizing the "length" into an entity that carries its meaning on its surface. For the relevance of the events is experienced by the noetic consciousness of the men participating in them; it is not presented by the "length" as an object for everybody to observe. The assumption of both Hegel and Comte that by their time a true philosophy of history had become possible, because the length of the course had at last offered all the materials necessary for a philosopher to pronounce with finality on the meaning of history from its beginning to its end, is precisely this fallacy, frequently used by modern speculators as a screen that will hide the real motives of their work.

In the earliest instances of the symbolism, the Egyptian and Mesopotamian, the very time lag in the appearance of a mytho-speculation on history makes its motivation discernible as an unrest, or anxiety, aroused by the recent impact of irreversible events. For, long before historiogenesis, the societies in cosmological form possess an impressive array of symbolisms that purport to cope with the meaning of social order and disorder in time. In the New Year festival and coronation ceremonies, for instance, we find rituals which adjust the order of society to the rhythm of cosmic order. The established order, both of cosmos and empire, is experienced as threatened by new outbreaks of the chaos and its forces that had been suppressed by the original creation of the cosmos and the foundation of empire; and the rituals mentioned serve the rhythmical renewal of social order through the analogical repetition of the creation of cosmic order. Through centuries before historiogenesis appears, the precarious existence of society between order and chaos was experienced as adequately expressed and protected by the rituals of foundation and renewal. Hence, the study of single cases of historiogenesis will have to ascertain the events that caused the older symbols to be considered wanting in the new situation. Whatever these events concretely are, the result is manifest: Historiogenesis implacably places events on the line of irreversible time where opportunities are lost forever and defeat is final.

Some implications of a symbolism that places a far from linear manifold of events on a single line of time become plain in the Sumerian King List, probably conceived about 2050 B.C., after the expulsion of the Gutaeans and the Sumerian restoration of empire through Utu-hegal of Uruk. Thorkild Jacobsen has unraveled the method of its construction.[2] The Sumerian Empire was a manifold of city-states under local dynasties, with an imperial organization superimposed, whenever one of the cities, not always the same, gained ascendancy over the others through conquering expansion. Whereas a critical historian would have to relate the parallel histories of the cities, as well as the changes of ascendancy, the authors of the King List constructed a unilinear history of Sumer by placing the parallel city-dynasties in succession on a single temporal line of rulers, issuing into the restored empire of their own time. The parallel histories of the cities were abolished, but nevertheless absorbed into an imaginary, unilinear history of empire. One cosmos, it appears, can have only one imperial order, and the sin of coexistence must be atoned by posthumous integration into the one history whose goal has been demonstrated through the success of the conqueror. If it, then, be remembered that the imaginary line of kings is extrapolated to its absolute point of origin in divine-cosmic events, so that nothing extraneous to it has a chance of disturbing the one and only course admissible, the construction appears as an act of violence committed against historical reality. The relevant course of events descends ineluctably from the cosmic origin down to the present of the authors whose society is the only one that matters. To the aggressive overtones,

---

[2] Thorkild Jacobsen, *The Sumerian Kinglist*, Assyriological Studies, No. 11 (Chicago, 1939).

finally, there corresponds an undercurrent of obsessive anxiety above which
the authors attempt to rise by the imaginative conversion of a temporal gain
into a possession forever. The construction is a metastatic device, meant to
sublimate the contingency of imperial order in time to the timeless serenity of
the cosmic order itself.

The deliberate distortion of historical reality and the anxiety aroused by the
vicissitudes of imperial order, together with the metastatic magic of eclipsing
the disturbing reality by projecting an imaginary second reality on a timeless
line of time that comes to its end in the everlasting meaning of the author's
present, form a syndrome worth some attention, because it characterizes not
only the Sumerian King List but also such modern enterprises of historiogenetic speculation as Hegel's *Vorlesungen ueber die Philosophie der Geschichte*. The technical problem Hegel had to face resembled closely that of the
Sumerian symbolists. The eighteenth century had broken with the traditional
construction of history as one line of meaning running from Creation through
the history of Israel, Judaism, Christianity, Rome, and the Western *sacrum
imperium* to the present; the last construction of this type, Bossuet's, had been
superseded by the critical work of Voltaire; the parallel histories of China and
India, the Islamic world and Russia, had emerged so visibly that a philosopher
of history no longer could overlook them. Hegel, however, wanted to continue
the Christian historiogenetic symbolism on the new level of a Neoplatonic,
immanentist speculation on the *Geist* which dialectically unfolds in history
until it reaches its full self-reflective consciousness in the wake of the French
Revolution and the Napoleonic Empire. Hence, from his position in an imperial present, Hegel had to cope with a manifold of pragmatic events even
less amenable to being brought on a single line of time than the parallel
histories of the Sumerian city-states. And yet, he achieved the feat by interpreting the great civilizational societies as successive phases of the unfolding *Geist,* simply disregarding their simultaneity and succession in time.
Especially striking is the treatment of Egypt and Mesopotamia. Chronologically, they would have to be placed at the beginning. But that would have
disturbed the westward march of empire toward ever-increasing freedom,
proceeding from China and India, through Persia, Greece, and Rome, to the
Germanic World with its climax in the empire of the French Revolution.
Hegel resolves the problem by demoting the early Near Eastern empires to
subsections of the later Persian Empire that had conquered them; and the same
fate he inflicts on Israel and Judah. By ingenious devices of this kind—the
inclusion of "Mohammedanism" in the "Germanic World" deserves to be

remembered—he manages to herd the errant materials on the straight line that leads to the imperial present of mankind and to himself as its philosopher. The modern technique of historiogenetic construction, it appears, is still the same as the Sumerian.

As the comparison between the Sumerian King List and Hegel's *Philosophy of History* shows, historiogenesis as an autonomous symbolism has by now a lifetime of four thousand years. Once it is recognized as a type, it proves of unsuspected importance indeed because of its virtual omnipresence. The earliest instances occur in the Mesopotamian and Egyptian empires. Since in these cases the speculation is conducted well within the range set by the primary experience of the cosmos, one might expect historiogenesis to be peculiar to societies in unbroken cosmological form. This expectation will be disappointed, however, for the symbolism also occurs in the Israel which, by its covenant in freedom under God, has broken not only with the cosmological order of Egypt, but with the myth of the cosmos itself. It then appears in the context of ecumenic empires in China, India, and Rome as an instrument for coping with the history of social order. It adapts itself, furthermore, to the ambiance of polis and philosophy; assumes a curious form in the "utopia" of Euhemerus, in connection with the imperial expansion of Alexander; gains a new Near Eastern life, through the speculations of Berossus and Manetho, in the time of the Diadochic empires. It even informs the little-known speculation of Clement of Alexandria, where it becomes an odd weapon in the fight against polytheism. By Judaism and Christianity, finally, it has been transmitted to the medieval and modern Western civilization where, since Enlightenment, it has proliferated into the bewildering manifold of progressivist, idealist, materialist, and positivist speculations on the origin and end of history. The symbolism, thus, displays a curious tenacity of survival—from cosmological societies proper to contemporary Western societies whose understanding of the world can hardly be described as inspired by the primary experience of the cosmos. Historiogenesis is one of the great constants in the search of order from antiquity to the present.

§ 3. EXISTENCE AND NON-EXISTENCE

The preliminary presentation of historiogenesis as a millennial constant has revealed structures in the history of consciousness which are not accessible to a conventional description of symbols as phenomena: Noetic consciousness, the life of reason, is active within the medium of the cosmological myth and produces the types of mytho-speculation; a speculation within the cosmo-logical style of truth occurs also in societies that have broken with the myth of the cosmos; a noetic speculation on the *arche* of being that we associate with the beginnings of Hellenic philosophy has its equivalent in the early cosmological empires; a conception of unilinear history that by conventional assumption belongs in the orbit of Israelite-Christian revelation is to be found not only in cosmological and ecumenic empires but also in the supposedly non-mythical and non-theological, contemporary Western society. The con-stancies and equivalences adumbrated work havoc with such settled topical blocks as myth and philosophy, natural reason and revelation, philosophy and religion, or the Orient with its cyclical time and Christianity with its linear history. And what is modern about the modern mind, one may ask, if Hegel, Comte, or Marx, in order to create an image of history that will sup-port their ideological imperialism, still use the same techniques for distorting the reality of history as their Sumerian predecessors?

The problems of this class will be treated throughout the present volume. For the moment, I shall concentrate on the immediate issue, that is, on the inconsiderate Sumerians and Egyptians who speculate on linear history, though they are Orientals who ought to be content with cyclical time. This requires a brief exposition of what is meant by the primary experience of the cosmos, as well as reflections on the pressure of anxiety which tends to disrupt the primary experience.

1. The Primary Experience of the Cosmos

The cosmos of the primary experience is neither the external world of objects given to a subject of cognition, nor is it the world that has been created by a world-transcendent God. Rather, it is the whole, *to pan,* of an earth below and a heaven above—of celestial bodies and their movements; of seasonal changes; of fertility rhythms in plant and animal life; of human life, birth and death; and above all, as Thales still knew, it is a cosmos full of gods. This last point, that the gods are intracosmic, cannot be stressed strongly enough, because it is almost eclipsed today by such facile categorizations as polytheism and monotheism. The numbers are not important, but rather the consciousness of divine reality as intracosmic or transmundane. In the Mem-phite Theology, imperial order is established by a drama of the gods that, by virtue of the consubstantiality of all being, is performed on the human plane as the drama of Egypt's conquest and unification. In the Sumerian King List, kingship is created in heaven and then lowered to earth; and two thousand years later, in Jewish apocalypse, there is still a Jerusalem in heaven, to be lowered to earth when the time for God's kingdom has come. Yahweh speaks from Mount Sinai, out of a fiery cloud; the Homeric Olympians dwell on this earth, on a mountain reaching into the clouds, and they have quarrels and agreements affecting the historical destinies of peoples in Asia and Europe. The Hesiodic gods Uranus and Gaea are indistinguishably heaven and earth themselves; they enter into a union and generate the gods, and the generation of gods in their turn generates the races of man. This togetherness and one-in-anotherness is the primary experience that must be called cosmic in the pregnant sense.

In cosmological empires, the understanding of history is dominated by this primary experience of the cosmos. The events of history are worth remembrance, because man engaged in action is conscious of his existence under God. The ruler of a cosmological empire acts by a divine mandate; the existence of the society, its victories and defeats, its prosperity and decline, are due to divine dispensation. When the Hittite king, Suppiluliumas (*ca.* 1380–1346), tells the story of his campaign against Tusratta, the king of the Mitanni, he speaks as the executor of a divine decree and renders account to the Stormgod, whose favorite he is, so that posterity may know of the victory willed by the god. When, in the Behistun Inscription, Darius I (521–486) reports the victory over his domestic enemies, the war assumes the form of a struggle between the Lord of Wisdom and his opponents, between Truth and Lie, so that posterity may know the truth about the Truth that has prevailed. An especially forceful document of this class is the report of Queen Hatshepsut (*ca.* 1501–1480) on the restoration of order after the explusion of the Hyksos:[3]

> Hear all ye people and folk as many as they may be,
> I have done these things through the counsel of my heart:
>
> I have not forgetfully slept, but have restored what had
> been ruined.
> I have raised up what had gone to pieces,
> when the Asiatics were in the midst of Avaris in the
> Northland,
> and among them were nomads, overthrowing what had
> been made.
> They ruled without Re; and he (Re) did not act through
> divine command down to my majesty.

---

[3] Translation by John A. Wilson in James B. Pritchard (ed.), *Ancient Near Eastern Texts Relating to the Old Testament* (Princeton, 1950), 231; hereinafter cited as *ANET*.

I am established on the thrones of Re.
I was foretold for the limits of the years as the one
                              born to conquer.
I am come as the uraeus-serpent of Horus, flaming against
                              my enemies.
I have made distant those whom the gods abominate,
              and earth has carried off their footprints.

This is the command of the father of (my) fathers
              who comes at (his) appointed times, of Re,
and there shall not occur damage to what Amon has commanded.

My (own) command endures like the mountains—
the sun-disk shines forth and spreads rays over the titles
                              of my majesty,
and my falcon is high above (my) name-standard for the
                              duration of eternity.

When the god commands, by virtue of the divine substance flowing through him the king will command; when the command of the god remains in abeyance, the king is not able to act as a ruler. The will of the god thus becomes manifest, through action or inaction of the ruler, in the order or disorder of society. The king is the mediator of cosmic order that through him flows from God to man; and the historical report bears witness to the dispensation of the gods that govern the existence and order of society in time.

One man's victory is another man's defeat. The proud reports glowing with righteousness were rendered by the victors; the defeated, who have left no monuments, were probably less inclined to praise the splendor of divine-cosmic order. Moreover, the pharaohs who defeated the Hyksos knew that the Hyksos had defeated their predecessors. There is a hint of theodicy in the text when it speaks of the god "who comes at (his) appointed times" and sometimes, for reasons of his own, will not come as desired by man; however glorious and durable the order may be in other realms of being, in history there sways the god who is "the setter up and plucker down of kings." On such occasions, the cosmological style becomes transparent for a truth about God and history beyond the truth of the cosmos. In spite of its embracingness, the shelter of the cosmos is not safe—and perhaps it is no shelter at all. The pride inspiring the reports of victory can barely veil an undercurrent of anxiety, a vivid sense of existence triumphant over the abyss of possible annihilation.

These reflections suggest a tempting assumption concerning the experience that will disrupt the cosmological style of truth. The vicissitudes of social order in history, with their undercurrent of anxiety, will ultimately destroy the faith in cosmic order. Since cosmological societies conceive their order as an integral part of cosmic order, the argument would run, the realm of history is the area from which the sense of precariousness, once aroused, will expand to the cosmos as a whole. A severe crisis of empire might arouse apprehensions of a twilight of the gods who are part of the cosmos just as much as man and society; and it might shake the faith in the stability of the cosmic order itself. If doom is the fate of empire, why should it not be that of the cosmos?

The assumption is not quite wrong. The revulsion from imperial rise and fall enters, indeed as a motivating factor, the spiritual movements which supersede the truth of the cosmos by the truth of existence; and the mood of despair induced by a senseless succession of empire can even engender a symbolism like the Daniel Apocalypse, with its metastatic hope for a divine intervention that will put an end to the grotesque disorder of cosmologically ordered society and history by crushing it out of existence through the world-filling kingdom of God. Nevertheless, the mood of distrust in the cosmos aroused by the vicissitudes of empire is not sufficient cause to explain the dynamics of the cosmological style of truth with its longevity, its stability and resistance to disillusionment, its internal changes and ultimate disintegration. For skepticism regarding cosmic order caused by the breakdown of empire, as well as states of existential alienation, are attested by a rich literature even for the third millennium B.C., and yet nobody ventured a break with the truth of the cosmos. During the worst disorders of the Intermediate Periods in Egypt, no prophets arose to proclaim a new truth of existence under God instead of the pharaoh; nor do we hear of revolutionary movements proposing alternatives to the traditional type of empire. Pragmatic events, it appears, can arouse the negative existential states of bewilderment and revulsion, alienation and despair; the existential moods in their turn can make the minds of men receptive for a pertinent attack on the truth of the cosmos when it comes; but neither the events nor the moods by themselves will change a style of truth. Changes can come only through noetic advances which let more compact symbols appear inadequate in the light of more differentiated experiences of reality and their symbolization. A style of truth can be challenged only on its own ground through confrontation with a more differentiated understanding of reality.

The challenge must meet the primary experience of the cosmos on its

own ground and show its truth to be inadequate in the light of more differentiated insight. The old truth and the new are closely related because,
after all, they are two verities about the same reality; they are equivalent
symbolizations, to be distinguished by their place on the scale of compactness
and differentiation. Considering this close relation, the "own ground" of the
primary experience is of considerable importance, as it is the same ground on
which the challenging differentiations have to move. What this common
ground is, I shall try to determine by an examination of the symbols used in
cosmological societies to express their integration into the cosmos. For this
purpose I shall consider one or two symbolisms of kingship.

If a king uses the style of a ruler over the four quarters of the world, he
wants to characterize his rule over a territory and its people as an analogue
of divine rule over the cosmos. In fact, however, the analogy is not supplied
by the cosmos itself but by phenomena of the physical universe, more specifically by the earth and the celestial bodies whose revolutions determine the
four quarters. The analogy makes cosmological sense only because the world,
in the physical sense, and with it the gods, kings, and societies are conceived
as consubstantial partners in a cosmos that embraces them all without being
identical with any one of them—though in this particular symbolism one
must note a tendency, to be further explored, to let the embracing cosmos
blend into the external universe. Another instance: If the king is symbolized
as the mediator of divine-cosmic order, perhaps even himself as god or at least
as son of god, again the analogy does not stem from the cosmos itself but
rather from the gods. And again it makes cosmological sense only because
gods and kings are consubstantial partners in the cosmos—though this time
one must note a tendency to let the embracing cosmic order blend rather
with the gods. The intracosmic areas of reality, one may say, provide one
another with analogies of being whose cosmological validity derives from
the experience of an underlying, intangible embracingness, from a something
that can supply existence, consubstantiality, and order to all areas of reality
even though it does not itself belong as an existent thing to any one of these
areas. The cosmos is not a thing among others; it is the background of reality
against which all existent things exist; it has reality in the mode of non-
existence. Hence, the cosmological play with mutual analogies cannot come
to rest on a firm basis outside itself; it can do no more than make a particular
area of reality (in this case: society and its order in history) transparent for
the mystery of existence over the abyss of non-existence.

The "own ground" of the primary experience, the ground it has in common with all differentiated experiences of the same reality that will challenge it, turns out to be the fundamental tension of all reality experienced: the tension of existence out of non-existence.

Existence out of nothing as the primary experience of early societies might be suspect because it reminds one of modern existentialism. The parallel is well observed, but the suspicion of a modernistic interpretation of ancient materials is unfounded. Rather, inversely, the resemblance is caused by a consciousness of groundless existence acutely reawakening among modern thinkers who have rejected doctrinal metaphysics and theology without being able to recapture non-doctrinal trust in cosmic-divine order. The flood of anxiety and alienation released under such conditions of intellectual and spiritual disorientation causes the modern situation to resemble that of the third millennium B.C., with parellel symptoms of spiritual disease as striking as the modern philosophies of history and the Sumerian King List. Existence out of nothing is indeed the fundamental experience of reality in early societies just as much as in later ones. The fact is attested by the special set of symbols for its expression. For at the center of the cosmological myth of order there opens the rich field of symbolism that Mircea Eliade has explored in his *Mythe de l'éternel retour* (1949). It is the field of the previously mentioned rituals of renewal that has, as Eliade observes, the function of abolishing time, of undoing its waste and corruption, and of returning to the pristine order of the cosmos through a repetition of the cosmogonic act. He speaks of the purpose of the New Year rituals, as the *'statisation' du devenir,* as the attempt to bring becoming to a standstill, to restore being to the ordered splendor that is lethally flowing away with the flow of time. The people living in the truth of the myth sensed the cosmos threatened by destruction through time; and the ritual repetitions of cosmogony purported to "annul the irreversibility of time." The experience of a cosmos existing in precarious balance on the edge of emergence from nothing and return to nothing must be acknowledged, therefore, as lying at the center of the primary experience of the cosmos.

In his *Principes de la nature et de la grâce* (1714), Leibniz has formulated the two questions the metaphysician will have to ask regarding the sufficient reason for the universe of things: (1) Why is there something, why not nothing? and (2) Why do things have to be as they are and not different? In their context, I should warn, the "metaphysician's" formulations are handicapped by the "physicist's" assumption of things as given without their dimension of non-existence; they have the polemical color of an endeavor to rescue reality from its destruction through the advance of scientism. It is perhaps this critical pressure, however, that has forced the questions to their brilliant starkness, so that they are immediately recognizable as the questions aroused by the primary experience of reality as a tension between existence and non-existence. In modern philosophy, they have become centrally motivating questions: A century after they were formulated in the little discourse for Prince Eugene of Savoy, in the work of Schelling; and again a century later, in Heidegger's existentialism. Hence, from enlightened deism and theodicy, through Romantic theogony, to the contemporary existentialism in terms of being, time, and anxiety, the motivating structure in philosophical consciousness is the same as in the consciousness of cosmological thinkers, however widely the answers to the questions may differ between and among the ancients and moderns. The answer of Leibniz: "This ultimate reason of things is called God" (*Principes,* 7–8).

I have introduced the questions as formulated by Leibniz, in order both to establish and distinguish the relation between the primary experience of reality, the questions arising from it, and the answers given as a constant in the dynamics of consciousness. First, there is the experience, variously expressed as follows: Whatever comes into being must perish; the things return to where they have come from; nothing that exists is its own ground of existence; existence is an intermediate movement (*planeton*) between being (*on*) and not-being (*me on*) (*Plato*); pure being and pure nothing are the same, and their truth is the movement from the one to the other, *i.e.,* becoming (*Hegel*). From the variously articulated experience, then, arises the aetiological question, the question of the ground: What is this mysterious ground the existent things don't carry within themselves but nevertheless carry with them as a sort of matrix of existence? At this point "logical" difficulties can arise either through insufficient linguistic articulation of the problem, or through hypostatic derailments, or, a possibility Hegel has pointed out, through fear of the answer. For whatever the ground is, it must be something; but as soon as the term *something* is introduced it suggests a "thing" of the type of existent things; but as the ground is not an existent thing, it only can be "nothing"; but as "nothing" is really nothing in terms of existent things, the question of the ground is illusionary; and so forth, until the pole of non-existence in the experienced tension of reality has dissolved in hypostatic negations of its reality. Nothing seems so difficult to grasp as the "sufficient reason" for the universe of things, especially if one is afraid that the answer could be that of Leibniz. Once these obstacles on the way are surmounted, either by noetic analysis or by simply ignoring them, one can arrive at answers. The ground can be a Platonic world-soul animating the cosmos; or an equally Platonic Father-God about whom we know so little that he has never been worthily praised by man; an Aristotelian *prote arche* to the aetiological chain which discloses itself as the divine Nous of *Metaphysics;* an Israelite creator-god; the pre- and transmundane God of the Christian dogma; a Neoplatonic world-soul, improved by Hegel's dialectically immanent *Geist;* a Bergsonian *élan vital;* the epigonic Being for whose parousia Heidegger waited in vain; or the Amon-Re for whose parousia Queen Hatshepsut did not wait in vain. I am enumerating answers indiscriminately, not because one is as good as another, but in order to make it clear that we get nowhere by putting one against the other, or by treating them as materials for doxographic dissertations. For the answers make sense only in relation to the questions they answer; the questions, furthermore, make sense only in relation to the concrete experiences of reality from which they have arisen; and the concrete experiences, together with their linguistic articulation, finally, make sense only in the cultural context which sets limits to both the direction and range of intelligible differentiation. Only the complex of experience-question-answer as a whole is a constant of consciousness. Moreover, this consciousness is not an abstract entity facing an abstract reality, so that any mode of experience at random would be possible at any time; rather it is the consciousness of a concrete man, living in a concrete society, and moving within its historically concrete modes of experience and symbolization. No answer, thus, is the ultimate truth in whose possession mankind could live happily forever after, because no answer can abolish the historical process of consciousness from which it has emerged—however frequently and fervently this fallacy may be entertained by doctrinaire theologians, metaphysicians, and ideologists. But precisely because every last answer is a penultimate in relation to the next last one in time, the historical field of consciousness becomes of absorbing interest; for it is his participation in the history of consciousness that confers on man's existential encounters with the reality of which he is a part the ultimacy of meaning which the penultimate answers, torn out of the complex experience-question-answer, do not have.

2. The Cosmological Style of Truth

The preceding remarks are meant to bring the cosmological style of truth into focus as an historical process of consciousness. Under the surface of millennial stability, noetic consciousness is at work on a truth that is unstable because its compact mode of symbolization will not do justice to structures of reality apprehended implicity but not yet fully differentiated. The critical points, as they become visible on the occasion of the historiogenetic symbolism, are (1) the search for mytho-speculative answers and (2) the appearance of a variety of times—rhythmical, linear, infinite, cyclical—in the response to the problem of non-existence.

The cosmological style of truth is fundamentally unstable because the tension in reality between existence and non-existence, though experienced as real, does not become sufficiently articulate. In the mode of cosmological compactness all reality is symbolized as a cosmos of intracosmic "things." The existent things become consubstantial partners in the divinely ordered cosmos, and the non-existent divine ground is symbolized as the intracosmic gods. The cosmos is as much in the things it embraces as those things are in the cosmos. As a matter of fact, the things are so much the cosmos itself that in the earlier phases of cosmological thought there is not even a word for cosmos, though there appear symbols for its pervasive order, like the Egyptian ma'at who is imagined as a further intracosmic divinity. One should especially note that in this style of symbolization, the poles of the tension in reality must be dispersed as "things" over areas of reality conceived as equally intracosmic.

The compression of existence and non-existence into intracosmic things meets the counterpressure of reality. Even before processes of differentiation set in, the conflict makes itself felt in the peculiar pattern governing the play of mutual analogies. This play, in which the several areas of reality supply one another with analogies of being, is possible only because gods and men, celestial phenomena and society are conceived as intracosmic things, i.e., as consubstantial partners in the community of being, so that they all can represent the cosmos that is present in them all. In the practice of symbolization, however, this claim to equal representativeness is superseded by distinctions of representative rank in which the apprehended but not differentiated tension in reality imposes itself on the compactly symbolized areas of intracosmic reality. For, as the examples of cosmologically symbolized kingship have shown, the existent king holds his position not in immediacy under the non-existent cosmos but has it analogically mediated through the celestial universe and the intracosmic gods. The universe and the gods assume the function of the non-existent ground; they are more cosmic than man and society. The pressure of the tension in reality, thus, tends to disrupt the ordered whole of intracosmic things, but the disruption is prevented by according some of the things a higher rank of representativeness. This device proves of considerable importance for understanding the symbolism of a "cosmos." For the primary experience of reality is the experience of a "cosmos" only because the non-existent ground of existent things becomes, through the universe and the gods, part of a reality that is neither existent nor non-existent. The tension of reality has been absorbed into the wholeness of the intermediate reality that we call cosmic. The In-Between of cosmic reality encloses in its compactness the tension of existence toward the ground of existence. Hence, the cosmos is tensionally closed. I am stressing the *tensional* closure, for to this day the understanding of cosmological thought is made next to impossible by the fundamentalist fallacy of imagining the cosmos of the primary experience to be *spatially* closed.

The disruption, though, cannot be prevented forever. The compression of the tension into the In-Between of cosmic reality becomes critically untenable when the astrophysical universe must be recognized as too much existent to function as the non-existent ground of reality, and the gods are discovered as too little existent to form a realm of intracosmic things. In the hierarchical order of realities that governs the symbolization of kingship there become visible the lines along which the cosmological style will crack until the cosmos dissociates into a dedivinized external world and a world-transcendent God. At this point, however, one must be careful not to overstate the results of differentiation and dissociation. What cracks is the cosmological style of truth as far as it tends to conceive all reality after the model of In-Between reality; and what dissociates is the cosmos of the primary experience. But neither of these consequences of differentiation affects the core of the primary experience, *i.e.,* the experience of an In-Between reality. On the contrary, it is still with us. For in the *Critique of Practical Reason,* in the "Conclusion," Kant must acknowledge: "Two things fill the mind with ever new and increasing admiration and awe: the starry heaven above me and the moral law within me." Kant's "starry heaven" is the celestial universe transparent for its divine ground, and his "moral law" is the presence of a divine reality that has become transmundane in the conscious existence of a man who has become mundane. The In-Between reality of the primary experience has been critically pruned; it is no longer the model for symbolizing all modes of reality; but it is still there. Moreover, the two areas of In-Between reality that resist compliance with the victorious model of existent things are still the same that are accorded higher representative rank in the cosmological symbolization of kingship. Hence, the cosmological style of truth is not simply a flight of imagination to be discarded in the light of later and better insight, but indeed a style of symbolization with a core of reality experienced in truth. And inversely, the differentiated existent thing has become the core of truth in a style that symbolizes all reality after this model; and again the style will crack under the pressure of the reality that remains unrecognized, this time the In-Between reality, as it does in the twentieth century A.D.

Reality can be experienced either as the whole in which it is transparent for the presence of the divine ground, or as the manifold of existent things in tension toward the non-existent ground. If one of the experiences is made the model of all reality at the expense of the other, the resultant style of truth will be unstable and require epicyclical symbolizations for its balance. In the case of the cosmological style, this balance is achieved by the mytho-speculative symbolisms which extrapolate the areas of intracosmic reality toward the ground by telling the story of their genesis from the beginning. Nothing need be added at this point to what has previously been said about the equivalence of mytho-speculation to the noetic symbolizations of the divine ground of being.

3. The Modes of Time

There remains to be considered the variety of times in the responses to the problem of non-existence. As far as the sources are concerned, there is no doubt that more than one conception of time appears within the cosmological style of truth. The obscurities surrounding the matter do not arise from enormous difficulties in the problems to be explored, but from the unsatisfactory state of contemporary science, burdened as it is with ideological mortgages and the consequences of specialization. One of the more rugged obstacles is the aforementioned topical block, according to which cosmological thought is characterized by cyclical time, while linear time is peculiar to Judaeo-Christian history. As a proposition in science, the topos can be roundly dismissed as nonsense; and yet it survives, because it carries the ideological overtones of a progress from the cyclical to the linear conception. Cyclical time is more primitive, suitable for pagans like Plato who did not have the benefit of either Revelation or Enlightenment; linear time is more advanced, the true time of history in which God reveals himself to Christians and the ideologists reveal themselves to mankind. The sequence is an historiogenetic construction; as such it has become, beyond the Christian orbit, an ideological *idée force*. Hence, it will be apposite to clarify the issue of a plurality of times as far as it is obscured by the topos.

The construction of the topos conceives time, whether circular or straight, as a line on which things can be arranged. The obscurities caused by the topos will dissolve, if one refrains from hypostatizing time as a line on which items of reality can be placed in succession. If, in a more contemplative mood, one permits time to be the lasting of reality itself, one will expect as many modes of time to appear as there are modes of reality experienced. The time of the cosmic whole before its dissociation is not the time of existence and non-existence after the tension of reality has differentiated; the time of existent things is not the time of the non-existent divine ground; the time of seasonal rhythms is not the time of society in political action; the time of biological evolution is not the time of history; the lifetime of a man who adjusts to cosmic reality is not the lifetime of an apocalyptic who expects the end of the cosmos next week; and so forth. The variety of times, thus, is correlative with reality experienced in the various modes of compactness and differentiation, of existence in truth as well as of existence in a state of alienation and deformation. Since the cosmological style of truth is an abbreviating term for symbolisms developed in social fields which extend over thousands of years, and since, furthermore, within these fields there run the processes of consciousness which issue in the classic and Christian differentiations of the non-existent divine ground of existence, one can expect a considerable number of times to appear as the experience of reality moves through the field of differentiation and deformation, constituting it in the process. It would be rather a surprise if, in this field of variant experience, the symbolization of time should prove to be the one invariable.

The topos is still so strong that it not only eclipses the appearance of irreversible time in historiogenetic speculation, but also subsumes all the other modes under the head of "cyclical" time. It owes this strength to the truth it originally derived from the concrete opposition of the early Christian thinkers to the then-dominant conception of the cosmos as an entity that would come to its end through the catastrophe of *ekpyrosis,* and experience rebirth, an indefinite number of times in indefinite time. This conception, however, is not characteristic of the cosmological style as a whole, but represents its late phase of deformation which runs chronologically parallel with its disruption through the newly differentiating truth of existence in classic philosophy, Judaism, and Christianity. The deformation is a rather complex process: I shall select only the factors that have an obvious bearing on the issue of so-called cyclical time.

There is to be distinguished, first, the phantasy of the course of history as an entity with a beginning and an end, recurring periodically in infinite time. As far as I know, the earliest unequivocal articulation of this conceit is to be found in *Problemata,* XVII, 3 where Aristotle reflects: Should we really say that the generation of the Trojan War lived prior to us and that those who lived earlier were prior to Troy, and so on ad infinitum? Aristotle rejects the idea of infinite regression. The course of history is finite; the later we are placed in it, the closer we are to its next period. Hence, we may be prior to Troy, if Troy should happen to lie at the beginning of the course while we are situated near its end. The passage is a precious demonstration of the problems that will arise when the cosmos of the primary experience dissociates and the existent thing, placed in the dimension of indefinite time, space, and causality, emerges as the model of being. History is for Aristotle a course of events with an intelligible meaning. If the model of the existent thing is applied to the meaning of history, it clashes with the indefinite regress which, for Aristotle, deprives reality of its meaning. The solution through recourse to historiogenetic speculation is no longer possible, the recourse to eschatology not yet. Hence, history has to become a finite thing set in an indefinite dimension; and as it is a necessary part of cosmic order, it is forced to repeat itself. Whether it makes sense to apply to this construction the term *cyclical time,* as if it were the real time of a mode of reality experienced, is at least doubtful. The term looks rather like a misnomer, if one considers that, on the one hand, we have no experience of a finite course of history that would repeat itself and that, on the other hand, the problem arises from the transfer of the indefinite time-dimension of existent things to the In-Between reality of history. The symbolism does not articulate any reality experienced at all but is characteristically a deformation of reality through secondary speculation. If one wants to speak of cyclical time in this connection nevertheless—which may be a convenience—one must acknowledge that the term denotes a speculative deformation of reality.

In *Problemata,* the deformation of In-Between reality through the model of the existent thing does not extend beyond the course of history; Aristotle leaves the cosmos intact. In post-Aristotelian philosophy, especially with the Stoics, the cosmos itself becomes an object in the dimensions of indefinite time and space; a plurality of worlds, including the course of history, succeed one another in time and coexist in space. In this radical form, the deformation dominates the following centuries, well into the Christian period, when the lifetimes of Marcus Aurelius (121–180) and Clement of Alexandria (*ca.* 150–215) overlap. That is the late phase of cyclical time when the extravagancies of secondary speculation abound. Not only cosmos and history, but also individual men will repeat themselves indefinitely; the life of a person will recur in the minutest detail; at most one may admit differences in the number of freckles on a man's face. Again and again there will be a Socrates who has his quarrels with Xanthippe and must drink the hemlock. The repetitive sameness goes so far that logicians begin to worry about the problem of identity: Is the Socrates of one cycle identical with the Socrates of the next one? Some would be affirmative; others would have misgivings, for identity requires existence in continuity and the two Socrateses are not continuous. And so forth. Inevitably, Christian thinkers found the repetitive cosmos incompatible with the one world created by their God; and they could hardly approve of a history in which the epiphany of Christ is a recurrent event. Once imagination leaves the orbit of reality experienced, the imagery of a second reality can become grotesque. Nevertheless, in fairness to the ancients one must say that they were not more indulgent in this respect than the moderns are in their comparably structured state of existential disorientation, for, ever since the plurality of worlds has been introduced again to the general public through Fontenelle's *Entretiens sur la pluralité des mondes* (1686), Western society has descended to the vulgarian grotesque of flying saucers, an invasion from Mars, investment of public funds in listening to signals from other worlds, a wave of excitement that the pulsar emissions could be such signals, and the industry of science fiction that is based on this conceit.

Still, the imagery of cyclical time is not entirely unrelated to reality experienced. Though there is no cosmos that performs cycles in infinite time for an outside observer, there is the cosmos of the "starry heaven" that fills with admiration and awe the man who looks up to it; and when the man looks up, he can indeed observe cycles in the sense of a periodic return of celestial constellations. The experience of real cycles within the celestial cosmos forms the historical background to the hypostatic cyclical time in the late phase of the cosmological style. This background will come into view, if one ascends from the Stoic cosmos, through its more immediate ancestry in Heraclitean, Pythagorean, and perhaps Anaximandrian speculation, to the older and wider field of Near Eastern myths of catastrophes through conflagrations and floods followed by the renewal of the cosmos. The myths of this class have nothing to do with hypostatic speculation; they are, as the study by Giorgio de Santillana and Hertha von Dechend, *Hamlet's Mill* (1969), has shown with a wealth of materials, engendered as responses to the experience of certain celestial movements, especially of the precession of the equinoxes through the zodiac in the cycle of the Great Year. For the "world" of the early cosmological societies is symbolized by the "four quarters" which correspond to the "points" of the solar movement; and these points are oriented by the point of the spring equinox, *i.e.,* by the relation of the rising sun to the zodiacal constellation in which it rises at this time. This point of the equinox, however, is not at rest but precedes in the cycle of the Great Year, taking about 2,200 years to move through one of the twelve zodiacal constellations. Hence, the cosmos of the primary experience, far from being static, is experienced as unstable; the precession of the equinoxes, relentlessly disturbing its order, arouses the anxieties which can express themselves in the myths of cosmic catastrophes and restorations. Since the contents of the myths appear to refer to equinoctial movements as early as the precession from Gemini to Taurus, the astronomical observations presupposed in the experience must go back at least to 4000 B.C.

When the cyclical time of the topos is traced to its experiential origin, it dissolves into the time dimension of celestial cycles. The time of these cycles, however, is in itself no more cyclical than the time of vegetation rhythms is rhythmical, or the time of unilinear history is itself linear. By using the adjectives to denote modes of time, we do no more than acknowledge the diversification of reality as extending to the modes of lasting peculiar to each variant of reality. Nevertheless, the diversified modes of lasting reality are not random phenomena in an open field of variegated realities; they are not diversified as species of a genus, but as partners in the reality of the cosmos; and their relations are governed by their participation in the lasting of the whole. We experience the modes of reality and their times as hierarchically ordered, and we recognize their hierarchy through the institution of the calendar which relates the other modes ultimately to the time of celestial cycles. As distinguished from the other variants of reality, the celestial cycles appear to be the very time of their own reality; we approach a limit at which reality becomes time and numbers. Plato was aware of this limit when, in his late work, he assumed the ideas to be numbers. Moreover, he expressed his experience of this limit at which reality becomes transparent for its non-existent ground by symbolizing the cosmos as the *monogenes* of the Father, and time as the *eikon* of eternity.

§ 4. Numbers and Ages

When the cosmos becomes an existent thing that repeats its course in indefinite time, obviously a symbol that makes sense only in the context of the primary experience has been hypostatically deformed. The status of symbols, as well as their relation to the experiences they purport to express, is much less clear in the case of mytho-speculations which hold an intermediate position between cosmological compactness and noetic differentiation. Without losing their original meaning, the symbols of the myth become, as it were, raw material that has to be fitted into a new context of meaning—as for instance when intracosmic gods of various experiential origin become generations of gods in a theogony that has the purpose of differentiating the divine reality behind the intracosmic gods, or when the cosmic catastrophe of the Great Flood, originally engendered as a mythopoetic response to the precession of the equinoxes, becomes an historiogenetic event on the same level as the reign of a recent king. Several strata of meaning merge into a new whole, the one affecting the other in the process of composition. For the case of historiogenesis, the threads woven into this fabric must now be disentangled, as far as that is possible, through an analysis of the sources.

If the governance of society is experienced, not as a series of brute facts, but as part of an intelligible order under the dispensation of the gods, there will arise the question of the meaning that governs the flow of events in time. The thinkers who develop the historiogenetic symbolism try to find this meaning by extrapolating the course of events toward an origin in the divine-cosmic order, so that the present can be understood as the terminal situation into which the meaning flowing from the origin has issued. The present, however, is fleeting. Hence, the thinker may try to buttress it by projecting the course into the future toward its absolute divine-cosmic end.

An instructive instance of extrapolation into the past is the previously mentioned Sumerian King List, to be dated *ca.* 2050 B.C. On the basis of already existing dynastic lists of the city-states, as well as of epic and legendary materials, it extrapolates the dynasties of the fictitious empire back to the mythical Great Flood. The List was later expanded farther backward by prefixing to it an "ante-diluvian" Preamble which informs us about the dynasties of the five cities before the Flood. The Preamble opens with the formula: "When kingship was lowered from heaven, kingship was (first) in Eridu"; the List after the Flood begins: "After the Flood had swept over (the earth) (and) when kingship was lowered (again) from heaven, kingship was (first) in Kish." Both formulas symbolize the origin of governance as the lowering of kingship from heaven; history begins when the order ordained by the gods becomes incarnate in the temporal course of the world.[4]

A speculation on the total course, comprehending also the future, is im-

---

[4] Translation by A. Leo Oppenheim, *ANET*, 265f.

plied in the Biblical historiogenesis inasmuch as the date of the exodus from Egypt is placed in the year 2666 from the creation of the world, for the number 2666 is two-thirds of 4000. With the exodus, two-thirds of a world aeon of 4000 years, that is of one hundred generations of forty years each, have run their course.[5]

In this second case, there appear certain numerical relations which determine the length of the historical course as well as its division by epochs and periods. I shall, first, isolate this factor of numerical speculation.

It is highly probable that the numerical relations among the dynastic periods of the Sumerian King List reflect a principle of numerical speculation in their construction. For the dynasties before the Flood have eight kings with a total reign of 241,000 years; the dynasty of Kish after the Flood has twenty-three kings, with a total of a little over 24,510 years; then the dynasty of Uruk has twelve kings, with a total of 2,310 years. Within the dynasty of Uruk, however, the mythically excessive reigns break off with Tammuz and Gilgamesh; to their successors the List ascribes historically possible reigns of from 6 to 36 years. The three sums for the long mythical periods, expressly drawn in the text, present the following picture:

$$
\begin{array}{ll}
241{,}200 \text{ Years} & 67 \times 3{,}600 \\
24{,}510 \text{ Years} & 68 \times \ \ 360 + 30 \\
2{,}310 \text{ Years} & 65 \times \ \ \ 36 - 30
\end{array}
$$

Even though the mathematical calculations behind the construction of the periods cannot be clearly discerned in the text as it stands, the picture as a whole suggests that these numbers did not assemble by accident. The successive periods shrink in length roughly in the proportion 10 to 1; the basis of the calculation seems to have been the *saros* of 3,600 years; and the multipliers 67, 68, 65 oscillate around the value of 66.66 . . . (that is, of $\frac{2}{3}$ of 100.) Moreover, the number of 24,510 years for the middle period is reasonably close to the 25,800 years of the Great Year in which the cycle of the precession is completed. The periods, thus, appear to result from an attempt to fit the empirically observed precession of the equinoxes into a hexagesimal system of numerical speculation. The multiplier of $\frac{2}{3}$ of 100, then, recalls the $\frac{2}{3}$ of 100 generations used in the Israelite speculation on the date of the exodus. The proportion of 10 to 1, finally, that governs the relation between the periods is also the

[5] Gerhard von Rad, *Das Erste Buch Mose, Genesis Kapitel 1–22*, 9 in V. Herntrich and A. Weiser (eds.), *Das Alte Testament Deutsch.* Neues Goettinger Biblewerk, Teilband 2 (4th ed.; Goettingen, 1956), 54.

proportion that governs the sum of the three periods, inasmuch as the total of 268,020 years is about 10 times the cycle of the precession.

The probability that the Sumerian King List results from numerical speculation becomes a practical certainty, if one considers the second great case from the same cultural area, *i.e.,* the late Babylonian construction of Berossus under the reign of Antiochus Soter (280–262). The system of Berossus (*ca.* 330–250) has been reconstructed from the fragments by Paul Schnabel.[6] The first of its periods, beginning with creation and reaching to the primordial kings, has a time-span of 1,680,000 years. Then follow: the period of the primordial kings before the Flood, with 432,000 years; the period of the kings after the Flood, down to the death of Alexander the Great, with 36,000 years; and, finally, the period from Alexander to the end of the world through *ekpyrosis,* with 12,000 years. When the years are translated into Babylonian *saroi* of 3,600 years and *neroi* of 600 years each, the following series of periods will result:

1,680,000 Years	466 Saroi, 4 Neroi	From creation to the primordial kings
432,000 Years	120 Saroi	From primordial kings to Flood
36,000 Years	10 Saroi	From kings after the Flood to Alexander
12,000 Years	3 Saroi, 2 Neroi	After Alexander to end of the World
2,160,000 Years	600 Saroi	Duration of the World Aeon

Finally, there must be considered the construction of genealogical tables in the Israelite historiogenesis. Two different constructions are preserved for the table of the descendants from Adam, and even three different ones for the descendants from Shem, so that the fact of deliberate numerical speculation is beyond doubt.

For the Adamite table we have the version of the Masoretic text in Genesis 5:3–31 as well as a second one that is common to the Septuagint and Josephus:[7] The higher sum in the second column is achieved by raising the ages of the patriarchs at the birth of the first son by exactly one century in eight out of

---

[6] Paul Schnabel, *Berossos und die Babylonisch-Hellenistische Literatur* (Berlin, 1923), 176f.

[7] The following table by H. St. J. Thackeray in Josephus, *Jewish Antiquities* (Loeb Classical Library, *Josephus,* Vol. IV), 39f.

| *Age* | | *Age at birth of firstborn* | |
(Masoretic)		*Masoretic*	*LXX, Josephus*
Adam	930	130	230
Seth	912	105	205
Enosh	905	90	190
Kenan	910	70	170
Mahalalel	895	65	165
Jared	912	162	162
Henoch	365	65	165
Methusela	969	187	187
Lamech	777	182	188
Noah	950		
Age at Flood		600	600
Adam to Flood		1656	2262

ten cases. The same technique is used in the following Shemite table (Gen. 11:10–26). The dates of patriarchs, just as the reigns and periods in the Sumerian and Babylonian tables, are functions of the numerical schemata favored by various schools of symbolists.[8]

About the motives for introducing a numerical schema into the symbolism no more can be said than the obvious. Back of the schemata lies a mysticism of numbers which express the cyclical reality of the cosmos. Even in the early

| *Age* | | | *Age at birth of firstborn* | | |
(Masoretic)			*Masoretic*	*LXX*	*Josephus*
Shem	600	Firstborn	2	2	2
Arpachshad	438	after Flood	35	135	135
Kainan	—		—	130	—
Shelah	433		30	130	130
Eber	474		34	134	134
Peleg	239		30	130	130
Reu	239		32	132	130
Serug	230		30	130	132
Nahor	148		29	79	120
Terah	205		70	70	70
		From Flood to Abraham	292	1072	993

[8] The following table, *ibid.*, 73.

myth, thus, we encounter a conception of the cosmos as structured by numbers that was still alive in the philosophy of Pythagoras and Plato. The Israelite number of 4,000 years or the Babylonian 600 *saroi* of 3,600 years each appear to be sacred or perfect numbers, suitable to represent a cosmic aeon; and for the Sumerian King List I have pointed to the probable combination of an hexagesimal speculation with the Great Year. The existence of rival schools of symbolists is put beyond doubt by the Israelite tables, but about the rationale of their speculation we still know regrettably little. Most obscure are the lowest levels of the constructions. Why a king on the Sumerian List, or a patriarch on the Israelite genealogical tables, has been assigned this or that number for his reign or life can be surmised only rarely as, for instance, in the case of the short-lived patriarch Henoch (in the Adamite table) whose 365 years are probably due to a solar myth.

Between the global number assigned to an aeon and the single numbers of reigns and lives at the bottom of the construction, there lies a series of historical periods, which characteristically become shorter the closer they come toward the present. A little bit more can be said about this middle stratum of the schemata than about the global and the lowest numbers. I shall now turn to the question of the ages and their decreasing length.

First the facts: The Sumerian historiogenesis has three periods from the origin down to the historically possible dates. The first one has a length of 241,200, the second one 24,510, the third one 2,310 years. The factor of reduction is about 10. The reigns of the kings in the three periods have an average length of about 30,000, 1,000, and 200 years. The construction of Berossus has periods of 1,680,000, of 432,000, and of 36,000 years. No approximately constant factor of reduction is recognizable. The period from creation to the primordial kings has neither kings nor reigns; the 10 primordial kings before the Flood have an average reign of 12 *saroi;* the first 86 kings after the Flood, with a total of 34,090 years, have an average reign of 393 years; with the 8 Median usurpers and their total of 224 years we approach the historically possible. Though Israelite historiogenesis has no clearly decreasing periods, the principle of reduction is applied to the ages of the patriarchs within the periods:

(1) Adamites	*ca.* 700–1,000	Years
(2) Shemites	*ca.* 200– 600	Years
(3) Patriarchs	*ca.* 100– 200	Years
(4) Ordinary Men	*ca.* 70– 80	Years

The meaning of the decreasing periods will become apparent from the commentaries of Christian authors who, since antiquity, have had to face the question of the high ages of the patriarchs. To the commentators the question is delicate, because the durability of the patriarchs is reported in a work which claims to be a truthful and reliable account of the history of mankind, or, more cautiously, to which this claim is attributed—for it is by no means certain that the symbolists themselves have understood their creation as "true" history in a literal sense. For the elucidation of the problem, I shall draw on three commentators: St. Augustine, Martin Luther, and a contemporary theologian, Gerhard von Rad.

St. Augustine was, regarding this question, a fundamentalist. He felt obligated to make the longevity of the patriarchs credible by analogy with the giant stature of early man. While longevity cannot be proven, for the patriarchs are dead and no longer objects of observation, at least the giant stature of early man can, in his opinion, be empirically demonstrated as it is attested by the finds of fossilized bones of such men. And if the giants were real, why should the long-living patriarchs have been less real? Moreover, in the course of his demonstration he also adduces pagan testimonials in support of his plea, which, if they do not support his defense of longevity, at least bring to our attention the related symbolisms in Vergil and Homer. St. Augustine's reference to the heroic deed of lifting a stone which twelve men of the build the earth brings forth today could not lift (*Aeneid,* xii, 99 f; *Iliad,* v. 302), refers us to the historiogenetic elements embedded in the classic literature as a prospective field for the discovery of symbolisms of a similar type.[9]

Luther, in his commentary on the age of the patriarchs, has penetrated to the core of the problem: "Therefore this has been a right golden age, whereas our age hardly deserves the name of dirt, when nine patriarchs with all their descendants lived at the same time. . . . For this is the highest honor of the first world that there lived in it so many pious, wise, and saintly men in company at the same time. For we should not think that they were the common names of plain and simple people, but they were all men of heroic excellence." Luther, to be sure, was a fundamentalist too, but at the same time he was sensitive to the myth; and the dry genealogical tables became transparent to him for the golden age of the heroes.[10]

Gerhard von Rad, finally, who quotes Luther's passage in his commentary on Genesis, elaborates its insight further, stripping off the fundamentalist

[9] Augustine, *Civitas Dei,* XV, 9.
[10] Von Rad, *Das Erst Buch Mose,* 58 (Luther, *Weimarer Ausgabe,* XLII, 245f).

encumbrances. He thinks that the history of the patriarchs witnesses to the high vitality of the first mankind as it emerged from creation, and at the same time delivers a discreet judgment on our present, natural status. "We must consider, after all, that the Priestly document which contains the genealogical tables did not offer a story of the Fall, which theologically would account for the disturbance and decline in the created status of man and, as a consequence, for the transition to the status of Noachitic mankind. Here in the genealogical tables we find something approximately corresponding to the story of the Fall. The slowly fading ages of the patriarchs (most consistently in the Samaritan system) must be understood as the gradual decline of an original, miraculous vitality of man, in proportion to his increasing distance from the creational origin."[11]

As a first result of the commentaries we must note that the Hellenic symbolism has been drawn into the horizon of the inquiry. In the Mesopotamian and Israelite speculations on periods of decreasing length there is hidden the symbolism of the Ages of the World in the sense of Hesiod; and the decrease of vitality with increasing distance from the creational origin has its parallel in Plato's myth of the *Statesman* which lets the order of the world decline with its removal in time from the original impetus of order imparted by the God. Beside the Near Eastern there also exist Hellenic variants of historiogenetic speculation. Moreover, and this is the second result, the reflexions of von Rad make visible the type of experience which strives to express itself by means of the declining ages. For the Priestly document (P), which contains the speculation on the periods, offers no story of the Fall; and inversely, the story of the Fall in the Yahwist document (J) makes the expression by means of periods of declining vitality superfluous. Hence, the story of the Fall must be recognized as expressing, alternative to the speculation on periods, the experience of a tension between the destiny of man and his temporal status. The proposition can be generalized: The story of the Fall is an equivalent alternative, not only to the speculation of the Priestly document, but also to the Sumerian, Babylonian, and Hellenic, as well as to every related speculation in other societies. As one of the important motives of historiogenetic speculation there becomes manifest the experience of man's existence in time as imperfect: The stream of events, descending from the cosmic origin to the present, symbolizes imperfection as a state of existence that is "not-always-so-in-time"; in the Time of the Tale, golden ages and paradises can precede and follow the present that

[11] *Ibid.*, 55.

is imperfect. In the story of the Fall, the historiogenetic Time of the Tale begins to crack. The story, it is true, still moves in the time of the myth, but the
clumsy sequence of ages declining in length is abandoned in favor of the Fall
that has happened once for all, so that the time of history in which the structure
of existence after the Fall does not change can emerge.

§ 5. Imperial Mediation of Humanity

Though both the story of the Fall and the tale of decreasing periods symbolize the experience of imperfection in existence, the two symbolisms are
not wholly but only partially equivalent, for the story of Adam and his Fall
is the story of Everyman; it touches personal existence directly. The construction of ages assigns primary reality to the races and generations of man, so that
its bearing on man's concrete existence is mediated by his membership in the
successive collectives. Moreover, as the numerical speculations have shown,
the myth of declining ages is more closely related to the order of the cosmos
in the astrophysical sense than to the human sphere proper. Hence, though
both symbolisms appear in the context of Israelite historiogenesis, the story
of the Fall has more anthropogonic, the story of the ages more cosmogonic
character.

The overlapping and intertwining of symbolisms becomes of more than
taxonomic interest, when the question is raised why the construction of decreasing periods should survive, once the story of the Fall has been developed.
If in historiogenetic speculation no more were at stake than a search for
symbols that will adequately express the tension of imperfection-perfection,
one would expect the more cosmogonic symbol to disappear once the more
adequate of the Fall has been created. One might even expect a speculation
on the cosmic antecedents of history to become altogether superfluous, once
the divine command and man's disobedience have been understood as the
ineluctable tension of the human condition, once the experience of man's
existence under God has differentiated with such clarity as it has in the
prophecy of Jeremiah, during the decades before the fall of Jerusalem (585
B.C.). With the discovery of its motive in the experience of imperfection, the
time would appear to have come for the cosmological type of historiogenesis to
dissolve and to be superseded by an understanding of history in terms of the
truth of existence.

Such expectations, however, will not be fulfilled. Historiogenesis does not
dissolve. It even expands at the expense of the other types of mytho-speculation

that move in the cosmic, divine, and human realms of experience. The Old
Testament speculation, which in its final form belongs to the exilic and post-
exilic periods, takes over a variety of cosmogonic and anthropogonic myths,
as well as a wealth of legends; it divests all these materials, as far as possible,
of their autonomous mythical character and integrates them into its own symbolism as historical events. Moreover, the same process can be observed in the
Babyloniaca of Berossus, as it absorbs the myths of the creation of the world
and of its final conflagration, of the Flood as well as of culture-heroes who
have endowed humanity with the arts of writing, agriculture, city-building,
and with the sciences.[12] Historiogenesis, thus, not only persists but even displays a tendency to swallow up all other types of mytho-speculation. It is the
symbolism by which the cosmological style of truth survives most obdurately in
social fields whose style of truth is informed by philosophy and revelation.
Such pertinacity suggests the presence of an issue beyond the tension of
imperfection-perfection.

The cause of the expansiveness can most clearly be discerned in Egyptian
historiogenesis. Hence, I shall begin the analysis of this peculiar phenomenon
by adding the Egyptian case to the materials under consideration.

Egyptian historiogenesis extrapolates history back toward its origin by
prefixing a series of divine dynasties to the first dynasty of human kings. As in
the Israelite case, several variants are preserved; but in the Egyptian case, we
are fortunate enough to know at least something about the motives behind
the variety, inasmuch as the several speculations are recognizably the work
of the Priestly colleges of a number of important temples.[13]

A first variant lets the succession of divine rulers begin with the Ptah of
Memphis. It is to be found both in the Turin Papyrus, from the time of
Dynasty XIX (*ca.* 1345–1200), and in the *Aigyptiaka* of Manetho (*ca.* 280,
about contemporary with Berossus). A second, probably older variant lets the
succession of divine rulers begin with the Re of Heliopolis. It has been preserved through Diodorus, in his *Bibliotheke Historike,* I, 13 (*ca.* 50–30 B.C.).
A Theban variant, then, is contained in the account of Herodotus (II, 144–45),
if the Pan, whom he names as the first god, is correctly interpreted as the
Amon-Min of Thebes. The analysis of the variants by Egyptologists has shown

---

[12] Cf. the fragments in Schnabel, *Berossos und die Babylonisch-Hellenistische Literatur,* 251f.

[13] The account of facts follows Wolfgang Helck, *Untersuchungen zu Manetho und den
Aegyptischen Koenigslisten,* Vol. XVIII of *Untersuchungen zur Geschichte und Altertumskunde
Aegyptens* (Berlin, 1956), 4–9. Cf. Ludlow Bull, "Ancient Egypt," in R. C. Dentan (ed.), *The
Idea of History in the Ancient Near East* (New Haven, 1955), 1–34. The fragment of Manetho's
mentioned in the text is in W. G. Waddell (ed.), *Manetho* (Loeb Classical Library), 2ff.

that the symbolists let the human dynasties be preceded by three dynasties of gods. The first dynasty was drawn from the great Ennead of the gods of Heliopolis (with the exception that in the Memphis variant, the Ptah of Memphis precedes the Re of Heliopolis); the second dynasty was drawn from the Ennead of the "lesser gods" of Heliopolis, beginning with Horus; and the third dynasty comprised the "servants of Horus," the spirits of the dead. A fragment of Manetho, preserved in the Armenian version of Eusebius' *Chronica,* enumerates the personnel of the three dynasties as the gods, the heroes, and the *manes*—to be followed by the mortal rulers of Egypt down to Darius, the king of the Persians. The variants differ, for reasons unknown, in a noteworthy point, inasmuch as the Turin Papyrus and Manetho enumerate as rulers only the male gods of the Ennead, while the Heliopolitan version, as preserved by Diodorus, has the female gods too. These are the facts as far as they are relevant to our purpose.

The facts reveal an important relation, regarding both time and subject matter, between historiogenetic speculation and the Egyptian annalistic records. Although the Turin Papyrus dates from Dynasty XIX (1345–1200), with regard to its content a somewhat higher date may be assumed; the Papyrus may be the copy of a document from Dynasty XVIII (1570–1345). And from the preceding centuries, inscriptional and literary formulas such as "time of Re," "time of Osiris," "time of Geb," "time of Horous," are extant, possibly pointing to the earlier existence of speculations on the dynasties of gods. With the most generous assumptions, however, we can hardly move the date higher than the Middle Kingdom, or at best the First Intermediate Period (2200–2050). Long before the highest possible date for the content of the Turin Papyrus, however, lies the Palermo Stone of Dynasty V (2500–2350), which lets the rulers of Egypt, beginning with Menes, be preceded not by the dynasties of gods, but by the predynastic rulers of the still separate Upper and Lower Egypts, and even by a series of rulers of a temporarily united Egypt. The Palermo Stone proves that the annalists of the Old Kingdom had knowledge, probably through oral tradition, of a predynastic history of Egypt, of considerable length and political importance. The sources will permit us, therefore, to draw the conclusions that (1) historiogenetic speculation appears rather late in the history of Egypt and that (2) it represents a new interest which has no use for the predynastic history of Egypt as recorded by the older annalists. Moreover, the nature of the new interest becomes apparent from the fact that predynastic history was sacrificed. For in the new speculation, the human history of Egypt begins with the establishment of the

Egyptian Empire through the conquest attributed to Menes; before this human creation of order (which itself is the earthly counterpart of the drama of the gods in the Memphite Theology), there prevails the order of the divine rulers. Hence, by means of historiogenesis the history of Egypt is speculatively heightened to a history of divine order whose representative in cosmic time is the Egyptian Empire created by Menes.

In order to understand the peculiar data surrounding the origin of historiogenetic speculation, one must realize that a cosmological empire is more than one type of political organization among others. In its self-interpretation, imperial rule is the mediation of divine-cosmic order to the existence of man in society and history. Still in the third century B.C., Antiochus Soter (280–262), the new Macedonian king of Babylon, presented himself to the god Nebo in the same symbolic language in which twelve hundred years earlier the Egyptian queen Hatshepsut had presented herself to Amon-Re: The "first-born son of Seleucus" prays to the "first-born son of Marduk, child of Arua, the queen who fashioned all creation" for the god's "lofty command which is never revoked" to grant the stability of the king's throne, as well as the order of justice to the people, under the god's "lofty scepter which determines the borderline between the heaven and the nether world"; in return, the king will collect tribute from the countries and bring it home for the perfection of the god's newly founded temples of Esagila and Ezida.[14] Even at a time when the symbolism had lost a good deal of its strength in an environment of mystery religions and philosophical movements, empire thus was still the mediation of divine rule to the order of man. The god who determines "the borderline between the heaven and the nether world" determines thereby what is human order; the king as the mediator represents both god and man when, through his rule, he administers the cosmic order of reality; and the temple is the cosmic omphalos where the upper and the nether worlds meet. Hence, the breakdown of a cosmological empire entails more than the murderous unpleasantness of political disorder; it is a spiritual catastrophe, because the existential tension toward the divine ground of existence has not yet been sufficiently differentiated to function with social effectiveness as the *pièce de résistance* of order. For the order of his humanity, man has still to rely on the rather compact borderline drawn by the *summus deus* of the empire and administered by the king; only in the form of empire can man live in the truth of his humanity under the gods.

---

[14] Text translated by A. Leo Oppenheim, *ANET*, 317.

The implications of existence in imperial form did not become articulate all at once with the establishment of empire. The data and dates of the Egyptian case make it possible to give further precision to the questions, raised more than once previously, of the late date of historiogenesis as a mythospeculative type and its connection with political disorders. The history of empire had indeed to run a long course, at least long enough for a major catastrophe to occur, before the function of empire as the representative form of divine-human order came into focus with such clarity that historiogenesis could be developed as the adequate expression of the problem. The period between the decline of the Old Kingdom after Dynasty V and the restoration of order under Dynasties XI and XII (*i.e.,* the so-called First Intermediate Period, which has left the unforgettable impression of its trauma in the literature of the age) forms the background for the Egyptian historiogenetic speculation. The literary masterpieces of the time are well known. It will be sufficient, therefore, to refer to the *Prophecy of Nefer-rohu,* from the time of Amenhemet I (2000–1970), to illuminate the problem.[15] In the literary form of a prophecy dated back to the Old Kingdom, the work draws the great arc of experiences from the political catastrophe, through the time of troubles to the new order. The disorder is so profound that it has destroyed the divine origin of order; the Nome of Heliopolis, the birthplace of the gods, no longer exists; Re himself must lay the foundations for a new creation; and when the god has laid the foundations, Ameni will come, the messianic pharaoh, the triumphant; he will suppress the rebels, expel the Asiatics and Libyans, restore justice, and reunite the Two Lands. Disorder experienced in the spiritual depth of its horror appears to have been the force which raised the problem of order to the symbolic height of a new divine creation and the advent of a messianic king, much as the disorder experienced by the prophets of Israel inspired them to drive the problem of order to the heightened symbolisms of the new covenant, of the new heavens and the new earth, and of the messianic Prince of Peace.

In the light of the Egyptian data, then, further precision can be given to the preliminary characterization of historiogenesis as a speculative extrapolation of pragmatic events to their cosmic origin. For the Egyptian case, by its elimination of the well-known predynastic rulers, proves conclusively that the symbolist is concerned not with pragmatic history in general, but only with that sector of the *res gestae* that is representative of divine-human order. He is attracted neither by a society at random nor by a plurality of societies. The

[15] Text translated by John A. Wilson, *ANET,* 444f.

Sumerian King List, it is true, speaks of a kingship that has been lowered from heaven to one or the other of the Mesopotamian city-states. The object of interest, however, is not the respective autonomous city and its order, but the one imperial rule wielded in imaginary succession by the rulers of different city-states. The cities exist in the plural, the empire and its kingship only in the singular. In the Egyptian case, again the one society under one ruler is the carrier of true order; the Two Lands separately, a disintegration of empire, and the rise of local rulers are synonymous with disorder. To secure this oneness, the Egyptian symbolists, more radical than the Sumerians, do not deform preimperial history but throw it out altogether. The speculation on imperial order appears to be meant as a speculation on universal human order. Understanding this point requires an effort of imagination, because from our modern position we are accustomed to seeing an ancient society as one among many and we have, therefore, some difficulty in realizing that a Mesopotamian, Egyptian, or for that matter a Chinese symbolist, lives in the one organization of mankind when he lives in the empire surrounding him. The relation of a man's humanity to his membership in the imperial society was so close indeed that in some instances it was expressed by linguistic identification. The hieroglyph for *Egyptian,* for instance, also means *man;* and even more rigidly, the conventional phrase *son of a man* signifies the son of an Egyptian of social rank. Whereas from the modern position the close tie between human status and membership in a concrete society, or even in its ruling group, will appear as a regrettable restriction or discrimination, from the position of the ancient symbolists the idea of man was discovered on occasion of an imperial creation under the dispensation of the gods. For the enlargements of the social horizon from tribal society to city-state, and further on to an empire which comprises the whole area of a civilization, are not mere quantitative increases in the number of population, but qualitative jumps in social organization which affect the understanding of human nature. They were experienced as creative efforts by which man achieved a differentiated consciousness both of himself and of the divine origin of an order that is the same for all men. Through the hard reality of empire, there begins to shine forth, as the subject of history, a universal mankind under God.

Reading an historiogenetic speculation of the early Sumerian or Egyptian type backward from the author's imperial present, one arrives at the cosmic-divine origin of empire; reading it forward from the divine dispensation of governance, one arrives at the empire in the author's historical present. Human existence under the gods firmly remains in imperial form. There is no room yet for a differentiated human nature in the classic or Christian sense; nor is there an opening yet for tension between the dimensions of man's existence as the *zoon noetikon* and *zoon politikon*. On occasion of a breakdown, the empire can become transparent because of its character as the representative of true humanity; but the idea of a truly universal mankind which embraces not only the members of an empire and the members of contemporaneous societies, but all men living under divine dispensation in the past, present, and future, does not yet break the imperial form of humanity. The order of empire, though transparent for the idea of universal mankind beyond organization, becomes its prison. Hence, the question will arise: What kind of experiences are likely to break down the compactness of imperial existence? In the Egyptian and Mesopotamian cases, one finds next to nothing by way of an answer to this question. One could perhaps point to a loosening of imperial compactness through the mysticism of Akhenaton as, in his hymns, the pharaoh accepts Asiatics and Libyans as human beings in the society of the empire; but this modest crack in the wall does not affect the historiogenetic symbolism. In the Israelite case however, the idea of universal humanity has differentiated so far that theological interpreters speak of a radical break with the symbolisms prevalent among the other peoples of the Ancient Orient. This assumption goes too far, for in spite of the differences the common Near Eastern type of historiogenesis was not abandoned. Still, the radical antithesis favored by the theologians is so instructive that I shall begin the analysis of the Israelite case with its presentation.

In his commentary on Genesis, Gerhard von Rad writes:

> Israel has not simply drawn a straight line from primordial myth down to its own temporal existence. The straight line running back to the myth is characteristic for the religion of the polis, in which the political community can take seriously only itself. (The list of the old-Babylonian primordial kings begins: 'When kingship was lowered from heaven, kingship was in in Eridu. . . .') The conception of Genesis is different: The line from primordial times does not run without a break through Noah to Abraham, but issues first into the universe of nations. When Israel looks back from Abraham, there is a decisive break in the line running back to the point of origin, that is, the Table of the Nations (Genesis 10). This break means that Israel saw itself, without illusions and without a myth, in the world of the nations. What Israel experiences from Yahweh, will happen in the sphere of history. The insertion of the Table of the Nations means, for Biblical theology, the radical break with the myth.[16]

[16] Von Rad, *Das Erst Buch Mose,* 120f.

The passage elaborates the decisive point of difference with precision: The Table of the Nations in Genesis 10 introduces mankind to the Israelite speculation; Israel, though she is the Chosen People, is one people among many.

One can agree with von Rad on the point of difference and still have reservations regarding his conclusions. For it appears that von Rad has inverted the relation between a constitutive event and the symbolism expressing it. The Israelite experience of revelation, as well as the subsequent existence of the Chosen People under the Law of Yahweh, it is true, belongs to the historical rather than the cosmological mode of existence. But the genuinely historical character of Israel's existence under God must not be construed as a consequence of a universalist conception of mankind; rather one would have to say that revelation constituted Israel's history as a universally human form of existence; the Table of the Nations is the symbolism expressing this constitutive event. For the revelations from the Thornbush and Sinai are addressed to man and society directly; they abolish the ruler of the cosmological empire as the mediator of divine order to man by placing man immediately under God. The Israel constituted from Sinai was, representatively for mankind, endowed with a new insight into the truth of human existence that is valid for everyman. Through the Sinai event, man has acquired his consciousness of historical immediacy under God. The new insight, however, did not dissolve historiogenesis but, on the contrary, was absorbed into its symbolism. Historical consciousness, though its meaning was clear to the prophets, did not gain its full organizing force in the elaboration of symbols but had to submit to historiogenetic speculation of the cosmological type. The Table of the Nations notwithstanding, the revelations from the Thornbush and Sinai were integrated as events in an historiogenesis of the Chosen People.

The revelation from the Thornbush expresses an experience of personal immediacy, the revelation from Sinai an experience of social immediacy under God; both, then, are recorded as events in an historiogenetic construction which mediates the truth of existence through membership in the Chosen People. This combination of symbolisms brings to attention the plurality of the experiential motives that have affected the Biblical narrative.[17] Israelite historiogenesis has indeed, as distinguished from the Egyptian and Mesopotamian cases, not one but two organizing centers: the Davidic foundation of empire and the Sinaitic Covenant. The foundation of empire, though it was the later event, furnishes the chronologically first motive, for the famous

<hr />

[17] *Order and History*, Vol. I, Ch. 6, pp. 2–3.

David Memoirs (II Sam. 9–20; I Kings 1–2) form the core of the narrative; beginning with the rise of David, the narrative tells the story of the empire, as well as of the successor kingdoms, down to the fall of Jerusalem. As far as the foundation of empire as the motive and imperial history as the subject matter are concerned, the pragmatic part of the narrative has the same character as the corresponding parts in the historiogenesis of the neighboring Near Eastern societies. When it comes to the extrapolation of the *res gestae* back to their cosmic origin, however, the Israelite pattern differs radically from that of the cosmological empires, for in Biblical historiogenesis imperial history is preceded for centuries by events that have no parallel in Egyptian or Mesopotamian history, *i.e.,* the exodus from Egypt, the Sinaitic Covenant, and the conquest of Canaan through which Israel was constituted as the Chosen People. Their memory had been preserved through liturgies, the oldest extant of which is perhaps Deuteronomy 26:5b–9:

> A wandering Aramaean was my father;
> and he went down into Egypt, and sojourned there, few in number
> and he became there a nation, great, mighty, and populous.

> And the Egyptians dealt ill with us, and afflicted us, and laid
>   upon us hard bondage.
> And we cried unto Yahweh, the God of our fathers;
> and Yahweh heard our voice, and saw our affliction, and our toil,
>   and our oppression.

> And Yahweh brought us forth out of Egypt,
> with a mighty hand and outstretched arm,
> with great terror, and with signs, and with wonders.

> And he brought us into this place,
> and has given us this land,
> a land flowing with milk and honey.

The exodus from cosmological civilization and the entrance into freedom under God were historical events in the eminent sense whose memory had been preserved through liturgies and prayers. As they contained the meaning of Israel's existence, they could not be eliminated like the predynastic rulers of Egypt without destroying the people; once they were understood in the fullness of their meaning, they had to take spiritual precedence over any foundation of empire, even an Israelite one. Since the symbolists could not neglect either of the experiential centers, Biblical historiogenesis has the distinction of containing a pre-imperial history.

This concession, however, raised two problems of construction. In the first place, the symbolists had to meet the question of the carrier of order in history. If imperial society was not the sole carrier of order, who could appear as the acting subject of order in history? And second, they had to meet the question of the universal validity of revelation. If revelation was God's appeal to man to place himself under his order, could even a pre-imperial Israel be the subject of history?

The symbolists resolved the problems by recourse to the categories of tribal society. Mankind was conceived as a clan descending from the ancestor Adam; the foundation of empire was preceded by the history of the tribal federation back to the Covenant and, further back, by the history of the patriarchs, of Noachitic and Adamitic mankind. The mythical dynasties of Mesopotamian and Egyptian historiogenesis were replaced by the genealogical tables of the Adam clan; and the humanly universal intention of constructing an Adam clan was made explicit by fitting the Table of the Nations into the genealogy of the tribe. This empirically universal history was then again heightened to a representative universal history of mankind, by stressing the sacred line of the covenants of God with the receptive representatives of mankind, i.e., the covenants with Noah (Gen. 9:9) and Abraham (Gen. 17:1–8), and the Sinaitic Covenant, so that the epochal covenants divided the history of mankind into the four periods from Adam to Noah, from Noah to Abraham, from Abraham to Moses, and from Moses to the present. By the speculation on the four periods, the foundation of the empire that had been the primary motive for the historiographic enterprise was symbolically subordinated to the events relevant to all mankind. One should add that the Gospels have changed the pattern of epochs and periods so as to accommodate the Messiah from the house of David as a further representative event in the history of humanity: Matthew (1:17) counts four periods from Adam to Abraham, from Abraham to David, from David to the exile, and from the exile to Christ.

In Israelite historiogenesis, the history of an empire that is transparent for the order of human existence under God is replaced by the history of the relationship between God and man. If now again we ask the question previously raised—why the symbolists of exilic and post-exilic times, though they had a differentiated understanding of history, took upon themselves the yoke of historiogenesis—we encounter again the experiences of imperial catastrophe. During the period of the kingdoms, the differentiated insights into the existence of man and society in immediacy under God were by no means lost; they even were brought to new clarity by the prophets' opposition to both popular and royal backsliding toward Egyptian and Assyrian forms of the cosmological myth. Nevertheless, the insight into universal humanity was so firmly tied to its realization by the Chosen People and its political organization that the division of the empire, followed by the destruction of the divided kingdoms, became the motivating experiences for historiogenetic speculation. As the *Prophecy of Nefer-rohu* served to illuminate the spiritual climate from which Egyptian historiogenesis could grow, so Psalm 137 will show the disturbance of the soul from which the Israelite speculation could emerge:

> By the rivers of Babylon,
> there we sat, truly, and wept,
> when we remembered Zion.
> Upon the poplars, in the midst of her,
> we hung up our harps.
> For they who held us captive
> demanded songs,
> and they who mocked us, mirth:
> "Sing us one of the songs of Zion!"
>
> How could we sing a song of Yahweh
> on the soil of the stranger?
> If I forget you, Jerusalem,
> may my right hand forget me!
> May my tongue cleave to my palate,
> if I do not remember you,
> if I set not Jerusalem
> above my highest joy!
>
> Remember, Yahweh, to the sons of Edom
> the day of Jerusalem,
> they who said: Raze it, raze it,
> down to the foundations!
> Daughter of Babylon, destructive one:
> Blessed be he who requites you
> what you have done to us!
> Blessed be he who seizes your brood
> and smites it against the stone!

This memorable document, trying to involve God and his realm in the imperial wars of the Ancient Orient, betrays the emotional confusion from which emerged such widely different phenomena as the historiogenesis of the Priestly writings, the Deutero-Isaianic vision of the suffering servant, the Torah and Rabbinism, Maccabean zealotism, and irenic Christianity.

§ 6. THE HELLENIC CASE—EUHEMERUS' *Historia Sacra*

Historiogenesis is a mytho-speculative extrapolation of pragmatic history toward its cosmic-divine point of origin. Now that we turn to the Hellenic variants of the symbolism, it is well to recall the definition, because the study of the earlier Near Eastern variants may have induced the prejudice that all historiogenesis must start from an imperial present. If that were the case, there could be no Hellenic mytho-speculation of the historiogenetic type, because there was no Hellenic empire that could have furnished the pragmatic substratum for the symbolism. Historiogenesis, however, proves to be a symbolic form of extraordinary pertinacity, elasticity, and variability. In the Egyptian case it insisted on the imperial present so intensely that the predynastic pragmatic history, though well known, was simply thrown out; in the Sumerian King List, it integrated the city-states into imperial history by violent fragmentation and reshuffling of pragmatic materials; in the Biblical narrative, it extrapolated the pragmatic events of the Davidic empire and the successor kingdoms into tribal history and the revelatory events. Moreover, as the Israelite case demonstrates, mytho-speculation in the field of history is not even abandoned when universal humanity under God has differentiated from the order of the cosmological empire in which it had been compactly contained. God and man, world and society remain united as they are in the primary experience of the cosmos; and the lastingness of cosmic reality continues to find its expression in the cosmic Time of the Tale. By virtue of a revelatory experience of man's existence in society, its time dimension may be recognized as the history that is transparent for divine order; by virtue of noetic insight, the problem of beginning and end may be recognized as an antinomy attaching to the flux of time; but neither revelation nor philosophy dissolves the time and tale of the cosmos. Even when the realm of universal humanity in time is discerned ever more clearly as the history of man's encounter with God, the mytho-speculative form of historiogenesis survives.

The phenotypical differences between Hellenic and Near Eastern variants of historiogenesis are caused by the structural differences of pragmatic history. Beyond the Hellenic city-states there existed an Hellenic civilization, recognized by the Greek historians and philosophers as a society of the same type as the Mesopotamian, Egyptian, or Persian civilizations. Though it never went through the pragmatic process of organizing itself as a pan-Hellenic empire, it was understood as capable of organization in imperial form and, therefore, as a potential subject of historical successes and catastrophes of the same kind as the Near Eastern empires. Moreover, in this capacity it was the potential subject of historiogenetic speculation. I stress the potentiality of its becoming the subject of mytho-speculation, because its actualization was handicapped by the technical difficulty that the Greeks possessed neither annalistic records nor a sufficiently coherent traditional history, and above all that they had no chronology. As a consequence, there never was a known and datable Hellenic history of appreciable length beyond the fifty years which a man can recollect from his own experiences as well as from the memory of the older generation. The massive quantity of historical events at the disposition of Near Eastern symbolists was missing in Hellas because there existed no imperial or temple archives to preserve the facts and dates of Hellenic history. The attempts to construct a chronological skeleton for the comparatively few known facts began rather late, in the second half of the fifth century, when Hellanicus synchronized the lists of the priestesses of Argos both with the lists of the archons of Athens and the dates of Oriental history. As late as the fourth century, Timaeus (*ca.* 356–260) introduced, in his *History of Sicily,* the reckoning by Olympiads, the clumsy but necessary instrument for counting years; and only in the third century did Eratosthenes (*ca.* 284–200) engage in the enterprise of assigning definite dates to the main events of Greek history down from the conquest of Troy. The shortness of known history and the recency of its recording became exciting subjects of debate for the historians of the Hellenistic and Roman periods, when, after the Western conquest of the East, Oriental authors began to rebel against the prejudicial opinion that the Greeks had a monopoly of critical and reliable historiography. The *Contra Apionem* of Josephus, which perhaps originally bore the title *Against the Greeks,* is the renowned document of the Orientals' protest against Greek historians. I shall return to the problem of Josephus presently.

The Hellenic symbolism which must be recognized as historiogenetic bears the following characteristics:

(1) There is no course of the *res gestae* of millennial or even secular extent. From a comparatively narrow historical horizon, speculation can at best move through a few widely spaced epic and mythical events and then must jump immediately to the absolute point of origin.

(2) Hellenic historiogenesis is subject to the previously demonstrated regularity that speculations of this class are motivated by the experiences of political catastrophes and restorations.

(3) As the catastrophes do not concern imperial institutions, the universally human problem of spiritual and moral decay of existence becomes predominant. Moreover, as the recovery from disorder cannot issue in a restoration of imperial institutions, the inquiry tends to develop into a universally human philosophy of order.

(4) As Hellenic society, though living in the shadow of the Asiatic great powers, was not imprisoned by an imperial form of its own and, consequently, was not compelled to experience humanity as represented by existence in imperial form, it remained open for empirical mankind beyond the confines of Hellas. As Israel has created the Table of the Nations, so Hellas has developed, though from differently structured motives, the Periegesis, *i.e.,* the ecumenic survey of empirically known mankind.

Symbolisms created by Hesiod and Herodotus will serve as representative examples of the type.

The Hellenic type of historiogenesis is represented most purely by its earliest instance in Hesiod's myth of the Ages of the World. Strictly speaking, the *logos* told in *Erga,* 106–179, is an anthropogony, but not without reason has the tale of the races of man become known under a name that stresses its character as a mytho-speculation on history. For while the first three races of fabulous creatures owe their existence to the poet's intention of creating an anthropogony of three generations parallel to the three generations of gods in his theogony, this series of the golden, silver, and bronze races is followed by the Homeric heroes and by the present iron race of men. The fourth and fifth races clearly reveal the poet's intention to interpret the present disorder of mankind as a phase of history ordained by the gods. The *logos* displays the characteristics of the Hellenic type in purity: There is, first, the narrowest possible historical horizon, comprising no more than the misdeeds experienced by the poet himself in his local polis at the end of the eighth century; from this narrow horizon, second, the problem of order is lifted to the universal level of divine justice and human conduct; and from this narrowly circumscribed present, finally, the poet jumps to the heroic mankind of the Mycenaean period. One should especially note the complete lack of *res gestae* between Hesiod's present and the paradigmatic age of the heroes; between the race of the demigods, whose survivors were removed by Zeus to the Islands of the Blessed, and the present race of men the great Fall has occurred. Beyond the Homeric abbreviation of the Mycenaean society, Hesiod has no historical materials at all (Plato, in the *Nomoi,* goes farther back to Minoan legislation and its divine origin); the generation of the epic is preceded by three generations of creatures who hardly bear human features, even though they are called men. Since the three races before the heroes are created by the three corresponding races of gods in the theogony, the construction as a whole is closely related to the Egyptian historiogenesis which lets the human rulers be preceded by the three dynasties of gods.[18]

The Hesiodic myth of the Ages of the World can be described as an historiogenesis contracted to the bare minimum. It was created after the Greek dark ages, at the very dawn of Hellenic civilization proper. The extraordinary possibilities of further development contained in this attempt to interpret the order of human existence in society did not become visible before the fifth century, in the work of Herodotus.[19]

With Herodotus, the structure of the symbolism has remained, on principle, the same as with Hesiod, but the enormous bulk of the Periegesis has changed the phenotype so thoroughly that most readers will hardly become aware of the similarity of construction. His *Historiai* was written after the Persian Wars. Its motivating experience was the threat to the existence of Hellenic society and the restoration of a precarious balance of power through the victories of Marathon and Salamis. This experience, which as a motive is typical for every historiogenetic speculation, determines an historical horizon much larger than the Hesiodic. The disturbance of order is no longer a question of petty violations of justice in the small town of Ascra; the scene has become worldwide, and the conflict between Asia and Europe affects the whole of mankind that is relevant within the Herodotean horizon. Universally human order, which is present as a problem also in Hesiod, now receives a new carrier in ecumenic mankind. By his ecumenic interest—as it becomes manifest in the vast survey of peoples, their cultures, and histories—Herodotus goes not only beyond Hesiod, but also beyond the Near Eastern speculations, and even beyond the Biblical narrative which clings, in spite of the Table of the Nations, to the Chosen People as the representative carrier of order. Still, the ecumenic interest is not original with Herodotus. From the very beginnings of Hellenic civilization, it is present in the Homeric epics as they conceive the Achaean-Asiatic conflict as a disturbance of universal human order that is, under the dispensation of the common gods, the same for Acheans and Trojans. As early as the epics, there is manifest the Hellenic sense of tragedy in human existence that later permitted an Aeschylus, in his *Persians,* to deplore the fall of the enemy as the tragic fall from his greatness.

[18] On Hesiod, cf. *ibid.,* Vol. II, Ch. 5.
[19] On Herodotus, cf. *ibid.,* Ch. 12, § 1.

To the ecumenic enlargement of the horizon, however, there corresponds in the work of Herodotus no appreciable elongation of the time-dimension. The *res gestae* of the conflict begin with the campaign of Cyrus against Lydia in 547, and they end with the conquest of Sestos in 478, filling altogether barely seventy-five years. As Herodotus was born *ca.* 485, his temporal horizon extends not much farther back than the half-century before his birth. These are modest figures compared with the long pragmatic histories integrated in the Near Eastern speculations. The far-flung Periegesis, it is true, offers information on much earlier events, as for instance Egyptian. But the *res gestae* of non-Hellenic histories retain the status of *historiai,* of a written report concerning results of inquiries; they are neither integrated into an historiographic context, nor do they have any function in the main line of Herodotus' speculation. His main line jumps, just as abruptly as does the Hesiodic, from the Persian Wars to the age of the Homeric epic. But it does not end there. Herodotus draws the line farther back through several more European-Asiatic conflicts to the first disturbance of order. The result is a chain of violations of justice: rape of the European Io through Phenicians; rape of the Asiatic Europe through Cretans; rape of the Asiatic Medea through Greeks; rape of the European Helen through Trojans; Hellenic war against Troy; Persian war against Hellas. The series leads, on no more than three pages, from the origin of the conflict down to its present phase of the Persian Wars; at Book I, 6, begins the narration of the *res gestae,* embedded in the great Periegesis. The extrapolation of history back to the absolute point of origin, thus, occupies hardly more space than with Hesiod.

The extrapolation is characterized by the transformation of mythical and saga materials into historical events, resembling the Israelite transformation of the same kind of materials into patriarchal history. Unusual, however, is the subsumption of the materials under a philosophical hypothesis that was perhaps inspired by Anaximander. For the violations of order are arranged by pairs so that guilt and atonement will balance one another, in accordance with the dictum of Anaximander that things, coming forth from the Apeiron, should perish into that from which they were born, paying one another penalty and compensation for their injustice according to the decree of time. Herodotus himself lives in the spirit of the dictum when he lets his Croesus warn the conquering Cyrus: There is a wheel of human affairs that turns and will not suffer the same man to be always fortunate (*Historiai,* I, 207). Hesiod had to rely, for the construction of the origin, on anthropogonic and theogonic form elements; Herodotus could use an Ionian hypothesis concerning the *arche*

of things. Hence, his law that governs the course of events is free from mythical imagery; Herodotus needs no gods to start things moving. In the medium
of materials transformed into historical events, he can trace their chain back
to a first action understood as human. The chain of events itself goes forth from
the *arche* of Anaximander, from the Apeiron.

Hellenic historiogenesis proper has an Hellenistic sequel in the *Hiera
Anagraphe* of Euhemerus, a work conventionally classified as a "novel" or
"utopia." I shall, first, characterize the situation in which this peculiar symbolism originated.

The first characteristic distinguishing Greek from Oriental historiogenesis
is the briefness of known history, due to the lack of annalistic and traditional
sources as the basis of historiography. The Greek thinkers were well aware
of the fact—in his *Timaeus,* Plato lets the Egyptian priest say to Solon: "O
Solon, Solon, you Hellenes are always children; there is no such thing as an
old Hellene!" (22b). The second distinguishing characteristic, closely related
to the first one, is the breakthrough to the nature of man and the possibility
of recognizing mankind as its carrier. Only the Hellenes have made neither
an imperial society nor the open society of all Hellenes, but ecumenic mankind the subject of history. As a consequence there existed in Hellas, and only
in Hellas, the situation in which an historiogenetic symbolism of ecumenic
complexion could be applied to the European-Asiatic ecumene when it gained
imperial structure in the wake of Alexander's conquest. It is advisable to speake
vaguely of an "imperial structure" rather than of an empire, because organizationally the conquest could not be held together but had to suffer division
into the Diadochic empires. Moreover, one can hardly speak of an imperial
society, because the collection of populations never had time to acquire a
stable social structure. And, finally, there were neither imperial gods nor an
imperial cult common to the humanity united by imperial conquest. An attempt to create an historiogenetic symbolism for this ill-defined situation in
the shadow of Alexander's ecumenic plans inevitably would have to assume
a strange shape.

When Euhemerus, the friend of Cassander, made such an attempt, *ca.* 300
B.C., it assumed the form of a project for an ecumenically desirable social
order. The author pretended that his project was the order of an actually
existing society; and with diplomatic discreetness he placed the society on the
imaginary island of Panchaea in the Indic Ocean. As a project of social

order, the work of Euhemerus belongs to the class of "utopias" of the age
which preferably should be called "mirrors of the prince," because their intention of appealing to the new rulers of the ecumene is certain, whereas the
question of whether they really are utopias in the sense that Thomas More
has given to the word coined by him has to be investigated for every case
separately. In the present context, however, this question need be no more than
adumbrated, as we are primarily interested in that part of the work in which
Euhemerus, speculating on the origin of order, presents his social project as
the creation of an ecumenic god-ruler. In the manner of an Egyptian historiogenesis, he extrapolates the order of the island society, supposedly of universal
validity for ecumenic mankind, to its origin in the ordering achievement of a
dynasty of gods.

On the island of Panchaea, writes Euhemerus, there stands the temple of
Zeus Triphylius, founded by the god when he was still the ruler of the ecumene and dwelt among men. In the temple there is a stele of gold on which
are inscribed the deeds of Uranus, Cronus, and Zeus. Uranus was the first
king on earth, an equitable and beneficent (*euergetikos*) man, well versed in
the movements of the celestial bodies, the first to honor the Uranian gods
with sacrifices, and for that reason called Uranus (Heaven). He was followed
by Cronus, who was followed by Zeus. Going to Babylon, Zeus was entertained by Belus, "and after that he went to the island of Panchaea, which lies
in the Ocean, and here he set up an altar to Uranus, the founder of his family."
The principle of historiogenetic speculation, the extrapolation of history back
to its divine origin, thus is retained, but the course of pragmatic history itself
which under Hellenic conditions had never been of more than modest length,
is now reduced to zero; from his timeless project, the author has to jump
immediately back to the divine dynasties.[20]

Two features of Euhemerus' symbolism deserve particular attention. The
first one is the Egyptian character of the construction. While it may be safely
assumed that the idea of a divine dynasty preceding the mortal rulers is of
Egyptian origin, a complication arises from the fact that Euhemerus distinguishes between celestial gods who have always been gods and earthly
rulers who have been elevated to the rank of gods. The distinction is preserved,
via Eusebius, by Diodorus in his summary of Euhemerus' opinion prefixed
to the story of Panchaea: "As regards the gods then, men of ancient times

[20] Felix Jacoby, *Die Fragmente der Griechischen Historiker I-A* (Leiden, 1957), No. 63,
"Euhemerus von Messene," Fragment 2.

have handed down to later generations two different conceptions: Certain of
the gods, they say, are eternal and imperishable, such as the sun and the moon,
and the other stars of the heavens, and the winds as well and whatever else
posesses a nature similar to theirs: for each of these the genesis and duration
are from everlasting to everlasting. But the other gods, we are told, were terrestrial beings who attained to immortal honors and fame because of their
benefactions (*euergesia*) to mankind, such as Heracles, Dionysus, Aristaeus,
and the others who were like them."[21] The Hellenistic conception of the beneficent ruler, of the *euergetes,* to whom divine rank is accorded, thus, appears
to have blended into the Egyptian idea. Unfortunately, however, the Hellenistic character of the conception of an *euergetes* is itself doubtful in view of
the fact that Hecataeus of Abdera (about contemporary with Euhemerus), in
his *Aigyptiaka,* attributes the distinction between the two types of gods expressly to the Egyptians. It is the Egyptians who, according to Hecataeus, are
of the opinion that there exist, on the one hand, eternal gods of the heaven,
the celestial bodies, and the elements, and, on the other hand, earthly (*epigeios*)
gods, some of them bearing the same names as the Uranian gods who formerly
were mortals but have attained immortality as a reward for their *euergesia*.
Some of them even were supposed to have been rulers of Egypt. And then, in
the previously quoted passage on the Heliopolitan and Memphite variants of
Egyptian historiogenesis, Hecataeus continues to discuss the Egyptian dynasties of the gods. Whether his report is reliable, or whether he has modified an
Egyptian tradition under Hellenistic influences, we have no means to decide.
Certainly, however, the problems of Euhemerus are not so simple as the conventional account of Euhemerism as a manifestation of Greek skepticism,
bordering on atheism, would lead us to believe.

The second point concerns the title of Euhemerus' work, the *Hiera Anagraphe*. Apparently this title has played some part in the genesis of the concept
of *historia sacra*. Ennius (239–170) translated Euhemerus into Latin, and
Lactantius (*ca.* 260–340), when he quotes from the Latin translation, refers
to it as *Sacra Historia* or *Sacra Scriptio*.[22] Moreover, Lactantius mentions
Euhemerus as the author who collected *res gestae Jovis et ceterorum qui dii
putantur*.[23] As it appears from these references, the term *hiera anagraphe* was
understood to mean both a written record and the subject matter of the record,

---

[21] Preserved by Diodorus Siculus, VII, 1, 2–3.
[22] In Jacoby, *Die Fragmente,* see *Sacra Historia* in Fragments 14, 18, 20–25, and *Sacra
Scriptio* in Fragment 14.
[23] Jacoby, *Die Fragmente,* Fragment 17. Augustine, *Epistulae,* XVII.

and in both meanings to signify history in the sense of the historiogenetic symbolism. The double meaning agrees well with Diodorus' account according to which Euhemerus spoke of the *praxeis*, the *res gestae* of the gods which he found recorded on the stele in the sanctuary of Zeus Triphylius.[24] As the usage of Hecataeus of Abdera shows, the term *hiera anagraphe* itself was probably used, even before Euhemerus, for designating the Priestly records of Egyptian history. This assembly of facts makes it highly probable that the phrase *sacra historia* has penetrated into the Western vocabulary from the Egyptian usage, mediated through the *Hiera Anagraphe* of Euhemerus and its Latin translation by Ennius. Not much more can be said about the question at present, as the origin and meaning of the terms *historia sacra et profana,* which today are taken for granted, apparently have never been explored systematically. At any rate, Augustine, with whom the pair of concepts is conventionally associated, does not have it. In *Civitas Dei,* XVII, 8, there occur the expressions *scriptura sancta* and *libri divinae historiae,* signifying the writings of the Old Testament; in XV, 9, the expression *historia sacra* is used in the same sense; and in XVIII, 40, there occurs the opposition of the *litterae divinae* to the *litterae saeculares. Doctrina Christiana,* XXVIII, has *historia gentium* to signify the writings of pagan authors in opposition to the Gospel writings. In every instance, the usage agrees with the Egyptian usage of *hiera anagraphe.*

§ 7. Historiomachy

The early historiogenetic symbolisms were firmly bound to the societies in which they developed. When the older cosmological empires were conquered by the ascending ecumenic empires, a new constellation of problems formed, for the older symbolisms, though they continued to be cultivated, were now forced into competition with one another for ecumenically representative rank. The beginnings of the competition can be noted in the cases of Berossus and Manetho, the Babylonian and Egyptian priests who wrote the histories of their respective societies, both at about the same time after the conquest of Alexander. They still used the historiogenetic symbolism as it had grown in their societies, but their language was the Hellenistic *koine,* and they wrote in the new political situation when the Seleucid and Lagid dynasties tried to stabilize their recently established rule by promoting a syncretistic imperial

---

[24] Jacoby, *Die Fragmente,* Fragment 3. Lactantius, *Divinae Institutiones,* I, 11, 233.

culture. These first attempts at coming to terms with the new situation inevitably were disappointing, for the experience of an ecumenic mankind could hardly be symbolized by imprisoning it in a symbolism that had its roots in the Babylonian or Egyptian imperial form, or for that matter in Israel or Hellas. Still, the attempts were made and a pattern of competitive claims began to form. The points by which the rivals counted their respective superiority apparently were the autochthony and antiquity of their societies, for Diodorus who wrote his *Koine Historia*, his universal history of mankind, about the middle of the first century B.C., reflected on the pretensions of Hellenic and barbarian historians who each claimed the origin of mankind for his own people. Diodorus seems to have been a man of common sense; he decided not to get involved in the unresolved questions of rival chronologies and therefore reported the several traditions impartially.[25] Since the phenomenon of this competition for ecumenic rank through history has hitherto received no name, I shall call it *historiomachy*. In concluding this chapter, I shall outline the principal phases of the great struggle.

In the competition with their Oriental *confrères* the Greek historians were at a disadvantage, because there existed no reliable Greek history of appreciable depth in time. I have briefly referred above to the Hellenic attempts at reconstructing a Greek history back to the Trojan War from saga materials. The process began with the logographers of the sixth century B.C. and had substantially come to its conclusion with Eratosthenes (*ca.* 284–200). Apollodorus, then, cast the results of Eratosthenes into verse in his *Chronica* and dedicated his work to Attalus II of Pergamon (159–138); in this more pleasant form it was widely read. The Greeks, thus, had acquired something like a respectable history extending from Troy to the year 144 B.C. When the power of empire, and with it the obligation to have an impressive history, moved westward, the Romans found themselves in the same embarrassing situation in relation to the Greeks as the Greeks had been in, in relation to the Orientals. In the preface to his *Romaike Archaiologia*, Dionysius of Halicarnassus (*fl.* 30–7 B.C.) informs us about Greek public opinion in this matter:

> The early history of Rome is still practically unknown to the Hellenic public. The majority have been misled by the false view, which is based on nothing but hearsay, that the founders of Rome were uncivilized vagrants and outlaws who were not even free born; and that the secret of Rome's rise to world domination should not be sought in her righteousness, her fear of God, or any moral quality, but in the amoral automatism

[25] Diodorus Siculus, I, 9.

of Fortune, who has bestowed her greatest gifts on her most undeserving servants. The malicious make this indictment in so many words and blame Fortune for having imparted the privileges of the Hellenes to the lowest savages; and it is superfluous to speak of the general public when there are actually writers who have ventured to place this position on permanent record in their historical works.[26]

This was the state of opinion, against which Dionysius wrote his *Romaike Archaiologia*. In his work he let Roman history begin with the immigration of Greek tribes, of Oenotrians and Pelasgians, before the time of the Trojan War. The Romans, in brief, were Greeks, and their history was part of Hellenic history.[27] This attempt to make the Romans respectable will be better appreciated if it be remembered that, at approximately the same time as the Halicarnassian, Vergil connected the history of Rome with the Trojan War, though he did not share the ambition of Dionysius to make Greeks of the Romans.

After the Jewish revolt and the fall of Jerusalem (A.D. 70), Josephus Flavius considered it necessary to participate in the contest. One hundred years after Dionysius' *Romaike Archaiologia* he published, as a counterpart, his *Ioudaike Archaiologia*. He wrote from a position of strength inasmuch as he could top the earliest recollections of the Westerners with the story of the creation of the world itself. Moreover, to Greek and Roman archaeology, which had to rely on stories about gods and heroes, frequently of questionable decency, he could present, as a wholesome contrast, his lawgiver Moses who always spoke purely and truly of God, though the narrative of happenings in remote ages would have offered many opportunities to indulge in *pseude plasmata*. And finally, as he assumed Moses to have lived two thousand years before his own time, Josephus could point out with pride that even the most venturesome among the pagan poets had never dared to place the birth of the gods at so early a date.[28] But the pagan public apparently did not react favorably to Josephus' claims concerning the higher antiquity and greater reliability of Jewish history. At least, he became sufficiently irritated by the skepticism he encountered to resolve upon a general attack on Greek historiography. To this attack he devoted his late work, the *Contra Apionem*. The principal thesis of the brilliantly written book can be summarized as the superiority of Egyptian, Babylonian, Phenician, and Jewish historical work, resting as it does on the

[26] Dionysius of Halicarnassus, I, 4.
[27] *Ibid.,* I, 11ff.
[28] Josephus, *Jewish Antiquities,* I, 15–16.

early possession of the art of writing and the careful keeping of archives, over the inexact and aesthetic manner of Hellenic histories, put together without a basis in reliable sources.[29]

In the last act of historiomachy, the Christians appeared as dramatis personae. They concluded the contest in more than one sense. For, on the one hand, the Christians were the survivors in the competition for supplying an adequate symbolism of order to the Mediterranean ecumene; on the other hand, they metamorphosed the sterile struggle for representative rank through superior age almost imperceptibly into the endeavor to produce a chronology and history of ecumenic mankind through the comparative evaluation of all available sources. The transition becomes tangible in the *Stromateis* of Clement of Alexandria (*ca.* 150–*ca.* 215) in the chapter dedicated to chronology (I, 101–47). I shall first treat the historiomachic aspect of the chapter—which at the same time happens to be its comic aspect because of the discrepancy between the spiritual rank of Judaeo-Christian tradition and the attempt to prove it by priority in time.

In *Stromateis* 105, 1, Clement says: "It is proven therefore that Moses lived 604 years before the reception of Dionysus among the gods, if he really was received among the gods in the 32nd year of the reign of King Perseus, as Apollodorus reports in his *Chronica*." In 106, 2–3: "Prometheus, however, lived at the time of Triopas, in the seventh generation after Moses; it follows that Moses lived long before, according to the Hellenic myth, man had come into existence. Moreover, Leon, the author of the work on the Hellenic gods, says that the Hellenes called Isis by the name of Demeter who lived at the time of Lynkeus in the eleventh generation after Moses." In 107, 2 Clement agrees with the verse of Pindar that "only late in time came to exist Apollo." In 107, 6: "Thus we have demonstrated that Moses preceded in time not only the sages and poets but also most of the Hellenic gods." Regarding priority among the sages the argument in 130, 2 concludes: "Hence it is easily to be seen that Salomon who lived at the time of Menelaus (who lived at the time of the Trojan War) was by many years earlier than the Hellenic sages."

The collection of passages from *Stromateis* once more brings to attention a characteristic of historiogenesis that cannot be stressed often and strongly enough, *i.e.,* the absorption of mythical materials by the symbolism. It is through their integration into historiogenesis that the tales of the myth are divested of their original nature and transformed into facts of history. Isis

---

[29] Josephus, *Contra Apionem*, I, 6–27.

and Demeter, Dionysus and Apollo become historical personages with a definite date in time, with the consequence that Clement can let his inquiry concerning the gods be followed, without a break of method, by the arguments concerning the date of Christ. Whether it be the dynasties of gods of the Turin Papyrus or the creation myth of the Bible, or further on the gods of Euhemerus or Hecataeus of Abdera, or finally the Incarnation—all are pored over and bound together by the pseudo-reality of "history." They are petrified into "facts" by a fundamentalism or literalism that had been alien to the free mythopoesis, be it of the Memphite Theology, or the creations of a Homer, Hesiod, Aeschylus, or Plato. The symbols of the myth have their truth as an analogy of being; if this consciousness of analogical truth is now destroyed, one of the principal causes (there were others) must be seen in the "historization" of the myth through historiogenesis. The tone peculiar to the arguments of Clement, half comic, half embarrassing, stems from this grossness of destruction. The problem is still with us today in the debates on Biblicism and demythicization, as well as in the discussions on the "historicity" of Christ.

Historiomachy, though in itself an unprofitable occupation, has nevertheless borne an important fruit. For each of the parties to the contest had thoroughly to work through its own history as far as the sources would permit, in order to show it to the best advantage. Moreover, as the war was conducted by comparisons and argument, each of the parties, in order to be successful, had to become familiar with the materials and arguments of the other side. Moreover, the competition for higher antiquity resulted in a chronological schema of empirical history, however defective and inaccurate; and the schema began to be filled with the events about whose dates the contestants were arguing. In his *Stromateis* Clement did not rely on the Biblical narrative alone, but made encyclopedic use of all the available works of Hellenic (136-9) and barbarian (40-3) chronography, as well as of the history of the Roman emperors down to Commodus. Inadvertently there emerges from the historiomachic intention, however rudimentary in form, a history of the peoples of the ancient Near Eastern and Mediterranean area. There is in the making the new literary genus of chronography that has determined, through the *Chronica* of Eusebius of Caesarea (*ca.* 260-340), the Western picture of world history well into the sixteenth century. With the new chronographic genus of literature, however, we have reached the point at which the problems of historiogenesis change over into those of the genesis of world history.

CHAPTER 2

The Ecumenic Age

The Ecumenic Age will denote a period in the history of mankind which roughly extends from the rise of the Persian to the fall of the Roman Empire. Since the concept is not established in contemporary science, the study must begin with an exposition of the epochal events that made its creation necessary, that is, the fall of Israel and Hellas to the power of empire. For an epoch in the history of order was marked indeed when the societies which had differentiated the truth of existence through revelation and philosophy succumbed, in pragmatic history, to new societies of the imperial type.

Israel existed in the historical form in which it had been constituted through the revelations from the Thornbush and from Sinai in the thirteenth century B.C.; and in their search for origins its historians found this form to extend beyond the exodus from Egypt back to Abraham's exodus from Ur in the early second millennium B.C. From the crisis of the Hellenic world arose the symbolic form of philosophy; and again in retrospect the philosophers interpreted Hellas and their own existence as the end of an historical course that embraced the Minoan, Mycenaean, and Hellenic civilizations, thus paralleling in time the history of Israel from its first exodus. Moreover, both Israel and Hellas were conscious of being set off, by their leap in being toward attunement with transcendent order, from the empires which had not broken the cosmological form, and even more so from societies on the tribal level. Both had expressed the consciousness of their higher order by referring to the surrounding mankind as goyim and barbarians; and when in the Hellenistic and Roman world the two societies came face to face, they even included one another in these depreciatory classes. Nevertheless, the proud consciousness of a privileged status saved neither society from the fate of succumbing to the onslaught of imperial power. The kingdoms of Israel and Judah fell to the Assyrians and Babylonians, and the post-exilic temple, rebuilt by permission of the Persians and lasting through the Macedonian rule, was ultimately destroyed by the Romans. The Hellenic society, having weathered the first imperial attack of the Persians, lost its independence to the Macedonians and

Romans. The empires closed in again on the clearing they had left in history for Israel and Hellas to flower. The attempts at ordering society by the truth of existence, be it the revealed word of God or the philosopher's love of wisdom, appeared to have come to their end.

§ 1. The Spectrum of Order

The cosmological societies in imperial form were, in pragmatic history, not succeeded by societies formed through the truth of the prophets and philosophers, but again by societies in imperial form. The representative thinkers of Israel and Hellas were well aware that the pragmatic order of history did not go the way of their spiritual order. In the East, the clash with the Seleucid Empire provoked the grandiose response of the Daniel Apocalypse to the disorderly conduct of a history which does not follow the path of spiritual perfection; at the same time, in the West, the clash with the Roman Empire elicited the more cautious, more temperate, and analytically more astute response of Polybius. Both the author of the Daniel Apocalypse and Polybius were conscious of witnessing an epoch when the course of order in history divided into pragmatic and spiritual lines; and yet, the meaning of the epoch is obscure even today because of the extraordinary complexity of events. The unraveling of the problem will suitably begin with raising the questions (1) whether the attempts at forming societies by the truth of existence were broken by the new empires at all, or by some other factor and (2) whether the new imperial societies belonged to the same type as the older Near Eastern empires against which Israel and Hellas had set themselves off by differentiating the truth of existence.

Regarding the first question, neither the revealed word nor the love of wisdom, though they had appeared in Israel and Hellas, had ever truly penetrated the respective societies; and this failure of penetration, far from being caused by disturbances from the outside, was due to indigenous resistance. Moreover, under the pressure of continued resistance the representatives of the word and of wisdom had to admit, though reluctantly, that the societies in which they lived would never be truly formed by the order of revelation and philosophy. Communities of disciples would have to be founded as the nucleus of truly ordered societies of the future. Thus Isaiah withdrew from politics to form, with his disciples, the remnant that would be the core of the new Israel; and the philosophers who had started as critics of the polis ended as founders of schools. Even more, beginning to assume definite shape was the insight that concrete societies organized for action in pragmatic history were no proper vessels for the realization of transcendent order at all. For the word mediated by Deutero-Isaiah commanded Israel to go forth from itself and to become a light to the nations; and the late Plato became the Athenian Stranger who transformed the living word of his presence that had been rejected by Athens into the written word, in the Prooemia of the *Laws,* for all men desirous of creating true order. The men who had experienced the universality of transcendent order were in search of social carriers of order other than the finite societies of their origin, because membership in the finite society seemed no longer to exhaust the meaning of human existence. The prophetic existence of the servant of God was separated from the collective existence of the Chosen People under the Torah; the philosopher's *bios theoretikos,* from political life; universal humanity, from parochial humanity. There began to differentiate a spectrum of order which required membership in a plurality of societies as its adequate form. In faint outlines there began to appear the fundamental division of temporal and spiritual order, of state and church. Hence, the question whether the new empires really broke the attempts to realize the order of revelation in Israel, and of philosophy in Hellas, must be answered in the negative. They could not break an attempt that had been, on principle, abandoned as a mistake; they could only provide a new pragmatic scene on which the problems of order originating in the leap in being could be pursued with a better understanding of their nature.

The second question, whether the new empires belonged to the same type of order as the older Near Eastern societies, must also be answered negatively. To be sure, conventionally we speak of the Persian, Macedonian, and Roman empires, but these names do not refer to concrete societies organized in imperial form as were the Egyptian, Babylonian, and Assyrian. The new empires took their names from the comparatively small societies on the outskirts of civilization who, at intervals of about two hundred years, conquered the vast Near Eastern-Aegean civilizational area. In the sixth century, the Iranian tribal societies began their conquest of Mesopotamia and Asia Minor and extended their empire to the Indus Valley and Egypt; in the fourth century, Philip II of Macedon achieved the hegemony over Hellas, and Alexander conquered the Persian Empire with the exception of the interior of Asia Minor; and with the second century began the Roman intervention in Macedonian, Greek, and Asiatic affairs, followed by the eastward expansion of the empire to the boundaries drawn by Parthian and Sassanian power. In none of these cases did the conquerors belong to the societies organized by them; in none of them did the resultant empire organize a Persian, Macedonian, or Roman society. On the contrary, the conquerors were spread fairly thin over the vast territorial expanse and could keep their empires in being only with the aid of the subjects. In the Iranian case, the Hellenic *condottieri,* the military entrepreneurs, and their mercenaries supplied the Persians with effective and reliable fighting contingents. Alexander, then, fought his battles not only with Macedonians, but again employed Hellenic troops and later integrated the Iranians into his army. Even more mixed were the forces of his successors: The battle of Raphia (217 B.C.) between the Seleucid and Ptolemaean rulers was fought among Macedonians, Greeks, Egyptians, Iranians, Celts, Thracians, and Arabs. And Rome, finally, could not even supply rulers for its empire: The Roman Julians and Italian Flavians were followed by Iberian, African, Syrian, Arabic, and Illyrian emperors. The empire as an enterprise of institutionalized power, thus, had separated from the organization of a concrete society and could be imposed as a form on the remnants of societies no longer capable of self-organization.

The answers to the two questions suggest a curious convergence of trends. The carriers of spiritual order tend to separate from the societies of their origin because they sense the unsuitability of the concrete society as a vessel for the universality of the spirit. And the new empires apparently are not organized societies at all, but organizational shells that will expand indefinitely to engulf the former concrete societies. The universality of spiritual order, at this historical epoch, meets with the indefinite expansion of a power shell devoid of substance. From the one side, the universality of spiritual order seems to reach out for the human ecumene rather than a concrete society as the field of its realization. From the other side, the new empires tend to expand over the whole ecumene and to provide an institutional order ready to receive the spiritual substance.

For the present, it would be unwise to go beyond this suggestion. The basis of materials must be broadened before a survey of the ecumenic problem can be attempted. And for the purpose of broadening the basis, I shall now examine more closely the nature of the new type of empire, this peculiar power shell which apparently has no substance of its own.

§ 2. The Pragmatic Ecumene—Polybius

The new empires originated, not in a ferocious will to conquer, but in the fatality of a power vacuum that attracted, and even sucked into itself, unused

organizational force from the outside; it originated in circumstances beyond
control rather than in deliberate planning. I shall examine the Iranian, Macedonian, and Roman cases under this hypothesis.

Comparatively simple is the Iranian beginning. The internecine wars between Assyria and Babylonia within the Mesopotamian area, in conjunction
with the Assyrian penetration of the Iran in the middle of the seventh century
B.C., set the stage for a Babylonian-Median alliance which in 612 destroyed
Nineveh and the Assyrian power. In his attempt to recover northern Assyria
and the city of Harran from the Medes, Nabonidus, the last ruler of Babylon,
then induced the Persian Cyrus to revolt against his Median lord and grand-
father Astyages; the result was the deposition of Astyages in 550 and the incorporation of Media into the Achaemenian Kingdom. Since Media was allied
with Lydia, Croesus opened hostilities against Cyrus—with the result that in
546 Lydia became part of Cyrus' empire. In 538 fell Babylon; and in 525
Cambyses conquered Egypt.

More complicated is the Macedonian case, because now the Achaemenian
Empire was already in being and the network of power relations had become
more intricate. Only a few of the relevant points will be touched. With the
fall of Lydia the Ionian Greeks had come under Persian rule; with the completion of the Asiatic-Egyptian conquest under the first two Achaemenians,
and with the consolidation of the empire and the extension of its borders to
the Indus in the early years of Darius I, the open frontier of expansion had
moved toward Hellas. From the end of the sixth century, one may say, Persian
is Greek history and vice versa. The suction of the power vacuum did not fail
to make itself felt. In 510 the Peisistratides in Athens were overthrown and in
508 Cleisthenes could inaugurate his democratic reform of the constitution.
The aristocratic faction promptly appealed to Sparta for help and received it.
In 507 Cleisthenes was temporarily expelled from Athens. In this predicament
the Athenians appealed to the Great King in Sardes for help, and the delega-
tion offered earth and water, the Persian symbol of submission. Though the
agreement was not ratified by Athens, the symbolic submission had been offered, and the refusal to obey the royal order of 506 to reinstate Hippias had
to be considered by the Persians an act of rebellion on the part of a vassal. In
499 the Ionian revolt began and received naval support from Athens. That
made the measure full. When the revolt had been broken in 494, the prepara-
tions of Darius for a punitive expedition against the rebels began. And Hippias, the Peisistratide expelled from Athens in 510, guided the Persian fleet
toward the plain of Marathon in 490. The pattern that became manifest on

this occasion governed Greek-Persian relations through the fifth and fourth centuries B.C., to Philip and Alexander. It is overshadowed in western historiography by the Greek victories of Marathon and Salamis, as well as by the Athenian culture and political achievements in the wake of the Persian War. But the new type of empire inaugurated by the Achaemenians had a long breath; the victories that meant so much for Hellas and the future course of history barely affected the Persian power. After the Athenian Empire had been exhausted and broken by the Peloponnesian War (431–404), the Hellenic situation again resembled closely that of 510. When in 387 the Spartan Antalcidas negotiated in Sardes a general settlement of Greek relations with Persia, it assumed the form of a royal decree, transmitted from Ecbatana to Sardes, providing that the Greek cities had to be autonomous with the exception of those in Asia which remained under Persian rule. The provision of autonomy for the Greek cities meant in practice that any federation of poleis of serious proportions would provoke Persian intervention. The power vacuum thus was held open.

Not all was well, however, with the Persian Empire itself. While its diplomatic skill and enormous financial resources were more than sufficient to keep a fratricidal Hellas in perpetual agony, the empire was debilitated by harem intrigues, abundant murders in the royal family, and internal revolts, and its military power had weakened so badly that after 404 Egypt was practically independent. Moreover, the battle of Cunaxa (401), won by Cyrus with the help of his Hellenic mercenaries against the royal army, had left a profound impression in Hellas through Xenophon's relation of the events in his *Anabasis*. Though the victory was abortive because Cyrus was killed in battle, there seemed a fair chance that a Hellenized monarch with an Hellenic army was a match for Persian power. Whether the empire was still strong enough in the fourth century to resist a united Hellas under competent leadership that wanted to get rid of the incubus was the question to which Alexander furnished the answer. By the middle of the fourth century there must have occurred to more than one Greek the idea that the only way out of the Hellenic misery was the formation of a league under the hegemony of the rising Macedonian monarchy. The suction of the power vacuum was again at work.

The open letter of Isocrates to Philip, the *Philippus* of 346, is the great document of the Hellenic state of mind that met halfway the plans of the Macedonian king. With admirable acumen Isocrates reduced the political issue to its relevant terms. In the first place, the leading Hellenic poleis—Athens,

Sparta, Argos, and Thebes—had failed in their attempts to provide self-organization for the Hellenic society, and there was no hope that future attemps would be more successful. Secondly, the misery of the cramped and frustrated poleis, exhausted by permanent wars and further aggravated by population pressure and political expulsion was appalling. Bitterly Isocrates remarked that a powerful army could be recruited in Hellas more easily from the displaced persons than from the citizen population (*ek̄ ton planomenon e ton politeuomenon*, 40). The remedy for the first evil was a panhellenic alliance under the leadership of Philip (Isocrates discreetly refrained from going into details, but it is doubtful that he would have liked the League of Corinth); the remedy for the second one was a war against Persia that would liberate the Ionians and open Asia Minor as a frontier of settlement for the overcrowded cities and the tens of thousands of refugees. The two proposals had to be carefully linked, for the Macedonians were not considered Hellenes (Isocrates avoids calling them barbarians, but uses the euphemism "not of the same kin," *ou homophylou genous*, 44), and the leadership of Philip would be acceptable only in the name of a panhellenic enterprise directed against Persia. One should not assume, however, any influence of Isocrates' program on the Macedonian plans. The idea of organizing the power potential of the Hellenic vacuum for the purpose of toppling the Persian colossus that stood on feet of clay was in the air. The *Philippus* proves no more than a political and intellectual climate in Hellas that conspired with the policies of Philip and Alexander.

The new type of empire, expanding westward from Asia to the Aegean area, ultimately drew Rome into its fatality. When Alexander's conquest had been divided among the successors, the large territorial state organized as a military monarchy had become the dominant power in the Eastern Mediterranean and the Near East. Although the division of the empire let the peoples of the Western Mediterranean escape the fate of incorporation that Alexander had intended for them, if we trust the *Hypomnemata*, even these Diadochic empires were formidable enough to motivate the organization for self-defense of power units in the West of comparable size and military potential. Under the impact of the events in the East, the Western Mediterranean area had to restructure itself politically into the potential organizers of territorial states and the potential subject populations. From this struggle for political organization on a scale that could resist the Eastern danger, Rome emerged as the dominant power after the Second Punic War (218–201). Once this position had been achieved, the expansion of what may be called the First Roman Empire toward the East was again governed by the suction of the power vacuum. For one must speak of a power vacuum in the East, inasmuch as the succession states were overshadowed by the idea of the empire of which they were the fragments. The political map was not final, but subject to change by anybody who had the power and enterprise to attempt it. In these Eastern conflicts the smaller powers, when their very existence was at stake, were liable to request the assistance of the rising Western power. This situation occurred in 201 when Pergamon, Rhodes, and Athens appealed to Rome against Philip V of Macedon and Antiochus III of Syria. With the Macedonian War of 200–197, the expansion began that brought Rome to the Parthian borders within two hundred years.

In describing the genesis of empire I have used the method developed for that purpose by Polybius in his *Histories*. I shall now introduce both the method and theory of Polybius (201–120) into the analysis of the phenomenon, in accordance with the principle that the self-interpretation of a society is part of the reality of its order.[1]

When analyzing a course of events (*praxeis*), Polybius (III, 6) insists that one must distinguish between its cause (*aitia*), its pretext (*prophasis*), and its beginning (*arche*). The student who cultivates the discipline of pragmatic history (*tes pragmatikes historias tropos,* I, 2, 8) must not be satisfied with a description of events, but must penetrate behind the spectacle as well as the pretexts in order to lay bare the first causes. In the case of the Macedonian Empire, for instance, Polybius distinguishes the retreat of the Greeks under Xenophon in 401 and the Asiatic raids of Agesilaus in 396/395, which revealed the weakness of Persia, as the cause; the vengeance on the Persians and the liberation of Ionia as the pretext; and Alexander's crossing to Asia as the beginning of the events (III, 6).

This pursuit of the first cause cannot become, however, an autonomous principle of historical method. For the chain of cause and effect recedes indefinitely; and through seeking the cause of the cause one would never

---

[1] The following analysis of the *Histories* differs in many respects from the treatment accorded to Polybian problems by the classical scholars, because I have concentrated on the problem of the ecumene. While such standard treatises as Kurt von Fritz' *The Theory of the Mixed Constitution in Antiquity: A Critical Analysis of Polybius' Thought* (New York, 1954) form the basis for all historical detail, the accents of interpretation fall differently. The interested reader should compare my treatment of the principal topics with the corresponding passages in the recent work of F. W. Walbank, *Polybius* (Berkeley, 1972). I should like to stress, however, that on the critical Book VI, Walbank's conclusions do not differ from mine—if I have understood the author's language of sophisticated caution correctly.

arrive at an object of history (I, 5, 3). Hence, the search for causes can be undertaken only when the object of history is already given; the search must be governed and limited by the spectacle (*theorema*, I, 2, 1) of which we want to obtain an adequate view (*theoria*, I, 5, 3). While the cause (*aitia*) precedes the beginning (*arche*) of the spectacle in time, the beginning precedes the cause in the logic of the analysis; and the beginning of the spectacle must be a matter of general agreement and knowledge; it must be self-apparent (*ex auten theoreistai*) from the events (III, 5, 4). Polybius chose as the object of his study the "extraordinary and grand spectacle (*paradoxon kai mega theorema*)" of the Roman imperial expansion (I, 2, 1). He delimited it at first as the half century from the beginning of the Second Punic War in 218 to the end of the Third Macedonian War with the battle of Pydna in 168 (I, 2–3), but then extended it to embrace the period from the beginning of the First Punic War in 264 to the destruction of Carthage in 146. In his search for first causes he limited himself to the motives of the Romans' "first crossing of the sea from Italy" in 264 (I, 5, 1). Thus far the method of Polybius and its application.

The crucial issue for the study of the period seems to be the delimitation of what Polybius calls the *theorema*, the spectacle. For its solution he lays down the principle that the object of the study has to emerge as self-apparent from the events themselves. (That is the very principle which in its general form—that the order of history emerges from the history of order—is employed throughout the present study.) When the principle is applied, however, to the specific question of empire, the delimitation of Polybius apparently does not agree altogether with our own. I shall now consider the points of agreement and disagreement in order to clarify further the nature of the new type of empire.

In the case of the Macedonian Empire, there is no overt difference of opinion regarding the various aspects (*aitia, prophasis,* and *arche*) of the phenomenon. Still, the agreement is weakened by the fact that Polybius treats the Macedonian case only incidentally, as an example for the application of his method, but does not place it, as we have done, in the larger context of imperial expansion, moving over the whole civilizational area from east to west, from Iran to Rome. He prefers, for the purpose of his study, to isolate the *theorema* of the Roman conquest; and as a consequence he must assume separate *theoremata* for the single cases that we intend to link into the one grand phenomenon of ecumenic empire. Such disagreement seems to cast a shadow on the objectivity of the method employed; for, if such differences of opinion are possible, the delimitation of the spectacle is perhaps not so self-apparent as the method assumes it to be. But if we examine the Polybian procedure in detail, the difference will appear less serious. In our analysis, we assumed the beginning of the Second Macedonian War (200–197) as the *arche* of the Roman expansion, and treated the formation of the Diadochic empires as the *aitia* which induced the defensive formation of corresponding territorial states in the Western Mediterranean and ultimately the Roman intervention in eastern affairs. Polybius, however, hesitated in his fixation of the *arche* between the beginnings of the Second Punic War in 218 and of the First Punic War in 264. This preference of Polybius for the earlier dates, as well as his hesitation between them, betrays the pressure of the problem inasmuch as it permitted him to study the wars in Greece and the Near East that were conducted parallel in time with the Second Punic War, and interlocked with it, as prelude to the Roman eastward expansion proper that began in 200 B.C. The device of the earlier *arche* enabled him, despite the concentration on the Roman *theorema,* to establish the connection between the rise of Rome and the earlier imperial history of the Eastern Mediterranean. And once this purpose was achieved, Polybius was even willing to admit that only the victory over Carthage at Zama in 202 emboldened the Romans to reach out toward Hellenic and Asiatic areas (I, 3, 6), thus setting the *arche* in 200 after all. The conflict, thus, dissolves on closer examination. Nevertheless, there remains the fact that Polybius saw the nature of empire concentrated in the Roman expansion. Hence, we must now turn to this part of his theory.

The attention of Polybius was caught, above all, by the extraordinary character of events (*to paradoxon ton praxeon*), by the unprecedented constellation of power that was gaining shape before his eyes. The events were unheard of, unprecedented, extraordinary, or unique inasmuch as the Romans, within the short span of half a century, subjected "almost the whole inhabited world (*oikoumene*)" to their sole rule (I, 1, 5). Previously the events of the ecumene (*tes oikoumenes praxeis*) had been conducted, as it were, in separate compartments, without unity of purpose, achievement, or locality, whereas now history had acquired an organic character (*somatoeides*) and the events of Italy and Libya had become interlinked with those of Hellas and Asia, all leading up to one end (*telos,* I, 3, 4), *i.e.,* toward the end of Roman supremacy (*hyperoche,* I, 2, 1). Polybius, then, supported the thesis of the extraordinary character by a comparison of the Roman expansion with empires (*dynasteia*) of the past. For a time, it is true, the Persians acquired an extensive rule (*arche*) and empire (*dynasteia*), but whenever they ventured beyond the confines of Asia, they endangered not only their rule but even their existence. The Lacedaemonians gained the hegemony of Hellas after the Peloponnesian War, but held it undisputed for no more than twelve years. And the Macedonians had, after the conquest of Asia, acquired the greatest empire both in extent and power that ever existed, but they still left the larger part of the ecumene, *i.e.*, Libya, Sicily, Sardinia, and Western Europe, outside its boundaries. Only the Romans subjected not parts but almost the whole of the ecumene to their rule (I, 2). And, finally, Polybius considered that a new literary form was required to meet the unprecedented events. When Fortune (*tyche*) herself made the affairs (*pragmata*) of the whole ecumene converge toward one end, it behooved the historian to respond with a study (*pragmateia*) that would bring into view the scheme of the whole ecumene (*tes holes oikumenes schema*) (I, 4, 6). The structure of the Roman expansion made all special histories of peoples and their affairs inadequate and obsolete; what the historian wanted to study was the general and comprehensive economy (*ten de katholou kai syllebden oikonomian*) of events (I, 4, 3); and for that purpose was needed the new form of a general and common history (*tes katholikes kai koines historias*, VIII, 2, 11).

The inquiry into the nature of ecumenic empire can now be resumed, taking into account the Polybian theory.

The nature proves elusive, because there exists no concrete society that can be considered the subject of imperial order. Polybius confirms this observation: No single society, but the whole geographical and civilizational horizon of the Mediterranean and Near Eastern peoples, from the Atlantic to the Indus, becomes the theater of pragmatic history. This new phenomenon requires a new terminology, for one can no longer speak of societies and their order when the events converge toward their destruction. What takes their place is the ecumene. The term *ecumene,* which originally means no more than the inhabited world in the sense of cultural geography, has received through Polybius the technical meaning of the peoples who are drawn into the process of imperial expansion. On this Polybian stratum of meaning could later be superimposed the meaning of the mankind under Roman jurisdiction (Luke 2:1; Acts 17:6; 24:5), and ultimately of the messianic world to come (Heb. 2:5). But this ecumene, as Polybius understands it, is an object of organization rather than a subject; it does not organize itself for action like Egypt, or the Chosen People, or an Hellenic polis. Moreover, it does not develop a symbolism by which its thinkers articulate their experience of the new order (though both an order and symbols can be imposed on it, as we shall see); above the ecumene there rises no cosmological symbolism as from the Near Eastern empires, no symbolism of world history as from Israel's present under God, no philosopher's theory of the polis as from the Athens of Plato and Aristotle. Instead of the philosopher who articulates the order of the soul, there appears the historian who articulates the dynamics of political events, of the *praxeis;* instead of the Platonic dialogue or the Aristotelian treatise, there is the Polybian *pragmateia.* The terms *praxis, pragmatike historia,* and *pragmateia* again have received their technical meanings through Polybius.

The man, finally, who created the new meanings of *ecumene* and *pragmatic history* was not a prophet or philosopher concerned with the order of his society, but a victim of the upheaval that he studied. Polybius was born in Megalopolis as the son of Lycortas, the statesman of the Achaean League. After the battle of Pydna in 168 he was among the one thousand Achaeans deported to Rome to await trial for opposition to Roman rule. Luckier than the others who were imprisoned in country towns, he was allowed to stay in the house of Aemilius Paullus as the tutor of his sons. Only in 151 was he permitted to return home, together with the three hundred Achaeans who had survived the waiting for the trial that never·was instituted. Two years later he was in Roman diplomatic service, accompanied Scipio Aemilianus, his former pupil, on the campaign against Carthage, and witnessed by his side the destruction of the city in 146. He returned to Greece in time to alleviate somewhat the harshness of the executions and destructions inflicted by L. Mummius on Achaea after the last uprising of the League had been broken; and he received statues as a benefactor from the surviving cities whose administration he reorganized under Roman authority. His was the life of a skillful and intelligent man in an age when fools can neither rule nor accept rule; he kept his admiration and hatred of the Romans in balance; and he let emotions not blur his view of events though they destroyed the order in which he had grown up.

The ecumene is not a subject of order but an object of conquest; and this is the reason that its status as an object of theory is unclear. Nevertheless, the events are inclined by Fortune toward a recognizable *telos.* For the expansion of the conqueror's dominion, though it is unlimited on principle, finds its limits in the ecumene itself—one cannot conquer more than there is. Hence, the object of the *pragmateia* becomes self-apparent after all as the establishment of the ecumenic empire. Polybius' concentration on the Roman *theórema* must be understood in the light of this self-limitation of the events. His comparison of the Roman with the Persian and Macedonian empires proves that he was quite aware of the comprehensive ecumenic drama, as well as of the connection between its phases. But the Persian Empire had fallen; and the Macedonian conquest had come to a halt with the death of Alexander and had not resumed its impetus for a century. With the rise of Rome the entelechy of the process seemed to unfold fully; an end came in view with no horizon of further ends beyond it; Polybius sensed around the events the aura of finality which later became articulate in the Vergilian symbol of the *imperium sine fine*. This character of consummation of an end justifies theoretically the concentration on the Roman *theorema;* not the ecumenic drama as a whole, but the agent and events of its consummation are the object of the *pragmateia*.

The concentration on the final act and actor, however, raises further questions. In the first place, it must be asked why the Romans should have succeeded where the Persians and Macedonians had failed. Moreover, a man of the philosophical culture of Polybius knew that, the finality of the Roman conquest notwithstanding, nothing is final in this world. Hence, the question of meaning forcefully intruded itself into the study of a process of destruction which apparently had no meaning even if it had inevitably to come to an end when everything in reach was destroyed. Both questions become topical in the work of Polybius; the first one in the form of reflections on the merits of the Roman constitution; the second one in the form of apprehensive remarks by the actors in the drama on the transience of their success.

The answer to the question of the Roman success is furnished by the disquisition of the Roman constitution in Book VI of the *Histories*. This part of Polybius' work is more famous than clear and conclusive; and it is further obscured today by the misunderstanding of not-too-careful interpreters. The premises of the argument are given in two blocks of text concerning a general theory of the forms of government (VI, 3–18) and a comparison of the Roman with other constitutions (VI, 43–58). Wedged in between the two blocks is a study of the Roman military organization (VI, 19–42). The conclusions which follow from the premises, however, are nowhere clearly drawn.

The text of VI, 3–18, is a curious assembly of topics which deliberately does not rise to the level of a theory. Polybius first relates the Platonic-Aristotelian classification of the forms of government. The good forms are kingship, aristocracy, and democracy; the corresponding bad forms are monarchy (tyranny), oligarchy, and ochlocracy. The forms appear historically in this order, beginning with kingship; each good form gives way to its corresponding bad form, the bad form to be followed by the next good form, and so forth; so that the whole series of constitutions in a society runs from kingship to ochlocracy. These transformations ensue by nature (*kata physin*, VI, 5, 1). The classification is torn out of the theoretical context which it has in the respective works of Plato and Aristotle. Polybius summarizes the results as *topoi* that will be suitable "to pragmatic history and the common understanding" (VI, 5, 2); today we would say it is an account in textbook fashion. To the whole series of forms he applies the Stoic category of the cycle; every society has a *politeion anakyklosis*, a cycle of constitutions that returns to its beginning (VI, 9, 10). The *topoi* of the forms of government and the cycle of constitutions then are supplemented by the *topos* of the mixed form of government that had been developed by the Peripatetic Dicaearchus of Messene (*fl. ca.* 320–310), in his *Tripolitikos*, for the case of the Spartan constitution. Every constitution that is constructed according to only one principle (the monarchic, oligarchic, or democratic) will rapidly decay; the inevitable decay can be staved off by mixing and balancing the three principles so that the decay of every single element will be checked by the countereffect of the two others (VI, 10). Polybius found this fortunate mixture realized in the Roman constitution. He assumed the consuls to represent the monarchical, the senate the aristocratic, and the tribal assembly the democratic element. To the checks and balances among the three elements he attributed the effectiveness of Rome in her struggle for empire (VI, 11–19).

The purpose of this account of *topoi* is not immediately apparent. To be sure, torn out of their context the *topoi* provide fine material for a history of ideas and one can learnedly present them as the political theory of Polybius. But they have a context; and the reader of Book VI cannot help wondering what precisely the author wanted to demonstrate. For, in the first place, Polybius recognized that Sparta, though her constitution was an example of the best form of government, was not successful in her struggle for supremacy in Hellas for the reason that other internal factors, which had nothing to do with the three constitutional elements, operated against it (VI, 48–50). Hence, if the inquiry into the best form was supposed to reveal the cause of the Roman success (VIII, 2, 3), the demonstration had broken down. Second, he knew that his law of change of all things had no exceptions (VI, 57, 1). The constitution of Rome, though it has the best form, will decay like any other under the pressure of victory and prosperity (VI, 9, 12–14); new wealth and extravagance will ruin the morale of the people and precipitate the development of ochlocracy (VI, 57); and the symptoms of the corruption are quite visible even now (XVIII, 35). Hence, the best constitution seems to enable a people only to create the circumstances that will ruin it in the end. And finally, Polybius did not even attempt to carry out his declared intention, *i.e.,* to show why Rome succeeded where Persia and Macedonia failed, for in the comparison of the Roman with other constitutions in Book VI Persia and Macedonia are not so much as mentioned.

The almost incredible futility of this part of Polybius' work, which as far as I know has not been observed, is worth some attention, for it reveals the appalling decline of philosophy barely two hundred years after Plato and Aristotle. Philosophy had given way to the *koine epinoia,* the common understanding to which Polybius blandly appealed when he replaced the analysis of order by a topical summary of the resulting terms; and the problem of order had been reduced to a calculus, as confused as confusing, of the dynamics of institutions. With the ruin of societies, of the subjects of order, apparently the sense of the order of the psyche itself had been dulled. The older societies were being smashed by the blows of pragmatic history; the ecumene into which they were dissolving had not yet sufficient life of its own to react against the orgy of obscene destruction except by the desperate outbursts of slave revolts; and the pragmatic historian was too fascinated by the *theorema* of success to appraise the events in terms of order. As far as Polybius was concerned, what did not count in the game of power did not count at all. In his comparative study of the best constitution he flatly refused to pay any attention to Plato's model politeia—for what is a lifeless thing compared with living beings (VI, 47, 7–10). There was already in the making the attitude of Cicero who with a sneer dismissed the best polities of the Hellenic philosophers as fancies of no importance by the side of the best polity that was created on the battlefields by the *imperatores* of Rome. The intellectual and spiritual atmosphere forcefully reminds one of Stalin's dictum: How many divisions has the Pope?

The second body of text (VI, 43–58) makes more sense than the first one. The *topoi* of the best constitution recede into the background. Polybius now announces the principle that the condition (*stasis*) of a polity is determined by customs and laws (VI, 47, 1–6). If the private lives of men are righteous and their public lives are just, then the polity may be said to be good; if they are the opposite, then the polity will be bad. Rome is in good condition because an aristocracy with high standards is in charge of affairs; if the standards should decline and the people no longer consent to obey—which inevitably will happen sooner or later—then the polity will be on its way toward och-

locracy (VI, 57, 6–9). Of the qualities of the Roman aristocracy, first mentioned should be a trait which always makes for worldly progress: The
Romans take what they can get and never give anything to anybody if they
can help it (XXXI, 26, 9). Polybius then gives an account of the funeral
rites by which the excellence of the aristocratic leaders of Rome and their
ancestors is impressed upon the people, thus systematically strengthening the
authority and prestige of the ruling class (VI, 53–54). He explains that a
surprising degree of honesty in public service distinguishes Rome from Carthage, but that nevertheless a deft hand at acquisition of property has endowed Rome with the means for military expansion that were lacking in
Sparta (VI, 50 and 56). The policy of confederation and alliance in Italy
supplies Rome with her excellent recruits of peasant stock for the army, while
Carthage has to rely on mercenaries (VI, 52); and a long section is devoted
to the Roman military system and its advantages (VI, 19–42). And finally,
Polybius stresses as the most important trait of the Roman commonwealth
the *deisidaimonia* of the people. The term *deisidaimonia,* usually translated
as superstition, means in this context rather god-fearing or religious. Polybius
treats the matter as an enlightened Greek. The religiousness would be an
object of reproach among other peoples, but in his opinion it preserves the
cohesion of the Roman polity. The Romans, he suggests with a sophistic touch,
adopted the propagation of religiousness for the sake of the common people.
"If one could form a polity of wise men, this course would not be necessary;
but since every multitude is unstable, full of lawless desire, unreasoned passion, and violent anger, the many must be reined in by invisible terrors and
suchlike pageantry." The ancients were right when they introduced among
the people beliefs in the gods and the terrors of the underworld; and the
moderns are foolish in destroying such beliefs (VI, 56, 6–12).

Though the two bodies of text were supposed to supply the premises for
conclusions concerning the causes of the Roman success, Polybius nowhere
drew them clearly. That is not to say that they could not be drawn. But the
topoi proved to be a handicap rather than a help; moreover, some of the conclusions were not pleasing to Romans, and the possibility must be considered
that Polybius did not care to go beyond adumbrations. Since the terms of
the problem were set by the theory of the cycle, the natural victor in a pluralistic power field would have to be the commonwealth that happened to be at
the prime of its effectiveness. Polybius made the point strongly in his comparison between Rome and Carthage: "For as every body, or commonwealth,
or project of action has its natural periods first of growth (*auxesis*), then of its

prime (*akme*), and finally of decay (*phthisis*), and as everything in them is at its best when they are in their prime (*akme*), the difference between the two commonwealths became manifest for that reason at that time" (VI, 51, 4). Since Carthage had embarked on its course earlier than Rome, it was in its decline while Rome was still in its prime. In Carthage the multitude was already influencing policies, while in Rome the senate still had control of affairs; and in the rivalry between the people and the best, the superior quality of the Roman aristocracy had to prevail (VI, 51, 5–8). Hence, the Roman success had nothing to do with Roman merits, but was due to the relative time positions of the two commonwealths in their respective cycles; the success was a fluke of history.

This conclusion, however, could not have been drawn bluntly—not only because that would have been impolitic, but because it was wrong. I have pointed out the futility of the argument based on the *topoi* of the cycle and the mixed form of government. Polybius knew that Sparta also had the mixed form of government; and if the time position in the cycle could be used as an argument in the comparison between Rome and Carthage, it fell flat when the Spartan case was taken into consideration. Obviously other factors besides the mixed form and the position in the cycle had something to do with imperial success. Hence the importance which Polybius attributed to the funeral rites and the *deisidaimonia*. As a Greek he must have been struck by the substantive solidity of the Roman order; he was aware that Rome had not experienced the disintegration of the civic creed which characterized the Athenian fifth and fourth centuries. And that disintegration was not merely a problem of the cycle, but of the specifically Hellenic development of philosophy. The civil theology of Rome had not yet dissolved under the impact of the physical theology of the philosophers, as Varro was to formulate the issue a century later. Polybius, thus, at least touched the true *paradoxon* of the role of Rome in the history of mankind: that a comparative primitive commonwealth on the outskirts of Hellenic civilization, still animated by the tough and not at all pleasant ethos of the peasant, had the staying power to survive the almost deadly struggle with Carthage, the political genius to master the ecumene organizationally, and the ability to assimilate Hellenic culture.

If the causes of the Roman success were by far too complex to be subsumed under the *topoi* about constitutions, the theory of the cycle had nevertheless its limited validity. For the prime of the Roman republic indeed was passing rapidly; and the symptoms of decline were multiplying before the eyes of Polybius. The pragmatic historian, however, while faithfully recording the symptoms, refrained from interpreting them as a philosopher. To be sure, he saw that the events were senseless in terms of order; and he shuddered at the workings of Fortune; but in his work at large the mood of acceptance prevailed. Again one must consider the possibility that Polybius did not reveal all his thoughts; for the Romans themselves had their misgivings about the course of events and, through his close association with the Roman ruling group, the historian was thoroughly familiar with the topics of political conversation. The Second Punic War had shaken the social structure of Rome through the population losses, the increase of the urban proletariat and the number of slaves, the transition from the peasant economy to the establishment of latifundia, and the rise of a new financial estate, of the *equites*. Moreover, a group of conservative senators under the leadership of Scipio Nasica declared the destruction of Carthage undesirable, since Rome would lose an opponent that kept her in form—though to no avail. The wanton destruction of two cities of the importance of Carthage and Corinth in 146 was understood as a loss of measure foreboding ill for the future. Furthermore the social unsettlement through the mass deportations and enslavements must have been terrific. When Tarent was reduced in 209, for instance, 30,000 Tarentinians were made slaves; and after the battle of Pydna in 168, Aemilius Paullus destroyed seventy Macedonian towns and sold 150,000 persons into slavery. The revolt of the slaves on the Sicilian estates, under the leadership of the Syrian Eunus, required a formal war of three years, 135–132, for its suppression. And above all, Rome herself was becoming a past to the Romans of the second century, to be held up as an archaizing model of conduct by Cato to his contemporaries.

Polybius knew all that. Nevertheless, he did not attempt a coherent account of the problems of Roman order, but expressed his awareness of incalculable disorder by means of a few reflections on Fortune which he attributed to various persons. On the occasion of the defeat of Perseus he let the last king of Macedon recall a prophetic passage from Demetrius of Phalerum, written about 317 B.C. (XXIX, 21):

> If you take not an indefinite time, nor many generations, but just the last fifty years, you will see in them the cruelty of Fortune. Fifty years ago do you suppose that either the Macedonians and the King of Macedon, or the Persians and the King of Persia, if some God had foretold them the future, would ever have believed that by the present time the Persians, who were then the masters of almost the whole ecumene, would have ceased to be even a name, while the Macedonians, who were then not even

a name, would be rulers of all? Yet this Fortune, who never keeps faith
with our life, but transforms everything against our reckoning and displays
her power by the unexpected, now makes it clear to all men, or so it
seems to me, when she endows the Macedonians with the wealth of Persia,
that she has but lent them these good things until she has decided to dispose differently of them.

Aemilius Paullus, the victor of Pydna, then was assigned by Polybius the role
of exhorting his countrymen, in the presence of the defeated Perseus, to remember the extremities of Fortune in the hour of success and to preserve the
measure of prosperity (XXIX, 20). The theme recurs for the last time on
the occasion of the destruction of Carthage when Polybius, looking down on
the burning city by the side of Scipio, heard from his pupil the confession of a
dread foreboding that Fortune who had made an end of Troy, of the Assyrians and Medians, of the Persians and Macedonians, and now of Carthage,
would prepare the same fate for Rome (XXXVIII, 22).

On the basis of the materials thus far assembled, at least a first step can
be taken toward the clarification of concepts.

That the term *ecumene* was actually used by the contemporaries of the
events for the purpose of their interpretation is established through the work
of Polybius. Originally the term meant the inhabited world as it was known
to the Hellenic observer. In the critical period it acquired, in addition, the
meaning of a power field into which the peoples were drawn through pragmatic events. The ecumene in this new sense, however, was not an entity
given once and for all as an object of exploration. It rather was something that
increased or diminished correlative with the expansion or contraction of imperial power; and it furthermore had degrees of intensity correlative with the
degrees of direct jurisdiction or indirect political control maintained from the
ruling center. In the Persian case, the ecumene of the empire included Hellas
in the sense that the area of Hellenic civilization was well within the range
of Persian diplomatic control, even though only the Asiatic Greeks were
temporarily included within the organization of the satrapies. In Alexander's
case, his empire included Hellas, in addition to the larger part of the previously Persian domain within its jurisdiction; but the western Mediterranean
was included in the ecumene only diplomatically, toward the end of the
conquerors' reign, if we accept the *Hypomnemata*. In the Roman case, finally,
the empire included the whole Mediterranean area, as well as Gaul, Western
Germany, and Britain, within the jurisdiction. And the expansion was vast

enough to acquire for the term *ecumene* the juridical meaning of the *orbis terrarum* that was coextensive with the jurisdiction of Rome. The emperor, as a consequence, became the protective godhead of the empire in his capacity of the *agathos daimon tes oikoumenes,* of the good divinity of the ecumene.[2] However, though the Romans expanded the ecumene prodigiously toward the west and north, the Mesopotamian, Iranian, and Indian territories slipped from the imperial grip. Nevertheless, the eastern peoples, even if they did not belong to the ecumene in the jurisdictional sense, still were part of the pragmatic ecumene inasmuch as pragmatic events of major proportions in one part of the vast field affected the power structure in the other parts.

The coherence of institutionalized power was supplied to this shifting and changing phenomenon of the ecumene by the empires. To be sure, not all of the peoples that, in the course of more than a millennium, became with varying degrees of intensity part of the pragmatic ecumene were ever united under the jurisdiction of one empire. The pragmatic ecumene came into being through a succession of imperial expansions from such widely distant centers as Iran, Macedon, and Rome. All three of these power centers built ecumenic empires in the sense that their imperial constructions participated in the process of creating one and the same ecumene. Hence, on the one hand, the ecumene comes into being through the pragmatic events of empire building; and, on the other hand, the empires become individuals of a species through the ecumene which they produce. As a consequence, the Iranian, Macedonian, and Roman character of the three empires is subordinate to their ecumenic function, while the ecumene never rises to the rank of a self-organizing society. The ecumenic empires are not successive organizations of the same society, even though their organizations extend to the same ecumene, because the ecumene is no concrete society. The peculiar structure of this social field forces us to speak of an Ecumenic Age, meaning thereby the period in which a manifold of concrete societies, which formerly existed in autonomously ordered form, were drawn into one political power field through pragmatic expansions from the various centers. This process has a recognizable begin-ning with the Iranian expansion; and it has its recognizable end with the decline of Roman power, when the ecumene begins to dissociate centrifugally into the Byzantine, Islamic, and Western civilizations.

---

[2] W. Dittenberger (ed.), *Orientis Graeci Inscriptiones Selectae,* No. 666. The inscription refers to Nero. No. 668 refers to the same emperor as the *soter* and *euergetes* of the ecumene. Marcus Aurelius is the *kyrios* of the ecumene in A. Boeckh (ed.), *Corpus Inscriptionum Graecorum,* No. 2581.

§ 3. The Spiritual Ecumene

The problems of the ecumene are not exhausted by the creation of the phenomenon through the events of pragmatic history. The ecumene, it is true, was not a subject of order but an object of conquest and organization; it was a graveyard of societies, including those of the conquerors, rather than a society in its own right. Nevertheless, while the former societies disintegrated, new experiences of order, new symbolisms for their articulation, and new enterprises for their institutionalization were developed by the victims of pragmatic destruction. Mankind in search of order had not been abolished. The ecumenic was the age in which the great religions had their origin, and above all Christianity. I shall now introduce the problem of the ecumene as it becomes apparent in Paul's self-understanding of his mission to the pagans.

1. Paul

The basis of Paul's missionary action is furnished by the passage of Matthew 24:14 which reads: "And this gospel of the kingdom shall be preached over the whole ecumene, as a testimony to all the nations (*ethnesin*); and then the end (*telos*) shall come." The ecumene in the pragmatic sense is established; but beyond the Polybian *telos* of the process through the Roman conquest, there becomes now visible a further *telos* through the spreading of the gospel. The ecumene is not rejected at all, but its establishment is reduced to the rank of a prelude to the drama of salvation. The differentiation of the new meanings becomes manifest in the temptation scene of Luke 4:5, where Satan offers Jesus power over "the kingdoms of the ecumene." This would be the imperial power over the ecumene in the pragmatic sense; but if this preparatory ecumene is taken for the end, it becomes Satanic. The kingdom that is truly the end, as Paul sets forth in his speech at Athens, will come with "the fixed day on which God will justly judge the ecumene through a man whom he has appointed, and whom he has guaranteed to all men by raising him from the dead" (Acts 17:31). Though the date of this day cannot be exactly fixed by human calculations—"for the Day of the Lord is to come like a thief in the night" (I Thess. 5:2)—it is impending in the near future. Paul assures the Thessalonians who grieve about their dead, because they will not see the coming of Christ and be members of his kingdom, that the dead will come to life too on the day: "For we can assure you, on the Lord's own authority, that those of us who will still be living when the Lord comes will have no advantage over those who have fallen asleep. For the Lord himself, at the summons, when the archangel calls and God's trumpet sounds, will come down from heaven, and first those who died in union with Christ will rise, then those of us who are still living will be caught up with them on clouds into the air to meet the Lord, and so we shall be with the Lord forever" (I Thess. 4:15-17). The day thus will come before the presently living have all passed away; and the dead, if they have died in union with Christ, will be the first to be raised into the kingdom.

Still, the dead must have died in union with Christ in order to be raised into his kingdom. And how can men die in Christ if they have never heard of him? Hence, all men must be reached by the gospel as fast as possible. To bring the gospel to the whole ecumene is the work of salvation incumbent on the apostle; and time is short, for the ecumene is large; Christ will come within the time of the living, and the life of an apostle is brief. Hence the constant pressure under which Paul is traveling as a missionary, working against time. "I have completed the preaching of the Gospel of Christ all the way from Jerusalem around to Illyricum. In all this it has been my ambition to preach the good news only where Christ's name was unknown, so as not to build on foundations other men had laid" (Rom. 15:19-20). The work of the apostles must not be duplicated; only main centers of regions will be touched, with the further spreading of the gospel being left to the new communities; frequent visitations are impossible. "This is why I have so often been prevented from coming to see you. But now there is no more work for me in this part of the world, and as I have had a great desire for many years to come to see you, when I go to Spain I hope to see you on my way there, and to have you see me off on my journey, after I have enjoyed being with you for a while" (Rom. 15:23-24). Whether Paul has really carried out his program to visit the whole ecumene from the eastern borders of the Roman Empire to Spain is not certain, because there are no sufficient sources for the last years and the death of the apostle. But it is at least probable in the light of I Clement 5:5-7: "Through jealousy and strife Paul showed the way to the prize of endurance; seven times he was in bonds, he was exiled, he was stoned, he was a herald both in the East and the West, he gained the noble fame of his faith, he taught righteousness to all the world (*kosmos*) and when he had reached the limits of the West he gave his testimony before the rulers, and thus passed from the world and was taken up into the Holy Place,—the greatest example of endurance." Since the letter was written from Rome, the center of the empire, the "West" most probably refers to Spain; and after his return from the extreme of the ecumene Paul seems to have suffered his martyrdom in Rome. For in pragmatic history his prosecutors accused him of being "a pest and a disturber of the peace among Jews all over the ecumene" (Acts 24:5).

Paul's conception of his apostolate showed that mankind, when it was forced by events into the senselessness of pragmatic coexistence, could resort to self-help. To be sure, a reactionary revolt on the pragmatic level, with the purpose of re-establishing the independent order of a former concrete society, was doomed to disaster in the face of imperial power; but the ecumenic co-existence of peoples, of Paul's *ethne,* could become transparent for a universal order of humanity beyond the pragmatic order of empire. In the shadow of the world-shaking events, of the Polybian *praxeis,* one could build a new society that had its source of order beyond the world. That attempt, however, was fraught with difficulties, as the texts just quoted clearly show. For the society envisaged by Paul was a community of the faithful in Christ, who waited for the day on which the earthly ecumene under the emperor would be superseded by the "ecumene to come" (Heb. 2:5) under the Lord. This life of a community in expectation of the Parousia had to run into two problems. The first one made itself felt in the comfort extended by the Apostle to the Thessalonians—that they need not grieve about their dead since those who had died in union with Christ would be raised to life and be as much members of the new kingdom as those who were still living at the coming of the Lord. That assurance, while it may have calmed the worries of affectionate relatives and friends, stirred up the larger question of whether the kingdom to come was open to all men or whether it was restricted to the contemporaries of Christ and his apostle. Even if the apostolate were successful in penetrating the whole ecumene with the gospel, what happened to the men who had lived and died before the advent of Christ? And this question, which could remain subliminal during the heat of eschatological expectation, would become more burning with the passing of the apostolic generation. When the "living" had all died and the Parousia had not occurred, what sense was there left in an ecumene that waited for its ultimate transformation? The adjustment of the ecumene to the delay of the Parousia is the second problem inherent in Paul's conception of his mission. To the questions raised thereby, various answers could be found, according to the context of experience and symbolization in which the problem of the ecumene arose. In a cosmological civilization, as for instance the Indian, metempsychosis became the Buddhist solution to the problem of how the ecumene of the presently living was related to past and future mankind. In the orbit of Judaeo-Christian anthropology this solution was impossible; the answer had to be found by the descent of Christ to the dead, through the conceptions of a *praeparatio evangelica* and a *civitas Dei*, and generally by means of a philosophy of history.

The various symbolisms developed as answers to the problem, however, are not our present concern; rather we are concerned with the problem itself, *i.e.*, the tension between the universality of spiritual order and the ecumene, which embraces the contemporaneously living. That is a problem, both theoretical and practical, of the first magnitude indeed. It is a theoretical problem for every philosophy of history, since the universal order of mankind can become historically concrete only through symbolic representation by a community of the spirit with ecumenic intentions—that is the problem of the Church. And it is a practical problem in politics and history, since the attempt at representing universal order through a community with ecumenic intentions is obviously fraught with complications through the possibility that several such communities will be founded historically and pursue their ecumenic ambitions with means not altogether spiritual. Since contemporary science possesses no critical vocabulary for the treatment of these problems, it is necessary to introduce the terms *ecumenicity* and *universality* for the purpose of distinguishing between the two components in the type of spiritual community that originates in the Ecumenic Age. *Ecumenicity* will mean the tendency of a community which represents the divine source of order to express the universality of its claim by making itself coextensive with the ecumene; *universality* will mean the experience of the world-transcendent God as the source of order that is universally binding for all men. To the spiritual communities of this type we will apply the term *ecumenic religions*, paralleling the term *ecumenic empires*. The term *ecumenic religions* is preferable to *universal religions* or *churches*, not only because it stresses the connection of the communities with the problem of the ecumene, but also for reasons of empirical description of the phenomena. For in the various ecumenic religions, the experience of universality is not always too well differentiated from the desire for ecumenic expansion. As a matter of fact, the tendency to expand pragmatically by means of violence can sometimes preponderate so strongly, as in the case of Islam, that it will become difficult to draw the line between an ecumenic empire and an ecumenic religion. The term *universal religions* would prejudge the crucial issue of the degree to which a spiritual community with ecumenic ambitions has clarified and actualized its character as a representative of universal, transcendent order.

2. *Mani*

While universality provides the experiential momentum for the expansion of an ecumenic religion, its ecumenic ambition makes it effective in the field of social order. I have isolated the ecumenic stratum of Christianity in Paul's conception of his mission and shall now further pursue the problem of ecumenicity, disregarding for the present the question of universality.

The pragmatic ecumene that had been created through the Iranian, Macedonian, and Roman conquests extended considerably farther east than the jurisdictional ecumene of the Roman Empire to which Paul had confined his missionary work. This incongruity between the field of Christian mission and the actual extent of the ecumene continued for more than two hundred years; by the middle of the third century A.D., Christianity still had not notably advanced into Mesopotamia, Persia, and India. Hence, if ecumenicity were made a test of true universality, Christianity was a failure. The time seemed to have come for the neglected sector of the ecumene to take matters in its own hands and to found a new religion which could prove the superiority of its universal truth by the greater effectiveness of its ecumenic expansion. That was the position assumed by Mani, the new apostle of Jesus, who appeared in northern Babylonia under the reign of Ardashir, the founder of the Sassanian dynasty.[3]

The fundamental text for the understanding of Mani's position is to be found in the *Shabhuragan,* the only work written by the prophet in Persian, for Shapur, the son and successor of Ardashir: "Wisdom and deeds have always from time to time been brought to mankind by the messengers of God. So in one age they have been brought by the messenger called Buddha to India, in another by Zaradusht to Persia, in another by Jesus to the West. Thereupon this revelation has come down, this prophecy in this last age, through me, Mani, messenger of the God of truth to Babylon."[4]

The single themes on which this text touches only briefly are elaborated in the *Kephalaia.* The sequence of the messengers and their religions is not merely a succession in time, but something like a confluence of independently rising waters into the one great river of truth represented by Mani:

[3] For the section on Mani in general cf. Henri-Charles Puech, *Le Manichéisme* (Paris, 1949). For the self-designation of Mani as the *Apostolus Jesu Christi*, cf. F. Chr. Baur, *Das Manichaeische Religionssystem* (1831), 368f.; C. Schmidt and H. J. Polotsky, *Ein Manifund in Aegypten* (Sitzungsberichte der Preussischen Akademie der Wissenschaften, Phil.-Hist. Klasse, 1933), 26f.; Puech, *Le Manichéisme*, 61f. The principal source is Augustine, *Contra Faustum*, XIII, 4.

[4] Quoted from F. C. Burkitt, *The Religion of the Manichees* (Cambridge, 1925), 57. The source is Al-Bairuni's *Chronology*, trans. and ed. by C. E. Sachau (London 1879), 190. I have not been able to obtain a copy of Al-Bairuni.

The writings (*graphe*) and the wisdom (*sophia*) and the apocalypses (*apokalypsis*) and the parables (*parabole*) and the psalms (*psalmos*) of all the earlier churches (*ekklesia*) have assembled at all places and have come (*katantan*) to my church and have associated with the wisdom revealed by me. As water comes to water and becomes a great water, thus have the ancient books come to my writing and have become a great wisdom, the like has never been announced among the ancient generations (*genea*). Never have been written nor have been revealed the books, as I have written them.[5]

The primary symptom by which the defectiveness of the earlier religions can be recognized is their regional limitation:

Who has elected his church (*ekklesia*) in the west, his church has not reached the east; who has elected his church in the east, his election (*ekloge*) has not reached the west; so that there are some among them whose name has not even become known in other cities (*polis*). My hope (*elpis*) however will go to the west and will go to the east. One will hear the voice of its annunciation in all languages, and one will announce it in all cities (*polis*). My church is superior in this first point to all earlier churches, for the earlier churches were elected in single places and in single cities. My church will go out to all cities and its message will reach every country (*chora*).[6]

The last quoted text suggests that the earlier religions did not achieve more than local importance because their technique of communication was insufficient. Buddha, Zoroaster, and Jesus, the predecessors of Mani, had in common that they did not write themselves, but left the fixation of their message to their disciples. "The fathers of justice (*dikaiosyne*) have not written their wisdom in books." That alone had to lead to difficulties, because variant traditions inevitably become a source of schisms. The restraint of the earlier founders with regard to writing, however, was more than a sin of omission. The predecessors deliberately did not write because "they knew that their justice (*dikaiosyne*) and their church would perish from the world (*kosmos*.)"[7] The earlier religions thus remained limited, not by technical accident, but in accordance with a divine plan of revelation. They remained in good order for awhile, as long as "pure leaders" were in them; but after the death of the leaders, confusion spread, together with negligence in discipline and work. But this fate will not befall "the religion that I have elected." And after that

[5] Carl Schmidt (ed.), *Kephalaia* (Manichaeische Handschriften der Staatlichen Museen Berlin; Stuttgart, 1940), Ch. 154. Schmidt-Polotsky, *Ein Manifund in Aegypten*, 42.

[6] *Kephalaia*, Ch. 45.

[7] *Ibid.*, Introduction, 7f.

assurance the argument returns to ecumenism as the test of superiority. The earlier religions spread in only one country and one language; but Mani's will spread in every country, in every language, in the distant countries. And this lastingness will be assured through the writing of the message in books, written by Mani himself, and to be propagated by living writings, teachers, bishops, elect, and hearers, so that the wisdom and work of Mani will last to the end of the world.[8]

Mani's special concern was the decline of Christianity, the work of Paul, and his own improvement on the apostolic office. In Chapter I of the *Kephalaia* "On the Coming of the Apostle," he deals with "the mystery of the Apostles who are sent into the world to elect the church."[9] Paul also went out and preached, but "after Paul the Apostle gradually, day by day, the whole mankind was seduced into sin. They left justice behind them, and the narrow difficult way, and preferred to walk on the broad way." Thus "the world was left without a church, as a tree from which you pluck and take away the fruits that are on it, so that it is left without fruit." But when the church of the savior (*soter*) had been taken away, "then my apostolate (*apostole*) happened, about which you have asked me. From this time the Paraclete (*parakletos*), the spirit of truth, was sent, who has come to you in this last generation (*genea*), as the savior has announced: When I shall go, I shall send you the Paraclete."[10] And again the argument turns from the apostolic succession, culminating in Mani the Paraclete, to the problem of ecumenicity. "At the end of the years of Ardashir, the king, I went out to preach. I traveled by ship to the country of the Indians and preached them the hope (*elpis*) of life and elected there a good election." From India he went to Persia, Babylon, Mesene, and Susiana. Shapur received him with honors and permitted him to travel through the whole realm in order to preach. His mission took him to "the land of the Parthians, up to Abiadene, and to the border districts of the territory of the realm of the Romans." He went "from east to west, as you see;" and he went toward the north and the south to cover all regions of the ecumene (*oikoumene*). "Not one of the Apostles has ever done such a thing."[11]

The heavy accent that falls on the ecumenicity of Mani's work may leave the impression that earthly success was the main concern of the apostle. It will be well therefore, in conclusion, to remember that ecumenic mankind is the

---

[8] F. C. Andreas and W. Henning, *Mitteliranische Manichaica aus Chinesisch-Turkestan II* (Sitzungsberichte der Preussischen Akademie der Wissenschafter Berlin, 1933), 294–362, 295.

[9] *Kephalaia*, Ch. I, 15,

[10] *Ibid.* 13f.

[11] *Ibid.*, 15f.

symbol of universal mankind. When the message has filled the ecumene the time will be ripe for the eschatological events. Two sections of the Manichaean Psalm 223 will illuminate this ultimate purpose of Mani's work. The first section is concerned with the ecumenic achievement:[12]

> Lo, thy holy churches have spread to the four corners
>   of the world (*kosmos*).
> Lo, thy vine-trees have filled every place.
> Lo, thy sons have become famous in all lands.
> Lo, thy Bema has become firmly established in every place
> ... river now that flows in the whole earth.

The second section adumbrates the eschatological mystery:[13]

> This whole world (*kosmos*) stands firm for a season,
> while there is a great building being built outside
>   this world (*kosmos*).
> So soon as that builder shall finish,
> the whole world (*kosmos*) will be dissolved and set on
>   fire,
> that the fire may smelt it away.

From the Manichaean texts emerges a conception of history strongly resembling the Polybian. A period of pragmatic history seemed to Polybius to be well demarcated by the succession of the Persian, Macedonian, and Roman empires; the unity of the period was self-apparent from the effect that it wrought, that is, from the creation of the ecumene; and the period was reaching its climax through the Roman conquest inasmuch as its *telos,* the transformation of the cultural ecumene into the ecumene of pragmatic history, was approaching its full unfolding. A period of spiritual history seemed to Mani to be equally well demarcated by the succession of the religions founded by Buddha, Zoroaster, Jesus, and himself. The period began, just as the Polybian, in the sixth century B.C.; its unity was again self-apparent as the ecumenism of the religions; and the period was approaching the full unfolding of its *telos* through Mani, the "Seal of the Prophets," whose church would overcome the regionalism of the predecessors and establish the last and fully ecumenic religion. This parallelism does not surprise the philosopher of history who is willing to accept his sources as the authoritative guide to the understanding of a period. The builders of empires and the founders of religions in the age that

---

[12] *A Manichaean Psalm-Book,* Vol. III of Manichaean Manuscripts in the Chester Beatty Collection, ed. by C. R. C. Allberry (Stuttgart, 1938), Psalm 223, lines 3–7, p. 11.

[13] *Ibid.,* lines 20–24, p. 13

we have called the Ecumenic Age were indeed concerned with the society of all mankind that had become visible beyond the confines of the former concrete societies; they were concerned with the order of a human mass that had been drawn into the vortex of pragmatic events; and in the symbolism of an ecumenic order in the making they both met. In the process of events the term *ecumene* gained the spectrum of meaning that we have touched on several occasions. The cultural was transformed into the pragmatic ecumene; the latter then became transparent for the universal order of all mankind—past, present, and future; the universal order found its symbolic representation in the order of an ecumenic church embracing the contemporaneously living; and by its ecumenicity a religion, finally, reached again into the rivalries of communities on the pragmatic scene. The *telos* of the period developed the parallel spectrum of meanings: From the finality of the Roman Empire to the eschatological finality of a transfigured mankind; and from the transcendent finality, in which the universality of the church expressed itself, back to the ecumenic finality of the last of the apostles. The ecumene thus was the point of convergence for empire and church. By its ecumenic expanse the empire ascended from the atrocity of a raw conquest to the dignity of the representative organization of all mankind; by its ecumenic apostolate the church, which represented the universal source of order, descended to the rank of an ordering force in society and history. The pragmatic shell and the transcendent substance were destined to meet sooner or later on the level of ecumenic organization, as they actually did in the meeting of the Maurya Empire with Buddhism or of the Roman Empire with Christianity.

3. Mohammed

The blend of pragmatic conquest and spiritual apostolate affected the epiphany of Mohammed toward the end of the Ecumenic Age. By the seventh century A.D. the alliance between Rome and Christianity had settled in the Byzantine form, while a similar though more precarious blend characterized the Mazdakist Empire of the Sassanian dynasty. The Byzantine and Sassanian models of an ecumenism which combined empire and church formed the horizon in which Mohammed conceived the new religion that would support its ecumenic ambition with the simultaneous development of imperial power. The case is of special interest as there can be no doubt that Islam was primarily an ecumenic religion and only secondarily an empire. Hence it reveals in its extreme form the danger which beset all of the religions of the Ecumenic Age, the danger of impairing their universality by letting their

ecumenic mission slide over into the acquisition of world-immanent, pragmatic power over a multitude of men which, however numerous, could never
be mankind past, present, and future.

A selection of pertinent passages from the Koran will best elucidate the
problem of ecumenism as it appeared to Mohammed.[14] His conception of
spiritual history and its finality was on the whole the same as Mani's. There
was a series of divine revelations to a succession of messengers (III, 78):

> Say:
> We believe in God, and what has been sent down to us,
> and what has been sent down to Abraham and Ishmael,
>   Isaac and Jacob, and the Tribes,
> and in what was given to Moses, Jesus, and the Prophets,
>   from their Lord,
> We make no difference between them;
> and to Him are we resigned (*muslim*).

To the succession of messengers corresponds the succession of the messages
(III, 2):

> He has sent down to you the Book in truth,
> confirming those which precede it.
> Aforetime he sent down the Torah and the Gospel as
>   guidance to man,
> and now he has sent down the Illumination (*furquan*).

In the history of the "Book," the last one is superior to the preceding ones
(X, 38):

> This Koran could not have been devised by any but God.
> It is a confirmation of what is revealed before it,
> and a clearing up of the Book—there can be no doubt—
> from the Lord of all creature.

In the succession of messengers Mohammed assumes the rank of the last one,
as the "Seal of the Prophets" (XXXIII, 40); he is the apostle to the ecumene
(VII, 157-58):

> Say:
> O men! Verily I am the Messenger of God to you all,
> Whose is the kingdom of the heavens and of the earth.
> There is no God but He! He gives life and makes to die!

[14] For the phrasing of the following texts I have used the translations by J. M. Rodwell in *The
Koran* (Everyman's Library) and by Arthur J. Arberry, *The Koran Interpreted,* 2 Vols. (London-
New York, 1955).

> Therefore believe in God and in his Messenger
> —the unlettered prophet who believes in God and His word—
> and follow him so you will be guided aright.

The apostolate has its function in the economy of creation. The world was created by God and to him it must return. "He produces forth creation, then causes it to return again," the righteous to be recompensed, the infidels to be punished (X, 4). The drama of creation is a struggle between truth and falsehood in which truth, with the aid of the messengers, will prevail (XXI, 16–18):

> We created not the heaven and the earth,
> and what is between them, for sport;
> had We wished to find a pastime,
> We had surely found it in ourselves, had We willed.
> Nay, but We hurl the truth against falsehood,
> and it smites it and, lo!, it shall vanish.
> Then woe to you for what you profess (of God).

The militancy of the passage is not metaphoric. The struggle between truth and falsehood has to be conducted on the battlefields between the armies of Mohammed and his adversaries. The realm of God in history is difficult to distinguish from a closely knit community of warriors (XLVIII, 29):

> Mohammed is the Messenger of God,
> and those who are with him are hard against the infidels,
> merciful among themselves.

The infidels must desist from their unbelief or the tension between truth and falsehood in the world will be removed by energetic action (VIII, 40–41):

> Fight them until there is an end of strife
> and the religion is all God's.
> Then, if they desist, God surely will see what they do;
> but if they turn their back, know that God is your pro-
>   tector:
> Excellent protector! Excellent helper!

For "surely the worst beasts in the sight of God are the ingrate who will not believe" (VIII, 57); if taken in war they must be treated in such a manner that their followers will disperse (VIII, 59). The faithful must prepare for war and strike terror into God's enemy who is theirs; and they need not shun expense, for "all that you shall expend for the cause of God shall be repaid you; and you shall not be wronged" (VIII, 62). There may be even a profit in the business of expanding religion over the ecumene, but the missionary work of the sword must not be undertaken for that reason alone (VIII, 78):

> It is not for any Prophet to take prisoners
> until he has made a great slaughter on the earth.
> You desire the passing fruition of this world,
> but God desires the world to come.

The taking of prisoners for sale is permitted only after an earnest of the spiritual intention has been given by a conscientiously extensive slaughtering of infidels. And even then the profits of the common man are somewhat impaired by the 20-percent rule (VIII, 42):

> Know you that, whatever booty you take,
> the fifth part belongs to God and his Messenger,
> to the near of kin, and the orphans, and the needy,
> and the wayfarer.

That rule, however, was probably seen by the faithful in the light of a welcome tax reduction, since under the pre-Islamic custom the chieftain was entitled to one-fourth of the loot.

§ 4. The King of Asia

The compact order of cosmological empires is refracted into the spectrum of a pragmatic and a spiritual ecumene, *i.e.,* into indefinitely expanding power organizations without spiritual meaning and humanly universal spiritual movements in search of a people whose order they could form. This millennial process of dissociation of order, its vicissitudes to the end in the rise of orthodox imperial civilizations, is what we have called the Ecumenic Age.

In the preceding sections, the process had to be presented in the perspective of comparatively late phases when the course of events had unfolded sufficiently far for the participants, both active and passive, to become aware of its entelechy and to express their consciousness through the symbolism of the ecumene. The procedure is philosophically necessary, because there is no reality of order in history except the reality experienced and symbolized by the noetic consciousness of the participants—there would be no Ecumenic Age identified by its problems of order, unless they had been identified through symbols by somebody who had experienced them. But in using the procedure one must beware of imposing the perspective of the participants—inevitably limited by their position in time and space, by their access to materials, and by the pressure of events in daily immediacy—as a limit on the present study. In the Polybian *pragmateia,* for instance, Rome succeeds not to cosmological empires but to the ecumenic effort of Persians and Macedonians. The Achaemenian beginnings of the Ecumenic Age whose entelechy the Polybian Rome is destined to consummate remain in the dark. Moreover, though both Polybius and Scipio appear to apprehend the senselessness of conquest vividly, the fatality of the ecumenic *telos* is taken so much for granted that questions do not arise regarding what kind of society the populations collected in the empire would be and what kind of substantive order they would have. These, however, were the questions that plagued Alexander when the course of events catapulted the king of the Macedonians to the kingship of "Asia" and forced a consciousness trained by Aristotle to find out of what he now was king. And finally, Polybius had never heard of his great contemporary, the author of the Daniel Apocalypse, who had written off history as a senseless succession of empire and expected the restoration of order to human existence in society from a divine intervention that would make an end of history. Not until St. Augustine wrote his *Civitas Dei* was a symbolism found that integrated the pragmatic and spiritual orders into a whole of meaning, at least after a fashion, at least for Western Christian civilization, at least for a time.

We must now ascend from the Polybian and later phases of the process to the origins when, in the wake of the Achaemenian conquest of Babylon, the ecumenic problems of order became articulate for the first time and when, in the wake of Alexander's wresting the title of a king of Asia from Darius Codomannus, the nature of the society on which the imperial form was to be imposed became a problem. The presentation of these two issues will be followed by a survey of the Graeco-Indian aftermath to Alexander's penetration into the Punjab, to the point of its fading out in the East at about the same time that Polybius recognized the ecumenic *telos* of the Roman Empire in the West.

1. Achaemenian Prologue

The presentation of the Achaemenian sources will have to be introduced by a general statement of the experiential motivations that are liable to dissociate the compactly cosmological form of order into power and spirit.

A society in cosmological form is experienced by its members as an analogically ordered part of the divinely ordered cosmos. The symbolization of its order as an analogue of cosmic order has nothing to do with the size of its population or territory; nor does it carry an obligation to subjugate foreign populations or to expand the territory; and the coexistence of a plurality of such analogues is not experienced as an unbearable contradiction to the oneness of the cosmos. In this sense, therefore, societies in cosmological form are completely self-contained. Nevertheless, under the pressure of pragmatic events the form can lose its firmness. When a cosmological empire expands beyond the ethnic orbit of its origin, as Egypt did after the campaigns of Thutmosis III, the experience of one imperial order extending over several peoples can arouse the spiritual consciousness of one divine order common to all men. In the Hymns of Akhenaton a movement of this type becomes tangible in the coordination of Libyans and Asiatics with Egyptians as members of the same cosmic-divine analogue, though it did not go so far as to proclaim a universal-divine source of order for all men. The experience of expansion, of a pragmatic ecumene in the making, however, need not have this effect: In the Assyrian and Babylonian cases of truly ecumenic displacements and transplantations of populations, no trace of an ecumenic conception of empire is to be found in the symbolism. The complexity of the matter becomes manifest in the case of Moses. The divine declaration, through the mouth of Moses, that not the pharaoh but Israel is the Son of God links the symbolization of the Chosen People firmly to the latent ecumenism of the Egyptian empire. Moreover, contemporary with the epiphany of Moses, the Amon Hymns of Dynasty XIX begin to differentiate the unknown universal God behind the known intracosmic gods. Man's participation in divine reality, whether in the form of noetic penetration and illumination of its problems (more accentuated in the Amon Hymns) or of overwhelming divine irruptions (more accentuated in the revelations to Moses), is apparently an independent factor in the disintegration of the compact cosmological empire, however much the differentiating experience of participation may in turn have been stimulated, and made convincing, by pragmatic events.

The matter of experiential motivation is further complicated by the possibility of literalist or hypostatizing derailments inherent to all symbolization. An analogic rule over the four quarters of the world is always exposed to imaginative derailment into a literal rule over an indefinitely expanding territory; literalism was perhaps an ingredient in every aggressive expansion of a cosmological empire back to the third millennium B.C. Such literalist degradation of cosmological symbols does not differ, in principle, from the degradation the symbolism of a universal mankind under God suffers from its derailment through ecumenic ambitions. As a universal order of mankind can be fallaciously considered capable of realization through the imposition of an ecumenic empire on the contemporaneously living, so a cosmological order can be thought capable of realization through an indefinite expansion of power. The universalism of man's existence in presence under God, compactly contained in the truth of existence through membership in a society ordered as a cosmic analogue, is just as capable of literalist derailment before as after its differentiation. The literalism of translating transcendent-divine order into man-made immanent order is structurally the same phenomenon as the immanentist derailment of a philosophy of being in the transition from the Parmenidean vision of *Is!* to the immanentist speculation of the Sophists. The possibility of making immanentist nonsense of symbols which express the experience of divine presence in the order of man's existence in society and history is always present.

If the various factors are taken into account, what we have called in abbreviating language, the "transition" from cosmological to ecumenic empires, or the "succession" of the later type to the earlier one, becomes a highly diversified process of disintegration under pressure of a considerable variety of experiences. When a cosmological empire is attacked by neighboring tribes and remains victorious, the result may be an expansion without ecumenic intentions or any literalist derailments whatsoever. The experience of an actual expansion, then, can, but need not, shake the firmness of the cosmic analogue; it can, but need not, become a stimulant for differentiating experiences of participation in divine reality. When such spiritual breakthroughs occur, they can remain subordinate to the imperial form as in the case of the Amon Hymns; or, if they are carried to the length of tampering with the established empire god, as in the case of Akhenaton, the movement can be aborted through indigenous resistance of the establishment. There must be noted, furthermore, late in the history of cosmological empires, the frenzied Assyrian and Babylonian outbursts of something like a pragmatic ecumenism *de facto,* not accompanied by a differentiated understanding of the phenomenon as a *telos,* as well as the reaction to the general disturbance and unsettlement, among conquerors and conquered alike, through archaizing movements.[15] Considering this diversified field of phenomena, the case of Moses and the Chosen People merits attention as the only case before the rise of ecumenic empires wherein a differentiated advance beyond the cosmic analogue has succeeded in creating a new type of order both pragmatically and spiritually. The distinctive factor in this unique occurrence appears to be the finding of a suitable ethnic carrier for a spiritual

---

[15] For Israelite, Assyrian, and Egyptian instances of archaism cf. *Order and History,* I, 378f.

outburst, as Moses found in the tribes he led from bondage; the spiritual exodus from cosmological compactness seems to require the pragmatic exodus of a subject-people, if a differentiated type of order is to be established for a society in history.

Regarding the Achaemenian beginnings, it will be helpful to ascertain the parallels with, and differences from, the exodus of Moses and his people. In neither of the two instances does the new type of order result from the internal development of a society in imperial form; in both cases the carrier is a small people within the civilizational orbit of the empire. Moreover, the spiritual movement of Moses in the Israelite case is paralleled by the spiritual movement of Zoroaster in the Persian case. Pragmatically, however, the Persian movement is the reverse of the Israelite, for the exodus of Israel from Egypt is countered by the Persian conquest of Babylon, Egypt, the Indus Valley, and Anatolia. As a consequence of the pragmatic exodus, furthermore, Israel gained its status as a people under the kingship of God, but got involved in the fatal struggle for survival in the world of pragmatic power; while, as a consequence of the pragmatic conquest, the Achaemenians gained an empire but got involved in the problem of making spiritual sense of an order that was neither an analogue of the cosmos nor the order of a people.

The Achaemenian expansion is characterized by the combination of a derailment from the cosmic analogue to the indefiniteness of pragmatic conquest with the spiritual movement of Zoroastrianism. I shall, first, trace the literalist derailment as far as the scanty inscriptional sources permit.[16]

At the time when Cyrus the Great conquered Babylon, he was king of Anshan; through the conquest he became king of Babylon in addition. At this phase of the Achaemenian expansion, the cosmological symbolism of the Babylonian empire still governed the proceedings. When Cyrus "took the hands of Marduk" he could say of himself:[17]

> I am Cyrus, the King of the All (*kiš-šat*), the great King, the
> mighty King, King of Babylon, King of Sumer and Akkad,
> King of the four quarters of the world,
> Son of Cambyses, the great King, King of the city of Anshan,
> Grandson of Cyrus, the great King, King of the city of Anshan,

[16] F. H. Weissbach, *Die Keilinschriften der Achaemeniden* (Leipzig, 1911). Ernst Herzfeld *Altpersische Inschriften* (Berlin, 1938). For the unsolved problems of the Behistun Inscription cf. F .W. Koenig, *Relief und Inschrift des Koenigs Dareios I am Felsen von Bagistan* (Leiden, 1938).

[17] Cyrus inscription on clay cylinder. Weissbach, *Keilinschriften*, 5.

Great-grandson of Teispes, the great King, King of the city
    of Anshan,
the eternal seed of the Kingdom whose dynasty is beloved by
    Bel and Nabu,
whose Kingdom they desired for the enjoyment of their heart.

With the expansion of the empire through Cyrus, Cambyses, and Darius I, however, the pressure of pragmatic events made itself felt. The speed and violence of the conquest shook perhaps the static symbolism of the rule over the four quarters. At any rate, in the Behistun Inscription the dynamics and the actual movement of the expansion can be sensed; in § 6 Darius speaks of the countries which "came forward to serve" by the will of Ahuramazda; and then he enumerates them: "Persia, Elam, Babylon, Assur [Syria], Arabia, Egypt, those of the sea [the Greek islands], Sardes, Ionia [Cyprus and the Cilician coastal cities], Media, Armenia, Cappadocia, Parthia, Drangiana, Areia, Chorasmia, Bactria, Sogdiana, Gandara [Paropamisadae], Saka, Sattagydia [Punjab], Arachosia, Maka—twenty-three countries in all."[18] Here speaks no longer the king of the four quarters in the cosmological sense, but a ruler who has gone beyond the boundaries of his original kingdom to engage in an indefinite conquest which by this time has already gathered in twenty-three countries. The trend toward ecumenism articulates itself, then, in the Naqsh-i-Rustam Inscription NRa, where Darius speaks of himself as the "King of the countries of all tribes, the King of this farflung earth."[19] In the immediately following enumeration (§ 3) he refers to the countries of which he took possession "outside Persis"; the number of countries has increased to twenty-nine, not counting the Persis. And a similar formula, followed by the enumeration, occurs in the Persepolis daiva Inscription of Xerxes.[20] The ecumenic intentions of Xerxes, finally, are attested by the speech which Herodotus attributes to him. Through the conquest of Hellas Xerxes intended to make the Persian territory (*gen*) coextensive with the Aether of Zeus. "No land that the sun beholds will lie on our border, but I will make all to be one country, when I have passed over the whole of Europe." And the pragmatic character of the ecumene is

[18] Weissbach, *Keilinschriften*, 11–13. In the translation of *patijaiśa as* "came forward to serve" I am following Koenig, *Relief*, 62, who assumes the word to belong to the court language. The delegates of the countries, with their gifts, come forward to meet the king as his servants; the ceremony is also to be found in pictorial representation. In the list of the countries I have put the identifications suggested by Koenig in brackets, *ibid.*, 62 f. For the order of the enumeration and its relation to the Iranian picture of the world cf. *ibid.*, 63 f.

[19] Darius, Naqsh-i-Rustam Inscription (NRa), § 2. Weissbach, *Keilinschriften*, 87.

[20] Xerxes, Persepolis daiva, § 3. Herzfeld, *Altpersische Inschriften*, No. 14, 34.

stressed by Xerxes' opinion that no polis or people will be left to meet him in battle, once Hellas is conquered.[21]

Beyond the ecumenism, through the pressure of pragmatic events, there makes itself felt, second, the symbolism of a universal order of justice or truth by the will and grace of Ahuramazda. The Behistun Inscription as a whole is the glorification of the victory of Ahuramazda, represented by Darius, over the realm of the lie (*drauga*), represented by the false Smerdis and the other rebels. The Naqsh-i-Rustam Inscription NRb, as deciphered by Herzfeld, then praises the order created by Darius as the work of Ahuramazda:[22]

> A great god is Ahuramazda
> who has created this all-surpassing work,
> that has become visible,
> who has created the peace for men,
> who has endowed with wisdom and good-being Darius the King.

This Preamble is followed by the king's *autolouange,* beginning with the lines:

> Says Darius the King:
>   By the will of Ahuramazda I am of this kind:
>   What is right I love,
>   not-right I hate.
>   Not is it my pleasure,
>   that the lower one suffers injustice because of the
>   higher one,
>   nor is it my pleasure,
>   that the higher one suffers injustice because of the
>   lower one.
>   What is right that is my pleasure.
>   The man of the Lie I hate.

The *autolouange* covers what in Aristotelian language would have to be called the excellences or virtues of the king; and it concludes (§ 3) with the assurance that the king's achievements are due to the virtues which are the gift of Ahuramazda. This self-praise of the king (which should be read in full) goes far beyond the conception of the ruler as the mediator of cosmic order in the pharaonic scene. It rather recalls a mirror of the prince in the manner of David's Last Words.[23] For the god has formed the king's character; the king has become a person with distinct excellences in the image of the personal god.

---

[21] Herodotus, VII, 8.
[22] NRb, § 1. Herzfeld, *Altpersische Inschriften,* No. 4, 9.
[23] *Order and History,* I, 473.

The substance of order that fills the far-flung empire through the conquering and administrative action of the king is no longer cosmic but the spiritual and moral substance of Ahuramazda.

This new, differentiated experience of order is most strongly present in the Persepolis daiva Inscription of Xerxes.[24] After the enumeration of the countries under his rule (§ 3), Xerxes relates that some of these provinces of the empire rebelled at the time he became king. They were subdued with the help of Ahuramazda; and since some of them had previously worshipped the *daiva*, Xerxes now "levelled these *daiva* stables to the ground," prohibited the worship of the *daiva*, and established in its place the cult of "Ahuramazda with Rtam the brazmanic" (§ 4). The meaning of the formula "Ahuramazda with Rtam the brazmanic" is difficult to determine, as its occurrence in the present inscription is unique. Still, Rtam is known as the central concept of Zoroastrianism, meaning the divine truth of order. The *Rtam-Vahu* prayer (Yazhd 27, 15) says:

> The truth is the perfectly good (literally: the best good);
> by its own will is, by its own will for us
> may become the perfect order (*rtai*), the truth (*rtam*).[25]

The prayer for the realization of the truth of order for us on the earth is, in substance, the Lord's prayer that the realm of God may come. Originally the transfiguration of the world through the coming of the truth was considered imminent; but Zoroastrianism, like Christianity, had to shift its eschatological hopes to the indefinitely distant end of the world, thus giving room to the historical interlude of an order in the spirit of truth.[26] The meaning of *brazman* is rather obscure in the context. It certainly is the same word as the Indian *brahman;* but then the meaning of *brazmanic* would be so close to that of Rtam that at the present state of knowledge a distinction cannot be made.[27] It is certain, however, that with the formula "Ahuramazda with Rtam the brazmanic" Xerxes introduced Zoroastrian symbols into his conception of imperial order. And on this occasion the universal substance of order was

---

[24] Xerxes, Persepolis daiva. Herzfeld, *Altpersische Inschriften*, No. 14, 27–35.

[25] The *Rtam-Vahu* prayer, as transliterated by Herzfeld, *Altpersische Inschriften*, 288, Y.27, 15:
> rtam vahu vahištam asti
> uštā asti uštā ahmāi
> hyāt rtāi vahištāi rtam

[26] Herzfeld, *Altpersische Inschriften*, Glossary *s.v. Rtam*, 288: "Ursprünglich wird diese verwirklichung, gāth. haᶿyā-varštāt-. wie im Urchristentum, jeden augenblick erwartet; die spätere theologie folgt der traurigen realität der geschichte, indem sie sie in weite ferne ans weltende rückt: die apatiyārakīh oder das frašam, vgl. s.v."

[27] *Ibid.*, Glossary *s.v. Brazmani.-*

personalized, not only in the king but also in the subjects of the empire. For the Inscription continues:[28]

> You, in the future, when you think "I want to be
> peaceful in life and blissful in death," walk in
> the laws that have been set by Ahuramazda. Worship
> Ahuramazda with Rtam the brazmanic. Who walks in
> the laws that have been set by Ahuramazda, and wor-
> ships Ahuramazda with Rtam the brazmanic, will be
> peaceful in life and blissful in death.

With these last admonitions Xerxes has moved farther than any of the other Achaemenian kings from cosmic-divine order in the direction of transcendent-divine order. The Rtam as such is an old cosmological symbol, in its function not different from the Egyptian Maat or the Chinese Tao; its new meaning as the universal source of order over all men as persons was created by Zoroaster. With this new meaning, the symbol is now adopted by Xerxes when Ahuramazda becomes the god who not only forms the king and the empire—as did Akhenaton's god—but makes every man who worships him, without royal mediation, a participant in his Rtam so that in death he will be *rtava, i.e.,* blissful.[29] It may have been his spiritual fervor that made Xerxes, as far as we know, the only Achaemenian king who actively interfered with the older worship of the *daiva* and replaced it with the cult of Ahuramazda.

2. *Alexander*

The Macedonians were the successors to the Persian Empire. About Alexander's conception of his imperial conquest we are better informed than about that of the Achaemenians, though not too well since the considerable body of literature produced by the companions of the campaign has perished with the exception of such fragments as are preserved by later historians, especially by Arrian (*ca.* A.D. 96–180) in his *Anabasis of Alexander*. The campaign started, as far as the official propaganda was concerned, as a war of

---

[28] Persepolis daiva, end of § 4. Herzfeld, *Altpersische Inschriften*, 35.

[29] Herzfeld, *Altpersische Inschriften*, Glossary *s.v. Rtavan-*. Herzfeld, *s.v. frašam.*, p. 164: "In dem eschatologischen § 34 des *MāhFrav.,* paraphrase der saušyantverse des *Yt.* XIX, 89, werden amaršantam azaršantam mit mp.amurg ut azarmān 'frei von tod und alter' übersetzt, vgl. s.v. mrδ-, und das voraufgehende frašam ebenso richtig mit abēš ut apatiyārak 'frei von befeindung und bekämpfung (durch das Böse).' Der frašam-zustand ist in jüngerer sprache die apatiyārakīh, das 'nicht-mehr-bekämpft,' das 'über-den-kampf-hinaus-sein,' die 'kampflosigkeit.' In ihm haben die auferstandenen als 'rtavano das ziel des 'rtam, das absolut-gute 'erreicht.' In *Xerx.Pers.daiv.* sind die gläubigen auf erden šyātā 'quieti' frei von kampf. šyātiš 'quies' ist das durch die annahme der religion auf erden verwirklichte frašam."

revenge against the Persians and of liberation of the Ionian Greeks. What the
real objectives were, if a definite plan existed at all, can only be inferred from
the growing resistance of the Macedonian staff officers, whom Alexander had
inherited from Philip, and especially of Parmenio, to the submerging of
Macedonian force in the Asiatic vastness. In the minds of Philip and his
officers the objective had probably been limited to the conquest of the Anatolian coast and enough of the hinterland of Asia Minor to create a territorial
state that could hold its own strategically against any attempts of the reduced
Persia to regain the lost position and was large enough to allow for settlement
by the overflow of Hellenic population, but not so large that it could not be
militarily controlled by the limited Macedonian manpower. What Alexander's
ideas were at the beginning of the campaign we do not know, but it is quite
possible that the program which later unfolded was already envisaged by him
in its general outlines.

The first indication of objectives considerably larger than the ones harbored
by his conservative staff came after the battle of Issus when he had to answer
Darius' offer of a treaty of friendship and alliance. The letter of Alexander to
Darius, which is preserved by Arrian (II, 14), is a source of the first importance
inasmuch as it is the only extant document in which we hear the voice of
Alexander himself. Having rejected Darius' plea of a defensive war on his
part and having accused him of aggression, Alexander continues:

> As I am the Lord of all Asia, you come to me! If you fear lest by coming
> you receive ungracious treatment by me, send some of your friends to re-
> ceive my pledges. When you come to me, request and receive your mother,
> wife, and children, and what else you may wish. What you persuade me
> to give, shall be yours. And for the future: When you address yourself
> to me, address me as the King of Asia; do not approach me on equal
> terms, but speak to me as the lord of all that is yours if there is anything
> you need; otherwise I shall take steps concerning you as an offender. But
> if you still contend for your kingdom, stand and fight for it, and don't
> run—for I will reach you wherever you are!

This letter is less a source than the fascinating moment of the *translatio
imperii* itself.

The role of the king of Asia in succession to Darius could not be played
for long. As a consequence of its phantastic speed the conquest threatened to
become an amorphous mass of territories and peoples, without definite institutional and symbolic form. Tarn summarized the problem neatly when

he wrote: "In Egypt Alexander was an autocrat and a god. In Iran he was an autocrat, but not a god. In the Greek cities he was a god, but not an autocrat. In Macedonia he was neither autocrat nor god, but a quasi-constitutional king over against whom his people enjoyed certain customary rights."[30] The continuation, with some modifications, of the Persian administrative organization by satrapies could not obscure the fact that Alexander's dominion as a whole, as well as his own position as the ruler, had no form. The fragmentary sources concerning Alexander's intention to create such a form are numerous, but none of them is conclusive by itself. We can do no more than form a mosaic and let it suggest as much of a picture as it will.

The first text to be considered is the summary of Alexander's ecumenism given by Plutarch (ca. A.D. 46–120) in his *Fortune and Virtue of Alexander*. The work is an epideictic speech, using rhetorical *topoi* in praise of Alexander's virtue. One of the *topoi* is the elevation of the king above the philosopher for the reason that the king realizes through action what the philosopher only dreams and talks about. It is the commonplace that we saw in the making in the work of Polybius. In the pertinent section of the speech (I, 6; 329a–d) Plutarch first summarizes the "much admired *Politeia* of Zeno, the founder of the Stoic sect (*hairesis*)" in the postulate: Men should not live separated under the laws of their respective poleis and peoples, but form one polity and people with a common life and an order common to all. What Zeno only dreamt, Plutarch continues, Alexander put into effect; for to Zeno's reason (*logos*) he supplied his deed (*ergon*). Alexander did not follow the advice of Aristotle to treat the Hellenes as their hegemon, the barbarians as their master, but was convinced that "he was sent by the gods (*theoten*) to be the general harmonizer (*harmostes*) and reconciler (*diallaktes*) of the All." When he brought men together not by reason (*logos*), he forced them by arms (*hoplois*); and thus he mixed their lives and characters, their marriages and habits, as in a loving cup. He bade them consider "the ecumene (*oikoumene*) their fatherland, his army their citadel (*akropolis*) and protection, all good men their kinsmen, and all bad men not of their kin (*allophylous*)." They should not distinguish, as formerly between Hellenes and barbarians by customs and apparel; rather, what is excellent (*arete*) should be recognized as Hellenic, what is iniquitous (*kakia*) as barbaric. To this summary must

[30] W. W. Tarn, "Alexander: The Conquest of the Far East" (*Cambridge Ancient History, Volume VI, Ch. 13, 1927*), 432 ff.

be added the information (I, 9; 330e) that it was the plan of Alexander "to gain for all men harmony (*homonoia*) and peace (*eirene*) and community (*koinonia*) among one another."

If no sources were extant but this account by Plutarch, it would be difficult to estimate its reliability. Did Plutarch perhaps attribute Zeno's ideas to Alexander merely for rhetorical effect? The suspicion is nourished by the fact that Alexander could not have added his *ergon* to Zeno's *logos*, as Zeno came to Athens only ten years after Alexander's death and at the time of his arrival could not have been more than twenty-one or twenty-two years old. But even if we disregard the anachronism and assume the account of Alexander's convictions and beliefs, which in part goes back to Eratosthenes (*ca.* 275–*ca.* 195 B.C.), as substantially correct, it is still unsatisfactory because we learn nothing about the concrete situations in which Alexander spoke of himself as the reconciler and harmonizer of the world in such a manner that the declaration could have become a matter of common knowledge. Did Alexander make speeches on philosophical topics? Or did he use such language in his table talk? And were they reported by his companions? In brief: We should like to know what the Old Testament scholars call the "setting in life" in which these symbols occurred.

Fortunately there are preserved, principally by Arrian, a number of episodes which prove that Alexander entertained such ideas indeed, even if he never gave them the generalized form related by Plutarch. We shall analyze the three episodes in which Alexander's conceptions of the empire, of the ruling class, and of his own position become tangible.

The first of these episodes related by Arrian in his *Anabasis of Alexander* (VII, 7, 8–9) was the Banquet of Opis. After the mutiny at Opis had ended with a reconciliation between the king and his Macedonian veterans, Alexander offered sacrifices and arranged a great feast. Sitting around him at the banquet were the Macedonian companions, next to them the Persians, and then the delegates of the other tribes according to their precedence in reputation and excellence. Alexander and his comrades drank from the same bowl and poured the same libations, the Greek seers and Persian Magians opening the ceremony. The ritual reached its climax when Alexander rose to say the famous prayer. The text of the prayer quite possibly is not complete, though its tradition goes back to Ptolemy; moreover its grammar bears more than one translation. According to the reading accepted by most scholars Alexander "prayed for the other good things and for Homonoia between, and partnership in rule (*koinonia tes arches*) between, Macedonians and Persians." If this reading be accepted, the king prayed for no more than harmonious relations in the joint Macedonian-Persian rule of the empire. In his extensive analysis of the pertinent texts, Tarn considers this interpretation incompatible with the situation of the banquet, where representatives of the various peoples of the realm were present to the number of nine thousand; the Homonoia must have been requested for the vast mixed population under Alexander's rule, as suggested by the Plutarch passages which probably render the tenor of the prayer. Tarn wants to translate therefore: Alexander "prayed for the other good things, and for Homonoia, and for partnership in the realm between Macedonians and Persians." "Homonoia in the prayer has to stand alone as a substantive thing, and not merely be tacked on to the words 'Macedonians and Persians'."[31] As far as I can see, Tarn's reading is quite as justified as the first, more commonly accepted one, especially as it is supported by the Plutarch passages. But I suspect that the energy expended on the argument that either of the two readings has to be the correct one is wasted. For the text as it stands almost certainly does not render Alexander's prayer literally—it must have been differently composed and longer[32]—and we do not know in what direction its meaning has been changed through the abbreviated tradition. Instead of pressing the preserved form as if it were the authentic text of the prayer, one should treat it as a mutilated text from which the probable meaning of the original has to be reconstructed as far as that is possible. In our attempt to arrive at such a probable meaning we shall avail ourselves of the grammatical opportunity to understand the *Makedosi kai Persais* as a *dativus commodi* and assume the king to have prayed, not for fellowship *between* Macedonians and Persians, but for the blessings of the gods *for* Macedonians and Persians. Among these blessings the prayer then singled out the *homonoia kai koinonia*

---

[31] W. W. Tarn, *Alexander the Great*, II: *Sources and Studies* (Cambridge 1948), 444. For Tarn's discussion of the problem connected with the prayer, as well as for the literature on the subject, see pp. 434–49. Ernest Barker, *From Alexander to Constantine* (Oxford 1956), 6, has translated the prayer: "Alexander prayed for blessings, and especially for the blessing of human concord (*Homonoia*) and of fellowship in the realm (*koiononia tes arches*) between Macedonians and Greeks (*sic*!)." Fritz Schachermeyr, *Alexander der Grosse* (Graz-Salzburg-Wien, 1949), 411, renders the substance of the prayer: "one prayed, for Macedonians and Persians, for concord and community of their rule." This translation introduces the possibility of construing the *Makedosi kai Persais* as a *dativus commodi*, about which presently more in the text. Against Tarn he decides (Note 256) that Homonoia cannot stand alone as a substantive thing, but stresses that the prayer for concord in the ruling circles does not contradict Alexander's wishes for the Homonoia embracing all mankind.

[32] Tarn, *Alexander*, 443.

tes arches. If we make this assumption, we create a context of meaning that is intelligible both intellectually and pragmatically. For the formula of the specific blessing transfers the categories of *homonoia* (being of one *nous,* likemindedness) and *koinonia,* which Aristotle had developed for the polis, to Alexander's creation, *i.e.,* to the empire that embraced not only Macedonians and Persians, but also Greeks, Egyptians, Phrygians, Phoenicians, Arameans, Babylonians, Arabs, Indians, and so forth. That such a vast agglomeration of culturally variegated peoples was in dire need of a community of the spirit (*nous*) to become the people of an empire will hardly be doubted.

Moreover, that Alexander prayed for the unity of empire in favor of Macedonians and Persians also made sense in this situation, for he intended the two peoples, which together were no more than a small minority in the population of the empire, to be its common ruler. This program of Alexander's, to provide a ruling class for the empire through the amalgamation of Macedonians and Persians, however, met with considerable resistance. His first measure, that his companions should share the honors of administrative office and military command with their recently defeated enemies, was in the nature of the case not to their taste. A further complication, then, was introduced through the relation between Alexander as a quasi-constitutional king and his Macedonian soldiers who were at the same time something like an assembly of the people. Alexander's reorganization of the army so as to include Asiatic contingents on the same footing with the Macedonians could be understood by the latter only as a symptom of his intention to abandon his kingship of Macedonia in favor of the kingship of Asia. The Macedonians felt rejected by their king for whom they had won his victories; and the mutiny at Opis was not a conspiracy of officers but an emotional outbreak of the aggrieved common men. And finally, the intended amalgamation of the two peoples into one ruling class required measures more substantial than the appointment of Persians to positions that might have gone to Macedonians. Hence, Alexander propagated a mixture of customs and manners, adopted partly Asiatic garb, and introduced elements of Persian court ceremonial. The climax of these endeavors was again, as at Opis, a banquet with a ritual act, the great marriage feast at Susa. By royal command, eighty of his companions married daughters of the Persian and Median nobility, and ten thousand Macedonians had to take Asiatic women. Alexander himself married Barsine, the eldest daughter of Darius. The mass wedding was celebrated according to Persian custom.[33]

---

[33] Arrian, *Anabasis,* Vol. VII, Ch. 4, pp. 4–8.

What the husbands by command thought about this royal intervention in their most personal affairs is not known.

Alexander's conception of his own position as the ruler of the empire is the obscurest point of all inasmuch as it is veiled, since antiquity, by the confused reports about the questions of proskynesis and deification. The works of the companions of the campaign may have been more elaborate and clear, but the historians of the Roman period—who are our only source—report so obscurely that apparently the nature of the issue has escaped them.[34]

The proskynesis before the king was part of the Persian court ceremonial; it did not imply any recognition of the king as a god. Since in Greece, however, obeisance was made only to the gods, Alexander's attempt to introduce the Persian ceremonial could be, and perhaps had to be, understood by the Macedonians and Greeks as a pretension of divinity. The inevitable clashes, as for instance the oratorical conflict between Anaxarchus and Callisthenes, or the terrible scene with Cassander,[35] are broadly reported by the ancient historians because they make good stories. But whether these scenes touch the core of the issue is rather doubtful. If such a core exists, it is to be found in one more of the ritual banquet scenes which Alexander seems to have favored for the creation of his imperial symbolism. It is preserved in two versions which both probably go back to the episode as related in a work of Chares, Alexander's master of ceremonies. Neither of the two versions is very illuminating by itself as they both concentrate less on the ceremony than on the obstreperous conduct of Callisthenes; but they supplement one another, and it is possible therefore to reconstruct the scene with high probability.

One of the versions is given by Plutarch in his *Life of Alexander* (LIV, 3-4):

> Chares of Mitylene says that once at a banquet Alexander, after drinking, handed the cup to one of his friends. He, on receiving it, first stepped before the altar (*hestia*) and, when he had drunk, prostrated himself (*proskynesai*), then he kissed Alexander and resumed his place. As the others were doing the same Callisthenes in his turn took the cup—the King paid no attention as he was conversing with Hephaestion—drank and then went towards the King to kiss him. But Demetrius, surnamed Pheido, cried: "O King, do not agree the kiss, for he alone has not prostrated himself before you." When Alexander declined the kiss, Callisthenes exclaimed in a loud voice: "Then I shall go away the poorer by a kiss."

[34] *Ibid.*, IV, 10–11.
[35] Plutarch, *Life of Alexander*, LXXIV.

The second version is given by Arrian in his *Anabasis* (IV, 12, 3–5): "Having drunk from it Alexander sent round a golden cup, first to those with whom he had arranged about the proskynesis. The first one rose to drink and prostrated himself, and received a kiss from Alexander; and so they did one by one in order." Then again follows the embarrassing scene with Callisthenes.

From the two versions combined it appears that this was not an accidental episode, but the carefully planned occasion on which the ceremony of proskynesis was to be introduced. The banquet, though we do not know where it took place, had been arranged among Alexander and his closest friends. The ceremony was to be executed first by the companions in his confidence, and then the others, it was expected, would follow suit. The ritual itself apparently had the following phases: (1) The king would drink from the loving cup, the *phiale,* and pass it around; (2) the recipient would rise and step before the *hestia;* (3) he would drink and prostrate himself before the *hestia;* (4) then he would approach the king to receive the kiss; and (5) he would resume his seat. The meaning of the ritual clearly depends on the meaning of the *hestia.* This *hestia* now has been identified as part of the Achaemenian royal symbolism.[36] The great king was distinguished from ordinary men through the cultic possession of a royal fire, symbolizing the divine force that pervades the cosmos. Not the king, but his fire was divine. When the king went on a campaign it preceded him, carried on a silver altar.[37] It even went into battle with him.[38] And it was extinguished only at his death.[39] Alexander had taken over this symbolism, as we know from his order to extinguish the sacred fire on the death of Hephaestion as if he were a king.[40]

The introduction of the divine-royal flame into the ritual of the proskynesis is of interest in several respects. In the first place, it reveals to what degree Alexander had entered into the Persian conception of divine order, kingship, and empire. Second, it proves his skill as a psychological manipulator. For the proskynesis, which was repulsive to Macedonians and Hellenes, was to be executed before the altar with the flame, not before the king; the courtiers were to prostrate themselves before the symbol of divinity, but the king himself remained human. Or so it seemed at least, if the Macedonians and Hellenes could be taken in. But the resistance of Callisthenes was perhaps motivated by

[36] F. Jacoby, *Kommentar zu den Fragmenten Griechischer Historiker,* 436. Fritz Schachermeyr, *Alexander der Grosse* (Graz-Salzburg-Wien, 1949), 310.

[37] Xenophon, *Cyropaedia,* VIII, 3, 12.

[38] Curtius, *History of Alexander,* III, 3, 9.

[39] Diodorus Siculus, XVII, 114, 4.

[40] *Ibid.*

his understanding that this clever arrangement implied precisely what it seemed to reject. For this ritual, third, reveals something about Alexander's conception of his own divinity. The Persian proskynesis was executed before the king who was a man; Alexander's proskynesis was executed before the royal flame which was divine. The association, through the ritual, of the king with the divinity of the flame well justified the cry of Demetrius in the Plutarch version that Callisthenes had not executed the proskynesis "before you", *i.e.,* before Alexander. In devising his ritual Alexander, while using the Persian court ceremony, had gone far beyond it and subtly introduced the claims of his divinity.[41]

Alexander's conception of his own divinity is obscure, and considering the state of the sources it probably will remain so. Still, it is possible to classify the variegated materials and issues so that the difficulty itself will be circumscribed somewhat more clearly than it is in the extensive debate on the question.[42]

(1) It is fairly certain that Alexander's request of 324 B.C. to be recognized as a god by the cities of the League of Corinth was an administrative measure which had no bearing on the issue of his own conception. As hegemon of the League, he was bound by the covenant not to interfere in the internal affairs of the cities; but such interference, for the purpose of resettling refugees, had become necessary, and the jurisdiction which he did not have as the hegemon he could have as a god.

(2) Closer to the issue of Alexander's understanding of his divinity would be the influence of Aristotle's conception of the man distinguished by *arete* who is "like a God among men" (*Politics,* 1284a11)—if such an influence existed. Since the debate about this phrase, which Hegel had assumed to refer to Alexander, apparently will not come to rest, it is necessary to articulate our own position in the matter. As I have indicated earlier in this study, nothing

[41] The debate about the precise meaning of the passages in question is still going on: Did Alexander demand the proskynesis before the fire or before himself? In the text I have adopted the interpretation given by Schachermeyr in his first Alexander monograph of 1949 because, considering the circumstances, it appears to me to be the most plausible. This interpretation, however, has met with criticism. In his new *Alexander der Grosse* (Vienna, 1973), Schachermeyr still prefers his earlier interpretation of a proskynesis before the fire, but admits the circumstances of the scene to be so complex that the proskynesis before the king is also possible. For the complexities of the circumstances, see now the extensive presentation in the *Alexander* of 1973, pp. 370–385. Cf. also Appendix 7 on *"Das persische Koenigsfeuer,"* 682ff.

[42] For the sources and the extensive debate cf. Tarn, *Alexander the Great,* II, Appendix 22 on "Alexander's Deification."

in the text of Aristotle explicitly supports a reference to Alexander.[43] However, since this leaves the possibility open that the phrase ought to be understood in this sense, even without an explicit reference, I must now add that the argument, in the course of which this phrase occurs, is crystal clear, that this argument has nothing to do with Alexander, and that the question can only arise if the phrase is tortured out of context. A summary of the argument follows:

In the critical chapter of *Politics* (1284a3–1284b34) Aristotle deals with the institution of ostracism as a safety device that will eliminate from political society persons who outrank by Arete their fellow citizens so far that their presence is a silent reproach (that will perhaps not always remain silent) to the constitutional provisions of the respective poleis which do not allow them public status in accordance with their personal rank: "They will be treated unjustly if ranked as equals, being unequal by virtue and political ability—for such a man is like a god among men." "There is no Nomos for them, since they are themselves Nomos." In such cases "political justice" will require the removal of the embarrassing persons from the scene; and this necessity is independent of the constitutional form. Tyrants will proceed more brutally; but oligarchic or democratic poleis, while they use the gentler means of ostracism, proceed according to the same principle. An imperial polis like Athens furthermore uses the same device to suppress potential resistance in her subject poleis; and the king of the Persians uses it to prevent revolts among the Medians, Persians, and other proud populations of his empire. Only one exception to this principle of "political justice" can be considered, that is, in the case of the best constitution (*ariste politeia*) where it would indeed be improper for the others to rule over such a man. For that would be like claiming rule over Zeus and parceling his powers (*tas archas*). In the best constitution men should obey such a man gladly so that there would be kingships of such men forever in these poleis.

The summary, though brief, is exhaustive. The argument contains no references, explicit or implicit, to Alexander. Moreover, the language of gods among men, as well as the consideration of their status in the best politeia, resumes the language and problem of Plato's *Laws* 739b–740a; Aristotle is moving within a theoretical context set by Plato; and the theoretical motivation is sufficient reason for the form which the argument assumes in Aristotle's context. In view of the theoretical cohesion of the argument, it is not only

---

[43] *Order and History*, III, 311.

unnecessary but methodologically improper to cast around for political allusions of a sensational nature. And, finally, it must be stressed that any attempt to apply the phrase "like a god among men" to Alexander flatly contradicts the explicit contents of Aristotle's argument. For conclusions can indeed be drawn from this chapter with regard to Alexander, because the casuistry of the passage also covers the case of an Asiatic empire. The king of Persia too engages in the removal of men of superior excellence from his realm in the interest of constitutional order, with Aristotle's approval of such "political justice," precisely because he is *not* "like a god among men" himself; and the same reasoning will apply to his Macedonian successor in the kingship of Asia. To be sure, Aristotle does not draw this conclusion explicitly and we do not know, therefore, whether he had it in mind—but there is no reason to put it beyond him. Moreover, Aristotle develops the type concept of the *pambasileia*, of the autocratic monarchy "over a polis, a people, or several peoples," and characterizes it as an *oikonomike basileia,* a household kingship (1285b30–33), so that there can be no doubt that this type of political organization is not the "best polis," and not even a polis at all, in which the man of superior *arete* could be recognized as ruler. We conclude, therefore, that the much debated phrase not only does not apply to Alexander, but that the context excludes such application and perhaps even suggests, to anybody who wants to draw conclusions, the rather dim view which Aristotle took of the activities of his former pupil.

(3) The only passages that seem to have a bearing on Alexander's occupation with his own divinity or semidivinity are connected with his journey to the oracle of Ammon in the oasis of Siwah. Plutarch, in his *Life of Alexander,* XXVII, *in fine,* reports the remark of the Egyptian philosopher Psammon that "all men are under the royal rule of God"; Alexander, he continues, responded with the "more philosophical" reflection that "God is the common father of all men, but makes the best ones peculiarly his own." The formula of God as the common father of all men recalls the Homeric Zeus who was "the father of men and gods" (*Iliad,* I. 544), as well as Aristotle's use of the passage to illustrate the royal rule of a father over his children (*Politics,* 1259b14). What is new in the saying attributed to Alexander is the opposition of the fatherhood of God to his royal rule as the cosmocrator, and the singling out of the best as "peculiarly his own." The attitude revealed in the remark, assuming it to be authentic, agrees well with the general picture of Alexander's ecumenism as drawn by Plutarch in his *Fortune and Virtue of Alexander,* I, 6: Hellenes and barbarians have become a common humanity whose fatherland is the

ecumene and whose acropolis is Alexander's army. But one can assert not much more than this agreement. To go further and to speak of this saying as the epochal first declaration of the "Brotherhood of Man," as Tarn does,[44] is an ideological exaggeration which distorts the situation with regard to both the past and the future. For, as far as the community of mankind is concerned, there is nothing in the dictum that cannot be found in the late sophistic fragments on equality and harmony;[45] and as far as the fatherhood of God is concerned, there is nothing that would betray a spiritual breakthrough beyond Plato and Aristotle. Alexander's experience of universal order, though loosened up by the task of organizing a multicivilizational empire, remains in bondage to the ecumenism of the conqueror.

This bondage becomes apparent if one considers Alexander's conviction that God "makes the best ones peculiarly his own" in the context of its utterance—that is, on the occasion of the conquest of Egypt, the assumption of the pharaonic succession, and the visit to Ammon. Arrian relates (III, 3, 1–2) that Alexander was overcome by the desire to visit the Libyan Ammon, partly because he wanted to consult the infallible oracle as Heracles and Perseus had done before him, partly because he traced "something of his descent" (*ti tes geneseos tes heautou*) from Ammon and hoped to learn more about himself. What the conqueror learned from the god we do not know; Arrian only says that the answer was "according to his heart" (*thymos*) (III, 4, 5); but it can hardly have been anything but a more elaborate explanation, on the part of the priest, of the pharaonic sonship of god, just acquired by Alexander in Memphis, which must have been mysteriously disturbing to a young man of Macedonian-Hellenic education. Plutarch indeed relates that the priest greeted Alexander as the son of god;[46] and Diodorus Siculus interprets the priestly information as the grant of the empire of the world: "From Ammon was granted him the dominion of the whole earth."[47] The cosmological dominion of the pharaoh had been converted—whether by the priest, or by the historians—into an ecumenic dominion.[48]

All this is much less than we should like to know, but beyond this point lies nothing but the Pothos of Alexander, his desire or yearning. Arrian, as we

---

[44] Tarn, *Alexander*, II, 437.

[45] *Order and History*, II, 323–28, especially 326.

[46] Plutarch, *Life of Alexander*, XXVII.

[47] Diodorus Siculus, XVII, 93, 4.

[48] That is all that can be extracted from the texts. For an imaginative presentation of the Ammon episode in the context of Alexander's life see Schachermeyr, *Alexander der Grosse* (Vienna, 1973), 242–56; cf. also Appendix 5 on *"Umstrittene Orakel,"* 672ff.

have seen, tells that a Pothos overcame Alexander to go to the Ammon in
Libya, presumably to learn from the god himself more about his new sonship.
As far as we know, Alexander himself coined the meaning which the word
pothos acquired in his usage, the meaning of a forceful desire to reach out
indefinitely toward the unknown and unheard of; and it is probable that he
used it in this sense for the first time, when the Pothos gripped him to visit the
Ammon in the desert.[49] For the understanding of Alexander's consciousness of his ecumenic role, we are ultimately referred to the daemonism of his
genius.

3. Graeco-Indian Epilogue

In the wake of Alexander's campaign in the Punjab, the scene of imperial
foundations expands to India. The following survey will be confined to the
events most closely connected with the Macedonian rule in "Asia," *i.e.,* the
complex of the Maurya and the Graeco-Indian empires. It will not extend to
the Yuechi and other nomad foundations, as they belong to a chain of events
that originates in the foundation of the Chinese Empire; nor will it extend
to the later, indigenously Indian rise of the Gupta Empire. Moreover, as in the
preceding sections, I shall refrain from drawing the all-too-obvious parallels
with the phenomena of imperial retreat and expansion we can observe in our
own time.

At the time of Alexander's campaign the area of Indian civilization was
politically still a manifold of tribal republics and principalities of various size
and power. One of the larger units was the kingdom of Maghada, under the
Nanda dynasty, in the Ganges Valley. Plutarch, in his *Life of Alexander*
(LXII, 4), relates the following episode: "Andrakottos, when he was a youth,
saw Alexander himself. And we are told that he often said later that Alexander had narrowly missed the conquest (*ta pragmata*), since the King was
hated and despised because of his baseness and low birth." The Andrakottos
of this episode was the Maurya Chandragupta, the founder of the first Indian
Empire. He had incurred the displeasure of the Nanda king,[50] to whom
possibly he was related, and had become a fugitive in the West. Among other
Indian princes he had come to the camp of Alexander at Patala, 325 B.C.
About eight years later, in 317 B.C., when the last Macedonian satrap left India,

---

[49] On Alexander's Pothos, cf. Victor Ehrenzweig, *Alexander and the Greeks* (Oxford, 1938),
52–61; and the Appendix on "Pothos" in Fritz Schachermeyr, *Alexander der Grosse* (Vienna,
1973), 654ff.
[50] Justin, XV, 4.

Chandragupta established himself in the new power vacuum with the help of northwestern tribes and then descended on the kingdom of Maghada; deposed the last Nanda king who, according to his account, had been distinctly unpopular; and exterminated his house. His adviser in this domestic revolution was Chanakya, surnamed Kautilya, to whom the redaction, if not the authorship, of the *Arthasastra* is attributed.[51] A critical moment came for the new foundation *ca.* 305–303. When Seleucus Nicator had established himself finally in "Asia," he undertook a campaign to recover the Indian satrapies and to penetrate perhaps deeper into India than Alexander had done. The course of events is not too well known, but it ended certainly with the Seleucid and the Maurya coming to an understanding. Seleucus received a contingent of war elephants in exchange for the recognition of the Paropamisadae, Aria, Arachosia, and possibly Gedrosia as parts of the Maurya Empire. Chandragupta received a Macedonian princess, whose precise relation to Seleucus Nicator is not known, in marriage. Megasthenes sojourned as the Seleucid envoy for some time, *ca.* 302–298, at the Maurya court in Pataliputra; and the extant fragments of his work have become one of the important sources for understanding the society and organization of the Maurya Empire.

The Maurya Empire had begun to crumble immediately after the death of Asoka in 233, but it came to its end only in 184, when a general of the last Maurya ruler, the Brahman Pushyamitra Sunga, assassinated his master. Again an imperial power vacuum was created, comparable to the earlier one, after the death of Alexander, when the Macedonians abandoned the Indian satrapies; and as the earlier vacuum had attracted the Maurya Chandragupta, so the present one invited Demetrius, the king of Bactria, to conquering action. But before this second Greek attempt at penetrating India can be sketched, a word on the kingdom of Bactria is necessary.

In the Bactrian satrapy of the Seleucid Empire, Euthydemus of Magnesia had become the founder of an independent dynasty. The prehistory of the dynastic independence is not too clear. As much as can be discerned, thanks to the brilliant analysis of numismatic and literary sources by W. W. Tarn, the satrapy had always enjoyed a privileged status as the eastern shield of the

---

[51] All dates are insecure. I am following the reconstruction of the Maurya chronology by P. H. L. Eggermont, *The Chronology of the Reign of the Asoka Morya. A Comparison of the Data of the Asoka Inscription and the Data of the Tradition* (Leiden, 1956). Cf. Vincent A. Smith, *The Early History of India: From 600 B.C. to the Muhammadan Conquest* (4th ed.; Oxford, 1924); and Chapters XVIII–XX, on the Maurya dynasty, by F. W. Thomas in *The Cambridge History of India,* Volume I (New York, 1922).

empire against the nomads.[52] The satrap Diodotus was given in marriage a sister of Seleucus II around 246. Diodotus II, his son probably from an earlier marriage, assumed the kingship, broke with the Seleucids, and entered into an alliance witth Tiridates of Parthia. It was presumably the Seleucid queen-widow who then took matters in hand, married her daughter to Euthydemus who at the time can have been no more than a satrap of Diodotus II, had Diodotus killed and Euthydemus made king. The relations with the Seleucid ruler Antiochus III cannot have been free of suspicion, but at least the alliance with the Parthians who were the enemies of the Seleucids was ended. Euthy-demus was a ruler of unusual ability. Apparently he succeeded where Alexander had failed in achieving an amalgamation of the Bactrian native rulers with the Macedonians and Greeks, and thus laid the basis of a Bactrian power that could be used, after his death in 189, by his son Demetrius to expand the kingdom through the conquest of the Seleucid provinces in eastern Iran. In 184, with the end of the Maurya dynasty, came the great opportunity to imitate Alexander by embarking on the conquest of the India that Alexander had seen beyond the Hyphasis but was not allowed to enter.

The imponderables of the situation appear to have contributed more importantly to the success of the enterprise than the military strength of Demetrius, his sons, and his generals. For Chandragupta, the founder of the Maurya dynasty, had married a Seleucid princess and Demetrius was related to the Seleucids on the distaff side. Though this did not make him exactly the heir of the Maurya, it made him at least the most closely related dynast, if dynastic relationship was. to be counted by relationship to Alexander's successors in "Asia." Furthermore, there entered into the situation the indigenous conflict between the Brahmans and the Indian warrior caste, the Kshatriya. The resistance to Alexander in India had been organized and fought most ferociously by the Brahmans, while the Kshatriya princes had soon been willing to come to an agreement with the conqueror. Moreover, Asoka, the grandson of Chandragupta and the Seleucid princess, had been the great propagator and protector of Buddhism; and the Buddha himself, as well as Asoka, had been Kshatriya. Buddhism appears to have had its primary appeal to the Kshatriya, while the Brahmans were opposed to it. The Sunga prince

---

[52] All data and dates in the following presentation of processes which are typical for the Ecumenic Age are based on W. W. Tarn, *The Greeks in Bactria and India* (1938; 2nd ed.; Cambridge, 1951). For a more recent historical survey cf. George Woodcock, *The Greeks in India* (London, 1966), with bibliography.

Pushyamitra, who had killed the last Maurya king, was a Brahman; and the later Buddhist legend depicted him as a persecutor of Buddhism who wanted to undo the work of Asoka. The Greeks and Macedonians, however, were classified by the Indians regarding their caste status as a slightly inferior variety of Kshatriya. And finally, this time the Greek invaders brought with them an experience and technique of treating "natives" that Alexander had not possessed. All these factors must be taken into account in order to understand that the invasion of India by Demetrius met with considerably less resistance than the military strength of India could have afforded.

The plan of Demetrius emerges with reasonable clarity from its execution. The core of the Maurya Empire had been the kingdom of Maghada; it had been ruled from Pataliputra on the Ganges, while viceroyalties had been established in Taxila for the Northwest and in Ujjain for the West. Demetrius started his conquest from Bactria and had to preserve the connection with his home base. Hence, he first occupied the Northwest and took his seat in Taxila, and then let two armies advance southeast toward Pataliputra and southwest toward the coast and Ujjain. It was a pincer movement which, if it had been concluded, would have brought the "India" that was known to the Greeks through Megasthenes under the jurisdiction of Demetrius. Taxila would have been the capital, Pataliputra and Ujjain the viceroyalties. The southeastern army under Menander, the general and son-in-law of Demetrius, reached Pataliputra indeed; the former capital of the empire was in Greek hands at least from 175 to 168 B.C. The southwestern army under Apollodotus, probably a brother of Demetrius, certainly penetrated into the general area of Ujjain. But the pincers were never closed; Vidisa, the home kingdom of Pushyamitra, that was lying between the jaws of the pincers, escaped occupation.

The campaign must have been supported by something like a liberation propaganda. At least two of the princes, Apollodotus and Menander, adopted on their coinage the style of "Soter." This is a new symbolism of the Ecumenic Age. The style "Soter" had been used only twice before: once by Ptolemy I of Egypt who styled himself the Savior when he had saved Rhodes from Demetrius the Besieger; and a second time by Antiochus I when he had saved Asia Minor from the Gauls. Apollodotus and Menander must have posed as the Saviors of Buddhists from the Brahman Pushyamitra. A few years later the style of Savior was to be used against them, when Antiochus IV Epiphanes became the Soter who saved the Seleucid east from the Euthydemid princes. An age of ecumenic imperialism throws up of necessity, it appears, the curious phenomenon which today is called "liberation," *i.e.,* the replacement of an obnoxious imperial ruler by another one who is a shade less obnoxious—or at least nobody is permitted to say otherwise. In the case of Apollodotus and Menander, their assumption of the role of Saviors of Buddhism does not mean that they became Buddhists themselves. Nevertheless, the relations to the Buddhist community must have been friendly and intimate, or Menander could not have become the hero of the Buddhist legends which are preserved under the title of *Milindapanha*.

At its climax, the domain of Demetrius extended from Turkestan through Afghanistan and Belutchistan, to the Maurya "India." The conquest, however, never did come to a close, for at the latest in 168 began the campaign of Eucratides, the general and cousin of Antiochus IV, to recover the Seleucid East. The imponderables that had favored Demetrius in his advance toward India, now favored Eucratides in his attack on the Bactrian base of Demetrius. He too was related to the Seleucids, and more closely than Demetrius. Moreover, he came by the command of the ruling Seleucid king, and probably himself appointed a sub-king to deal with a rebellious usurper. The Macedonian loyalties in Bactria turned from Demetrius to Eucratides; and the strength of the Euthydemids in their relation to the native population now turned against them, for among the Macedonians and Greeks of this generation there probably could be found a good number who were quite as recalcitrant to the fusion with barbarians as were the companions of Alexander. Eucratides was another Savior, this time of Macedonians and Greeks from a ruler who favored the native barbarians. This would explain the success of Eucratides with forces which cannot have been strong. By 167 he was in possession of all territories west of the Hindukush. The Indian conquest of Demetrius and his sub-kings had to be halted. Demetrius himself returned to Bactria to meet Eucratides, was defeated and killed. Menander and Apollodotus had to abandon their advanced position, in order to meet the danger from across the Hindukush.

The chronology of the subsequent events is uncertain. At the latest in 165 Eucratides crossed the Hindukush in order to conquer India in his turn; after 163, when Antiochus IV died, he separated his destiny from the Seleucid Empire and became king in his own right; in 160 the Parthian Mithridates got involved in the events and conquered Bactria; Eucratides had to return to meet the danger in his back, and in 159 was killed in battle. For reasons unknown, then, the Parthians withdrew from Bactria, so that the dynasty of Eucratides could maintain itself in the country until the Saka and Yuechi conquered Bactria, *ca.* 130–129. South of the Hindukush, now cut off from the Bactrian basis, Menander could organize a kingdom that comprehended the

West and Northwest of India. He died *ca.* 150–145. On one of his bronze coins appears the symbol of the wheel which indicates that he understood himself as an Indian Chakravartin; and after his death the cities accorded his ashes the Chakravartin honor of Stupas. His role in the Buddhist legend has been mentioned already. He tried, it appears, to create an Hellenistic-Indian empire, with the imitation of Asoka as a strong factor in his conception. The Saka invasion of India, beginning *ca.* 120, gradually corroded the Greek possessions; by *ca.* 30 B.C. the last remnants of Greek rule in India had disappeared.

(identity which brings "redemption" Too. —

CHAPTER 3

The Process of History

The men living in the Ecumenic Age were forced by the events into reflections on the meaning of their course. The reflections of the participants in the process, then, forced the preceding studies into digressions extrapolating the issues raised. And these issues of a philosophy of history, which could be treated only incidental to the main line of analysis, must now be made explicitly thematic.

§ 1. The Process of Reality

The issue that appeared to take precedence over all the others was the problem of identity. A process has to be the process of something, but the something of which the Ecumenic Age was the process proved elusive. It could not conceivably be the history of either the cosmological empires which disappeared or of the ecumenic empires which rose in its course. It was not the history of Babylon or Egypt, of Persia, Macedonia, or Rome, of the Greek or the Phoenician city-states, of the Maurya or the Parthian empires, of Israel or the Bactrian kingdoms, though all of these societies were somehow involved in it. If the something could not be found, could history possibly be the history of nothing? Could there be such a thing as the historical process of history? The question requires serious consideration and will receive it, but for the moment we must store it away. During the Ecumenic Age itself, at any rate, the violent diminution, destruction, and disappearance of older societies, as well as the embarrassing search, by the conquering powers, for the identity of their foundations, was the bewildering experience that engendered the "ecumene" as the hitherto unsuspected subject of the historical process.

This new symbol, however, was plagued with ontological difficulties. For the ecumene was not a society in concretely organized existence, but the *telos* of a conquest to be perpetrated. In the pursuit of the *telos,* then, the ecumene in the cultural sense turned out to be much larger than expected, and the conquest never reached its goal. Moreover, one could not conquer the non-existent ecumene without destroying the existent societies, and one could not destroy them without becoming aware that the new imperial society, established by destructive conquest, was just as destructible as the societies now conquered; the whole process seemed devoid of sense. When finally enough contemporarily living human beings were corralled into an empire to support the fiction of an ecumene, the collected humanity turned out to be not much of a mankind, unless their universal status as human beings under God was recognized. And when universal humanity was understood as deriving from man's existence in presence under God, the symbolism of an ecumenic mankind under an imperial government suffered a serious diminution of status. Philosophically, the ecumene was a miserable symbol.

1. The Subject of History

The problem of identity just adumbrated was never completely thought through during the Ecumenic Age itself. The high point of its penetration was reached by St. Augustine when he discerned the movement of *amor Dei* as the existential exodus from the pragmatic world of power—*incipit exire, qui incipit amare*[1]—and, consequently, conceived the "intermingling" of the *civitas Dei* with the *civitas terrena* as the In-Between reality of history. In the construction of his *Civitas Dei,* however, he subordinated these great insights to an historiogenetic pattern whose unilinear history came to its meaningful end in the dual ecumenism of Church and Roman Empire. Beyond the dual ecumenism of his present, history had no meaning but the waiting for the eschatological events. Nevertheless, not only the insights concerning the existential exodus and the historical *metaxy* are relevant to the present analysis, but the construction of the whole as well. For St. Augustine tried to solve the mystery of meaning by attributing to certain events and societies an eschatological ultimacy beyond the meaning of their existence in the historical *metaxy,* and this attempt as a type recurs frequently in the construction of identities for the subject of history.

In the long course of Western history since St. Augustine, the problem has changed its appearance but not its structure. The contents of the Augustinian historiogenesis, it is true, have crumbled under the pressure of a vastly enlarged knowledge of history, but the symbolic form itself has survived the demise of its Christian-imperial substance; for the speculative thinkers of Enlightenment and Romanticism continued to use the form for the construc-

---

[1] *Enarrationes in Psalmos* 64, 2. For further analysis of this problem cf. the chapter on "Immortality: Experience and Symbol," in *In Search of Order,* Vol. V of *Order and History.*

tion of unilinear histories that would lead up to the imperial present of their respective choice, *i.e.,* one or the other variety of ideological ecumenism, endowed like the Augustinian dual ecumenism with eschatological ultimacy of meaning. As for the Augustinian insights concerning the historical *metaxy,* they did not fare too well. Rather than being further developed they were badly deformed by what Hegel has called the "Protestant Principle" of relocating the world of divine intellect (*die Intellektual-Welt*) in the mind of man, so that "one can see, know, and feel in one's own consciousness everything that formerly was beyond."[2] That is to say, the historical *metaxy* was perverted into a dialectical movement in the intellectual's consciousness. As a consequence of the fate that has befallen the *Civitas Dei,* we are today still in suspense between the assumption that history must be the history of something—empires, city-states, nation-states, civilizations, or ecumenic mankind—and the uneasy suspicion that the process of history cannot be predicated on societies which appear and disappear in its course. Each of the supposed subjects of the process has become suspect of being an hypostasis.

The temptation to hypostatize historically passing societies into ultimate subjects of history is strongly motivated. At its core there lies the tension, emotionally difficult to bear, between the meaning a society has in historical existence and the never quite repressible knowledge that all things that come into being will come to an end. A society, one might say, has always two histories: (I) the history internal to its existence and (II) the history in which it comes into and goes out of existence. History I is greatly cherished by the members of a society; History II encounters emotional resistance and preferably should not be mentioned. In the debate around Toynbee, this phenomenon of emotional resistance could be well observed in its more or less grotesque aspects. By developing his concept of civilizations as "the intelligible field of study," Toynbee had irritated both the national historiographers and the believers in a progressive history of mankind. The national historians felt the subject of history that is dear to their hearts threatened by its reduction to a phase in the civilizational cycle, wedged in as a time of troubles between the growth of a civilization and its end in a universal state; the progressivists were aroused by the assumption that Western civilization, distinguished in their historiogenetic speculation by the eschatological index "modern," should have to go the way of all civilizations, down to interregnum and dissolution. Moreover, the critics had comparatively easy play, because Toynbee had laid

---

[2] Hegel, *Vorlesungen ueber die Geschichte der Philosophie* (Stuttgart, 1965), Vol. 3, (*Jubilaeumsausgabe,* ed. Hermann Glockner, Vol. 19), 300.

himself wide open to attack through his own eschatological dream: The four universal religions, since they correspond to the four psychological types of Jung, would achieve a new ecumenism of globally balanced humanity. It is not difficult to diagnose the fear of life and death at the bottom of the irritation caused by Toynbee's violation of the taboo. The dreamers of a society that will live happily forever after once it has come into existence are reluctant to face the insight of Anaximander's dictum (A 9; B 1): "The origin (*arche*) of things is the Apeiron. . . . It is necessary for things to perish into that from which they were born; for they pay one another penalty for their injustice (*adikia*) according to the ordinance of Time."

2. *Anaximander's Truth of the Process*

In their exposed position of Hellenic city-states neighboring on Asiatic empires, the Ionians had ample opportunity to experience the violence of the Ecumenic Age. The Anaximandrian fragment happens to be the earliest extant pronouncement by a philosopher on the process of reality and its structure. Moreover, Anaximander's compact experience and symbolization of the cosmic process has informed the understanding of the process in the realm of society and history from Herodotus and Thucydides down to Polybius. The fragment, thus, has become the key symbolism for what may be called the tragic experience of history. I shall briefly set forth the implications of the compact text and then indicate some important points in the subsequent differentiation of consciousness.

Reality was experienced by Anaximander (*fl.* 560 B.C.) as a cosmic process in which things emerge from, and disappear into, the non-existence of the Apeiron. Things do not exist out of themselves, all at once and forever; they exist out of the ground to which they return. Hence, to exist means to participate in two modes of reality: (1) In the Apeiron as the timeless *arche* of things and (2) in the ordered succession of things as the manifestation of the Apeiron in time. This dual participation of things in reality has been expressed by Heraclitus (*fl.* 500 B.C.) in the terse language of the mysteries (B 62):

> Immortals mortals
> mortals immortals
> live the others' death
> the others' life die.

Reality in the mode of existence is experienced as immersed in reality in the mode of non-existence and, inversely, non-existence reaches into existence.

The process has the character of an In-Between reality, governed by the tension of life and death. Thus far one can go in an analytical elucidation of the texts, but no farther; any attempt at paraphrasing their meaning would destroy their compactness. On the contrary, one must beware of identifying the immortals as gods, the mortals as men, or life and death as that of human beings, or the things (*ta onta*) as inorganic objects, organisms, men, or societies, and so forth. It is true, the symbols mean all these "things"; but beyond the diversification of the process of reality in the several realms of being, and beyond the diversification of things in these realms, they compactly mean the process as the Whole, or the One, in whose structure the things existent in the realms of being participate with their diversified structures. A paraphrase would destroy an experience and truth that must be accepted in its compactness as preceding and founding all differentiated experience of the process in its variants in the realms of being, particularly in the realm of society and history.

Moreover, paraphrastic interpretations would obscure the historical stratification in the meaning of symbols. For experiences and their symbolizations are not self-contained units, carrying the whole of their meaning in themselves; they are events in the process of reality and as such related to past and future events. A paraphrase would destroy that part of meaning that accrues to symbols through their position in the history of consciousness. The Ionian truth of the process is present in the background of consciousness, when the later thinkers explore specific structures for the case of societies in history. An Herodotean formulation concerning the process of history, for instance, presupposes the "Ionian hypotheses," even though the names of Anaximander and Heraclitus are not mentioned. If, in such a case, the fact that the earlier symbolisms are connoted were overlooked, if such a passage were read as if it contained nothing but what it offers in its immediacy, its meaning would not be fully realized. Neither can Plato's analysis of the *metaxy* structure in reality be fully understood, unless the reader is as conscious of the Ionian symbolism in the background as was Plato. Hence, the compact truth of reality does not become obsolete when later thinkers explore the structure of the process in the several realms of being; on the contrary, it supplies the context in which alone the specific insights make sense. The truth of the process is historically stratified inasmuch as the later specific insights connote the earlier wholeness as the context in which the differentiating work is conducted.

Even more, the historical stratification of truth is reflected in a structure of philosophical language that has remained a constant to this day. For one still uses the symbol "things" in the sense of the Ionians, as for instance Heidegger does when he makes his careful pre-Socratic distinction between *das Sein* (*to on,* ultimately the Anaximandrian Apeiron) and *das Seiende* or *die seienden Dinge* (*ta onta*); and the work of Whitehead vibrates with the historical tension of truth, when he lets his "process of reality" gain its weight of meaning from its oscillation between the process of physical reality and the wholeness of the cosmic process. On the other hand, serious disturbances in the understanding of reality are inevitable, if and when the consciousness of the contextual wholeness is lost in the turmoil of exuberant differentiations, as it was in the wake of Enlightenment and, in particular, of Kant's epistemological skepticism. In this "climate of opinion," to be characterized as a state of public unconsciousness, it becomes incumbent on the true philosophers, who are always rare, to regain consciousness through regaining its historical stratification. The existential problem of the philosopher who finds himself in this situation was explored by Nietzsche who, in his *Schopenhauer als Erzieher,* described the problem of regaining consciousness as the task of finding the way that rises "from the height of skeptical discontent and critical resignation up to the height of tragical meditation."[3] Such personal efforts, however, have not yet made much of a dent in the climate of opinion. As the debate around Toynbee shows, the "tragical meditation" on the process of reality has by far not yet been restored to public consciousness.

3. The Field of Noetic Consciousness

Surrounded by the mysteries of Apeiron and Time, things come into being and perish. That any one of the things that come into being could stop the process and master it for ever after is an absurdity, not to be entertained as long as a man's apperception of reality is not badly disturbed. Still, however unexceptional the Anaximandrian insight may look, it has nothing to say on the inevitable question regarding its own status: Is a truth concerning the process a "thing" that appears in it? Or is the truth found from a position beyond the process? The issue of historical stratification in consciousness, previously intimated, must now be further pursued.

First, there are to be eliminated a few conventional misunderstandings. The truth of the process must not be hypostatized as an "absolute" truth. It is not a gem of classical wisdom to be pocketed as a possession forever and on occasion to be exhibited to an impresssionable audience; nor is it a cheap truth

---

[3] Friedrich Nietzsche, *Unzeitgemaesse Betrachtungen* (Werke, Leipsig, 1899, I, 1) 409.

to be used for introducing sentimental meditations on the vanity of all things under the sun; nor is it a documentary truth to be used as evidence in erudite ponderings on the pessimism of the Greeks. Regarding the third of these hypostatic abuses, a special warning will be apposite. For "pessimism" and "optimism" are neologisms of the eighteenth century which denote certain "modern" moods of existential response to reality. To apply these mood categories to Greek philosophers is an anachronism—the Greeks were not "modern men"; they were men who faced the process of reality without undue pessimism or optimism. From the rejection of the various absolutisms it does not follow, however, that now one should look for this or that relativistic alternative. None of the ideological Isms is acceptable in a critical investigation.

The Ionian discovery constitutes a field of noetic consciousness in which the thinkers advance from the compact truth of the process to the differentiated truth of the discovering consciousness. What begins as an insight into mystery and structure of the process leads on to the experience that has become articulate in the insight, and further on to its recognition as an act of consciousness by which man participates in the process of reality. The "thing" that is called man discovers itself as having consciousness; and as a consequence, it discovers man's consciousness as the area of reality in which the process of reality becomes luminous to itself. Moreover, as the field of noetic consciousness unfolds in time through a succession of thinkers, the field itself comes to be recognized as belonging to the structure of reality. The process is not an unconscious succession of "things"; rather it is structured in time by the progress of noetic consciousness. A mute process about whose meaning one could be in doubt becomes a process increasingly articulate about its meaning; and what is discovered as its meaning is the emergence of noetic consciousness in the process. The differentiating discoveries, then, engender the language symbols for their articulation: The Psyche becomes the site of conscious participation in reality; the Depth becomes the dimension of the Psyche from which new insights are drawn up; the Nous becomes the faculty of apperceptive participation in the process; Philosophy, the love of wisdom, becomes the tension of man's existence in search of truth; and so forth. Throughout the centuries in which noetic consciousness unfolds from the Ionian beginnings to the climax in Plato and Aristotle, however, the origin of the movement in the Anaximandrian truth remains alive. The differentiation of consciousness makes reality both luminous and meaningful against the background of the compact truth; it does not overreach itself into a beyond of the process. The philosophers' truth does not become a possession; it remains the truth of the search (*zetesis*) in erotic tension toward the mysterious ground of existence. The philosophers' noetic consciousness of existence in erotic tension, thus, becomes the closest neighbor to the Augustinian *incipit exire qui incipit amare, i.e.,* the revelatory consciousness of the exodus from Babylon as the meaning of existence.

§ 2. The Dialogue of Mankind

The phenomena of Greek philosophy are well known on the doxographic level. Not so well known is the constitution of a field of noetic consciousness through Anaximander's truth of the process and the historical stratification of truth in this field. And practically nothing is known about the constitution of the field as a subprocess in the larger process of the Ecumenic Age, or about its importance for the discovery of meaning in history, or about the intimate relations between existential exodus and imperial conquest. Hence, in order to lay the foundations for further analysis, it will be necessary to establish the historical stratification of truth in the noetic field of consciousness through the selection of a few representative examples.

1. Herodotus

The truth of the process imposes itself once it is discovered. But it is a compact truth of the cosmos as a whole. In order to unfold its implications, it must be recognized in its variant modes in the several realms of being. The first differentiating step to be considered will be, therefore, the transition from the truth of the whole to its manifestation in the realm of man, society, and history.

In *Histories* I, 207, Herodotus lets Croesus give his advice to Cyrus:

> If you deem yourself immortal, as well as the army that you lead, it is not for me to give advice to you. But if you know yourself man, as well as those whom you rule, know this above all: There is a wheel (*kyklos*) of human affairs which, turning, does not suffer the same man to prosper always.

The first part of the advice, the wheel on which the affairs of man revolve, corresponds to the Anaximandrian becoming (*genesis*) and perishing (*phthora*) of things. The conclusion, that the movement of the wheel will not suffer the same man to prosper always, corresponds to Anaximander's conclusion—that by perishing, things pay one another penalty for the injustice of their coming into being. The advice as a whole, thus, is modeled on the Anaximander fragment B 1.

About the earlier symbolism in the background of consciousness there can be no doubt; but the relation is not as pellucid as it might be, because the Herodotean pronouncements on the process of history are impaired by a distinct lowering of spiritual and intellectual quality. Herodotus had an eye for the wheel of human affairs, but he did not know how to cope with the Apeiron. The divine *arche* has been replaced by the conventional symbolism of immortals and mortals; and the convention has become ambiguous through its juxtaposition with the advice that derives from the Anaximandrian dictum. For the immortals of the passage are not the Homeric gods who debate and resolve on human affairs on the Olympian council; they are introduced only to be dismissed as irrelevant once they have served the rhetorical function of directing attention to the really important issue of human affairs and their fatality. But this rhetorical dismissal looks as if it were no more than rhetorical indeed. If the immortals were really to be discarded as an obsolete symbolization of the divine *arche,* then the mortals of the passage would have to become something like the immortal-mortals of Heraclitus. That, however, was apparently not Herodotus' intention. For the Croesus who makes short shrift of the immortals when he speaks in the council of Cyrus, is the same who had addressed the conqueror, when he fell into his hands: "Now that the gods have made me thy slave, oh Cyrus" (I, 89). The gods seem to have a hand in human affairs after all.

The ambiguities and inconsistencies are caused by a deformation which the truth of the process has suffered in the transition to the realm of history. In the work of Herodotus, the men who with authority pronounce on the structure of the historical process are not philosophers; they are persons like Croesus, Cyrus, Xerxes, and their advisers. These imperial entrepreneurs of the Ecumenic Age understand the meaning of life as success (or prosperity, *eutychia*) in the expansion of their power and consider every setback to be caused by the intervention of a divine super-power. In the various discussions of this imperial personnel on the possibility or actuality of disaster, the recurrent theme is the "envy (*phthonos*) of the gods." No doubt the great design of conquest would succeed, unless there was lurking in the background the divine "envy" as the limiting factor (I, 32; III, 40; VII, 10; and the conclusion of VII, 46). This "envy of the gods" is an old motif of the myth, inasmuch as the man who overreaches himself, or rises too high, the man who is guilty of *hybris,* attracts the wrath of the gods. The tragedians have used the motif more than once in this sense, as for instance Aeschylus in the great scene of Agamemnon's return (*Agamemnon,* 855–974); and Sophocles even has absolutized this wrath of the gods into the anonymous force of the Jealous (*ho phthonos, Philoctetes,* 776). But only in the work of Herodotus, in connection with the Ionian truth of the process, has it become the pervasive symbol for the shadow that falls on the splendor of royal existence. The truth of the process, thus, is preserved as far as the pattern of becoming and perishing is concerned, but the mystery of Apeiron and Time has been eclipsed by the imagery of a power tension between mortals and immortals. The reality of the process is not denied, but the "thing" called man does not participate in it with the whole of his existence. A part of man has been exempted. For man has split into a power-self that is his own and another part of his self that cannot escape participation, though its participation is experienced as a victimization by the process. If this divided self of the imperial entrepreneur is held against the two centers of the *amor sui* and *amor Dei* which St. Augustine has distinguished in the psyche, with the victim-self of the conqueror taking the place of the *amor Dei,* a serious deformation of existence can be discerned as the cause behind the deformation of truth.

In the *Histories,* Herodotus lets the historical figures be the speakers on the process of history and its structure. To what extent their reflections are indeed their own and not those of Herodotus is an intricate problem. Certainly, their utterances are not "historical" by the standards of critical historiography. The Croesus, for instance, who died *ca.* 540 introduces his advice to Cyrus with the reflection: "My sufferings (*pathemata*) have turned to wisdom (*mathemata*)" —a formulation that sounds suspiciously as if Croesus had been reading Aeschylus who lived 525–456. It does not follow, however, that the various speeches express the position of Herodotus. They may well be historical in the sense that the general conception of the process attributed by Herodotus to his figures was geographically as widespread as the Persian Empire was far-flung and had a time range of several centuries. Unless one wants to assume that the spectacular events of conquest and defeat following the expansion of Cyrus had escaped the attention of the contemporaries who were engulfed by them, some such view of the *fortuna secunda et adversa* in human affairs must have been rather common by the time of Herodotus' writing. Moreover, since the conception is general enough to accommodate such diverse concretizations as the dialogue of Xerxes and Artabanus at the Hellespont (VII, 45–53), or the letter of Amasis to Polycrates (III, 40), or the story of Mycerinus (II, 129–

33), Herodotus quite possibly has faithfully recorded a common view with its manifold variations. The reliability of the record would not be impaired by the fact that he himself shared the view, with a variation of his own.

This personal variation can perhaps be touched in the conclusion of the *Histories*, in IX, 122. There Herodotus tells the story of the Persian situation after Cyrus had deposed Astyages in 550 B.C. One Artembares counseled the victor to embark on further conquest: Persia is a poor and rugged country; one should go forth from it and occupy one of the fertile lands in the neighborhood. "Who that had the power would not so act? And when shall we have a fairer time than now, when we are lords of so many nations, and rule all Asia?" But Cyrus rejected the counsel: He warned the Persians that they could not continue to be rulers in the fertile countries, for soft countries give birth to soft men. With the loss of their warlike spirit they would fall to the rule of others. "So the Persians departed with altered minds, Herodotus summarizes, confessing that Cyrus was wiser than they; and chose rather to dwell in a churlish land, and exercise lordship, than to cultivate plains, and be the slaves of others."[4] This conclusion of the *Histories* is appended to the account of the Greek operation against Sestos, in 478 B.C., that ended the Persian Wars. In this operation, the grandson of the Artembares who had given the advice to Cyrus was killed.

Conquest is exodus, for one must leave behind what one has in order to conquer; and this expansion of existence beyond the order of existence achieved arouses the envy of the gods. This is the moral of the story. Herodotus, it appears, has shrewdly discerned the problem of a concupiscential exodus from reality under the apparently realistic surface of ecumenic conquest.

2. *Thucydides*

In the *Histories*, the mystery of the process is eclipsed by the imagery of a power game played by gods and men. Man's humanity has been contracted to his libidinous self, and the gods have shared his fate. Still, the Herodotean figures are not quite insensitive to the mystery. They know enough about right and wrong to know that something is wrong with the success (*eutychia*) of expanding power; whatever it is, this wrong attracts the disastrous intervention of the gods. Herodotus, then, has discerned the nature of the wrong as the concupiscential exodus from reality. Of the mystery, thus, at least a shudder is left.

---

[4] Rawlinson's translation.

No shudder is left in the Melian Dialogue of Thucydides. The eclipsing imagery is elevated to the rank of reality itself (V, 105):

> Of the gods we believe, and of men we know, that by a necessity of nature they rule wherever they can. We neither made this law nor were the first to act on it; we found it to exist before us and shall leave it to exist forever after us; we only make use of it, knowing that you and everybody else, if you were as strong as we are, would act as we do.

The Anaximandrian process in which the "things" participate has become the law by which the power-self acts. Even more, the process hypostatized into a law is a necessity of nature operative in the very man who commits the hypostasis: A fictitious identity of conquest with reality can be achieved by identifying reality with a humanity contracted to its libidinous self. By this game of transforming reality in the image of deformed existence, history has found the subject that can master it—at least until Aegospotami. Those who are not the subject, in this case the Melians, have the choice beween submission and massacre.

The games by which the power-self makes itself the fictitious master of history are still played today. The modern parallels of political situations in which the subject of history has identified itself come easily to mind. What needs emphasis is rather the difference of spiritual and intellectual rank. For the Athenian negotiators admit, and even stress, the horror in its starkness; they do not make the slightest attempt at smearing it over with idealisms, ideological verities, or speculative systems. It is true, they have deformed their existence and created an imaginary reality that will allow them "to do their thing," but in the background of this imaginary reality there is still the tragic consciousness of the process. They have not sunk to the untragic vileness of the ideologist who cannot commit the murder he wants to commit in order to gain an "identity" in place of the self he has lost, without moralistically appealing to a dogma of ultimate truth.

Thucydides lets his Athenian ambassadors make a special point of this starkness. They open the negotiations with the request to dispense with all pretenses of justice and honorable conduct which nobody believes anyway. They do not derive any right of empire (*arche*) from their victory over the Persians, nor do they accuse the Melians of having done any wrong. Empire is just empire, the ultimate reality (V, 89). At this point the succession of empire comes into view as the experience that causes the truth of the process to be deformed in the transition to the realm of history. The succession of empire in the Ecumenic Age—from the Babylonian and Egyptian to the

Persian, to the Athenian, to the Macedonian and the Diadochic and finally to the Roman empires—is an impressive spectacle indeed. Those who witnessed it as it unfolded could not help but become conscious of it. Herodotus was so much aware of it that he used it as the pragmatic skeleton around which he arranged his *Histories*. His Periegesis, the historical survey of the cultural ecumene known in his time, is in fact a series of digressions from the nodal points of succession that brought the regions and peoples surveyed into the ecumenic expanse of the Persian Empire. Having started from the Lydians as the neighbors of the Ionian cities, and the overthrow of the Lydians by the Persians, he formulates the principle of his construction (I, 95): "The course of my studies now compels me to inquire who this Cyrus was by whom the Lydian empire was destroyed, and by what means the Persians had become the lords of Asia."[5] And then he sets forth the succession of Syrians, Medes, and Scythians, down to the Persians, with an interesting side note on the "collection" of a number of formerly insignificant tribes into the ruling nation of the Medes (I, 101). The Herodotean observation of the phenomenon is substantially already the same as the later, more famous one in the Daniel Apocalypse.[6]

As it continued through century after century, the succession impressed the contemporaries with its daimonic senselessness. Moreover, this impression could grow so strong that it would block out all meaning of reality: From the phenomenon of succession, the senselessness expanded over all history and, beyond history, over the cosmic process as a whole. Later in the Ecumenic Age, this senselessness of all reality became so worldfillingly oppressive that the mood vented itself in the extreme responses of apocalypse and gnosis. The blackness of such extreme despair can be felt rising behind the icily controlled account of the Melian Dialogue.

3. Plato

The truth of the process has indeed constituted a field of consciousness, but the explorers of the process in the realm of history have uncovered deformations of the truth rather than its further differentiation. Since in their historiographic work Herodotus and Thucydides let the imperial entrepreneurs of

[5] On the Herodotean Periegesis, on its connection with ecumenic empires, as well as on the continuity of the problem in historiography to the present cf. Manfred Henningsen, *Menschheit und Geschichte, Untersuchungen zu A. J. Toynbee's "A Study of History"* (Munich, 1967).

[6] For the symbolism of "succession" from Herodotus to Daniel, cf. Martin Hengel, *Judentum und Hellenismus* (Tuebingen, 1969), 333. For the continuation of this problem through the Middle Ages, cf. Werner Goez, *Translatio Imperii* (Tuebingen, 1958).

the Ecumenic Age dominate the stage, this result is not surprising. For, at any time, the course of history will be hardly more than a cause of despair, if its reality is restricted to the phenomena of concupiscential exodus and succession of empire. The process cannot become luminous with meaning through a study of men who contract their humanity into a power-self and invent Second Realities for the purpose of obscuring the reality that has meaning. It will reveal its meaning only where men are open toward the mystery in which they participate by their existence and allow the reality of the process to become luminous in their consciousness. After the crippling of the truth through existential closure, it becomes the philosopher's task to heal and restore it by opening his existence to the divine ground of reality.

In the *Philebus* (16c–17a), Plato has both restored and further developed the Anaximandrian truth. Socrates introduces his exposition of the differentiated symbols with a brief reminder of their revelatory character:[7]

> There is a gift of the gods to men, so at least it appears to me. From their abode they let it be brought down by someone like Prometheus, together with a fire exceeding bright. The men of old, who were better than we are and dwelt nearer to the gods, passed on this gift in the saying: That all things that are ever said to exist have their being from One and Many, and conjoin in themselves Limited (*peras*) and Unlimited (*apeirian*).

These gods of Plato are not envious. On the contrary, they cause the light to be brought to men, to be received by those who are nearest to the gods, and by them to be passed on to mankind at large. The new Prometheus does not have to steal the fire; the exceeding bright (*phanotaton*) fire of the truth is freely given. In the symbolic form of the myth, thus, Plato recognizes the philosopher's role in history as that of the man who is open to reality and willing to let the gift of the gods illuminate his existence.

In the exegesis of his differentiated experience, then, Plato symbolizes the mystery of being as existence between the poles of the One (*hen*) and the Unlimited (*apeiron*). Where the One changes over into the Many (*polloi*) and the Unlimited into the Limited (*peras*), there arises, between the two poles, the number (*arithmos*) and form (*idea*) of "things." This area of form and number is the In-Between (*metaxy*) of the One (*hen*) and the Unlimited (*apeiron*) (16d–e). The *metaxy* is the domain of human knowledge. The proper method of its investigation that remains aware of the In-Between status of things is called "dialectics"; while the improper hypostasis of In-

---

[7] On the revelatory character of the Platonic myth, cf. the chapter on "The Gospel and Culture," in *In Search of Order*, Vol. V of *Order and History*.

[handwritten margin notes: ✓ Noetic consciousness by man himself— to wake up to the divine in his own Soul]

Between things into the One or the Unlimited is the characteristic defect of the speculative method that is called "eristics" (17a).

For Anaximander, the poles of being were Apeiron and Time. The Apeiron was the inexhaustibly creative ground (*arche*) that released "things" into being and received them back when they perished; while Time with its ordinance was the limiting pole of existence. In the differentiated truth of Plato, the One has become the cause (*aitia*) that is present in all things (30b), to be identified with wisdom and mind (*sophia kai nous*) (30c–e); the Limit, then, has moved into the *metaxy;* and to the Apeiron is left the function of an infinite and formless *materia prima* in which the One can diversify itself into Many of the "things" with their form and number. From the differentiation, there emerges the new symbolism of an In-Between reality, of the Metaxy, that receives its specific meaning from its constitution through the divine ground, *i.e.,* the Nous.

The differentiation is clear and to the point. But how was it achieved? What kind of Prometheus brought the revised edition of the Anaximandrian dictum down to Socrates-Plato? These questions will find their answers, if one remembers that the truth of the earlier symbolism could constitute a field of noetic consciousness, because it expressed a philosopher's experience of the reality in which he participates with his existence. What actually had to be differentiated from the earlier experience was the noetic consciousness implied in the compact dictum. Once the truth of man's existence had been understood as the In-Between reality of noetic consciousness, the truth of the process as a whole could be restated as the existence of *all* things in the In-Between of the One and the Apeiron.

The symbolization of the erotic tension in man's existence as an In-Between reality is to be found in the *Symposion*. In the myth told by Diotima, Eros is the son of Poros (riches) and Penia (poverty); he is a daimon, something between god and man; and the spiritual man (*daimonios aner*) who is in search of truth is somewhere between knowledge and ignorance (*metaxy sophias kai amathias*) (202a). "The whole realm of the spiritual (*daimonion*) is halfway indeed between (*metaxy*) god and man" (202a). The spiritual powers "interpret and convey things human to the gods and things divine to men; carrying prayers and sacrifices from below, the answers and commandments from above; being themselves midway between the two, they bring them together and weld them into one great whole. . . . For god with man does not mingle; only through the mediation of the spiritual powers can man, whether waking or sleeping, have converse with the gods" (202e–203a).

The truth of existence in erotic tension is conveyed by the prophetess Diotima to Socrates. The dialogue of the soul between Socrates and Diotima, reported by Socrates as his contribution to a dialogue on Eros that is a dialogue in Plato's soul, retold to friends by one Apollodorus who, years ago, had heard it from Aristodemus, who, years ago, had been present at the Banquet, is the artfully circumvallated setting for the truth of the Metaxy. For this truth is not an information about reality but the event in which the process of reality becomes luminous to itself. It is not an information received, but an insight arising from the dialogue of the soul when it "dialectically" investigates its own suspense "between knowledge and ignorance." When the insight arises, it has the character of the "truth," because it is the exegesis of the erotic tension experienced; but it does arise only when the tension is experienced in such a manner that it breaks forth in its own dialogical exegesis. There is no erotic tension lying around somewhere to be investigated by someone who stumbles on it. The subject-object dichotomy, which is modeled after the cognitive relation between man and things in the external world, does not apply to the event of an "experience-articulating-itself." Hence, the Socrates of the *Symposion* carefully refuses to make a "speech" on Eros. Instead, he lets the truth unfold itself through his dialogue with Diotima as he reports it. Moreover, he makes it a point to let his report begin with the very question that had come up last in the preceding dialogue with Agathon. The Socratic dialogue of the soul continues the dialogue among the companions at the Banquet and, inversely, this continuity secures to the preceding dialogue the same character of the "event" in which the erotic tension in a man's soul struggles to achieve the articulate luminosity of its own reality. Hence, the dialogue of the soul is not locked up as an event in one person who, after it has happened, informs the rest of mankind of its results as a new doctrine. Though the dialogue occurs in one man's soul, it is not "one man's idea about reality," but an event in the Metaxy where man has "converse" with the divine ground of the process that is common to all men. Because of the divine presence in the dialogue of the *daimonios aner,* the event has a social and historical dimension. The Socratic soul draws into its dialogue the companions and, beyond the immediate companions, all those who are eager to have these dialogues reported to them. The *Symposion* presents itself as the report of a report over intervals of years; and the reporting continues to this day.[8]

Moving dialogically in the area between riches and poverty, between

----

[8] On the parallel problem of information and event in the Gospel, cf. *ibid*.

knowledge and ignorance, between the gods and man, the soul discovers the meaning of existence as a movement in reality toward noetic luminosity. Back of this movement there shines the exceeding bright fire that accompanies the gift of the gods, brought down by the Platonic Prometheus to the men who are willing to receive it—perhaps intimating a light experience of the mystic. And in the farther background of Plato's noetic consciousness, there burns the Heraclitean fire that rules the cosmos with its movement of waxing and waning between need (*chresmosyne*) and satiety (*koros*) (Heraclitus, B 64–65).

4. Aristotle

When the soul discovers existence to have meaning as a movement toward noetic consciousness, it discovers the discovery to have meaning as an event in history.

Plato recognizes the historical field constituted by the event, and he articulated its structural points through symbols. In the *Symposium*, the philosopher who moves in the realm of the spirit (*pan to daimonion*) receives the name of a *daimonios aner*; for the man who lives in the older, more compact form of the myth he preserves the *thnetos*, the mortal of the epics; and the man who has become familiar with the new insight but resists it, he simply calls an *amathes*, an ignorant man. Though the terms *thnetos* and *amathes* were previously in use, they now acquire a new meaning through the relation of the existential types they denote to the historically new type of the *daimonios aner*. A new field of meaning thus emerges, when older or resistant types are made intelligible as compact or deformed in the light of noetic consciousness. Moreover, Plato recognized the discovery of the Metaxy as constituting a Before-and-After structure in history; the event is an epoch which divides history into two periods. In the myths of the *Gorgias* and the *Statesman*, he developed the symbolism of an intelligible advance of meaning in the process of history, marked by the irreversible appearance of the philosopher. No return is possible from differentiated noetic consciousness to the more compact forms of the people's myth. A meaning in history that was questionable or altogether wanting as long as the process was seen in the perspective of the imperial entrepreneur, thus, becomes recognizable in the perspective of the philosopher's consciousness.

The Platonic discoveries

    a) of the Metaxy as the area of reality in which the cosmic process becomes luminous for its meaning;

b) of the progression of consciousness to noetic insights as the historical dimension of meaning; and

c) of the structures emerging in the Metaxy through the progression of consciousness as lines of meaning in history

have established the vast field in which the investigations concerning the meaning of history still move today. The periods, or stages, or ages of consciousness, the *Bewusstseinslagen,* have remained the constants of inquiry even into the "eristic" deformations of the "dialectical" problems through the speculative systems of the eighteenth and nineteenth centuries.

In the sequel to the Platonic discoveries, the relations between the symbolic forms of philosophy, of the older myth, and of the Ionian symbolization of the process proved in need of further clarification. There is more than one symbolic form, because the experience of reality varies in the dimensions of compactness and differentiation, as well as of deformations through contraction of existence and fallacious hypostases. These various modes of experience require different symbols for their adequate expression, while the reality experienced and symbolized remains recognizably the same. In dealing with this issue, Aristotle discovered the relation of equivalence between symbolic forms. Two symbolisms are equivalent in spite of their phenotypical differences, if they refer recognizably to the same structures in reality.

Aristotle identified the search for the divine ground as the reality symbolized by the various forms under consideration. Going back to Anaximander's B 1, as Plato did in the *Philebus,* Aristotle gave his rendering, both paraphrastic and argumentative, of the truth that had constituted the field of noetic consciousness. In *Physics,* III, 4 (203b7ff) he stated:

> Everything either is the beginning (*arche*) itself or is from the beginning. Of the Unlimited (*apeiron*), however, there is no beginning, or else it would have a Limit (*peras*). As far as it is a beginning, furthermore, it is ungenerated and imperishable, for whatever is generated of necessity must come to an end and there must be an end to every perishing. Therefore, as we say, it has no beginning (*arche*) but is itself the beginning of all things, embracing and governing all things as those thinkers declare who accept no other causes (*aitias*) besides the Apeiron, such as mind (*nous*) or love (*philia*). And this (Apeiron) is the Divine (*to theion*), for it is immortal and imperishable, as Anaximander and most of the natural philosophers (*physiologoi*) maintain.

The passage is of special value for the present analysis, because it does not merely enumerate philosophical "positions" but enters into the "dialogue"

that leads from the Anaximandrian compactness to the differentiating symbols of Democritus, Anaxagoras, Empedocles, Plato, and Aristotle himself. In
the primary experience of Anaximander, the divine mystery of the process
in which things come into being and perish was still intact, so that the Apeiron
in its character of an *arche* could still be translated, without hesitation, as the
"origin" of all things. In the post-Sophistic passage of Aristotle, the *arche*
must be translated as "beginning," because the experiential accent now falls
on the things as they exist in time, so that the Apeiron is pushed into the
position of an odd sort of reality which has no beginning in time but is the
beginning of itself. The Apeiron is no longer the unquestioned presence of
the divine in the compact experience of the process; its quality of a divine
ground of things must rather be argumentatively deduced, through negation,
from the "real" things that have a beginning and end in time. The situation
is in the making in which the so-called proofs for the existence of God appear
necessary. Besides the model of "things-in-time" there makes itself felt, furthermore, the experiential accent on the form-matter constitution of things. Under
the dominance of this second model, the Apeiron is pushed in the direction of
a *materia prima,* as in the so-called "materialism" of Democritus. This pressure
on the Apeiron in the direction of matter, then, can motivate the introduction
of a second *aitia* that will act formatively on the supposedly formless inertia
of matter, such as the *nous* of Anaxagoras. The introduction of a second *aitia,*
however, deprives the Apeiron of its quality as the "originating" *arche* which it
has in the truth of Anaximander, so that the debate arrives at the tension of
the process between the One and the Unlimited in the *Philebus* passage. In
brief, the great "dialogue" about the causes is on the way to its climax in the
Aristotelian recognition of the *prote arche* as the divine Nous. The search of
the divine ground, thus, is indeed recognizable as the constant in the symbolisms from the *physiologoi* of the sixth to the *philosophoi* of the fourth
century; from Anaximander to Aristotle, the divine ground, *to theion,* moves
from the Apeiron to the Nous. The force that pushes the "dialogue" on its
differentiating course is supplied by the experiential accents on the various
models of reality—on the things that exist in time, on the things that consist
of form and matter, and ultimately on the thing that has consciousness. The
"dialectical" advance through the phenomena of the Metaxy loosens the compactness of the early truth and permits the divine *arche* to be discerned as the
divine Nous that is present in man's search of the ground.

Consciousness is the area of reality where the divine intellect (*nous*) moves
the intellect of man (*nous*) to engage in the search of the ground. Aristotle

has carefully analyzed the process in which the divine and human intellect (*nous*) participate in one another. In his language, man finds himself first in a state of ignorance (*agnoia, amathia*) concerning the ground (*aition, arche*) of his existence. Man, however, could not know that he does not know, unless he experienced an existential unrest to escape from his ignorance (*pheugein ten agnoian*) and to search for knowledge (*episteme*). Since a general term, corresponding to the later *anxiety,* did not yet exist in the Greek of the classic philosophers, Aristotle must characterize this unrest through the more specific terms *diaporein* or *aporein* which signify the asking of questions in a state of confusion or doubt. "A man in confusion (*aporon*) or wonder (*thaumazon*) is conscious (*oietai*) of being ignorant (*agnoein*)" (*Metaphysics,* 982b18). From this restlessness in confusion arises the desire of man to know (*tou eidenai oregontai*) (980a22). In the restless search (*zetesis*) for the ground of being (*arche*), then, there must be distinguished the components of desiring (*oregesthai*) and knowing (*noein*) the goal and, correspondingly, in the goal (*telos*) itself the aspects of an object of desire (*orekton*) and of an object of knowledge (*noeton*) (1072a26ff). The search, thus, is not blind; the questioning is knowing and the knowing is questioning. The desire to know what one knows to desire injects internal order into the search, for the questioning is directed toward an object of knowledge (*noeton*) that is recognizable as the object desired (*orekton*) once it is found. Or, as Aristotle phrases it, the object of the search, the *noeton,* is present in the search as its mover. "The mind (*nous*) is moved (*kineitai*) by the object (*noeton*)" (1072a30). The search from the human side, it appears, presupposes the movement from the divine side: Without the *kinesis,* the attraction from the ground, there is no desire to know; without the desire to know, no questioning in confusion; without the questioning in confusion, no knowledge of ignorance. There would be no anxiety in the state of ignorance, unless anxiety were alive with man's knowledge of his existence from a ground that he is not himself.

"Thought (*nous*) thinks itself through participation (*metalepsis*) in the object of thought (*noeton*); for it becomes the object of thought (*noetos*) through being touched and thought, so that thought (*nous*) and that which is thought (*noeton*) are the same" (1072b20ff). In the exegesis of the search that I have just reproduced, the human participates in the divine and the divine in the human Nous. Since Aristotle uses the symbol *metalepsis* to signify this mutual participation in the event of the process becoming luminous, it will be appropriate to characterize the noetic exegesis of man's existence, as well as the symbols engendered by it, as events belonging to the realm of metaleptic reality.

The symbolisms that appear in the philosophers' dialogue are equivalent in spite of their phenotypical differences, because they express the same reality in various modes of compactness and differentiation. The reality that remains recognizably the same is the search of the ground (*aitia, arche, prote arche*). In his *Metaphysics*, Aristotle extends the relation of equivalence beyond the manifold of the philosophers' symbols to include the symbols developed by the mythopoets, in particular by Homer and Hesiod. The Socrates of the *Theaetetus* had observed that the experience (*pathos*) of wondering (*to thaumazein*) is the mark of the philosopher. "Philosophy has indeed no other beginning (*arche*)" (*Theaetetus*, 155d). Aristotle resumes the observation but acknowledges the *thaumazein* as a general human possibility. Everybody's existence can be disturbed by the *thaumazein*, but some express their wondering through the myth, some through philosophy. By the side of the *philosophos*, therefore, stands the *philomythos*—a neologism which our philosophical language unfortunately has not preserved—and this "*philomythos* is in a sense a *philosophos*, for the myth is composed of wonders (*thaumasion*)" (*Metaphysics*, 982b18ff). The linguistic thread that leads from the *thaumasia* of the myth to the generally human *thaumazein* in which philosophy originates, then, is spun further into the reflection that the philosopher, though he has no use for the *thaumasia* of the myth, has a wonder (*thaumaston*) of his own in the happiness he experiences when he is engaged in his theoretical action (1072b26). Though the philosopher, once noetic consciousness has been differentiated, cannot accept the gods of the myth as the *arche* of things, he can understand what Homer and/or Hesiod are doing when they trace the origin of the gods and all things to Uranus, Gaea, and Okeanos: For by their theogonic speculations they are engaged in the same search of the ground as Aristotle himself (*Metaphysics*, 983b28ff).[9]

For obvious reasons, one will hardly ever encounter the name of Aristotle in twentieth-century debates on meaning in history. For the line of meaning that emerges from the Platonic-Aristotelian exploration of noetic consciousness is the dialogue of mankind on the divine ground of existence, consciously conducted in the Metaxy, in the metaleptic reality in which *to theion* is the moving partner. The modern climate of opinion, on the contrary, is dominated by the

[9] For the further study of the problem of equivalences, cf. the chapter on "Equivalences of Experience and Symbolization in History," in *In Search of Order*, Vol. V of *Order and History*.

equally conscious revolt against the dialogue. Ever since the eighteenth century, this revolt has expressed itself by means of imaginary histories, created
from the position of a contracted or alienated self. That is not to say, however,
that the relation of equivalence no longer applies, for the revolt is quite
articulate regarding its purposes and, therefore, recognizable as such by its
construction of immanentist counter-grounds to the divine ground of existence, such as the positive consciousness of Comte, or the dialectical consciousness of Hegel, or the *Produktionsverhaeltnisse* of Marx. The search of
the ground, thus, remains recognizable as the reality experienced even in the
modes of deformation. However much the symbolisms of deformation may
express existence in untruth, they are equivalent to the symbolisms of myth,
philosophy, and revelation. In particular, one should remember Plato's characterization of "eristic" speculation as the fallacy of hypostatizing this or that
piece of In-Between reality through identification with the One or the Apeiron.
These fundamental possibilities of "eristic" hypostasis are prototypically represented by Hegel's blending of the Metaxy into the One and by Marx's
blending of the Metaxy into the "matter" of the Apeiron. Moreover, both
thinkers characteristically pervert the meanings of terms when they let the
symbol "dialectics" signify what in philosophical language is called "eristics."

The modern obsession with deforming reality through the contraction of
man's humanity into the libidinous self, through the murder of God, and
through the refusal to participate in the dialogue of mankind in which God
is the partner, can hardly be realized in its full violence, unless it is contrasted
with the great openness of the classic philosophers. Aristotle, it is true, did
not accept the gods of the myth as the *arche* of things, but from his last years
there is extant the fragment of a letter: "The more I am by myself and alone,
the more I have come to love myths." A "modern age" in which the thinkers
who ought to be philosophers prefer the role of imperial entrepreneurs will
have to go through many convulsions before it has got rid of itself, together
with the arrogance of its revolt, and found the way back to the dialogue of
mankind with its humility.

§ 3. Jacob Burckhardt on the Process of History

When the process of reality becomes luminous, a line of meaning appears
in history. But no more than that. Noetic consciousness does not stop the
process in which it is an event. The process goes on; and the new luminosity,
if anything, makes its mystery more tantalizing than ever. Hence, the fire

exceeding bright must not be used to obscure the darkness that comprehended it not.

These observations would have appeared all too obvious to the people of the Ecumenic Age, especially to the philosophers who differentiated noetic consciousness. In our time they need emphasis, for the lights of the various speculative systems which dominate the public unconscious are used precisely for the purpose of obscuring the reality of the process and of pretending that it can be stopped. It will be apposite, therefore, to refer to Jacob Burckhardt, one of the rare modern historians who has faced the issue and analyzed it.

In his 1868 lectures *On the Study of History,* Burckhardt reflected on the conventional judgments that weigh progress in history against the price to be paid for it in human misery. "The greatest example is the Roman empire . . . accomplished through the subjection of Orient and Occident with immeasurable rivers of blood. Here we discern, on a large scale, a world-historical purpose, obvious at least to us: The creation of a common world-culture, making possible the expansion of a new world-religion, both to be passed on to the Germanic barbarians as the future cohesive force of a new Europe" (263).[10] Such weighing, he decides, though suggestive, is not permissible, because it rests on the fallacy that world-history is performed for the benefit of the person who indulges in the weighing. "Everybody considers his own time to be, not one of the many passing waves, but the fulfillment of time. . . . All things, however, and we are no exception, exist not for their own sake but for the whole past and the whole future. . . . The life of mankind is a whole; its temporal and local vicissitudes appear as an up and down, a fortune and misfortune, only to the weakness of our understanding; in truth they belong to a higher necessity" (259f). The formulations are deceptively mild, but behind them stands Burckhardt's hard insight into the existential motivation of such weighing: It is "our profound and most ridiculous selfishness" (259). The suffering of the many is treated as a "passing misfortune"; one refers to the undeniable fact that periods of lasting order are, in most cases, the sequels to atrocious struggles for power; and one belongs, by one's own existence, to an historical present that has been gained from the suffering of others (259). The profound methodological debates about the history that has to be written anew by every generation from the position of its own present,

---

[10] Jacob Burckhardt delivered his lectures, *Ueber Studium der Geschichte,* in the winter of 1868 and repeated them in the winter of 1870/71. His notes were edited and published by Jakob Oeri, in 1905, as *Weltgeschichtliche Betrachtungen.* The page references in the text are to the Kroener edition by Rudolf Marx.

and about the "values" of historians which determine different conceptions of history, are wiped out by Burckhardt's insight into their existential root in "our profound and most ridiculous selfishness." The suffering is real and so are the violators who inflict it on the victims. This violence is evil; and it does not become less evil, if a power situation that has been created by such evil is taken into the cure by better men, so that in the end mere power is "transformed into order and law" (263). Still, Burckhardt does not indulge in "pessimism." He has an eye for ages, peoples, individuals, who destroy the old and make room for what is new without being capable of a happiness of their own. "Their renovative power has its source in a permanent discontent that is bored by every achievement and presses onward toward new forms" (262). One is reminded of the Herodotean insight into the concupiscential exodus. Nevertheless, such restless striving, however important its consequences, still has the form of "the most unfathomable human egoism, which imposes its will on others and derives its satisfaction from their obedience, even though no obedience and veneration are enough for its taste and it will permit itself every act of violence" (262). Moreover, Burckhardt can imagine worse things than the evil of egoistic violence: "The domination of evil has a high significance, for only if there is evil there can be disinterested goodness. It would be an unbearable spectacle, if on this earth goodness were consistently rewarded and evil punished, so that evil men would start to behave respectably as a matter of rational caution; for they still would be around, evil as they are. One might want to pray Heaven to grant impunity to the evil, so that they would appear again in their true character. There is enough hypocrisy in the world as it is" (264). Burckhardt, thus, accepts the Anaximandrian truth of the process in the fullness of its mystery. Neither will he deny to ecumenic empires and religions the meaning of an intelligible advance in the self-understanding of humanity, nor will he justify evil as a means to the end of the advance. If you ask people, he observes ironically, they are rarely interested in a renovation of the world, if it is to be brought about by their extermination and the immigration of barbarian hordes. And then again uncompromisingly: "Becoming and perishing are the general fate on this earth; but every true single life that is cut short before its time by violence, must be considered irreplaceable, and even not replaceable by another just as excellent" (267f).

Burckhardt's uncompromising stance was necessary in opposition to a climate of opinion in which nonsense, both hypocritical and illiterate, on the issue abounded; and today it is even more necessary than it was a hundred years ago. And yet, if this were to be the last word in the matter, it would reduce the mystery of the process to the alternatives of stagnant goodness and criminal progress, something like the Platonic alternatives of a polis for pigs and the feverish polis. Moreover, it would create the illusion of a choice where no choice exists and, thus, foster precisely the vulgarity of moralistic egoism which Burckhardt detested most. Hence, one must distinguish with some care between the two lines of thought that in his reflections intersect.

There is, first, the line of attack on the "egoists" who want to appropriate history and its meaning to a situation of their preference. All speculative constructions of "world-history," whether of St. Augustine, or Hegel, or of the progressivist thinkers, are brushed aside as "impertinent anticipations." For "Eternal Wisdom" has not informed us about its purposes. The "philosophies of history" which pretend to a knowledge of the "world-plan" are not unprejudiced but "colored by ideas which the philosophers absorbed when they were three or four years old" (5). Setting aside the hyperbole, the passage is important, because it puts the finger on the strain of infantilism in the public unconscious of our time. What Burckhardt criticizes is the attempt to construct a meaning of history from the position of what I have previously called History I, for such constructions have the purpose of obscuring History II—that is to say, the reality of the process in which the phenomena of History I are no more than "passing waves." He wants to eliminate the fallacy of identifying subjects of history by endowing a phenomenon in History I with an eschatological index.

In his second line of thought Burckhardt is concerned with the reality of the process as it presents itself to the thinker once the deforming constructions of meaning are removed. In his attempt, however, he encounters certain difficulties. For the deformations of reality through speculative "philosophies of history" cannot simply be thrown out. They are also events in the process; and any categorization of historical phenomena will have to be general enough to include the deformations as intelligible events. Burckhardt was aware of this problem; as the passages quoted have shown, he uses the category of "egoism" or "selfishness" to characterize both the violent conqueror and the violent constructor of world-historical meaning. But "egoism" as an existential category, though it carries conviction because of its generally correct intent, does not have sufficient analytical weight as a concept. "Egoism," like "optimism," "pessimism," "nihilism," "altruism," and so forth, belongs to the new-speak of Enlightenment; and while it makes good sense in the self-articulation of a subjectively deformed existence, one hesitates to use it in critical language.

To dispose of Napoleon's conquest and Hegel's system as two manifestations of "egoism" is not quite satisfactory, even if the characterization is not all wrong.

The difficulty encountered by Burckhardt is the generally unsatisfactory state of noetic analysis. The great issues of existential maturity and immaturity, formation and deformation, primitivism, infantilism, imbalance, escapism, and so forth, are badly neglected, because in the modern climate of "secularization" (a polite word for "deculturation"), the questions of "ethics" or "morality" have separated from the structures of existence. In the ethics of the Ecumenic Age, they belong together. The issue of Aristotle's *Ethics* is not "morality" but the standard of conduct set by the existentially mature man, by the Aristotelian *spoudaios*. The analysis of ethical and intellectual virtues does not constitute a realm of autonomous insights but is dependent for its truth on the existential virtues of *dikaiosyne, phronesis,* and *philia;* that is to say, on their real presence in somebody's existence, as well as on the careful analysis of this reality. The virtues make no sense, unless they are understood as the trained habits (*hexeis*) of the man who consciously forms himself by the erotic tension toward the divine ground of his existence. Moreover, when Plato and Aristotle develop the meaning of mature existence as the practice of dying and of immortalizing (*athanatizein*), they are fully aware that a society is not a community of "mature men" but a manifold of "people," a Plethos among whom the mature men are always a minority and rarely a dominant one. The Plethos is a vast field of diverse existential types: adults and youngsters; men, women, and children; peasants, artisans, workers, businessmen, soldiers, and officials; artists, poets, and priests; soothsayers, rhetoricians, and sophists; the poor and the rich; and, not to forget, the "slaves by nature." The virtues of the mature man, while providing the standard of humanity, are not expected to be the virtues of everybody in the Plethos; both Plato and Aristotle even tentatively project a plurality of ethics for various fundamental types. This vast field of existential types and their problems is today obscured by the apocalyptic dream of one "morality" for a community of men who are all equal. This dream, however, is the syndrome of a serious deformation of existence, and its social predominance has consequences: Ethically, the dream is one of the important causes of contemporary disorder, both personal and social; intellectually, the fact that the Plethos does not live up to the apocalypse is an inexhaustible source of surprise for the dreamers. The damage inflicted on the intellectual and ethical virtues by the moralistic apocalypse is further aggravated by a "psychology" that eclipses the problems of metaleptic reality by the phantasy of a world-immanent "psyche." The treatment of the concupiscences as biological urges, the construction of a materialistically conceived libido which is in need of sublimation, of a doctrinaire ego and superego that have to eclipse the tensions of existence, of a personal unconscious which is not so unconscious that its contents cannot be made conscious by psychologists, of a collective unconscious loaded with "archetypes" that once upon a time, before the psychologists put them down there, were the conscious symbolizations of metaleptic reality—these are some of the items from the long list of imaginative constructions which serve the common purpose of making the In-Between structure of existence unrecognizable.

Nevertheless, in spite of such strenuous efforts to deform humanity by pushing metaleptic consciousness into the unconscious, reality asserts itself through the dialogue of mankind conducted by historians and philosophers. It proved possible to relate Burckhardt's remark on the "permanent-discontent" to the Herodotean conception of the concupiscential exodus. Conquest is not merely "evil," it is not merely a manifestation of "aggressiveness." While the most obvious strain in conquering expansion is the "violence" and "selfishness" which Burckhardt stresses, there is also in it the strain of "boredom" and "discontent" with every achievement and of imaginative enterprise that will assuage the unrest. The release of the tension on the line of ecumenic conquest and mass murder, though it is a derailment from existential order, is still an act of imaginative transcendence. The concupiscential exodus of the conqueror is a deformation of humanity, but it bears the mark of man's existential tension just as much as the philosopher's, or the prophet's, or the saint's exodus. The structure of the Metaxy reaches, beyond noetic consciousness, down into the concupiscential roots of action.

§ 4. EXPANSION AND RETRACTION

The relation between the concupiscential and the spiritual exodus is the great issue of the Ecumenic Age. In the present section, I shall survey the changes of ecumenic consciousness induced by the experience of conquering expansion and the limits put on the unlimited drive by the structure of reality. The outcome is a peculiar retraction of ecumenism, inasmuch as the symbolism retains the pretense of unlimited expansion while it accepts the actual limitation. The concupiscential exodus has to retract into the embarrassing consciousness of a non-ecumenic ecumene, of a limited unlimited. The experience of this untenable result prepares the situation in which the ecumenic rulers become ready to associate their empire with an ecumenic religion, in order to channel the meaning of a spiritual exodus into a concupiscential expansion that has become flagrantly nonsensical.

1. The Pseudo-Aristotelian De Mundo

During the five hundred years from Herodotus to the writings collected in the New Testament, the Greek word *oikoumene* has accumulated the variety of meanings which I have distinguished, through adjectives, as the "cultural," the "pragmatic," the "jurisdictional," the "spiritual," and ultimately the "metastatic" ecumene. The changes of meaning are not haphazard; rather, they mark the advance from a compactly mythical to a differentiated noetic and revelatory consciousness of cosmic reality, under the pressure of a desire to know and of new knowledge acquired that intensifies the desire. The inner connection between apparently disparate phenomena through a "desire" that urges on to its more successful realization was commonly known in the Ecumenic Age through a variegated literature for the information of an educated public. In the pseudo-Aristotelian *De Mundo,* an Open Letter to Alexander, written by an unknown author, *ca.* 50 B.C., one can read (391a8–13):

> As it proved impossible to reach the heavens by the body, or to leave the earth behind and explore the heavenly regions, as once the Aloadae designed in their folly: So by means of philosophy, taking the Nous as its guide, the soul went beyond its border and left its home behind, having found a path that will not fatigue, for it can bring together in thought the things widely distant in space.

The anonymous author of this passage displays a Nietzschean touch in smelling out the "will to power" as the source of energy that moves the giants to pile Pelion on Ossa and the philosopher to engage in the search of the divine ground. But when he reduces the difference between concupiscential and spiritual exodus to a question of instruments (the soul succeeding where the body fails) and overlooks the existential revolt in the one case and the acceptance of existence in the Metaxy in the other, when he flattens the experience of Metalepsis to a transcendence by which the soul leaves itself behind, he betrays the fundamentalist tendency to transform the symbols engendered by an experience of participation into doctrinal results that can be elegantly formulated by a good stylist. He conceives the philosopher indeed as a man who is privileged to apprehend the things divine (*ta theia*) and unenviously (*aph-*

thonos) reveals them (*propheteuousa*) to mankind, so that everybody can participate in his privilege (391a15–18).[11]

The conception is fascinating, because here one can observe in the making something like an inverted ladder of perfection: From the unenvious gods of Plato and his "Prometheus" who brings the truth, one descends to the unenvious philosopher, and further down to the unenvious author of *De Mundo* who casts the philosopher's "results" in a pleasing form for general enlightenment. On this ladder, inevitably, not only the truth of reality descends from its luminosity in the philosopher's noetic consciousness to the opacity of propositional knowledge that can be possessed by everybody, but also the quality of a god. Having graciously raised the philosopher to the rank of an *aphthonos* who dispenses truth like the gods, only at one remove, the literary popularizer himself becomes a little god at second remove who dispenses truth about the divine ruler of the cosmos on the same level of propositions as an information about the arctic and antarctic poles of the physical universe or about the probable configuration of land and sea on earth. A sacredness of contents, deriving from the fire exceeding bright in Plato's metaleptic consciousness, thus, enters into an unholy alliance with the giants' enterprise of transforming the mystery of reality into a human possession of enlightened knowledge. In *De Mundo,* this hybrid of truth and power does not yet fully actualize its explosive potential, because the weight of the mixture still lies with the sacred contents. There can be no doubt about the cosmic piety of the author, or about his genuine desire to propagate what he considers to be the truth of philosophy. The great explosion will occur only when the philosopher's truth as the substratum of propositional propaganda is replaced by the truth of the revolt against metaleptic consciousness in both its noetic and revelatory forms, as it happened in the eighteenth century. A comparison, under this aspect, of *De Mundo* with Condorcet's *Esquisse* would prove instructive.

Still, an explosion of sorts occurs even in *De Mundo* when, in Chapter VI, the anonymous author draws the famous parallel between the governance of the cosmos and the governance of the Persian Empire. The author's con-

---

[11] For the cultural context of *De Mundo,* and for the controversy about its date, cf. the translation and comments in A.-J. Festugière, *La Révélation d'Hermès Trismégiste,* Vol. II: *Le Dieu Cosmique* (3rd ed.; Paris, 1949), 460–520. Festugière's translation sometimes takes paraphrastic liberties, as for instance in the passage 391a8–13 quoted in the text. It seems to have been influenced by the eighteenth-century translation by the Abbé Batteux, *Lettre d'Aristote a Alexandre, Sur le Système du Monde* (Paris, 1768). The translation by D. J. Furley in the edition of the Loeb Classical Library is reliable, though it does not always do justice to the rhetorical smoothness of the original. The translations in the text above are my own. For the dating of *De Mundo* I have followed Furley's suggestion in the Loeb edition.

ception of the cosmos rests substantially on the Aristotelian combination of a geometrical view in which the earth is placed at the center of the cosmos, with an essential view in which the source of order in the cosmos is placed at its periphery. By an ancient tradition common to all men, he says, all things are from and through God who is the *aitia* that holds the whole together; this God, furthermore, is called supreme (*hypatos*), because his abode is at the highest and first place of heaven; and his ordering power, finally, pervades everything, but is apprehended most immediately in the movement of the celestial bodies as they are nearest to him, while terrestrial affairs appear to be full of discord and confusion as the earth is farthest removed from him (397b13–398a6). Since a cosmic order that decreases as the spatial distance from the divine source increases must have appeared somewhat peculiar, the author proceeds to make it plausible by comparing the peculiarity to the diffusion of order from a royal center in an empire. The king himself in Susa or Ecbatana "is invisible to all," living in a marvellous palace with walls of gold, electrum, and ivory; he is surrounded by layers of guards and officials and intelligence personnel, so that the Master and God (*despotes kai theos*) can learn about everything and issue his orders accordingly; the vast empire of Asia (*arche tes Asias*), extending from the Hellespont to the Indus, then, is divided into regions under governors, and so forth, so that the will of the Great King pervades the whole realm to its limits, even though the ruler cannot give his personal attention to the distant things himself (398a6ff). The empire, of course, must not be expected to work as well on the whole as the greater polis of the cosmos (400b27), for the pre-eminence (or majesty, *hyperoche*) of a king is not that of God; but with due regard for the difference, one must not lose one's sense of proportion, for the distance from a lowly subject to the king is as great as the distance from the king to God (398b3). The king, thus, is a being halfway between the lowly subject of empire and the God of the cosmos. The giants still have not reached heaven, but at least they have raised themselves as heaven-high above their victims as heaven is above the imperial giants.

The construction of the imperial giant closely resembles the earlier construction of the philosopher as a being halfway between such creatures as write *De Mundo* and the gods who are the original dispensers of truth. The philosophers and kings who are intermediate between man and god are a far cry from the Platonic philosopher-king. A new type of "In-Between existence" emerges in the process of history, when noetic consciousness is corroded by servility to power. Philosophy, the author declares, should not think "small" (*mikron*), but "greet the most excellent men with gifts worthy of them," such as the Open Letter to Alexander (391b7-8).[12] Moreover these constructions and declarations are not pardonable slips of an otherwise philosophically minded author. On the contrary, the degradation of philosophy to an *ancilla potestatis* is firmly rooted in a remarkable transformation of the Anaximandrian truth of the process: "Of the particular things some come into being, while others are in their prime, and still others are perishing. The generations (*geneseis*) balance the perishings (*phthorai*), so that perishing makes it easier for the things to come into being." This economy of change, with some things ascending to power while others decline from it, preserves the system as a whole from destruction for infinite duration (397b2-8). Justice and luminosity of existence are eliminated. The existence of things is reduced to power; and the process itself is hypostatized into a powerful existent thing. The mystery of reality has been deformed into a power game by which the power of the process keeps itself in existence.

2. Oikoumene *and* Okeanos—*The Horizon in Reality*

In *De Mundo,* the cosmos has become a concupiscential existence, a sort of Moloch which devours things in time, in order to secure timeless being for itself. The noetic quality of the work is deplorable; how one could ever have supposed that such stuff was written by Aristotle is almost inconceivable. And yet, the author is animated by sincere reverence for the wonders of the cosmos, by a joyful excitement and pride in describing its marvellous composition (*systema;* 391b9) from the heaven, through the strata of fire, air, and water, down to the centrally located earth, and especially the *oikoumene* (392b21) in its configuration of land and sea. Though they do not abolish the noetic confusion, these sentiments make the concupiscential deformation understandable, inasmuch as they are aroused by the enormous enlargement of the ecumenic horizon through the action of the conquerors. The expansion of empire expands the horizon of knowledge.

The *oikoumene* described by the author is the imperial ecumene as it disengages itself from the compactly experienced ecumene of the Homeric period. In the epics, the word *oikoumene* signifies the inhabited land that rises above the water; and in this sense the word is still used in *De Mundo* when the author divides the *oikoumene* into islands (*nesos*) and continents (*epeiros*). But the Homeric earth—consisting of the Mediterranean, its islands, and the border-

---

[12] For the parallel in the relation of Hegel to Napoleon *cf.* the chapter, "On Hegel: A Study in Sorcery," in *In Search of Order*, Vol. V of *Order and History*.

ing land masses—is limited and surrounded by the river Okeanos that returns into itself, while the *oikoumene* of the author is "surrounded by the sea (*thalassa*) that is called the Atlantic" (392b23). The new ecumene, comprising the islands and continents, is itself an island in the vast sea; and beyond, out of sight, there probably lie many more ecumenes (the plural is used!) like the one that we know. The Okeanos of Homeric times has become the ocean, linguistically still distinct from the various seas (*thalassa, pontos*) which, branching off from it, indent our island ecumene (393a17).[13]

Oikoumene and *okeanos* belong together as integral parts of a symbolism which, as a whole, expresses a compact experience of man's existence in the cosmos. Man is not a disembodied psyche. His experiencing consciousness is founded in a body; this body is part of the life process through the generations; the human life process is part of the life that also comprises the animal and vegetable realms; this larger life process is founded in the earth on which it takes place; and the earth is part of the whole of reality that the Greeks have called the cosmos. The *oikoumene,* in the literal sense, is man's habitat in the cosmos.

This cosmos has spatial extension and temporal duration. But it has them in the perspective of the habitat. The cosmos is not an object in time and space; extension and duration are the dimensions of reality as experienced from the habitat inside the cosmos. These perspectival dimensions are neither infinite nor finite, but extend toward an "horizon," that is toward a border where heaven meets earth, where this world is bounded by the world beyond. In the Ecumenic Age, this experience of the "horizon" was still compactly symbolized by cosmogonic, theogonic and historiogenetic speculations, by the myth of the creation of the world, by the myth of the Okeanos as the boundary of the Oikoumene, and so forth. Moreover, the horizon is movable. As long as it is compactly symbolized through configurations in space or events in time, the boundary line can be pushed farther out in space through the expansion of geographical and astronomical knowledge, and farther out in time through the expansion of historical, evolutionary, geophysical, and astrophysical knowledge. However, though the Horizon is movable, it cannot be abolished. Even when the Horizon recedes so far that space and time become the *eikon* of the spaceless and timeless ground of being, the experience of the horizon is not "superseded," or explained away as an "illusion," for no enlarge-

---

[13] On the history of the *okeanos* symbol, cf. Albin Lesky, *Thalatta, Der Weg der Griechen zum Meer* (Vienna, 1947), especially 79ff, on Plato's conception of the world in the myth of the *Phaidon* which closely resembles the conception of *De Mundo*.

ment of the horizon carries us beyond the boundary line. It is true, though, that every such enlargement can cause a so-called "spiritual crisis," because there are always the literally minded who will misunderstand a change of the boundary symbolism under the pressure of expanding knowledge as an abolition of the boundary and, with the boundary, of its divine beyond. This is especially true for the expansion of the astronomical horizon after Galilei which has become one of the contributive causes to the vulgarian belief that man is no longer living in the cosmos but in a "physical universe."[14]

In the Ecumenic Age, the older symbolism that had to yield to expanding knowledge was the *okeanos* as the boundary of the *oikoumene*. In the time of the epics, the *okeanos* marks the horizon where Odysseus finds the Cimmerians and the entrance to the underworld of the dead (*Odyssey,* XI); it is the border of the *oikoumene* beyond which lie the Islands of the Blessed (IV, 56ff). In the epics, thus, the *oikoumene* is not yet a territory to be conquered together with its population. The experience of the "horizon" as the boundary between the visible expanse of the *oikoumene* and the divine mystery of its being is still fully alive; and the integral symbolism of *oikoumene-okeanos* still expresses the In-Between reality of the cosmos as a Whole. The historical import of the events which disintegrated the symbolism in the Ecumenic Age would be badly distorted, however, if for its ancestry one were to go no farther back than the epics. For the symbolism, while it is familiar through Homer and Hesiod, is not of Homeric or even Greek origin. The word *okeanos* does not have an Indo-Germanic root; it is a foreign word in Greek. Like *thalassa,* it belongs to the vocabulary of the sea that the Greeks acquired when they reached the Aegean. While the actual linguistic filiation of *okeanos* is uncertain, the symbolism itself is attested as old through both the Mesopotamian and Egyptian myth.[15] Gilgamesh finds Utnapishtim in the Garden of the Sun on the border of the Ocean; and in an inscription of Thutmose III (1490–1436 B.C.), Amon addresses the pharaoh:

> I have come,
>   That I may cause thee to trample down the ends of the lands;
>   That which the Ocean encircles is enclosed within thy grasp.[16]

---

[14] For the further elaboration of this problem *cf.* the chapter, "The Moving Soul," in *In Search of Order,* Vol. V of *Order and History.*

[15] Lesky, *Thalatta,* 64ff. For the continuity between the classic Greek and the Mycenaean symbolism of the *okeanos,* cf. Robert Boehme, *Orpheus. Der Saenger und seine Zeit* (Bern-Munich, 1970), especially 183ff, 286ff.

[16] *The Hymn of Victory of Thutmose III* (1490–1436), *ANET,* 374; translation by John A. Wilson. I wondered what Egyptian word could be translated as "ocean" and begged Dr. Dietrich

By the fifth century B.C., the river Okeanos had become the ocean-sea that surrounds the land mass of the ecumene and the mankind inhabiting it. Herodotus pours his scorn on the older conception: "For my part I know of no river called Ocean, and I think that Homer, or one of the earlier poets, invented the name" (II, 23); and: "For my part, I cannot but laugh when I see numbers of persons drawing maps of the world without having any reason to guide them; making, as they do, the ocean-stream to run all round the earth, and the earth itself, to be an exact circle, as if described by a pair of compasses, with Europe and Asia just of the same size" (IV, 36). How intimately the expansion of geographical knowledge is connected with the expansion of empire,

---

Wildung, egyptologist at the University of Munich, to enlighten me on the point. The following is the information graciously given by him: The Egyptian term in this passage is *šn*. This word belongs to a family of concepts whose basic meaning is "to be round, to circle around, to surround"; others are derivations with the meaning of "circumference, surrounding," "circle of the earth (orbis terrarum)." In the Ptolemaic period *šn* can have the meaning of "the sea that surrounds the Islands of the Aegean." In the Middle Kingdom it appears only in connection with other terms, such as "the great *šn*," "all that is encircled by the great *šn*," meaning the whole world. The literal meaning of the words translated as "ocean" in this passage would be "the great encircling." It goes back to the Egyptian conception of an ordered world surrounded by the primordial water, the chaos. As a derivation from this original meaning, *šn wr*, "the great *šn*," can then signify the sea north of Egypt. That the "great encircling" is a water can be inferred only from the determinative (canal or waterlines), while otherwise *šn* can also appear in the expression "all that is circled by (*šn*) the sun," which also means "the world as a whole."—Since the Greek word *okeanos* has gone through a considerable differentiation of meaning from its Homeric-Hesiodian to its later usage in geographical and imperial contexts, the employment of "ocean" in the translation of Near Eastern texts is apt to obscure the connection between horizon and death, the spatio-temporal limit of existence, expressed compactly in the early myth. Gilgamesh is not yet the differentiated discoverer or conqueror in pursuit of the ocean as a spatial horizon, but still the mythical hero in pursuit of life beyond death. The waters he has to cross, in Tablet X, are not the Ocean, as translated for instance in N. K. Sandars' edition of the *Epic of Gilgameh* (Penguin Classics, 1964), in the sense of a border of the ecumene but the waters of death beyond the world of this life. Moreover, the translation of "water" or "sea" as "ocean" will obscure the experiential equivalence with other myths in which the accents of imagery lie less on wanderings in space but rather on the battle for life and death, as in the Ugaritic myth of the struggle between Baal and Yam-Nahar (sea-river) that ends with the establishment of Baal's everlasting kingdom (*mlk. 'lmk*). G. R. Driver, *Canaanite Myths and Legends* (Edinburg, 1956), 80–81; cf. also the new French translation by André Caquot and Maurice Sznycer, "Le poème de Baal et la Mer," in *Les religions du Proche-Orient asiatique* (Paris, 1970), 388. One part of the god Yam-Nahar (sea-river) is symbolized as Judge Nahar (river). Driver, *Canaanite Myths,* 12, assumes this title to reflect "the myth that the trial of the souls of the dead before admission to the netherworld takes place on the bank of the world-encircling river or ocean." A very compact experience of horizon-death, thus, can branch out into such diversified myths as Gilgamesh's crossing of the waters of death, the battle of Baal and Yam-Nahar, the establishment of the divine kingdom over the waters of the depth as one finds it, closely related to the Ugaritic myth, in the so-called Royal Psalms of the Old Testament, and the Judgment of the Dead in Plato's *Gorgias* and *Republic*. If these fundamental equivalences and diversifications are obscured, it becomes next to impossible to recognize the same experiences at work in such modern phenomena as the quest for "revolutionary immortality" (Lifton).

as well as with imperial expeditions for further exploration of the ecumene and the ocean, can be gathered from Herodotus' own account in IV, 37ff. Starting from the original habitat of the Persians, he moves toward the sea in the four directions, following the campaigns of the Persian kings. On the occasion of Egypt, he includes the circumnavigations of Africa and the Pillars of Hercules; on the occasion of India he is handicapped, because further east the country "is void of inhabitants, and no one can say what sort of region it is" (IV, 40).

Before the Indian campaign of Alexander, the Western conception of the culturally relevant ecumene, excluding the nomad hordes in the north and the south, was still substantially that of Herodotus a century earlier. The inhabited world worth being known and conquered was the domain of the Persian Empire plus the eastern Mediterranean. If we trust the report of Herodotus concerning the ambition of Xerxes to conquer Hellas because then his terrestrial empire would be coextensive with the Aether of Zeus, the Achaemenian program of ecumenic conquest cannot have been very different from that of Alexander, setting aside that the home base of conquest had shifted from Iran to Macedonia. When Alexander expanded into India he thought that he would reach the Okeanos in the east. His late campaigns had less the character of a conquest, or even of a rational military enterprise, than of an exploration of the limits of the ecumene. Inevitably he ran into disasters due to topographical and climatic difficulties. When, after the crossing of the Punjab, India turned out to be much larger than expected, what was left of the army refused to have itself further decimated merely to satisfy Alexander's *pothos*. On the Hydaspis he had to turn back. The desire to reach the Okeanos in the east had to be scaled down to the journey down the Indus to the Arabian Sea where the Greeks encountered for the first time the phenomenon of oceanic ebb and tide. Equally disastrous proved the trek through the Gedrosian desert, on the way back from India to Susa, as well as the parallel exploratory voyage of the naval force. Where a military commander, calculating rationally as Darius had done in his exploration down the Indus, would have sent small forces, Alexander committed whole armies to destruction through unknown natural obstacles. In the genius of Alexander, the power drive of the conqueror blended with the curiosity of the explorer, and with the deadly concupiscence of reaching the "horizon," in the existential tension that is called his Pothos. Through this outburst, the ecumene as seen from the West acquired an indefinite horizon beyond the Punjab, though the actual extent of the Indian civilization area, as well as of the Far East beyond, was still unknown.

The point of present concern is the connection between the expanding knowledge of the cultural and the creation of the pragmatic ecumene. In the measure in which the imperial conquest expands, the cultural ecumene comes into view; and the discovery of a vast humanity beyond the former limits of the horizon, in its turn, not only affects the idea of mankind the discoverers are forming, but also the program of the ecumenic conquerors. How Alexander would have responded to his discovery of the eastern dimension of the ecumene we do not know because his life was cut short. But we know at least that after the disaster in the east, his eyes turned toward the Okeanos in the west, for the west beyond Sicily, and especially the Atlantic coastline of Africa and Europe beyond the Pillars of Hercules, was not too well known a part of the ecumene either. If some historians prefer to interpret the plans of the *Hypomnemata* as programs of exploration rather than of conquest they are perhaps not wrong; conquest and exploration had become difficult to distinguish even on occasion of the Indian campaign.

After Alexander, there begin the subtle changes in the meanings of the ecumenic-imperial symbols, which reflect the impossibility of making the jurisdiction of an empire congruent with the expanding cultural and pragmatic ecumene. When Alexander acquired the kingship of Asia in addition to his possessions in Macedonia, Hellas, and Egypt, he still could believe himself to have established the empire of the ecumene. The conception became shaky when the expanse of the ecumene beyond the Indus was realized; and it had to evaporate when east and west of "Asia" the Maurya and the Roman empires began to consolidate. When after the Diadochic Wars Seleucus I Nicator assumed the style of King of Asia, the transformation of the one ecumenic empire into a plurality of empires within the pragmatic ecumene had begun. The change of meaning becomes abundantly clear from the events of 166 B.C., when Antiochus IV Epiphanes celebrated the double Charisteia in Daphne and Babylon and let himself be styled Savior (*soter*) of Asia. The triumphal parade of the army and the new style can only refer to the victories of Eucratides in the east over Demetrius who had built up a Graeco-Indian empire, partly at the expense of the Seleucid eastern provinces. Moreover, 168 was the year of Pydna and in 167 the conqueror of Macedonia, Aemilius Paullus, had celebrated his victory by the great festival of Amphipolis. Hence, the historians who assume the double Charisteia of Antiochus IV to have been a counterdemonstration to Rome's victory are probably right. These parallel victories and celebrations, as well as the title Savior of Asia at this juncture, show that a division of the cultural and pragmatic ecumene had been accepted in view of the unalterable fact of the Roman rise to power. The Asia of Darius I and Xerxes found nothing in the west but a divided Hellas that did not need to be conquered to be controlled, and nothing in the east but the tribal federations and principalities of India which apparently, beyond the Indus, had not aroused the interest of the Persians. The Asia of Antiochus IV was a great power, but it was bordered in the west by Rome, which had just warned Antiochus off Egypt, and in the east by new imperial organizations that seriously encroached on the Seleucid territory. From west to east, the expanding ecumene was filling up with rival empires.

3. The Polybian Symbolism Resumed

Polybius developed his symbolism of the *pragmateia* and the ecumenic *telos* of the Roman expansion at the time of the victories of Aemilius Paullus over the Macedonians and of Eucratides over Demetrius. The question must now be considered whether the Polybian formulation of the ecumenic problem is adequate or whether it needs correction in the light of what we know today about the course of events.

In the situation of Polybius, the Hellenic victim of ecumenic imperialism, Rome dominated the scene. It is true, he knew about the events in Asia and he related the wars of Antiochus IV, but his conception of the *pragmateia* was substantially restricted by the *theorema,* by the pragmatic spectacle, as it became "self-apparent" in the Roman expansion. Though he probably had the general knowledge of Asia and India that could be derived from the Hellenistic writers, that knowledge itself was rather limited. Nobody knew more about India than he could read in Megasthenes, and Megasthenes could know no more than he could see from the court of Chandragupta. At the time, it would have been difficult for anybody to have a clear conception of the rise, extent, and fall of the Maurya Empire. Moreover, Polybius knew no more than anybody else in the West about China, or that the lifetime of the Maurya Asoka overlapped that of Ch'in Shih-huang-ti, the founder of the Chinese Empire. That there actually existed a pragmatic ecumene reaching from the Atlantic to the Pacific was not yet known in his time. While the Seleucids shaped "Asia," the Maurya rulers "India," and the Ch'in and Han dynasties "China," Polybius formulated the ecumenic problem in terms of "Rome." From his point of observation in the West, in the second century b.c., the Rome that had already conquered the western Mediterranean appeared to be destined to engulf the former Persian and Macedonian possessions which to Polybius exhausted the ecumene he really knew. That is the reason why to him pragmatic history appeared to have an ecumenic *telos*. Obviously, the deeper we penetrate into the Ecumenic Age in space and time the more inadequate the Polybian conception will prove.

These remarks on the inadequacy of the symbolism, however, cannot be the last word in the matter. The criteria for an ultimate judgment must be furnished by the experience of the "horizon." It is true, conquest can expand the knowledge of the cultural ecumene; the larger horizon of knowledge can motivate further conquest; the conquerors can transform the cultural into a pragmatic ecumene; they can further attempt to transform the pragmatic into a jurisdictional ecumene; such attempts can be frustrated for various reasons; and a plurality of imperial enterprises can spring up in the cultural-pragmatic ecumene, each retaining its ecumenic claim while coexisting with the others. All of these events, however, occur *within* the spatio-temporal perspective of reality from man's habitat in the cosmos that we have called the ecumenic "horizon," while the horizon itself can neither be reached nor transcended. Hence, the inadequacy previously characterized affects the Polybian conception of Roman destiny only as far as it anticipates events *within* the ecumenic horizon; it does not affect the symbolism as far as it expresses the experiences of the horizon and of the concupiscential attempt to reach it by means of physical conquest. The fact that the prediction of a Roman ecumene was proved wrong a century later, through the collision of "Rome" with the "Asia" of the Parthians, does not impair the truth of the *telos*. The symbolism of the *telos* remains a brilliant insight into the meaning of imperial expansion as an attempt to represent universal humanity visibly through the organized social unity of mankind in its cosmic habitat. The attempt is bound to fail, as Polybius well knew, for the concupiscence of conquest cannot reach the horizon beyond which lies the divine source of human universality, but from this very failure emerge mankind and its habitat as the site where the universality of man has to be realized in personal, social, and historical existence.

Once the consciousness of ecumenic existence has differentiated from the compact experience of *oikoumene-okeanos,* its truth becomes independent of the actual extent of an empire. At the very time when the pragmatic ecumene was still growing through the foundation of the Chinese Empire, through the migrations of the nomadic tribes set in motion by the foundation, and through the repercussions the migrations had in the West, the ecumenic drive of the conquerors retracted into the limits imposed by topographic, ethnic, cultural, military, and administrative conditions on the imperial enterprise. And yet, the self-understanding of the new empires did not revert from ecumenism to cosmic analogy, but rather advanced toward the alliance with the new ecumenic religions which, in their turn, did not hesitate to understand their spiritual insights into universal humanity as a mission to expand ecumenically. Three of the new religions—Nestorian Christianity, Manichaeism, and Islam—indeed expanded from the Near East to China, while a fourth one —Buddhism—expanded from India to China and Japan. On the other hand, the ecumenic *telos* that had been brought into focus by Polybius remained the pathos and the formative symbolism of the Roman *orbis terrarum,* undisturbed in its imperial consciousness by the existence of ecumenic empires in "Asia," "India," and "China." The ecumenic symbolism loses its formative force no more than the cosmic analogy, even though the actual jurisdiction of the empire is noticeably less than "the whole world." When the concupiscence of expansion had exhausted itself, the new ecumenic consciousness could retract, in alliance with the consciousness of universal humanity, into its function as the formative force for the societies that had emerged from the imperial ordeal. A new type of society had come into existence.

Two reflections are necessary in conclusion.

That a new type of society has emerged from the imperial turmoil of the Ecumenic Age, though not unknown, is still obscured by the unsatisfactory state of analysis and terminology. The term most frequently used to designate the new societies is "civilization." We speak of Graeco-Roman, Byzantine, Western, Islamic, Russian, and Chinese civilizations. Unfortunately the term is also used to designate pre-ecumenic societies such as the Mesopotamian and Egyptian cosmological civilizations. Moreover, it is used to designate societies characterized not by their formative experiences and symbolizations of cosmic and social order, but by the continuity of ethnic and cultural traits such as the "India" or "China" that comprehends both the pre- and the post-ecumenic societies, though obviously the "India" invaded by Darius or Alexander was not the "India" that emerged from the formation through Buddhist and Hinduist empires, nor was the "China" of the Chou period the "China" that emerged from the Han empire in alliance with Confucianism. Nevertheless, this usage can plead good sense for itself, for in more than one instance, the ethnic and cultural continuities determine the lines along which overextended, "multicivilizational" empires like the Achaemenian, the Macedonian, and the Roman break up. But then, precisely this good sense brings to mind again the difficulties caused by the "identity" of these empires which undeniably are the great formative forces of the Ecumenic Age. The dissatisfaction with such conflicting usages sometimes surfaces in remarks like Momigliano's: Toynbee "has reproached Gibbon for not understanding that the Roman empire began to decline four centuries before it was born. Indeed, Professor Toynbee maintains that the crisis of Roman civilization started in the year 431 B.C. when the Athenians and Spartans came to grief in the Peloponnesian War."[17] And finally, none of the conventional usages allows civilizational status to such phenomena as the Greek diaspora which formed the social basis for the "Age of Hellenism," or the Jewish diaspora which provided the first basis for the missionary expansion of the Gospel. I do not intend to go further into these problems on the present occasion, but it should have become clear that the "civilizations" are hypostatic "subjects of history" which obscure rather than illumine the process of history.

Second, a reflection must be made on the further fate of the ecumene as the habitat of man within the horizon of the cosmos. The expansion of knowledge regarding the ecumene did not stop with the Ecumenic Age, even though the ocean-sea remained the boundary for centuries to come. The concupiscential expansion, which at the same time was an expansion of knowledge, was resumed with the Age of Discoveries, leading ultimately to the circumnavigation of the globe. From the Mediterranean *oikoumene* bounded by the Homeric *okeanos*, the boundary was pushed back beyond India, China, and America until the physical shape of the ecumene turned out to be a sphere. If one tries to reach the *okeanos*, with its Islands of the Blessed and its entrance to the underworld, one returns to the point from which one started. The superb irony of the ecumene having the shape of a sphere that brings the concupiscential explorer of reality back home to himself, and of this sphere being situated in a cosmic horizon of infinite extension and duration, has hardly yet entered the consciousness of a mankind that is reluctant to admit concupiscential defeat. For this ultimate expansion of ecumenic knowledge forces the mystery of reality on man's consciousness with an inexorability that can no longer be veiled by pushing back the horizon through physical action. The consequences of the new state of knowledge that made the medieval image of the world obsolete were realized quite early in the so-called modern period. Regarding the global ecumene, Thomas More gently observed that all places on earth are equidistant from heaven; and regarding the cosmic horizon, Nicolaus Cusanus noted: "The center of the world coincides with its circumference," for the *centrum mundi . . . qui est simul omnium circumferentia* is

[17] Arnaldo Momigliano, "Christianity and the Decline of the Roman Empire," in Momigliano (ed.), *The Conflict between Paganism and Christianity in the Fourth Century* (Oxford, 1963),1.

God.[18] But the concupiscential exodus must go on, and since it has become a bit silly to chase around the earth, one must engineer round trips to the moon. Moreover, since the center of the cosmic horizon is everywhere and nowhere, so that again one is thrown back to the earth as the physical center of meaning, the cosmos must be dotted with a few extra-ecumenes that will inject sense into concupiscential expansion. Hence, we live in the age of other worlds than our own, of invasions from Mars, and of flying saucers.[19] Anything will do, as long as it puts off the confrontation with the divine mystery of existence.

Still, such imaginative *divertissements* are harmless compared with the renewed concupiscential drive of imperial entrepreneurs, this time of the ideological variety, to make the jurisdiction of their respective empires coincide with the pragmatic ecumene. The situation is considerably more explosive than at the time of the Roman *imperium sine fine*, for the new imperialism starts from a position of existential revolt against the spiritual order which, in the earlier ecumenic empires, aided in the process of retraction. Imperial *hybris*, equipped with enormous material means, is again let loose on the impossible task of creating universal humanity by maltreating ecumenic mankind.

[18] Nicolaus Cusanus, *De Docta Ignorantia*, Vol. I of Hoffman-Klibansky (eds.). *Opera Omnia* (Leipzig, 1932), 100.

[19] Cf. C. G. Jung, *Ein moderner Mythus von Dingen, die am Himmel gesehen werden* (Zurich, 1958; English translation, *Flying Saucers*, New York, 1969).

CHAPTER 4

Conquest and Exodus

In the Ecumenic Age, pragmatic conquest and spiritual exodus are so closely related in forming new social fields that the borderline between them tends to lose its sharpness.

Under the successors of Cyrus the Great, the Achaemenian conquest of Babylon is metamorphosed into an exodus from its cosmological form, inasmuch as the new empire is conceived as the realm of peace and justice for all men under the universal Truth of Ahuramazda. The autolouange of Darius can well be compared to the Last Words of David (II Sam. 23:1–4); and the *Rtam-Vahu* prayer of Xerxes even extends the personal order of existence under the universal God from the king to the people, for everyman is supposed to walk in the ways of Ahuramazda "with Rtam the brazmanic."

The Macedonian conquest, then, continues the Achaemenian exodus. Though many details will remain controversial, the conception of an Homonoia of mankind does not continue the cosmological form of the older empires but moves on the line from the Platonic-Aristotelian to the Pauline Homonoia. Alexander certainly tried to transform his pragmatic conquest into an ecumenic community (*koinonia*) under the divine Nous, fortified by the older symbolism of God as the father of all men.

Even more striking is this close relation between conquest and exodus in the Israelite case. There is, first, a movement from spiritual exodus to conquest, inasmuch as the exodus from cosmological form into the immediacy of a people under God is not achieved through an internal transformation of Egyptian society, but through a pragmatic exodus, the conquest of a new territory, and the constitution of a new society in history. In order to survive in the field of pragmatic power, this new society, then, has to acquire a king like the other nations, and it expands, through conquest, into the Davidic-Salomonic empire. When the vicissitudes of history have reduced the pragmatic power of Israel to nothing, however, the new society does not disappear but erupts in a second spiritual movement through Deutero-Isaiah: The exodus from Egypt must now be completed through the exodus of Israel from herself.

In this second exodus Yahweh will reveal his *kabhod* fully so that "all flesh shall see it together" (Isa. 40:5). Israel will not be reconstituted as a small territorial enclave among imperial great-powers of the cosmological type, but as the center of an ecumenic mankind under Yahweh (Isa. 55:5).

Deutero-Isaiah is conscious of his prophecy as an event that illumines the process of reality with a new meaning. From his various reflections, it appears, the new line of meaning can be construed as a sequence of either two historical or three cosmogonic phases. In the historical construction he relates the present exodus to the first Exodus of Israel from Egypt: The Israel of the first Exodus belongs to the past (Isa. 43:18–19):

> Remember not former things . . .
> I am doing a new thing—

and the "new thing" will be the deliverance (*zedakah*) of man, moving through and beyond Israel to all mankind (Isa. 49:16):

> I will make you a light to the nations
> that my salvation may reach
> to the end of the earth.

In the cosmogonic construction he interprets both the Egyptian and the present exodus as stages in the drama of Creation: In a first act, God is the creator (*bore*) of the world (Gen. 2:33ff); in a second act, he becomes the "creator of Israel" (Isa. 43:15) through Exodus and Berith; and in a third act, he becomes the Redeemer (*goel*) (Isa. 41:14) whose deliverance reaches to the end of the earth, through Israel the suffering servant. In the third and last stage, righteousness rains from the skies and the earth opens to let it sprout as deliverance, for "I, Yahweh, have created it" (Isa. 45:8). Creation, thus, is consummated only when the earth has brought forth the ecumene of liberated man. The symbolism is noteworthy, because it is the earliest known instance of history being constructed as a meaningful sequence of three phases culminating in the perfect realm. The symbolism of the third realm appears historically as one of the expressions of ecumenic consciousness.

In the final phase of Creation in which God acts as the *goel*, the prophet assigns to the ecumenic conqueror the role of God's instrument: The Cyrus who breaks the power of Babylon is Yahweh's Anointed, his *mashiach* (Isa. 45:1). With the transition from cosmological to ecumenic rule, the empire that keeps in bondage has become the empire that sets free. For an historical moment at least, the destruction of the cosmological empire lets the prophet envisage the ecumene as the social field in which his spiritual exodus can become the formative force. The line of meaning discerned by Deutero-Isaiah assumes a *harmmonie pré-établie* between the universality of a spiritual exodus and the establishment of an ecumenic field through conquest. This assumption expresses, again historically for the first time, the experience of a connection between conquest and exodus that later will recur in such famous instances as the Pauline-Augustinian connection between Roman Empire and Christianity, of the Hegelian pre-established harmony between the Napoleonic Empire in the wake of the French Revolution and Hegel's own "reconciliation" of the spirit in the wake of the previous existential "diremption," or the twentieth-century assumption of a Marxist metastatic revolution centered in the Soviet Empire.

§ 1. Exodus within Reality

The brief recall of representative instances reveals both the issue and its need for clarification. As a matter of empirical historiography there can be no doubt that the age of ecumenic empires is also the age of the spiritual outbursts that has been named the "axis-time" of mankind; nor can there be any doubt that important thinkers, Jewish, Stoic, and Christian, have experienced the simultaneity of ecumenic empires and spiritual outbursts, not as a mere coincidence but as a providential convergence of events, full of meaning for the spiritual state and the salvation of man. And yet, by its mere repetition, the sequence of the structurally equivalent symbolisms of the Deutero-Isaianic exodus of Israel from herself into an ecumenic mankind under Yahweh with Cyrus his Messiah, the Stoic exodus from the polis into the imperial ecumene of the cosmos, the Christian exodus into a metastatic ecumene providentially prepared by the imperial ecumene, the Hegelian ecumenic reconciliation and the Marxian ecumenic revolution, destroys the finality of meaning claimed by each member of the series singly. The final answer to the meaning of history has been given not once but several times too often. There is a conflict, theoretically unresolved, between the meaning which the thinkers again and again discern in the convergence of conquest and exodus, and the historical non-finality of every attempt at ecumenic finality.

The problem cannot be resolved on the level of the equivalent symbolisms, which, by their succession, make it manifest. There would be no sense in adding one more "meaning of history" to the more than enough that we have, pretending that the new one at last will be the right one. Nor would it make sense to simply throw the symbolisms overboard, for the lines of meaning *in* history, even if fallaciously hypostatized into meanings *of* history, are still there. Nor is there any profit in joining the apocalyptic peddlers of historical crises who believe the world is coming to its end if it does not come to the end they have planned for it. If these various escapes are barred, the hard core of the question raised by Jacob Burckhardt in his study on *Glueck und Unglueck in der Weltgeschichte* intrudes itself again. His analysis of "selfishness" in the construction of imperial meanings of history certainly is valid. But is it complete? Is there not something more to the construction than a fallacious hypostasis motivated by the egoism of the *beatus possidens?* Does history not really offer the nauseating spectacle of meaningful advances, which even Burckhardt does not deny, achieved through the human misery and mass murder of conquest? The question is ineluctable.

The analysis is concerned with the experience of convergent meaning as it has become conscious in the Ecumenic Age and has remained a constant in Western history ever since. An analytically valid answer can be found only by referring the symbols of conquest and exodus back to the process of reality from which they emerge and to the experiences of the process which they try to articulate.

The noetic field of consciousness in which the philosophers' debate about reality moves, was constituted by Anaximander through the previously quoted dictum (B 1): "The origin (*arche*) of things is the Apeiron. . . . It is necessary for things to perish into that from which they were born; for they pay one another penalty for their injustice according to the ordinance of time." The reality experienced and articulated in the dictum comprehends the Apeiron, the things, the relation between Apeiron and things, and the relation among the things. What has not yet become articulate as an area of reality is the noetic consciousness in which the dictum emerges as the luminous symbol of reality.

If reality is understood in the comprehensive sense of Anaximander's dictum, obviously man can neither conquer reality nor walk out of it, for the Apeiron, the origin of things, is not a thing that could be appropriated or left behind through movements in the realm of things. No imperial expansion can reach the receding horizon; no exodus from bondage is an exodus from the *condicio humana;* no turning away from the Apeiron, or turning against it, can prevent the return to it through death. Any and every gigantomachia ends with the defeat of the giants. Conquest and exodus, thus, are movements *within* reality.

Nevertheless, the symbolism of a movement which transcends reality while remaining within it is not senseless, for reality is not a field of homogeneous extension but is aetiologically and directionally structured. There is first of all the articulation of reality into the two modes of being, of the Apeiron and of thinghood, which are known to man inasmuch as he experiences himself as existing not completely in either the one or the other of the two modes but in the metaleptic reality of the Metaxy. Moreover, the two modes are experienced not as two indifferently different varieties of the genus "being," but as aetiologically and tensionally related, the one being the unlimited *arche,* the origin and ground of things, the other having the character of a limited thinghood that originates in the Apeiron and returns to it. Hence, there is a difference of rank between the two modes of being, with the Apeiron being "more real" than the things. This tension of existence toward reality in an eminent sense becomes conscious in the movements of attraction and search analyzed by Plato and Aristotle. And finally, the consciousness of tension is not an object given to a subject of cognition but the very process in which reality becomes luminous to itself. The Apeiron and the things are not two different realities in a static relationship one toward the other; they are experienced as modes of being, or as poles of a tension within the one, comprehensive reality. Reality in this comprehensive sense is experienced as engaged in a movement of transcending itself in the direction of eminent reality. Reality is in flux; and the flux has such directional structures as become manifest in the unfolding of the noetic field of consciousness from Anaximander's dictum to the philosophy of history of Plato and Aristotle.

The result of the analysis can be formulated in two propositions: (1) Reality in the comprehensive sense is recognizably engaged in a movement in the direction of eminent reality. Note: Reality as a whole, *not* the two modes of being separately. (2) Conquest and exodus symbolize enterprises of participation in the directional flux of reality. Note: Enterprises of participation, *not* autonomous human actions that could result in the conquest of, or exodus from, reality. The two propositions, together with their safeguards against fallacious deformation, circumscribe both the sense of the participatory enterprises and the limits to their sense on principle.

Beyond the insight of the two propositions lie the concrete configurations of the movement in history of which the insight itself is a part. The philosophers who articulated the insight were very much aware of their limited role as participants in a movement to which they could respond by their own differentiating action but which they could not control. Plato and Aristotle were specifically conscious of the following factors beyond human control:

(1) The noetic luminosity of participation in the movement of reality

did not emerge in the history of mankind before it emerged in the philosophers' own differentiating acts. Reality is not a static order of things given to a human observer once for all; it is moving, indeed, in the direction of emergent truth. Man's existence as partner in the movement of reality toward consciousness is not a matter of choice.

(2) Noetic consciousness emerged in the context of Hellenic culture; it did not emerge in Egypt, Persia, or Scythia. The ethnic and cultural diversification of mankind is a factor in the historical configuration of the movement, inasmuch as some ethnic and cultural contexts seem to be more favorable to the emergence of noetic consciousness than others.

(3) By the fourth century B.C., Greek historical memory had a time-span of more than a millennium. Plato and Aristotle were aware that the unfolding of the noetic field had not occurred under the more primitive conditions of the Mycenaean period; in their opinion, only the civilizational saturation of the polis, first in Anatolia, then in Attica, provided the material culture in which the philosophical enterprise could flourish. A primitive tribal village is materially too cramped to leave room for the *bios theoretikos.*

(4) Participation in the noetic movement is not an autonomous project of action but the response to a theophanic event (the Promethean light exceeding bright, the Socratic *daimonion*) or its persuasive communication (the Platonic Peitho). To this revelatory movement (*kinesis*) from the divine ground, man can respond by his questioning and searching, but the theophanic event itself is not at his command. Nobody knows why it happens at this particular time in history, why not earlier or later; why in the cultural context of an Hellenic polis, why not elsewhere; why in the civilizational setting of a city-state, why not under more rustic conditions; why at all, if it has not occurred for thousands of years in the past.

(5) The response to the theophanic event is personal, not collective. The noetic field of consciousness is not a "people" in the ethnic sense; it is not identical with any of the poleis in which the philosophers were born. It is a new social field in history, proliferating through the "dialogue" and institutionalized through "schools"; wherever it spreads, it forms a cultural stratum within an ethnic society, though this stratum may be desperately thin and ineffective. When Aristotle analyzed the problem of social order by the standards of the mature man, the *spoudaios,* he observed plaintively that there was no polis in which as many as one hundred mature men could be found. The structure of the people as a Plethos—as a manifold of men and women, old and young, of passions, occupations, interests, and characters, of inertia and alertness, of ignorance and knowledge, of intelligence and studipity, of re-

sponsiveness, indifference, and resistance to reason—is not abolished by the noetic field of consciousness. One can ascend from the Cave to the light, but the ascent does not abolish the reality of the Cave. The emergence of meaning in history must be taken seriously: The truth of the process need not emerge, if it were there already; and when it emerges, it is not a possession beyond the process, but a light that casts the process in the role of the darkness from which it emerges. What becomes manifest is not a truth on which one can settle down forever after, but the tension of light and darkness in the process of reality.

(6) Finally, and not surprisingly, the future of the process was no more under the control of the philosophers than its past. Noetic consciousness had differentiated in the ethnic and cultural context of the Hellenic polis; hence, both Plato and Aristotle were concerned with making the life of reason an ordering force in the society of its origin. They devised their paradigms of the best *Politeia* for this purpose. At the same time, however, they were conscious of the pragmatic predicament of the polis: That the polis would fall to the advance of empire was foreseen by Plato and witnessed by Aristotle. The models of the best polis were developed in the shadow of a process in which the polis itself was to be superseded by a new type of society.

The classic philosophers, thus, had no illusions about their role in the process of reality. They knew their range of participatory action to be limited to a sensitive alertness to disorder in personal and social existence, to their preparedness to respond to the theophanic event, and to their actual response. They could not control either the revelatory movement itself, or the historical conditions which enabled them to respond; nor could they affect the order of the Plethos more deeply by their response than the method of dialogical persuasion, amplified by the literary work, would allow. The only flaw apparent in this otherwise impeccable realism is the philosophers' inclination to devise paradigms of order at all for a society which they knew to be spiritually unreceptive and historically doomed. Though the flaw is seeming only, it still is an issue in the climate of opinion in which the paradigms are interpreted as "ideals" or "utopias"; and since this misunderstanding obscures an important insight into the structure of reality, the point must be clarified.

§ 2. Plato on History

The paradigms are part of the classic inquiry concerning the process of reality; their meaning is dependent on the analysis of the process in which their construction becomes possible as an historical event. If they are torn from this context, and treated in isolation under such doxographic heads as "political ideas," the misunderstanding of their construction as a manifestation of "idealism" is practically inevitable. Moreover, such treatment deforms the paradigm into the topos of the "best form of government" at large, while in the inquiry it is a model of noetic order that can be concretely realized, if at all, in the polis, but not in societies of the historically preceding types or in the historically impending type of empire. The classic inquiry, though it is motivated by the emergence of the noetic field of consciousness in the polis, does not confine itself to the polis but broadly surveys the historical manifold of social order, including the empire, as it presented itself to a Greek observer in the fourth century B.C. The paradigms, thus, gain their meaning from their place in the philosophers' response to the problems of the Ecumenic Age in which they lived.

The philosophers are concerned with the place of meaning in reality. There is a meaningful luminosity of consciousness, emerging from a process that was deprived of it in the past and, quite possibly, will be deprived of it in the future. Why should the truth of reality, as far as it is accessible to a man, not always be present in its differentiated form? Why should man not always be able to articulate the noetic order of society through paradigms? Why, in brief, should certain periods in human history be privileged to receive illumination from noetic consciousness?

The questions of this class, though disturbing enough, were less disturbing to the philosophers of the fourth century B.C. than they were to Jacob Burckhardt in the nineteenth century A.D., because their differentiating consciousness was still more firmly embedded in the primary experience of the cosmos than Burckhardt's with its Christian lineage. Their noetic consciousness did not yet have the certainty of historical uniqueness and ineluctability that derives from the salvational fervor of Jewish apocalypse. Classic consciousness, one may say, still bears the index of a "thing" in the Anaximandrian process rather than an apocalyptic index, though the latter is not entirely missing as we shall see presently. This peculiar structure of consciousness, keeping the balance between primary experience and apocalyptic prophecy, becomes manifest in Plato's treatment of the issue in the *Laws*.

In Book III, Plato opens his inquiry concerning the *arche* of the polis and the best *Politeia* with a page of reflections on the unbounded expanse of time in which thousands of thousands of poleis have come into being and perished, with all possible variations and transformations from small to great, from great to small, from good to bad, from bad to good (676). In this *apeiria* of time (676b), whose infinity corresponds to the originating *apeiron,* the present enterprise of devising a paradigm would have been undertaken an uncounted number of times in the past, as it will be in the future. The emergence of meaning does not escape the primary rhythm of birth and death, of *genesis* and *phthora*. Only against this background of acquiescence in the cosmic process Plato, then, narrows the reflection to the particular historical process that culminates in the present construction of the paradigm by introducing the myth of cosmic catastrophies. Many times the world of man has been so thoroughly destroyed by flood and plagues that only a few survived and human history had to start again from its primitive beginnings, but the quest for the *arche* will take into account only the last course of history to which the speakers of the dialogue themselves belong. The uniqueness of emergent meaning, thus, can be lifted into the compact Anaximandrian experience by letting history begin after the cataclysm remembered in the myth of Deucalion (*Laws,* 677a).

Having cast the spell of cosmic rhythm on the uniqueness of meaning, Plato proceeds to characterize the phases in the evolution of social order, over periods to be counted in thousands of years, from the primitive to the present situation. They are four in number. After the cataclysm which destroyed the previous civilization and especially the cities of the plains with their material and governmental arts, the only survivors were mountaineers. They lived in stone-age conditions, in household and small-clan settlements under patriarchal chieftains. This first type of order is called *dynasteia* (677b–680e). In the next phase larger villages were formed through a synoecism of smaller clans. This foundation of larger groups required actions of law-giving and governmental organizations, with the former clan chiefs forming an aristocracy and perhaps one of them receiving a pre-eminent role. This second type of order Plato calls *basileia* (680e–681d). Slowly the shock of the cataclysm wore off. Under the pressure of increasing population, again cities in the plains near the sea were founded. This third phase Plato identifies with the Mycenaean bronze age, with Ilium and the Achaean poleis that participated in the war against her (681d–682c). The fourth and last phase, beginning with the troubles after the return of the Greeks from Troy, reaches into the present of the dialogue and its construction of the paradigm. It is burdened with the discrepancy between the order it is supposed to have in the light of Plato's noetic consciousness and the fall from this order that endangers the very existence of the Hellenic polis. The war-bands returning from Troy found a leader in the mythical Dorieus and reconquered the cities in which a younger generation had risen to power; they organized the Peloponnesian territory as a federation of the three strong poleis of Lacedaemon, Argos, and Messene; a new type of society, larger than the earlier cities of the plains, the territorial state of a people had come into existence. This fourth type Plato calls the *ethnos,* the federated people (682d–683b). The new *ethnos,* if it had lasted, would have been a military power of such strength that no Asiatic power would have dared to attack it, and even strong enough in its turn to dominate both Hellenes and barbarians (685b–e; 687a–b). The foundation failed, however, because in two of the member poleis the lawgivers had committed the Greatest Folly (*megiste amathia*)—not providing either a man guided by wisdom (*phronesis*) for the royal function or constitutional balances that would prevent the abuse of absolute power. Only Lacedaemon survived, thanks to its well-constructed *Politeia* (689a).

The conception of the historical course is not a self-contained theorem that, as a matter of literary composition, simply follows the opening page on the cosmic rhythm. In their sequence, the parts of the dialogue articulate an integral experience of reality with an amplitude from the depth of the cosmos to the height of the divine Nous. The primary experience reaches indeed from below into Plato's historical consciousness, just as the noetic differentiation rises above it toward apocalyptic uniqueness. This stratification of consciousness, which the account just given does contain, though it does not make it readily visible, requires a few comments.

There is to be noted, first, the ambiguity which to this day causes the misunderstanding of Plato's political intention. In part it is terminological, for Plato uses *polis* as the generic term for the phases of social order as they follow one another from the clan settlements, through the village aristocracy and the polis of the plains, to the federated people. If the interpreter of *Laws,* Book III, reads "polis" to mean "city-state," he destroys the sense of Plato's analysis, for the inquiry is not concerned with the genesis and *arche* of the city-state in the sense of the "polis of the plains" but of the *ethnos.* Such a federation, however, can be covenanted and maintained in existence only if the *megiste amathia* is avoided and the city-states of the Mycenaean period are replaced by a new type of polis that is willing to adopt the paradigmatic *Politeia.* The construction of the paradigm must not be separated from its purpose of providing a constitution for the member-polis of a functioning federation. Moreover, this Hellenic federation is supposed to hold its own against Persia; in the power field of the time it is to be a match to the ecumenic empire, as the earlier Doric federation was to be the European counterweight to the "Assyria" in the background of Troy (685c). Since the federated *ethnos* is devised as the noetic alternative, growing out of the culture of the Hellenic polis, on the imperial scale of power set by the Asiatics, this Platonic conception is truly a symbolism of the Ecumenic Age. It must be ranked as the Hellenic equivalent to the Polybian conception of Rome's imperial *telos*.

But does the paradigm really belong to the fourth phase and not rather to a fifth one that lies yet in the future? The question arises from the uncertainties surrounding the meaning of *ethnos*. For in Plato's account the *ethnos* is formed historically when the Achaean warriors returning from Troy organize as the Doric federation (682e). In this usage, the Achaeans apparently were not considered a people before they became the Dorians. The paradigm of the *Laws* is devised, furthermore, not for a Doric federation that failed centuries ago, but for the Hellenes of today who have gone through the ordeals of the Persian and Peloponnesian wars and are now threatened by Macedonians and Persians. In a state of political convulsions similar to that of the Achaeans after Troy, the Hellenes are admonished to form themselves into an organized *ethnos*. Are the Hellenes an *ethnos* now, or will they be one only in the future when the potential member-poleis will have stopped their internecine warfare and adopted the paradigmatic *Politeia*? If these various usages are to be compatible with one another, as well as with the conception of a fourth phase of political order, the course of history must be understood as an advance of civilization in time through inventions and arts, improvement of transportation and discoveries, population increase and density of settlement to the point when culturally homogeneous peoples in contiguous settlement appear as distinguishable units in history. In the Platonic conception, then, such units would require a political organization for the two purposes of securing peace within the *ethnos* and defense against organized units of a comparable size (683d–685). This requirement, however, cannot be satisfied in the same manner by every unit of ethnic size. Plato insists that a noetically satisfactory order is possible only if the unit in question is indeed culturally an *ethnos* and not a jumble of former peoples held together by a conquering power as in the Persian case; the population of a multicivilizational, ecumenic empire is not an *ethnos* that could organize itself as a federation of paradigmatic poleis (693a). The empirical observation of cultural differences and historical variants of civilizational evolution, thus, interferes with the generalization of the historical "advance" (*proeleluthe,* 678b) through technological progress and population increase. While the pattern of the advance holds true, the

cultural results differ as widely as Hellas and Persia. The historical course that
culminates in the federated *ethnos* becomes the uniquely Hellenic variant of
the general pattern. Only in the Hellenic case can the fourth phase actualize
its entelechy of noetic order through the paradigm. In the generation after
Plato, then, the pressure of events motivates the Aristotelian changes of
meaning: The generic term for the historical types of society is no longer
the "polis" but the "community" (*koinonia*); the "polis" becomes the ultimate
Hellenic type, following the *oikos* and the *kome;* and the "ethnos" becomes
the Persian type ordered by the *pambasilea.*

The farther one goes into the details of Plato's conception of history the
more it impresses one by its empirical range, as well as by its validity in terms
of twentieth-century historiography. The secret of the success is the openness
of a consciousness that includes the primary experience of the cosmos. Plato
did not have to keep a worried eye on a Bishop Ussher's date for the creation of
the world in 4004 B.C. that still moved Hegel to arrange his time schedule for
ancient history with circumspection. He had all the time not in the world but
of the cosmos, "vast and innumerable," a *chronouplethos* (676b), in which
to accommodate an evolutionary history of mankind from the stone age
through the metal ages to the present, and from primitive tribal communities
through cities and peoples to empires, with ages to be counted in thousands of
years (*myriakis myria ete*) (677d). Nor did he have to worry about an hypostatized meaning *of* history but could concentrate on the truly fascinating phenomenon of human actions which create meaning *in* history. The passage on
inventions (677c–d) sounds as if Plato had been less interested in a perpetually
perfect order of things than in a state of imperfection—to be produced, if necessary, by a cosmic catastrophe—in which there is room for the splendor of creative imagination. A world not in need of inventive genius would be a bore.
Moreover, Plato knew the ultimate mystery of reality to be the process of the divine cosmos itself; he did not impose an index of apocalyptic finality on the
meanings which, at this or that point of its course, flare up in man's consciousness. With equanimity he could observe, therefore, a meaning squashed by the
very process that had let it emerge; the truth of reality is not affected in its
validity by oblivion. In the *Republic* he even made it a point that a paradig-
matically ordered polis, the *kallipolis,* would begin to decline from the moment
of its establishment because it is beyond man's ability to translate the mystery
of the cosmos into perfection in history. This equanimity was further fortified
by Plato's insight that the culture of a society is always integral, expressing
its attunement and adjustment to the order of the cosmos regardless of its

position in the pattern of civilizational "advance." Good and bad are always
in balance. A small materially primitive tribe has the virtues that go with a
simple life; a city of materially advanced civilization is marred by the vices,
litigations, and corruption that go with urbanized life (679). Hence, he did
not have to worry about the unjust disadvantage at which societies are put if
they hold an earlier place in the history of progress rather than a later one
(Kant's problem), nor about the price of suffering the earlier societies have to
pay in order to put the later ones higher in the scale of progress (Burckhardt's
problem), *i.e.,* about the pseudo-problems arising from the hypostasis of meaning. And finally, since Plato was not tempted to elevate a particular event, as
for instance his own differentiation of noetic consciousness, to the rank of a
goal toward which all mankind had been moving from the beginning (Hegel's
temptation), he could acknowledge the plurality of parallel civilizations in the
field of history. It is true, he could rank the Hellenic variety of the historical
course he had outlined highest, because it had flowered in the luminosity of
consciousness; but he knew that the field was diversified by the Asiatic and
Egyptian varieties. A comparably open consciousness was reintroduced to
Western civilization only in the eighteenth century A.D. through Voltaire's
conception of parallel histories.

The primary experience of the cosmos which makes this admirable openness possible is brought to bear on the historical course through Plato's judicious
use of the myth. A myth is an intracosmic story that explains why things
are as they are. The myth in this sense can become an obstacle to the advance
of knowledge when areas of reality, hitherto not covered by the older myth,
are newly differentiated; but it also can become a highly flexible instrument in
the hands of a great mythopoet like Plato when he wants to link noetic consciousness back to the process of reality in which the event of its discovery
has mysteriously occurred. The philosopher must of necessity establish this
link if he wants to articulate his experience of reality integrally, because there
is no reality of noetic consciousness independent from the mystery of its
emergence. If the mystery is forgotten, consciousness loses a fundamental
dimension, or rather—since reality cannot be truly lost, or ignored, or destroyed
—the mystery will be relegated to the unconscious from where its presence
will make itself felt unpleasantly; a consciousness that puts the primary
experience into the unconscious is liable to become anthropomorphic; and the
contracted reality of which it remains conscious is exposed to the various
hypostatic distortions and literalist deformations. Plato guards against such
derailments by introducing, first of all, the lasting of the cosmos as the time

that comprehends the lasting of all things, including the historical course as well as the philosophers who differentiate noetic consciousness, discover meanings in history, and devise paradigms. In a cosmic lasting that outlasts all "things," however, meaning in history would become meaningless, if the lasting were speculatively constructed as a dimension in which everything has happened already, and not once but an indefinite number of times. Hence, Plato must protect the lasting of the cosmos against its hypostatic deformation into an infinite time in which history, and ultimately the cosmos itself, happens over and over again in an eternal return, and he does it by introducing the myth of the last cataclysm and of Deucalion. There is no reality but the reality of which we have experience and memory, and man's memory does not reach behind the last flood; by experience remembered we have knowledge only of the one history in which such meaningful events as consciousness becoming luminous occur. The myth of the outlasting cosmos, thus, is confined to its function of keeping consciousness open toward the reality in which it becomes luminous while not converting the mystery into a "thing" that can be examined from all sides. As far as the historical course is concerned, the cosmos lasts long enough if it outlasts memory and meaning.

The myth of Deucalion will do its duty, however, only if it is properly understood as an intracosmic story that explains the range of Greek historical memory. If it is literalized into a report of a cosmic cataclysm that sets a *terminus a quo* for history in general, it will clash with memories of a longer range than the Greek, as for instance the Egyptian, and lead to the same kind of difficulties as Bishop Ussher's literalism. But that is not a problem to plague a master of mythopoesis who knows what he is doing: In the *Timaeus,* Plato simply creates a further myth that explains why Egypt is exempt from such cataclysms. Cosmic conflagrations, like the one caused by Phaeton, cannot destroy the Egyptians because at such times the Nile saves them by rising high; and they are safe from floods, because in Egypt the water does not pour down from above but wells up in a natural manner from below (22d–e). Moreover, in this context Plato remarks that the stories of catastrophes carry the "form of the myth" (*mythou schema*) (22c) as no more than an appearance, while the truth behind this form "is a deviation (*parallaxis*) of the bodies that revolve around the earth in the heaven" (22c–d). Plato refers to the precession of the equinox and knows about the connection between this phenomenon of "deviation" and the myths of cosmic disasters. The Platonic use of the myth, thus, not only preserves the parallel histories of the several civilizations, but also acknowledges their different ages as determined by the time of their emergence

from the stone age into a remembered continuity of history. Far from merging
these parallel histories into one historical course with its climax in Hellas,
Plato even insists on the age difference as a decisive characteristic of civilizations. For in *Timaeus* 22b, he lets the Egyptian priest explain to Solon that the
Hellenes are always children; "there is no such thing as an ancient Greek";
they are young in their souls because they have no old beliefs handed on by
tradition, nor a science hoary with age. Though Plato, like his ancestor Solon,
was a Hellene, there is no indication in the text that he felt depressed because
his soul was young.

Plato was not a priest who lived by beliefs of long tradition. His soul was
young because he was sensitively open to reality in the present and mastered
the "serious play" of symbols old and new that would celebrate his participation
in the drama of a cosmos becoming luminous to itself through Nous. There
is more to reality than the process of things that come into being and perish;
the cosmos is divine, and above the rhythm of passing and lasting there rises
the thing called man in whose psyche the divine reality can become theophany.
Living in the present, with a soul that is young, means living as a man in
active response, not to ancient beliefs, but to the movement of divine presence,
and allowing the soul to become the site of the revelatory event. The history
of man, then, is more than a record of things past and gone; it is transacted in
a permanent present as the ongoing drama of theophany. The emergence of
meaning from the Anaximandrian process of reality is, from the divine side,
the history of incarnation in the realm of things. The historical course of *Laws,*
III, describes the slow and painful advance of order in reality up to the federated *ethnos;* this course must now be related as a present to the present in
which Plato devises the paradigm.

The great theme of the *Laws* is the question, whether paradigmatic order
will be created by "God or some man" (624a). Plato answers: "God is the
measure of all things" rather than man (716c); paradigmatic order can be
created only by "the God who is the true ruler of the men who have *nous*"
(713a); the order created by men who anthropomorphically conceive themselves as the measure of things will be a *stasioteia* rather than a *politeia,* a state
of feuding rather than a state of order (715b). But who is that ruling God
from whom the paradigm should take its name rather than from ruling men, be
they monarchs, aristocrats, or the demos (713a)? In order to answer this question, Plato uses the myth concerning the ages of theophany. He recalls his
earlier treatment of the question in the *Statesman* through the myth of the ages

of Cronos and Zeus and relates this more compact version to the present state of analysis: The man-made poleis described in *Laws*, III, belong to the age of Zeus now coming to its end; and the myth of the earlier age in which men lived under the direct guidance of the gods must now be revised so as to make the advance from the myth's to the philosopher's theophany intelligible (713b). In the new version (713c–714b) Cronos realized that human beings could not be given autocratic control of their affairs without becoming filled with pride and injustice; he therefore installed beings of a more divine nature, namely daimons, as the rulers of men. "This tale has a truth to tell even today"; for in a polis where not a god rules but mortals the people have no rest from ills. After the unhappy experiences with human government in the age of Zeus, the time has now come to imitate by all means life as it was under Cronos; and as we cannot return to the rule of the daimons, we must order our homes and poleis in obedience to the *diamonion*, to the immortal element within us. This something, "what of immortality is in us," is the *nous* and its ordering is the *nomos*. The new age, following the ages of Cronos and Zeus, will be the age of Nous.

The paradigm is not a construction of social order on the same level as the other types known, only better. Nor is it a utopia or ideal. It is the paradigm of order in the Metaxy, on the new spiritual level achieved in Plato's noetic consciousness. Nor can it be simply added as a new type in temporal succession to the types of the historical course in *Laws*, III. The paradigm belongs to a new age in the history of theophany. One should note the parallel between Plato's three ages of Cronos, Zeus, and Nous and the three Deutero-Isaianic phases of Creation, First and Second Exodus. With the third age of the Nous, Plato has come as close to an apocalyptic symbolism as he could come without losing the balance of a consciousness that also comprehended the primary experience of the process in which the things come and go.

§ 3. THE BALANCE OF CONSCIOUSNESS

Since the exodus from reality is a movement within reality, the philosopher has to cope with the paradox of a recognizably structured process that is recognizably moving beyond its structure. While this structure is static enough to outlast the philosopher's life between birth and death—in fact it lasts through the millennia of known history to this day—it is dynamically alive with theophanic events which point toward an ultimate transfiguration of reality.

In the exegesis of reality, this paradox is liable to derail into misconstructions. Of the two paradoxically linked experiences, for instance, the exegete may favor the one over the other by according it an index of superior reality that will relegate the other one to a state of untruth. As a consequence, existence in the lasting cosmos may become an untruth to be overcome by the truth of transfigured reality, as in apocalyptic movements; or the truth of transfigured reality may become a projection, an illusion imaginatively thrown up by the men who truly exist in the lasting structure, as in various psychologies of the nineteenth century A.D.; or, in another type of derailment, the two experiences may cancel each other out so that the paradox degenerates into a void of existence without meaning, as in a Sartrian existentialism.

The philosopher must be on his guard against such distortions of reality. It becomes his task to preserve the balance between the experienced lastingness and the theophanic events in such a manner that the paradox becomes intelligible as the very structure of existence itself. This task incumbent on the philosopher I shall call the postulate of balance.

The establishment of the balance through Plato and Aristotle, both in fact and as a postulate of reason, is one of the principal events, not in the Ecumenic Age only but in the history of mankind. It has determined the life of reason in Western civilization up to our own time. In the twentieth century, however, the climate of opinion has buried the postulate so deeply in the public unconscious that a statement of its meaning and its implications is necessary.

The difficulties in preserving the balance arise from the constitution of reason through revelation.

In his exploration of history, Plato properly takes into account the experiences of both the height and the depth in the process, of both the Nous and the Apeiron; but in this balance he must include the unbalancing movement toward the abolition of the structure, i.e., the "fire exceeding bright," a divine light presence, closely related to the theophanies to which Parmenides, Heraclitus, and Xenophanes had responded. The unbalancing theophanic event, thus, becomes part of the balanced structure. Even more, it constitutes the structure inasmuch as the discovery of noetic consciousness is accompanied by the consciousness of its meaning as the event in which the process becomes luminous for itself. And finally, since it is the structure of reality that becomes luminous on occasion of the noetic theophanies, the openness of man's existence toward the Logos of reality is constituted by the god when he reveals himself as the Nous. The life of reason, thus, is firmly rooted in a revelation.

The issue of revelation as the source of reason in existence is conventionally anesthetized by carefully reporting the philosophers' "ideas" without touching the experiences that have motivated them. In a philosophical study, however, the philosophers' theophanies must be taken seriously. The questions which the revelatory experiences impose must not be dodged, they must be made explicit: Who is this God who moves the philosophers in their search? What does he reveal to them? And how is he related to the God who revealed himself to Israelites, Jews, and Christians?

Unless we want to indulge in extraordinary theological assumptions, the God who appeared to the philosophers, and who elicited from Parmenides the exclamation "Is!", was the same God who revealed himself to Moses as the "I am who (or: what) I am," as the God who is what he is in the concrete theophany to which man responds. When God lets himself be seen, whether in a burning thornbush or in a Promethean fire, he is what he reveals himself to be in the event. In the compact vision of Parmenides, the accent falls on the Oneness of the *realissimum* from whom all reality originates. The Thornbush Episode (Exod. 3) more subtly distinguishes between the mystery of the divine abyss and the What as which the God lets himself be concretely known in the theophanic event. The flame in the thornbush seen by Moses is not God himself, but the "messenger of Yahweh"; from the flame of the messenger, then, sounds a voice proclaiming itself as the "God of the Fathers"; only when Moses has veiled his head is he permitted to approach and hear the command to lead Israel out of Egypt; the command, then, is endowed with added authority by the identification of the God of the Fathers with the "I am who I am"; and this differentiating revelation of the divine source of authority in depth finally leads to the revelation of the impersonal name of God as the "I am."

The advances in depth, in the Thornbush Episode, from the angelic fire to the divine voice and from the God of the Fathers, whose credibility is perhaps not unquestioned among the people whom he let fall into bondage, to *the* God who Is in his tetragrammatic depth behind whatever he reveals himself to be when he lets himself be seen by man; and, on the human side, from questions, hesitations, doubts, and resistance to ultimate surrender— these advances in depth magnificently articulate the complexities of a revelatory experience which truly moves toward more differentiated insights into the relation between God and man.

This concentrated articulation will aid in understanding the experiential connection between various symbols which in Plato's work are dispersed over several Dialogues. There is first to be noted the messenger, Prometheus,

through whose fire exceeding bright the gods convey the truth of the One
and the Apeiron to man (*Philebus*), as well as the force that compels the
prisoner in the cave to turn around toward the divine light (*Republic*). These
forces belong to the same foreground of theophany as the fire that moves
Moses to turn toward the Thornbush. The messengers, then, are followed
by the gods themselves. They are the gods of the fathers, together with their
helpers—Cronos with his daimons, Zeus with Hephaestus and Prometheus
(*Statesman*). But these gods of the fathers, Aristotle's *patrios doxa,* have now
to abdicate in favor of the new god, the Nous, whose voice speaks directly to
the *daimonion* in man (*Laws*). Beyond the old gods, the movement penetrates
further into the depth of divine reality toward the Demiourgos and Father
who has created the cosmos and employs the lesser gods as the rulers over man
and the mediators of his instructions (*Statesman*).

Thus far the ascent in the hierarchy of divine beings, from the messengers
to the Demiurge and Father, is clear. There is, however, a further movement
of ascent running through the Dialogues that betrays certain hesitations and
restraints. In the *Phaedrus,* for instance, Plato characterizes the Olympians as
a class of intermediate divine beings, as cosmographically intracosmic gods
who can ascend above the heaven that is their habitat to the roof of the cosmos
in order to contemplate the truly divine region and reality of the *hyperouranion.* Human beings, though, who want to follow the Olympians in this
ascent will encounter the utmost (*eschaton*) toil and struggle of the soul; as a
consequence, no poet within the cosmos has ever worthily praised this transcosmic divinity or ever will (*Phaedrus*, 247). We are still engaged in the
movement of the psyche, though the advance has become more arduous; but
it does not become clear from the texts whether the divine reality of the
hyperouranion should be flatly identified with the Demiurge of *Statesman*
and *Timaeus,* or whether it compactly co-represents a still deeper depth in the
movement of the soul toward God. One can only note that pseudo-Dionysius
(*ca.* A.D. 500) uses the compounds with *hyper,* such as *hypertheos, hypersophos,
hyperkalos, hyperousios,* and so forth, in order to symbolize the abyss of divine
reality beyond the What that the God lets enter into a man's experience
of his presence. Certainly, however, Plato conceived the Demiurge not as a
god who creates the cosmos *ex nihilo,* but as a god who is limited in his work
by the apeirontic forces of Heimarmene (*Statesmen*) or Ananke (*Timaeus*);
the Anaximandrian experience of the Apeiron extends its balancing effect
into the symbolization even of the God behind the Olympian gods. It is not
surprising, therefore, when the *monogenes,* the firstborn whom Plato's Father-

God chooses for his incarnation, is not a man as in the Gospel of St. John (1:14) but the cosmos itself (*Timaeus*). Only by persuasion (*peitho*), and within the limits imposed by the pre-existent raw material (*chora*) of the cosmos, can the Demiurge wrest order (*taxis*) from disorder (*ataxia*) and build the cosmos in the image of the Nous that is the creator-god's own (*Timaeus*).

Though this symbolism is consistent, it would be disappointing if it were the last word a thinker of Plato's spiritual stature had to say in the matter. There must finally be considered, therefore, the famous passage concerning the two world-souls (*Laws,* 896e) which is assumed to reflect a Zoroastrian influence. The forming of the *monogenes* in the image of the Demiurgic Nous requires its incarnation in the soul and body of the cosmos. The cosmos is Nous-in Psyche-in Soma (*Timaeus*). If Plato assumes two such world-souls, "one the author of good, the other of evil," the "other" world-soul can hardly be the one in which the Demiurgic Nous has become incarnate. In the Platonic context, the symbolism of the two world-souls implies a second divine being, corresponding to Zoroaster's Angra Mainyu, by the side of the noetic Demiurge who would correspond to the Spenta Mainyu of the *Gathas;* and this assumption would further imply a movement in depth toward the divine reality of the Ahura Mazda behind the two spirits of good and evil. The status of cosmic reality would have subtly shifted from a Metaxy determined by Nous and Apeiron (*Philebus*) to a Metaxy determined by two angelic figures, a savior and a satan, and their actions allowed by the one God. These vacillations and uncertainties of meaning in Plato's late symbols suggest that his revelatory experience had indeed moved toward the divine abyss beyond the Demiurge and his Nous. But the articulation of this movement was consummated only by Plotinus when he found for the experience of the abyss the symbol of the divine Monas *epekeina nou,* of the One beyond the Nous (*Enneads,* V, viii, 10).

But why should there be any uncertainties of meaning at all? Did Plato lack the powers of intellect and imagination to state more succinctly that a Nous limited by Ananke could not limit his, Plato's, psyche in its responsive quest of the divine ground? I do not advise this explanation because it would mean to commit the

crimen laesae majestatis,
majestatis genii;

I would rather suggest that the uncertainties were created deliberately. Plato was well aware that revelation had a dimension beyond the Nous; he wanted to bring this dimension unmistakably to attention; but he did not want to elaborate it further because he was afraid that the elaboration might disturb the balance of consciousness. Consider the ambiguity in the passages just quoted. When he writes in the *Phaedrus* that no poet has ever worthily praised the *hyperouranion* or ever will, the passage can be read either as an ironic anticipation of his own worthy praise of the trans-Olympian Demiurge in the *Timaeus,* or as a warning that there is more to the *hyperouranion* than even the *Timaeus* has to tell. Again, the passage concerning the two world-souls in the *Laws* can be read either as an erratic block of Zoroastrian influence or as a deliberate warning that there is more to divine reality than the definition of *theosebeia* as the belief in the doctrines of the soul as the deathless ruler and of the revelation of the *nous* in the celestial movements (967) would suggest. But if the ambiguities of this class are intentional indeed, if the uncertainties serve the purpose of protecting the noetic core of the theophany against unbalancing vagaries of hypernoetic enthusiasts, this matter is in need of further inquiry.

There can be no doubt about the core of the theophany that surrounds itself with uncertainties: It is the revelation of the God as the Nous in both the cosmos and in man. Aristotle elaborates on this question in the historical survey of his predecessors in *Metaphysics,* A: The Ionian speculation on the elements as the ground of being was unsatisfactory because it left the qualities of goodness and beauty in the things unexplained, and to attribute these qualities to some automatism or to accident hardly made sense; the way out of this impasse was shown by Anaxagoras who was the first to suggest that the Nous was alive not only in living things but in nature at large, that order in reality (*kosmos, taxis*) was caused by the in-being (*eneinai*) of the Nous in everything. The noetic theophany, thus, reveals the intelligible structure in reality as divine. The Nous that had been experienced as the ordering force in the psyche let himself be seen as the divine ground of all being. The process of reality can become luminous for its structure in noetic consciousness because both the cosmos and the psyche of man are informed (*eneinai*) by the same divine Nous (984b8–23).

This core of the theophanic event, however, is experientially unstable. Revelation is not a piece of information, arbitrarily thrown out by some supernatural force, to be carried home as a possession, but the movement of response to an irruption of the divine in the psyche. Moreover, the movement of irruption and response has a structure of its own. As I have formulated it elsewhere, the fact of revelation is its content. Hence, the movement will continue, though not necessarily in the same person, if the phase of the response that has reached the stage of symbolization is sensed to be no more than penultimate. Once the psyche has begun to move beyond the intracosmic gods toward the divine ground of all being, it will not cease moving before it has sensed the truly Tremendum, the ultimate, non-present Beyond of all divine presence. In the case of the noetic theophany, the experience of a God who embodies his Nous in the cosmos, limited by Ananke, cannot but point, by implication, toward the non-incarnate, acosmic abyss of the divine beyond the Demiurgic action. The paradoxical structure of the exodus which causes the experiential instability can now be re-formulated, with special regard to Plato's historical position in the noetic movement, through propositions like the following:

The movement beyond the Olympians toward the noetic ground reveals the structure of reality but, at the same time, reveals iself as part of the structure;

The history of theophanic incarnation becomes transparent for its meaning as a movement toward the Beyond of theophany and incarnation;

Beyond the noetically structured cosmos whose divine order is limited by Ananke there becomes visible a reality that is free from the struggle with the apeirontic forces;   *The Kun-Lun Mountain where the Heavenly Peachtree is*

The history of revelation reveals the Beyond of history and revelation.

The structure of "beyond" in the historical advance from the Olympians to the divine ground of being is an unstabilizing factor indeed, because it confronts the movement with a "Beyond" that threatens to invalidate the theophanic events together with the process in which they occur.

Plato was eminently conscious of this paradoxical structure of the exodus; in fact, he has created the symbolism of the *epekeina,* of the Beyond. And yet, when he characterizes the Agathon as the originating power beyond both the knower (*nous*) and the known (*nooumena*) (*Republic,* 508c), he displays the same restraint as in the *Phaedrus* and the *Laws.* On the one hand, he lets the objects of knowledge (*gignoskomena*) receive from the Agathon not only their being-known (*gignoskesthai*) but their very existence (*einai*) and essence (*ousia*), and makes the Agathon itself the power (*dynamis*) beyond existence and essence (509b). One can hardly come closer to the Thomasic distinction between the necessary being of God and the contingent being of things. On the other hand, the reading of the passage as a sketch of the Divine that is to be filled in with the Demiurge of the *Timaeus,* preferred by some authorities, is just as tenable as the alternative speculations on Plato's theology preferred by others.

The danger against which the Platonic restraint protects is well known: It is the flooding of consciousness with imaginations of transfigured reality that will devalue existence in the cosmos under the conditions of its structure. The extreme manifestation of this acosmistic *contemptus mundi* in the Gnostic systems was to characterize a later phase in the Ecumenic Age, but certain problems that became acute in Gnosticism were latently present even in Plato's work, as for instance the identity of the God who is radically "Beyond." The Gnostics recognized in the hitherto unknown God of the abyss a divine being different from the creator-god, in particular from the Yahweh of the Old Testament. In their conception of reality, an evil daimon had devised the prison of this world for the purpose of holding captive in it the spark of the divine *pneuma* in man. As distinguished from this daimon, the true God is so absolutely beyond the world that he has nothing to do with its creation; and still less would he care to incarnate himself in it. The Gnostic imbalance of consciousness, thus, causes a split to run through divine reality, separating the daimonic powers of the world from the pneumatic divinity Beyond. This split, then, entails the break with the "gods of the fathers." No longer can the psyche ascend, in response to a theophany, from the God of the Fathers to the God whose name is the nameless "I am," as in the Thornbush Episode; no longer can God reveal himself, first as the creator of the world, then as the creator of Israel, and finally as the redeemer of a liberated ecumenic mankind, as in Deutero-Isaiah; and no longer can the psyche ascend with the Olympians to the vault of the heaven and contemplate the *hyperouranion*. When the later pagans and Christians, Plotinus and the Patres, condemned the Gnostic movement in their parallel polemics, they had the same critical motive, for the Gnostics had disrupted both the pagan and Christian historical fields of theophany when they rejected both the Olympians and the God of the Old Testament. By surrounding the noetic core with his belt of uncertainties, Plato could prevent this potentially disruptive issue from disturbing his primary concern with the incarnation of the divine Nous in the structure of reality. In his conception of the ages in history, he let the Nous follow Cronos and Zeus as the Third God in the government of man, without raising the question of which stratum in the movement of the psyche each member of the sequence belonged to.

The theophany of the Nous could not constitute a new meaning in history, if the movement of the psyche toward the absolute Beyond were allowed to cast on all divine incarnation in the world the spell of daimonic evil. Neither the Platonic hesitations nor the pagan-Christian resistance to Gnosticism must be mistaken for quarrels about points in "theology"; whatever the surface arguments, they are motivated by the profounder worry about the actual destruction of structure in reality through the obsession with imagery of the Gnostic type. If life in the cosmos was indeed life in a daimonic prison, man's ordering of existence in this kind of world was reduced to the preparation of his escape from it; in particular, he had to acquire the knowledge (*gnosis*) that would enable his personal *pneuma* to return, in death, to the divine Pneuma. Consistently, this program could, as it did in certain instances, lead to the formation of communities of men and women who would live and die without offspring, in the hope that the communities would continue until all human beings had joined them, so that all human *pneuma* would be returned to the divine *pneuma* through the extinction of mankind. While Plato and Aristotle conceived participation in the noetically structured reality of the cosmos as man's action of immortalizing, and even devised paradigms of social order that would make the *athanatizein* possible, the flooding of consciousness with the Beyond induced the imagery of non-participation, to the extreme of abolishing human existence altogether. The libidinous outburst of bringing immortality under the control of man, by developing techniques for liberating the *pneuma* from its prison, is distinctly an ecumenic phenomenon. Beyond the concupiscential exodus of the conquerors into the vision of an imperially unified mankind, the spiritual exodus of prophets and apocalyptics into the vision of a mankind under God, and the noetic exodus of the philosophers into the immortalizing participation in the Nous of the cosmos, the Ecumenic Age has also produced the Gnostic imagery of an exodus into ecumenic death.

Plato's imagination, it is true, hardly anticipated the specific forms which the obsession with the Beyond would assume four or five hundred years after his time. But fanciful assumptions of this kind are not needed to explain his restraint. The *soma-sema* experience, a foreshadowing of Gnosticism, was part of the Hellenic tradition at least since the Pythagoreans; given an adequate stimulus, it could well become the center for an unbalancing movement toward the Beyond. Moreover, like the tragedians before him, Plato knew enough about the lability of man's mental equilibrium and the possibilities of spiritual disorder, the *nosos,* to tread cautiously where issues of this magnitude were involved. Obsessive deformations of existence were possible in general; one or the other variety could be actualized by the too eager exploration of the theophany whose core was the Nous; and they could destroy directly, or indirectly through the social pressure they would arouse, the noetic order of existence which Socrates-Plato had labored to establish. The death of Socrates, under the accusation of having introduced new gods, was a living memory. It will be suitable therefore, in conclusion, to restate the nature of the revelation whose core was so important that it required protection, as it were, against revelation itself.

When man responds to God's appearance as the Nous, the psyche is constituted as the sensorium of reality in the full range from sense perception to cognitive participation in the divine ground. This omnidimensional "desire to know," the unobscured openness toward reality, the readiness to move apperceptively hither and thither (*diaphora*) in order to participate through distinguishing knowledge (*diaphorein, gnorizein*) in the structures of reality, has been crystallized by Aristotle as the character of noetic consciousness in the opening paragraph of *Metaphysics*.

The openness, in all directions, of consciousness toward the reality of which it is a part—the responsive participation of man, through the Logos of his psyche, in the Logos of reality—is the joyous willingness to apperceive a reality that is informed by the same Nous as the psyche—that is all.

But that is considerably more than is conventionally realized. Under the title of "reason," or the theologically condescending title of "natural reason," this constitution of the psyche once achieved is so much taken for granted that its origin in a theophanic event has passed from public consciousness. Substantially, this oblivion has been caused by the theologians' eagerness to monopolize the symbol "revelation" for Israelite, Jewish, and Christian theophanies. Even in our own time, the inadequacy of theologians when they refer to issues of classic philosophy is sometimes extraordinary—and this charge applies to some of the most famous names in the field. Hence, in a climate of opinion that is negatively conditioned by millennial habits of symbolization, and actively bent on the murder of God, it is difficult to sense the fascination which reason, through its formation of mature humanity, held for the philosophers who were accorded its revelatory discovery.

I want to stress again, therefore, that structure in reality is not simply there to be seen by everybody under all personal, social, and historical circumstances; it rather is reality as it reveals itself to a psyche when it responds to Plato's Third God, the Nous. Structure as the face of reality becomes historically visible when the polymorphous aetiology of the divine in the myth gives way to the philosophers' aetiology of the divine as the *prote arche* of all reality, as it is eminently experienced in man's tension toward the ground of his existence. Cognitively structured reality, unencumbered by compact experiences and symbolizations of divine presence, is correlative to the theophany of the Nous; the openness toward reality at large depends on the openness of the psyche toward the divine ground. No science as the systematic exploration of structure in reality is possible, unless the world is intelligible; and the world is intelligible in relation to a psyche that has become luminous for the order of reality through the revelation of the one, divine ground of all being as the Nous.

Moreover, the revelation of the Nous as incarnate in both the psyche and the world is, for the classic philosophers, inseparably connected with the question of mortality and immortality. For the openness of man's existence toward the ground is dependent on the something in man that can respond to a theophany and engage in the quest of the ground. This something in man, as it is discovered on the occasion of the response, Plato has symbolized as the *daimon* (*Timaeus*, 90a), Aristotle as the *theion* (*Nicomachean Ethics*, 1177b28ff). This divinest part (*theiotaton*) in the psyche is the human *nous* that can participate in the divine Nous; and the nature and culture of the *theiotaton* through its engaging in the quest of the ground, in a *theoria theou*, is the action of immortalizing (*athanatizein*). The connection between man's tension toward the ground and his apperceptive openness toward the structure of reality, blended in his omnidimensional "desire to know," thus, becomes the connection between his noetic *athanatizein* and his existence in the world of becoming and perishing, of birth and death, in which alone the pursuit of immortality is possible. Man can immortalize only when he accepts the apeirontic burden of mortality. The balance of consciousness between the height and the depth, between Nous and Apeiron, becomes the balance of immortality and mortality in the *bios theoretikos*, in the life of reason in this world.

The danger that Plato wanted to ward off by his restraint can now be formulated more precisely as the state of spiritual disorder in which man attempts to separate the pursuit of immortality from the Ananke of existence in the Metaxy as the condition of the pursuit. It is the same danger that has agitated the Church, throughout its history, in its struggle against apocalyptic and Gnostic sectarians who want to find shortcuts to immortality. I have already reflected on some aspects of the Gnostic movement in the Ecumenic Age, with its split of divine reality into a truly divine Beyond and a daimonically structured world. While these early movements attempt to escape from the Metaxy by splitting its poles into the hypostases of this world and the Beyond, the modern apocalyptic-Gnostic movements attempt to abolish the Metaxy by transforming the Beyond into this world. When the pursuit of immortality in mortal existence, the philosophers' *athanatizein* or the Christian sanctification of life, has become impossible because man has closed himself against the divine ground, and as a consequence has lost the balance of his consciousness as the mortal-immortal, an imaginary immortality must be provided through action in an imaginary world-immanent reality invented for this purpose. Such imaginative constructions of Second Realities, then, will obscure the structured reality that has become visible through the philosophers. The most important instances of this type are the constructions of speculative histories, from the eighteenth century A.D. to the present, which grant an imaginary immortality through active participation in an imaginary process of history.

CHAPTER 5

The Pauline Vision of the Resurrected

Plato kept the theophanic event in balance with the experience of the cosmos. He did not permit enthusiastic expectations to distort the human condition. Regarding personal order, man can experience the pull of the Golden Cord, but reason still has to contend with the counterpull of passion; regarding society, the paradigms of noetic order are persuasively elaborated, but they will not put an end to the struggle with a less noetically minded Plethos; and regarding history, the vision of the federated *ethnos* is not expected to prevent history from going the way of empire. In sum, Plato did not allow the theophanic event to grow into the apocalyptic "great mountain that filled the whole world" (Dan. 2:35).

The balance was preserved; but it required an effort to hold it against the unbalancing dynamics of theophany. The theophanic event constitutes meaning in history; it reveals reality as moving toward a state undisturbed by forces of disorder; and imagination, following the directional movement, will express its goal by such symbols of transfigured reality as "a new heaven and a new earth." That is the point at which apocalyptic imagination can endanger the balance of consciousness by tampering with the mystery of meaning. For the directional movement in reality has the character of a mystery indeed: Though we can experience the direction as real, we do not know why reality is in such a state that it has to move beyond itself or why the movement has not been consummated by an event of transfiguration in the past; neither can we predict the date for such an event in the future or know what form it will assume. The event, as it can happen any time, hangs as a threat or hope over every present. In fact, nothing happens; and yet, it might happen. In the cosmological style of truth, the anxiety of existence over the abyss of non-existence engenders the rituals of cosmogonic renewal; in the style of existential truth constituted by theophanic events, the anxiety of falling into the untruth of disorder can engender the vision of a divine intervention that will put an end to disorder in time for all time. When the conflict between the revealed truth of order and the actual disorder of the times becomes too intense, the traumatic experience can induce the transformation of the mystery into metastatic expectations. The aura of possibility surrounding the mystery can be condensed into an expectation, with certainty, of a transfiguring event in a not too distant future.

§ 1. The Pauline Theophany

The potential of distortion through metastatic imagination, it should be understood, is inherent to the mystery of meaning. If the mystery were not real, the distortions would have no appeal. This tension inherent to the mystery has received its classic formulation through Paul in Romans 8:18–25. In the wake of the Fall, the whole creation has been submitted to a state of futility or senselessness (*mataiotes*) of existence (20). The whole creation exists in the earnest expectation (*apokaradokia*) of the revelation (*apokalypsis*) that will come to the sons of God (19). "We know that the whole creation is groaning in the one great act of giving birth; and not only creation but we ourselves, who possess the firstfruits of the spirit, groan inwardly as we wait for our bodies to be set free (*apolytrosis*)" (22–23). Together with creation, our bodies will be set free (or: ransomed) from bondage (*douleia*) to the fate of perishing (*phthora*) and enter into the freedom (*eleutheria*) and glory (*doxa*) of the children of God (21). In Anaximander's language, transfigured reality will have the structure of *genesis* without *phthora*.[1]

To exist in this tension of the truth revealed, certain virtues are required. Salvation in the sense of transposition into reality without *phthora* is not a matter of knowledge; it is not seen but rests on hope (*elpis*); if it were to be seen, hope would not be necessary (24). And if we hope for something that we do not see, we must expect it (or: wait for it) with patience (or: endurance, *hypomone*) (25). In Romans 5:3ff, Paul elaborates in more detail a ladder of existential order, rising from the joyful acceptance of affliction (*thlipsis*) in this world, from the sufferings in time (*ta pathemata tou nyn kairou*, 8:18), to their endurance (*hypomone*), further on to the character-forming perseverance (*dokime*), which in its turn is the foundation of hope (*elpis*). Existentially this ladder will hold up, so that hope does not give way to disap-

---

[1] All quotations from Paul in this chapter were translated from the original. The text used is Nestle-Aland, *Novum Testamentum Graece et Latine* (London, 1969). Whenever possible I have conformed to the language of the King James Version. For specific questions the standard commentaries were used, especially *Peake's Commentary on the Bible*, ed. Matthew Black and H. H. Rowley (London, 1962). Guenther Bornkamm, *Paulus* (Stuttgart, 1969), proved to be of considerable help for the understanding of Pauline questions.

pointment, because it rests on the grace (*charis*) diffused in our hearts by the holy spirit (*pneuma hagion*) that has been given us (5:5–6); and even though our prayer be inarticulate, the *pneuma* in the heart that is divine will carry it up to be articulate before God (8:26–7).

1. Noetic and Pneumatic Theophany

The Pauline analysis of existential order closely parallels the Platonic-Aristotelian. That is to be expected, since both the saint and the philosophers articulate the order constituted by man's response to a theophany. The accent, however, has decisively shifted from the divinely noetic order incarnate in the world to the divinely pneumatic salvation from its disorder, from the paradox of reality to the abolition of the paradox, from the experience of the directional movement to its consummation. The critical difference is the treatment of *phthora*, perishing. In the noetic theophany of the philosophers, the *athanatizein* of the psyche is kept in balance with the rhythm of *genesis* and *phthora* in the cosmos; in the pneumatic theophany of Paul, the *athanasia* of man is not to be separated from the abolition of *phthora* in the cosmos. Flesh and blood, the *soma psychikon,* cannot enter the kingdom of God; it must be changed into the *soma pneumatikon* (I Cor. 15:44, 55); for the perishing (*phthora*) cannot take possession of the imperishing (*aphtharsia*) (50). The change of reality to the state of *aphtharsia* is the Pauline exegesis of the *mysterion* (51–52). Plato, it is true, preserves the balance of consciousness, but he plays down the unbalancing reality of the theophanic event; his consciousness of the paradox is weighted toward the Anaximandrian mystery of Apeiron and Time, because he refrains from fully unfolding the implications of the directional movement. As a result, the status of the Third God in his conception of history is surrounded by the uncertainties analyzed. Paul, on the contrary, is fascinated by the implications of theophany so strongly that he lets his imagery of a *genesis* without *phthora* interfere with the primary experience of the cosmos. In I Corinthians 15 he lets his exultation rise to the apocalyptic assurance that "we shall not sleep, but we shall all be changed, in a moment, in the twinkling of an eye, at the last trumpet. For the trumpet will sound, and the dead will be raised imperishable, and we (who have not yet died) shall be changed." The *aphtharsia* is an event to be expected in the lifetime of his readers and himself. The metastatic expectation of the Second Coming has begun its long history of disappointment.

While the texts leave no doubt about the point of difference, the point is not thought through. Paul was not a philosopher; he was the missionary for the

Christ who appeared to him on the road to Damascus. If the analysis were to stop at this point, we would be settled with an unresolved conflict between noetic and pneumatic theophany, and the import of the difference for the understanding of history would be lost. This import will become clear only if the difference is placed in the context of agreement between Plato and Paul on the fundamental structure of reality.

Plato and Paul agree that meaning in history is inseparable from the directional movement in reality. "History" is the area of reality where the directional movement of the cosmos achieves luminosity of consciousness. They furthermore agree that history is not an empty time-dimension in which things happen at random but rather a process whose meaning is constituted by theophanic events. And finally they agree that the reality of history is metaleptic; it is the In-Between where man responds to the divine presence and divine presence evokes the response of man. Against this context of agreement the difference narrows to the content of Paul's theophany, to the vision of the God who has become man, of the God who has entered the Anaximandrian Time with its *genesis* and *phthora* and, having gone through the *pathemata* of existence, has risen to the glory of *aphtharsia*. The vision of the Resurrected convinced Paul that man is destined to rise to immortality, if he opens himself to the divine *pneuma* as Jesus did. To the vision he responded with the proclamation of Jesus as the Son of God (Acts 9:20); and this conviction he extended to everyman: "For all who are moved by the Spirit of God, are sons of God" (Rom. 8:14). "If the spirit (*pneuma*) of him who raised Jesus from the dead dwells in you, then the God who raised Jesus Christ from the dead will also give new life to mortal bodies by means of the spirit indwelling in you" (8:11). Faith in Christ means responsive participation in the same divine *pneuma* that was active in the Jesus who appeared in the vision as the Resurrected. "Justified through faith, we are at peace with God through our Lord Jesus Christ" (Rom. 5:1).

The problems of theophany are so badly obscured today by theological, metaphysical, and ideological overlayings that a remark to ward off conventional misunderstandings will not be superfluous. Stated flatly therefore: The present concern is not with points of christological dogma but with a vision of Paul and its exegesis by its recipient. Hence, there can arise no question of "accepting" or "rejecting" a theological doctrine. A vision is not a dogma but an event in metaleptic reality which the philosopher can do no more than try to understand to the best of his ability. As the vision occurs in the Metaxy, it must not be split into "object" and "subject." There is no "object" of the vision other than the vision as received; and there is no "subject" of the vision other than the response in a man's soul to divine presence. The vision emerges as a symbol from the Metaxy, and the symbol is both divine and human. Any attempt to break up the mystery of divine-human participation, as it occurs in a theophanic event, is fatuous. On the subjective side, one cannot "explain" the divine presence in the vision by a psychology of Paul. And on the objective side, "critical doubts" about the vision of the Resurrected would mean that the critic knows how God has a right to let himself be seen. One could imagine a questionnaire:

In a flaming thornbush?
    Yes; at least the flame did not
        start a brush-fire.

In a Promethean fire?
    No; myth is a superstition.

In the negative vôice of a Daimonion?
    Yes; the fate of Socrates
        will teach you to think positive.

In the authoritative command from a
    fire-spouting mountain?
        Too spectacular; and authoritarian to boot.

As an angel of the Lord?
    Perhaps; but are there really any angels?

As incarnate in a man?
    I don't know. But a dangerous precedent; the
        Hegels and Emersons are a pain in the neck.

This will make the scurrility of "critical" attempts more obvious than lengthy argument could do. But the questionnaire itself is not a scurrilous exaggeration; rather it is a meiosis compared with the debates actually conducted about Christ as an "historical figure," or about the "historicity" of Incarnation and Resurrection. Again stated flatly: There is no history other than the history constituted in the Metaxy of differentiating consciousness, as the analysis of the noetic field has made clear; and if any event in the Metaxy has constituted meaning in history, it is Paul's vision of the Resurrected. To invent a "critical history" that will allow us to decide whether Incarnation and Resurrection are "historically real" turns the structure of reality upside down; it flies in the face of all our empirical knowledge about history and its constitution of meaning. The misunderstandings arise from the separation of a "content" from the reality of the experience, and from the treatment of the content as an object of propositional knowledge. In its metaleptic context, Incarnation is the reality of divine presence in Jesus as experienced by the men who were his disciples and expressed their experience by the symbol "Son of God" and its equivalents; while Resurrection refers to the Pauline vision of the Resurrected, as well as to the other visions which Paul, who knew something about visions, classified as of the same type as his own (I Cor. 15:3–8).

2. *Vision and Reason*

The Pauline vision, it is true, must be accepted as a real event in the Metaxy, constitutive of history. Moreover, it must not be split into "object" and "subject," or be submitted to the variety of fundamentalist, positivist, and other hypostatizing distortions. From these enjoinders it does not follow, however, that visions have nothing to do with reason and lie beyond critical examination. The assumption that revelatory visions are "irrational," that they can only be "believed" *telquel* or not at all, is again a misunderstanding caused by hypostatizing alienation from the reality of the experience. Paul, who, as I have said, knew something about visions and related pneumatic phenomena, was well aware that the structure of a theophanic experience reaches from a pneumatic center to a noetic periphery. The encounter between God and man, for instance, can have a dead center of inarticulateness, resulting in a state of stupor or blindness, in his case lasting for three days; stupor and blindness, then, can be followed by a period of highly articulate interpretation of the event, in his case lasting for the rest of his life; and the change in a man's consciousness of reality can be so radical that it has to be symbolized as a renovation, or rebirth, or the donning of a new man. In less radical instances, the encounter can become manifest in a trancelike or ecstatic state of "tongue-speaking," of glossolalia, followed by an attempt, either by the tongue-speaker himself or by another person present, to translate the pneumatic gibberish into language intelligible in the community.

On occasion of an apparently excessive wave of untranslatable tongue-speaking in Corinth, Paul has given a remarkable analysis of the issue. He distinguishes between tongue-speakers (*lalon glosse*) and prophets (*propheteuon*) (I Cor. 14:1–3). The tongue-speaker speaks to God, not to other people, inasmuch as nobody understands him when he speaks mysteries in the spirit (*pneuma*); while the man who prophesies speaks to his fellow men for their improvement, encouragement, and consolation (14:2–3). The tongue-speaker talks for his own benefit, the prophet for the benefit of the community (14:4). Hence Paul's parliamentary code for tongue-speakers: Never more than one at a time; never more than three at a meeting; if nobody can intrepret the gibberish, he has to sit down and shut up, speaking in silence to God and himself. Even prophets have to take their turn, and never more than three at a meeting, though prophets can always control their *pneumata* (in the plural!). "For God is not a God of confusion but of peace" (I Cor. 14:26–33). Not that Paul is against tongue-speaking. On the contrary, he considers it one of the gifts (*charisma*) by which the spirit manifests itself in community (12:10), and he prides himself on his own charisma: "I thank God, that I can outspeak in tongues any of you" (14:18). Nevertheless, pneumatic glossolalia is of no particular benefit to the community; hence, Paul insists, "when I am in the presence of the community (*ekklesia*), I would rather say five words with my mind (*nous*) than ten thousand words in a tongue" (14:19); "for when I pray in a tongue, my *pneuma* is praying, but my *nous* remains barren" (14:14). And then he enjoins: "You must not become mentally (*tais phresin*) childish; you may be children as far as wickedness is concerned, but mentally you must be adult (*teleios*)" (14:20). Without prejudice to the existentially ordering force of *pneuma,* the life in community is governed by *nous.*

What does the Pauline *nous* mean? It would appear to be improper to press the texts too far, because Paul's language is no more than semitechnical. Still, the meaning intended becomes clear enough. *Nous* is not the mind of just anybody who speaks intelligibly and persuasively, perhaps on the level of worldly wisdom, in the community, but the *nous* of a teacher or prophet whose existence is ordered by the *pneuma.* This becomes especially clear from I Corinthians 2, where Paul opposes the spirit of the world (*to pneuma tou kosmou*) and the spirit that comes from God (*to pneuma ek tou theou*) (2:12). As the context (1:18–25) shows, the "spirit of the world" is to be understood as the "spirit" of the men "whose hearts are far from me" in the sense of the vision of Isaiah 29:11–21; specifically they are "the wise according to the flesh, men in position of power, or of noble descent" (I Cor. 1:26). The man who lives by the "spirit of the world" is the *psychikos* who has nothing but "human wisdom"; the gifts of the divine *pneuma* are beyond his understanding. The man who lives by the "spirit from God" is the *pneumatikos* who can express the gifts of the spirit in spiritual language, so that "we, the *pneumatikoi,* have the *nous* of Christ (*noun Christou echomen*)" (2:16).

Though the Pauline analysis of existential order through man's tension toward the divine ground is not so clear as the Platonic-Aristotelian, the equivalence of the result is clear enough. The Aristotelian *spoudaios* is the man who is formed by the existential virtues of *phronesis* and *philia;* as a result of this formation he achieves a consciousness of reality and insights into right human conduct which enable him to speak "truly" about the order of reality, as well as of human existence. The Pauline *pneumatikos* is formed by the divine *pneuma;* as a result he can "judge all things" (2:16) and articulate his knowledge "in words taught by the spirit" (2:13). The Pauline symbols of the *propheteuon,* the *pneumatikos,* and the *teleios* are the equivalents of the Aristotelian *spoudaios.*

The symbols are equivalent, but the dynamics of existential truth has shifted from the human search to the divine gift (*charisma*), from man's ascent toward God through the tension of Eros to God's descent toward man through the tension of Agape. The Pauline *pneuma* is, after all, not the philosopher's *nous* but the rendering in Greek of the Israelite *ruach* of God. Hence, Paul does not concentrate on the structure of reality that becomes luminous through the noetic theophany, as the philosophers do, but on the divine irruption which constitutes the new existential consciousness, without drawing too clear a line between the visionary center of the irruption and the translation of the experience into structural insight. Paul distinguishes between *pneuma* and *nous* when the order of the community compels him to do so, as in the case of the tongue-speakers, but he does not expand this effort into a philosopher's noetic understanding of reality; the dividing line will rather remain blurred as, for instance, in I Corinthians 2:16, with its quotation from Isaiah 40:13, where the *ruach* of Yahweh is rendered as the *nous* of the Lord, preparatory to the assurance that we, for our part, "have the *nous* of Christ." The theophanic event, one may say, has for Paul its center of luminosity at the point of pneumatic irruption; and the direction in which he prefers to look from this center is toward transfigured reality rather than toward existence in the cosmos.

This preference causes certain ambiguities in the Pauline symbolism. In the famous hymn to love (*agape,* I Cor. 13), for instance, Paul accords the highest rank among the three so-called theological virtues of faith, hope, and love to Agape for the reason that it outlasts existence under the condition of *genesis* and *phthora* and carries over into *aphtharsia.* Faith and hope, as well as the divine gifts (*charismata*), belong to the temporal sphere of imperfection; love comprehends and surpasses them all, because it reaches from the abiding

sphere of perfection into the imperfection of existence. "As for gifts of prophecy, they will come to an end; as for the gifts of tongues, they will cease; as
for knowledge (*gnosis*), it will come to an end" (8). For in knowledge and
prophecy we have only truth broken into parts (*ek merous*), we don't have
the whole in full view. "But when consummation (or: perfection, *to teleion*)
comes, what is only partial will pass away" (10). "For now we see as through
a glass darkly, but then we shall be seeing face to face. Now I know only in
parts; but then I shall know as fully as I am known" (13:12). As for faith and
hope, they are not needed when reality has moved beyond *phthora* and become
abiding (Rom. 8). The equivalent symbols, thus, cease to be equivalent when
the recipient of the theophany moves from participation in divine reality to
the anticipation of a state of perfection (*to teleion*). The *teleios* in the state of
perfection is no longer the existential *teleios* who could be said to be equivalent to the Aristotelian *spoudaios*. The "man (*aner*)" of I Corinthians 13:11
is not the man who has become mentally adult in 14:20. As Paul moves from
participation to anticipation, the symbols which express existence in the
Metaxy acquire a new dimension of meaning; and Paul moves from the one
to the other with such ease that the symbols change their meaning indeed
in the twinkling of an eye.

I am not interested in pointing out terminological inconsistencies in the
letters of the saint. On the contrary, the ambiguities in Paul's symbolisms
must be accepted as the expression of his immersion in the directional movement of reality. Paul's anticipations imaginatively extrapolate the intense
assurance of the direction he has received through his vision of the Resurrected. When reading the First Letter to the Corinthians, I have always the
feeling of traveling, with Paul, from *phthora* to *aphtharsia* in a homogeneous
medium of reality, from existence in the Metaxy as a way station to immortality as a goal, with death as a minor incident on the road. Death is indeed
reduced to "the twinkling of an eye" in which reality switches from imperfection to perfection.

3. Death and Transfiguration

Such assurance met with skepticism among the recipients of the message,
and Paul felt compelled to answer pertinent questions concerning the source
of his assurance. In I Corinthians 15:12–19, he established the connection
between his prediction (*kerygma*) of resurrection and his vision of the Resurrected. "If there is no resurrection of the dead, then Christ has not been raised;
if Christ has not been raised, then your faith is vain (*mataia*)" (16–17). "If

Christ has not been raised, our preaching is empty (*kenon*) and your faith is empty"(15). The argument closes with the revealing sentence: "If we have no more than hope in Christ in this life, then we are of all men the most pitiful" (19). This sentence is the key to the understanding of Paul's experience of reality—or so at least it appears to me. Hope in this life, in our existence in the Metaxy, not only is not enough, it is worse than nothing, unless this hope is embedded in the assurance that derives from the vision.

The vision of the Resurrected is, for Paul, more than a theophanic event in the Metaxy; it is the beginning of transfiguration itself. This understanding of the vision, however, is possible only if the experience of a reality which paradoxically moves toward the divine Beyond of its structure, if the movement of the psyche toward the divine depth, is pursued to the point at which existence under the conditions of *genesis* and *phthora* is revealed as an event in the history of the divine Beyond. The Resurrection can be the beginning of transfiguration because it is revealed to Paul as an event in the tale of death he has to tell: "For as through one man came death, so now through one man comes the resurrection of the dead. For as in Adam all men die, so in Christ all men shall be made alive" (22–23). What I have called the "homogeneous medium of reality" in which I felt Paul moving from *phthora* to *aphtharsia* is the same medium of the myth in which the Fall of Adam occurs. When Paul goes beyond the analysis of reality in the perspective of the Metaxy, in order to interpret his vision of the Resurrected in the perspective of the divine Beyond that reaches into the Metaxy, he must, like Plato, resort to the symbolic form of the myth. Only in this medium can he tell the plot of the cosmic-divine drama that begins with death and ends with life.

Paul tells the tale of death and resurrection to its end. Having established Adam and Christ as the dramatis personae, he can pursue the phases of the transfiguration that has begun with the Resurrection in their due order (*hekastos de en to idio tagmati,* 23): In a first act (*aparche*), Christ is raised from the dead; then, when the *parousia* has occurred, those who belong to Christ will be raised; then comes the end (*telos*), with Christ handing over his kingdom to God the Father after he has destroyed the principalities (*arche*), authorities (*exousia*), and powers (*dynamis*); "and the last of the enemies to be destroyed is Death (*thanatos*)" (26). All things having been subjected to Christ, then, the Son himself will be subjected to God, "so that God may be all in all" (28). The war with the rebellious cosmic forces ends with the victory of God.

This tale, placing the vision in the perspective of God's way with the cosmos and man, dominates the imagination of Paul so strongly that the perspective of the Metaxy recedes to comparative insignificance. The domination of the tale rather than the tale itself is the cause of the ambiguities which spread from the symbols "death" and "time" to the various strata of Paul's exegesis. For the death of the tale is not the death every man has to suffer even if he believes in Christ. The difference could become shadowy to Paul, because he was obsessed with the expectation that the men living in Christ, himself included, would not die at all but, in the wake of the Parousia, be transfigured in their lifetimes. The transfiguration, as it had begun in time through Jesus the Christ, would shortly be completed in the same time. The Pauline "time" is ambiguous inasmuch as it lets the time of existence blend into the Time of the Tale.

4. The Truth of the Pauline Myth

The mythopoetic genius of Paul is not controlled by the critical consciousness of a Plato. The uncritical encumbrances of the symbolism must be discounted if the hard structure of its truth is to be discerned clearly. Since the tale of death and resurrection is a myth, the degree of differentiation it has achieved in symbolizing the truth about God and man must be determined by relating it to the less differentiated theophanic events, as well as to the more compact types of myth developed in the course of their exegesis. Myth is a symbolism engendered by the experience of divine presence in reality. In its cosmologically compact form, it is an intracosmic story about the gods and the divine origin of things. Still within this form, but pressing toward the limit of noetic consciousness, there develop the mytho-speculative types. When the breakthrough toward the luminosity of consciousness occurs, as in the Hellenic development of the noetic field, the myth then will lose its cosmological compactness; it can no longer be an intracosmic story, when its symbolism becomes luminous as the exegesis of a theophanic event in the Metaxy. Hence, the Platonic myth, though it can be a myth of the cosmos and its order, is no longer a cosmological myth, but an *alethinos logos,* a "true story," of the Demiurgic presence of God in man, society, history, and the cosmos. This philosopher's myth is carefully devised so as to make the tale of divine presence in reality compatible with the existential truth of man's tension toward the divine ground. The compactness of the myth dissolves when the structure of reality as revealed by the noetic theophany becomes the criterion of truth for the *alethinos logos.* Even the Platonic myth, however, is not yet fully differentiated; for Plato, though he established the truth of existence as the criterion for the truth of the myth, refrained from developing the criterion completely. Plato was aware, as I have shown, of the divine abyss beyond the revelation of God as the Nous, but he surrounded this further movement of the psyche toward the depth of divine reality with the deliberate uncertainties. Since the truth of existence was restricted to the noetic structure of consciousness, the *alethinos logos* of God and man in the *Timaeus* did not go beyond the figure of a Demiurge whose noetic efforts remained limited by Ananke.

Compared with the more compact types, the Pauline myth is distinguished by its superior degree of differentiation. In the first place, his vision carried Paul irresistibly beyond the structure of creation to its source in the freedom and love of divine creativity. Paul differentiated the truth of existence, *i.e.,* the experience of its ordering process through man's orientation toward the divine ground so far that the transcosmic God and his Agape were revealed as the mover in the theophanic events which constitute meaning in history. Since the truth of existence, however, is the criterion of truth for the myth, the Platonic type was no longer suitable as the ultimate truth about God and man, once the pneumatic depth in divine reality beyond the Nous had been articulated. While the Platonic Demiurge could remain limited by Ananke, the Pauline creator-god had to emerge victorious from his struggle with the forces of resistance in the cosmos. Paul, furthermore, differentiated fully the experience of the directional movement by articulating its goal, its *teleion,* as the state of *aphtharsia* beyond man's involvement in the Anaximandrian mystery of Apeiron and Time. If the movement of reality is consistently extrapolated toward its goal, again a more differentiated myth than the Platonic is required to express the experiential insight. In the perspective of the goal, the myth must become the story of the fall from and return to the imperishable state of creation intended by divine creativity. It must become the drama of creation and fall, of fall and redemption, of death and resurrection, and of the ultimate return of creation to its imperishable glory. The movement, in order to have meaning, must come to an end. In the philosophers' noetic theophany, the problem of the end presented itself in the form of Aristotle's aetiological argument and engendered the symbolism of the *prote arche;* in the pneumatic theophany of Paul, with divine creativity differentiated, an eschatology is required to complete the meaning of the movement. The Pauline myth indeed pursues the drama of the movement to its conclusion in the eschatological events. And finally, Paul has fully differentiated the experience of man as the site where the movement of reality becomes luminous in its actual occurrence. In Paul's myth, God emerges victorious, because his protagonist is man. He is the creature in whom God can incarnate himself with the fullness (*pleroma*) of his divinity, transfiguring man into the God-man (Col. 2:9). The whole creation that is groaning can be redeemed, because at one point, in man, the sonship of God is possible (Rom. 8:22–23). The movement in reality, that has become luminous to itself in noetic consciousness, has indeed unfolded its full meaning in the Pauline vision and its exegesis through the myth. The symbolism of the man who can achieve freedom from cosmic Ananke, who can enter into the freedom of God, redeemed by the loving grace of the God who is himself free of the cosmos, consistently differentiates the truth of existence that has become visible in the philosophers' experience of *athanatizein*.

5. Truth and History

The truth of existence emerges from the theophanic events in history. Paul's exegesis of his vision, with its concentration on the dynamics of theophany, brings the historicity of existential truth into sharper focus than did the philosopher's exegesis of the noetic theophany. Regarding the relation of truth and history, a new accent falls on the area of "history" and its rank in the whole of reality. The account of the hard structure of truth, as I have called it, in the Pauline myth would be incomplete if this issue, with its rich potential for misunderstandings, and deformations, were not clarified.

In classic philosophy, the discovery of noetic consciousness is inseparable from the consciousness of the discovery as an event which constitutes meaning in history. The statement summarily refers to a field of relations in reality which now must be detailed. The discovery has "meaning," because it advances man's insight into the order of his existence. The meaning of the advance, therefore, derives from the "meaning" of existential order in the sense of man's openness toward the divine ground, as well as from man's desire to know about the right order of existence and its realization. This derivation of historical meaning from the meaning of personal existence should be noted as peculiar to the noetic experience of reality; in the Pauline context we shall find the relation inverted. The advance of insight, furthermore, is an "advance" indeed. For the discovery is not dumped as a block of meaning into a "history" in which previously nobody had ever been concerned with such problems of meaning. The discovery of noetic consciousness is intelligible as an "advance" in relation to the more compact experiences and symbolizations of existential order preceding it. In Aristotle's language, the *philomythos*

Theophanic events constitute history
because they are events of men in union with the divine
CAP. D,

252   THE ECUMENIC AGE

and the *philosophos* experience and symbolize the same structure of reality at different levels of differentiation. The "advance" of meaning implies the "equivalence" of symbolisms, in this case of myth and philosophy. What becomes visible in the new luminosity, therefore, is not only the structure of consciousness itself (in classical language: the nature of man), but also the structure of an "advance" in the process of reality. Moreover, the site of the advance is not a mysterious entity called "history" that would exist independent of such advances; the site rather is the very consciousness which, in its state of noetic luminosity, makes these discoveries. The theophanic events do not occur *in* history; they constitute history together with its meaning. The noetic theophany, finally, reveals consciousness as having the structure of metaleptic reality, of the divine-human Metaxy. As a consequence, "history" in the sense of an area in reality in which the insight into the meaning of existence advances is the history of theophany. This is the state of insight achieved by Plato in his symbolization of meaning in history through the three stages of theophany.

This complex of insights has a considerable number of implications. Not all of them were unfolded in the philosophers' exegesis of noetic theophany; and some of them have indeed not been fully articulated to this day. For the present, however, the analysis must restrict itself to the specific problem that can compel, if differentiated under the impact of further theophanies, the transition from the Platonic to the Pauline understanding of history. This subcomplex to which I am referring is the peculiar tension in noetic consciousness between the truth of existence as it has become articulate in the set of classical symbols—*i.e., zetesis* and *kinesis; eros, thanatos,* and *dike; elpis, pistis,* and *philia;* and so forth—and the truth of existence as a state of existential order that emerges in a man when he goes through a theophanic event. This tension between the exegetic surface and the experiential depth of the theophanic event lies at the core of the vast controversies about the topical issue "truth and history." The peculiar achievement of the Pauline differentiation will not be fully intelligible unless it is set off against the potential of misconstruction inherent to the tension.

In its experiential depth, a theophanic event is a turbulence in reality. The thinker who has become engulfed by it must try to rise, like the Aeschylean diver, from the depth to the surface of exegesis. When he has come up, he may wonder whether the tale he tells is indeed the story of the turbulence, or whether he has not slanted his account toward one or the other aspect of the complex event; and he will wonder rightly, because the outcome depends on the interaction of divine presence and human response in the depth, as well as on the cultural context of the surface that will bias his exegesis toward what appears at the time the most important part of the truth newly discovered. If the account is slanted toward structure in reality, the structure of the "man" who can rise from the turbulence with noetic insight will be of absorbing interest. Even though the philosopher does not lose sight of the process in metaleptic reality at all, the "structural" bias still can, on occasion, induce a symbol like the Aristotelian "definition" of man as the *zoon noun echon,* as the living being that has reason. If such a "definition" is, then, torn out of its analytical context, it can degenerate into a definition in the nominalist sense; *yes.* and a "nature of man" which by definition does not change will become a fixture in the "history of philosophy," as in fact it has become in Western "culture." If, on the other hand, the account is slanted toward the process in reality, a quite remarkable change is to be observed, inasmuch as "man" emerges from the turbulence with an articulate consciousness of existence in the Metaxy which he formerly did not have. The change is so remarkable indeed that it motivates the Platonic-Aristotelian preoccupation with a "history" in which such things can happen. Like the structurally fixed "nature of man," the "change" in his nature can, and does, degenerate into a definitional fixture in the "culture" of society, so that the paradox of a reality which moves beyond its own structure dissociates into the ideological controversy whether *yes* the "nature of man" does, or does not, change.

Moreover, the dissociation of the paradox into a quarrel about definitional fixtures which have cut loose from their experiential basis cannot be brushed aside as a harmless entertainment for mediocre thinkers. On the contrary, the dynamics of the tension in which the definitionally derailed symbols originate is still fully effective; the paradox in reality has not disappeared, and under its pressure the polarized definitions develop a life of their own. The definitions, one may say, are in search of a "turbulence" that will supply them with the meaning they lost when they cut loose from the theophanic event; and they find this source of meaning in the man-made turbulence of a "revolution." The revolution in "history" is made to substitute for the theophanic event in reality. The turbulence of the encounter between God and man is transformed into the violence of an encounter between man and man. In the imaginary reality of the ideologists, this killing of men in revolutionary action is supposed to produce the much desired transfigurative, or metastatic, change of the nature of man as an event in "history." Marx has been quite explicit on this point: Revolutionary killing will induce a *Blutrausch,* a "blood-intoxication"; and from this *Blutrausch* "man" will emerge as "superman" into the "realm of freedom." The magic of the *Blutrausch* is the ideological equivalent to the promise of the Pauline vision of the Resurrected.

In the preceding paragraphs I have made considerable use of quotation marks. They indicate that the respective terms have moved from their original state of bona fide mythical, philosophical, or revelatory symbols to the state of degraded symbols, as Mircea Eliade calls them. In the course of Western deculturation, acutely since the middle of the eighteenth century, the symbols have become transformed into figures in the alienation games played by ideologists. As these games have no philosophical intention, it would be a misunderstanding to treat them as philosophical aberrations. They deliberately transpose reality and the paradox of its structure into the medium of an imaginary "Second Reality" in which the mystery of cosmic-divine reality that must be lived through, and died through, can be speculatively solved and actively abolished by men whose existence has been disordered by their *libido dominandi*. The enterprise is, of course, grotesque; and this strand of the grotesque in Western deculturation cannot be stressed strongly enough. There is the Comte who replaces the Era of Christ by the Era of Comte, and who writes letters to the Russian Czar, to the Grand Vizier of the Sultan, and to the General of the Jesuit Order with the purpose of bringing the Orthodox Church, Islam, and the Catholic Church home into the fold of positivism. And there is the Hegel who presents himself to the world as the ultimate Incarnation of the Logos, in the sense of the gospel of John. Consistently, this generation of the new Christs is followed, at the distance of a century, by the practitioners of transfiguration into the millennium by mass murder and concentration camps, by the Hitlers and Stalins. To this grotesquerie of libidinous obsession belongs the conception of "history" as an area in reality in which *aphtharsia* for mankind can be achieved, if not in the twinkling of an eye, at least by the judicious acceleration of *phthora* for a sufficient number of human beings over a reasonable number of generations.

The philosophical and revelatory symbols engendered by the theophanic events, and the degraded symbols as they are used in alienation games, illuminate each other as well as the common structure they express equivalently. The new Christs who appear in the first half of the nineteenth century and compete with the Resurrected of the Pauline vision, are the best proof, if proof were needed, for the constancy of the problem of transfiguration in historical consciousness. The paradox of a reality which moves toward its transfiguration is the structure equivalently expressed. Since the comparative empirical study of the relations between symbols and experiences has barely begun in our time, this may sound odd at first hearing. What has a theophanic event in the Metaxy in common with the libidinous obsession of an alienation game? I should like to stress, therefore, the identity of structure in both the consciousness of the Metaxy and the consciousness of the alienated Messianic speculator. In the experience of existential tension toward the divine ground, the poles of the tension are symbolized as "God" and "man," while the In-Between of existence is expressed by such symbols as *methexis, metalepsis,* or *metaxy.* In the closed existence of the alienated speculator, the structure of the Metaxy remains the same, but the thinker must now, in Nietzsche's phrase, extend grace to himself. He must develop a "divided self," with one self acting the role of "man" who suffers the human condition and the other self acting the role of "God" who brings salvation from it. The Metaxy becomes, in Hegel's language, the state of *Zerrissenheit* (diremption) or *Entfremdung* (alienation); the elaboration of the speculative system becomes the act of salvational *Versoehnung* (reconciliation); and the man who performs the feat combines in his person the two natures of God and man in the sense of the Definition of Chalcedon; he is the new God-man, the new Messiah. The structure of reality does not disappear, however, because somebody engages in libidinous revolt against it. While the structure remains the same, the revolt results, personally, in the destruction of existential order and, socially, in mass murder. I do not care to go beyond this point. It would be tempting to characterize the "divided self" of the alienated thinker as "schizoid," but the relation of this type of pneumopathological deformation to the phenomena which in psychopathology are treated under the general head of "schizophrenia" are not yet sufficiently explored. Certainly, however, the comparison casts some light on the phenomenon that is conventionally called "immanentism."

In the modern state of alienation, the enterprise of self-salvation dominates the concern with history and meaning. Theophanic events are no longer permitted to constitute meaning in history through an advance of insight into the truth of existence. The "meaning of history" itself has now been discovered by the new Messiahs; and the meaning of existence derives from participation in the libidinous speculation and action of the self-saviors. In its modern degradation, thus, "history" symbolizes the *opus* of revolutionary transfiguration. This extreme contraction of "history" to the meaning of an alchemistic, or magic, *opus* of transfiguring reality through revolution will, in its turn, illuminate the shift of accent in the transition from the classic to the Pauline conception of history.

6. The Truth of Transfiguration

In the letters of Paul, the central issue is not a doctrine but the assurance of immortalizing transfiguration through the vision of the Resurrected. Transfiguration is experienced as an "historical" event that has begun with the Passion and Resurrection of Christ. This experience must now be pursued a few steps beyond the previous analysis.

In Galatians 1:11–17, Paul insists on the purely divine source of the good tidings he has to bring. The evangel he has to evangelize, he has not "received or learned from any man," especially not from the apostolic pillars in Jerusalem, but exclusively through the "visionary appearance (*apokalypsis*) of Jesus Christ" (1:12), accorded to him by the grace of God who "revealed (*apokalypsai*) his Son in me" (1:16). I am rendering these key passages literally, because paraphrases as one finds them in standard translations would obscure Paul's precision in articulating his experience of the God who enters him through the vision and by this act of entering transfigures him. The Pauline theophany is structured in depth into the vision of the Resurrected and the presence of the God beyond who, by means of the vision, calls Paul to his apostolate. Paul is, above all, a prophet who is called by God to his office like the prophets of Israel. When he expresses his experience of the call (Gal. 1:15), he uses the same formula as Jeremiah (Jer. 1:5) and Deutero-Isaiah (Isa. 49:1); and there is even some cosmological coloring to the formula as the prophets derived it from the Near Eastern formula for the call by which the god ordains the king in his office. Paul is, second, the apostle to the nations who has to announce the truth of the transfiguration that has begun with Resurrection. This truth he symbolizes as the *Evangelium Dei* (*euaggelion theou*), as God's "gospel about his Son" that has been promised long ago "by his prophets in the holy scriptures" (Rom. 1:1–3). The stratification into the call by God and the gospel about his Son is so important for Paul's self-understanding that he refers to it whenever he introduces himself formally as the "apostle," as in I Corinthians 1:1, in Galatians 1:1–5, and most elaborately in Romans 1:1–6. From this stratification he derives his style of "apostle," thereby distinguishing himself from the earlier prophets who held out the promise that now in him is fulfilled.

The meaning of transfiguration as an historical event is set forth in the Letter to the Romans, especially in the famous self-analysis of Chapter 7. Paul lives in a state of existential unrest. His anxiety is caused by the conflict between the divine law, the Torah, which demands perfect obedience, and hamartia (sin)

the weakness of the flesh which makes obedience to the letter impossible. "I delight in the law of God with my inner man, but I see another law in my members warring against the law that my reason (*nous*) approves, keeping me captive in the law of sin (*hamartia*) that is in my members" (Rom. 7:22–23). "I discover it as a law, then, that when I want to do right, only wrong is within my reach" (7:22). This conflict inevitably raises the question of identity: "I do not even recognize my action as my own. For I do not do the good I want, but the evil I hate." "I can will what is right, but I cannot do it" (7:19; 18). The conclusion: "Now if I do what I do not want to do, clearly it is not I who do it but sin (*hamartia*) that dwells within me" (7:20). Paul does not attempt to shirk responsibility; he meditates on the loss of the true self in existence when the horizon of order, the "righteousness" or "justification" of existence, is limited by a law which, though it remains holy, has become impermeable for divine presence. Paul is in search of God, like Plato and Aristotle, but he finds the movement of his soul obstructed by a law that, for him at least, has become opaque and prevents his existence in the Metaxy.

Moreover, Paul is very much aware that the obstruction to the free movement is an "historical" problem, peculiar to the Judaism of his time; the law was not always a screen that separated man from God. He knows himself as the successor to the prophets who prefigured the freedom that he has gained; and he knows about the Abraham who lived before the law and to whom his faith (*pistis*) rather than any deeds in fulfillment of a law was counted as righteousness (Rom. 4:3; Gen. 15:6). "The Law brings wrath, but where there is no Law there is no transgression" (Rom. 4:15). The deadly sense of living irreparably in sin under God's wrath can be overcome only by opening oneself in faith to the grace and love of God. This paradigmatic type of existence Paul finds realized in Abraham. God promised Abraham that he would be the father of many nations because of his faith, and his descendants would inherit the world (*kosmos*). This promise does not refer to the bodily descendants of the patriarch, but to all men who share in the faith of Abraham whether they belong to the circumcision or not. "For he is the father of us all" who live "in the presence of the God in whom he believed, who brings the dead to life again, and who calls into being what is not, as he called what is" (4:9–17). Abraham is the prototype of man's existence in truth. His universal humanity through faith in the universal God that made him the father of many nations was continued by Israel's prophets to the nations, and is now consummated by Paul as the apostle to the nations (4:23–25). The Pauline apostolate, finally, is the consummation of the historical promise that goes back to Abraham, because through the visions of the Resurrected God has revealed Jesus as his Son who could do what "the law, weakened by the flesh, could not do": Entering the form of sinful flesh, he could break the power of the flesh by the power of the divine spirit (8:3). Hence, from now on there is no judgment of condemnation for those who are united with Jesus Christ. "For the law of the spirit of life-in-Christ-Jesus has set me free from the law of sin and death" (8:1–2).

Paul's restlessness because of the weakness of the flesh, his finding of the pneumatic order of existence, and his consciousness of a history of faith that culminates in the vision of the Resurrected must be treated as a unit of experience, just as the Platonic-Aristotelian *zetesis,* the finding of the noetic order of existence, and the consciousness of the discovery as an event in the history of theophany are a unit that must not be torn asunder. The specific difference between the two units is the accent that falls, in the classic case, on the cognition of structure and, in the Pauline case, on the exodus from structure. The difference, then, expresses itself in the literary form. In classic philosophy, the reflections on history appear incidental to the analysis of structure. Aristotle wrote an *Ethics* and *Politics;* he did not write an *Historics.* With Paul, the history of faith dominates the Letter to the Romans, while the reflections on personal and political conduct in the short present before the Parousia are appended in Chapters 12–15. The classic meaning *in* history can be opposed by Paul with a meaning *of* history, because he knows the end of the story in the transfiguration that begins with the Resurrection.

The difference between the two conceptions, however, is not contradictory; it does not compel a choice between alternatives. On the contrary, the two conceptions together act out, in the luminosity of consciousness, the paradox of a reality that moves beyond its structure. Neither does the classic concentration on structure abolish the unrest of the movement that becomes manifest in the Platonic uncertainties, nor does the Pauline relegation of ethics and politics to the fringes of a history that has been contracted into the transfiguring exodus abolish the cosmos and its structure. When the paradox of reality becomes luminous to itself in consciousness, it creates the paradox of a history in suspense between the Ananke of the cosmos and the freedom of eschatological movement. That the two branches of the paradox are distributed, in the Ecumenic Age, over the noetic theophanies of Hellenic philosophers and the pneumatic theophanies of Israelite-Jewish prophets must be acknowledged, but cannot be explained. The process of history is a mystery as much as the reality that becomes luminous in it.

Vladimir Soloovyov
later — Kyrc Russia

To the symbol "history," it appears, there must be accorded an amplitude wide enough to accommodate all the theophanic events in which the paradox of reality breaks through to consciousness.

a man's cons cons life in an event

This insight should clarify at least some of the issues involved in the worrisome debate about the "historicity" of Christ. As far as Paul is concerned, there was hardly an issue, because he still moved, like Plato, in an open field of theophany. The Olympian gods were, for Plato, just as valid theophanic symbols as his Puppet Player, or the Demiurge, or the Nous, or the unknown Father-God in the Beyond of this diversified field of divinities. In the same manner, Paul moved in a world of principalities, dominations, and powers, of death and sin, among whom the ultimately victorious Son of God had his place under the unknown Father-God beyond them all. In Galatians 4:8-13 and Colossians 2:20, Christ is presented as a superior divinity in competition with the "elemental spirits (*stoicheia*) of the cosmos"; the recipients of Paul's letters are reproached for backsliding to the cult of *stoicheia* who "by nature are not even gods" after they "have come to know God, or rather to be known by God" (Gal. 4:8-9).

The openness of the theophanic field, though it came under pressure when the Church felt it necessary to distinguish its "monotheism" from the "polytheism" of the pagans, could be substantially preserved for almost three centuries. The early Patres, from Justin and Athenagoras, through Theophilus, Tertullian, Hippolytus of Rome, and Origen, to Eusebius (ob. 339) found one or the other subordinationist construction to be the most suitable symbolism for expressing the relation of the Son to the Father-God. In the language of Origen, for instance, though the Son is *homoousios* with the Father, only the Father is *autotheos*, the God himself, while the Logos is a *deuteros theos*, a second God. One should note, furthermore, that Origen still felt quite free to create a neologism like *theanthropos*, the God-man, in order to express the ✓ incarnation of the Logos in Jesus. I mention it especially, because it had a surprising career in the time of the new Christs, in the nineteenth century, when Feuerbach hauled the God whom man had projected into the Beyond back into projecting man, thereby transforming man into God-man. Up to Nicaea (325), when the Athanasian victory put an end to this generous openness, Christianity was substantially ditheistic.[2]

The history of the Patres puts it beyond a doubt that the symbol "Christ"

---

[2] For the pre- and post-Nicene patrology, as well as for the references given in the text, cf. Berthold Altaner, *Patrologie: Leben, Schriften und Lehren der Kirchenvaeter* (Freiburg, 1951).

changes its meaning in the transition from the open field of theophany to
the realm of dogmatic construction. If the question of the "historicity" of
Christ is raised with the "Christ" of the dogma in mind, difficulties will inevitably arise. For the "Christ" of Nicaea and Chalcedon is not the reality of
theophanic history that confronts us in the Pauline vision of the Resurrected;
and to invent a special kind of "history," disregarding the theophanic reality
on which the dogma is based, in order to endow the Christ of the dogma with
"historicity," would make no sense. The trinitarian and christological dogma ✓
can be made intelligible only in terms of its own history, as a protective device
that will shield the oneness of the Unknown God against confusion with the
experiences of divine presence in the myths of the intracosmic gods, in mytho-
speculation, and in the noetic and pneumatic luminosity of consciousness.

§ 2. THE EGOPHANIC REVOLT

In the eighteenth and nineteenth centuries, a new kind of "history" was
invented, in order to accommodate the degraded "Christ"-symbolisms of the
new Christs who rejected theophanic reality altogether. I have just mentioned
the degrading transformation of Origen's *theanthropos* into the God-man of
Feuerbach's projection-psychology. The structure of this specifically "modern"
problem, however, is not yet sufficiently explored; the study of noetic and
pneumatic experience, of compactness and differentiation, of deformation of
existence and degrading of symbols is still in its beginnings; and the presentation of the problem is handicapped by the want of an established technical
language. I have spoken of ideological thinkers and their alienation games, of
the way they use philosophical and revelatory symbols in a degraded form,
and of their "divided self" by which they reproduce the structure of the
Metaxy in the state of alienation. This conventional language, though, is no
more than topically descriptive; it does not analytically penetrate to the
counterforce that compels the rejections of the theophany. I suggest, therefore,
the term *egophany* as a suitable symbol that will express the pathos of thinkers
who exist in a state of alienation and libidinous obsession.

1. The Egophanic Deformation of History

If the turbulence of theophany gives way to the revolution of egophany, the
reality of theophanic history must be eclipsed by an imaginary egophanic
history which is devised to culminate in the apocalyptic self-realization of the
thinker, as in the "philosophies of history" of Condorcet, Comte, or Hegel.

It must be especially devised for this purpose, for a history constituted by the noetic and pneumatic theophanies of a Plato and Paul can advance to the further differentiations of mysticism and, correspondingly, tolerance in dogmatic matters; it can also leave ample room for egophanic deformations of existence and the mass murder of human beings; but it cannot be made to yield egophany and mass murder as the meaningfully differentiated climax of theophany. If "history" is to culminate in the egophany of the respective thinker, it must have been egophanic history from the beginning. In order to create this imaginary history, the theophanic events must be reconstructed as egophanic events; and to this purpose, the reality of the Metaxy must be made to disappear. As far as man's humanity is concerned, the maturity of the classic *spoudaios* and the Pauline *teleios* must become a state of immaturity, *Comte did this* of men benighted by theological and metaphysical conceits, so that the state of egophanic "science" (Fichte, Hegel, Comte, Marx) can appear as the perfection of a maturity previously intended but only imperfectly realized. As far as God's divinity is concerned, the symbols engendered by theophanic events must be understood as projections of an imperfectly evolved self-reflective consciousness; in the state of perfect self-reflection (Hegel) God is dead (de Sade, Hegel), and if he is not dead enough he must be murdered (Nietzsche), so that the egophanic God-man or superman (Feuerbach, Marx, Nietzsche) can establish the final realm of freedom in history. A radically egophanic "history" is constructed with the intent of leaving no room for theophanic experiences and their symbolization. Hence, when the varieties of egophanic history have come to dominate the climate of opinion, as they *The Jesus Seminar today etc* do in our time, not surprisingly the "historicity" of Christ has become a problem for thinkers, including a good number of theologians, who have succumbed to the climate.

The egophanic constructions, with their peculiar deformation of humanity and divinity, resemble in certain points the conception of history in which the imperial entrepreneurs of Herodotus and Thucydides indulged. The *tertium comparationis* is the concupiscential drive that is set free to create order in its own image when a society is in crisis because the spiritual and intellectual substance of its order has atrophied to the extent that the established institutions and symbols are felt to be no longer representative of cosmic-divine order and the truth of existence. The parallelism, however, is not always readily apparent, because the cultural contexts in which the two drives originate, and have to find their self-expression through symbols, differ widely. The modern egophanic exodus presupposes the events of the Ecumenic Age inasmuch as it has to be conducted on the level of noetic and pneumatic consciousness, of philosophy and revelation, that has become the cultural heritage of Western civilization. The ancient symbolisms of the giants who are struck down when they reach for heaven, or of the envy of the gods that strikes the man who in his envy of the gods raises himself beyond the stature allowed to man, it is true, still apply to the modern giants; but in their self-interpretation the new Christs are not in competition with Zeus or Apollo, they are envious of Christ. In particular, they are bent on achieving the state of transfiguration in "history" that had been denied to Paul in spite of his vision, and to everyman since, because he died before the Second Coming; and to this purpose they try to force the Parousia into history in their own person.

Hegel, the philosophically most competent and historically most knowledgeable of the egophanic thinkers, was very much aware of this purpose as well as of its ultimate derivation from the Pauline vision of the Resurrected. The Christ of Hegel is not the Resurrected of the vision itself but a doctrinally derivative God-man; he appears in the event of "the divine being becoming man (*Menschwerdung des goettlichen Wesens*)." This is "the simple content of absolute religion." The divine being is "known as spirit, as *Geist*"; this religion is "the consciousness of itself to be *Geist*." The divine being is now "revealed" inasmuch as one knows what it is; and it is known inasmuch as it is known as *Geist,* "as being that is essentially self-consciousness (*Selbstbewusstsein*)." It is revealed to self-consciousness in its immediacy, as it is self-consciousness itself. "The divine nature is the same as the human nature; and it is this unit (*Einheit*) that is seen (*angeschaut*)." "That the supreme being can be seen and heard as an existent self-consciousness is the perfection of its concept"; in this perfection it is as existent in its immediacy as it is essence.[3] Not too many steps more in the dialectical process are needed for Hegel to advance from his conception of Christ in the "absolute religion" to the conceptual realization of the divine in his own "absolute knowledge (*absolutes Wissen*)." Using Paul's language (I Cor. 2:10), Hegel achieves the "revelation of the depth" in the "absolute concept." "The *Geist* that knows itself as *Geist*" is absolute knowledge (*absolutes Wissen*); and "in this revelation" the depth of the Pauline wisdom that pertained to the knowledge of an impending transfiguration is abolished (*das Aufheben seiner Tiefe*) by the transfiguration achieved.[4]

Hegel is as deliberate in his deforming action as he is skillful at hiding it

[3] Hegel, *Phaenomenologie des Geistes,* ed. Johannes Hoffmeister (6th ed. Hamburg, 1952), 528ff.
[4] *Ibid.,* 564.

behind a respectable-looking facade of philosophizing. He is the egophanic manipulator *par excellence*. Since his tactics are representative for the egophanic movement at large, and since they are still a strongly effective cause in the contemporary confusion about history and theophany, a word of comment on the quotations is necessary.

Human and divine nature (*Natur*) are the same. In this declaration, while using the language of the dogma, Hegel flatly rejects the Definition of Chalcedon with its concern about making divine and human nature, which are supposed to be different, intelligible as copresent in the one person of Christ.[5] The motive, intention, and implications of this rejection by a thinker who otherwise insists on his orthodoxy are the subject matter of a great debate, especially among Protestant theologians, that goes on to this day and fills a library. Certainly, Hegel was not a simple "heretic." The rejection quite possibly is motivated by a sense of incongruity between the Christ of the dogma and the Son of God we meet in the Gospels and the letters of Paul. One can admire the technical perfection of the Definition of Chalcedon under the conditions of philosophical culture in the fifth century A.D. and still refuse to use its language when speaking of "Christ," because the philosophical terminology of "natures" has become inadequate in the light of what we know today about both classic philosophy and theophanic events. Moreover, that the return from dogma to the reality of experience is a strong component in Hegel's rejection is made probable, not only by his general insistence on this problem, but also by the post-Hegelian preoccupation of theologians with the "historical Jesus," the "historicity of Christ," the "existence" in faith, and the increasing awareness of the apocalyptic strand in the New Testament.

And yet, while all this must be acknowledged as possible and probable in the motivations Hegel had in common with an age that was in revolt against theological and metaphysical dogmatism, it must also be acknowledged that in fact he did not return from the dogma to theophanic reality but, on the contrary, proceeded to dogmatize his egophany. He rejected the dogma but continued to use its language. An ingenious device: By rejecting the dogma he could throw out the theophanic event it was meant to protect; by retaining its language, he could use it as a cover for his far-reaching egophanic enterprise. If anybody should draw from the declaration the conclusion that he has identified God and man, Hegel could throw up his hands in horror at such malicious slander by a person whose intellectual powers were not sufficient to

---

[5] For the import of the definition of Chalcedon on the christological issue, cf. W. H. C. Frend, *The Rise of the Monophysite Movement* (Cambridge, 1972).

understand a work of speculative philosophy; and he was quite good at righteous indignation. He has never identified God and man; he has only philosophically identified both their natures as "self-consciousness." This argument can be used effectively, of course, only ff in the surrounding society the dogma has lost its meaning as a protective symbolization of the original theophanic event, if it has so far ossified that its symbols can be used as pieces in a speculative game regardless of their original meaning. And a game it is indeed that in these pages of the *Phaenomenologie* Hegel plays with the German word *Wesen.*[6] At the beginning of the paragraph, the word is used to signify the Divine Being (*Wesen*), *i.e.,* God himself; in the immediately following sentences, the word becomes equivocal, so that one cannot be sure whether it should be translated as Divine Being or divine essence; toward the end of the paragraph, the meaning of *Wesen* as essence preponderates; and in its last sentence, the phrase *goettliche Natur,* divine nature, is used as synonymous with *goettliches Wesen,* Divine Being. Though the paragraph begins with the Incarnation of God in Christ and ends with the self-consciousness that operates its own transfiguration, by writing the *Phaenomenologie,* Hegel has talked, with the appearance of perfect innocence, about nothing but the *Wesen,* that is *Geist,* about the *Geist* that is *Selbstbewusstsein,* and about the *Selbtbewusstsein* that is the *Wesen* of the *Geist.* The game is rigged; you can't win once you let yourself be sucked into accepting Hegel's language.

The reader can't win. But there is no doubt about the winnings of the egophanic manipulator. He has abolished the theophanic event, together with the consciousness of existence in the Metaxy in which it becomes luminous; and most importantly, he has abolished the stratification of divine reality in depth. Whether it is Plato or Paul, whether the noetic or the pneumatic theophany, whether God reveals himself as the Demiurge of structure or as the Redeemer from structure, revelation is experienced, not as identification with, but as participation in, divine reality. Beyond the theophanic presence experienced there lies, in the language of Aquinas, the tetragrammatic depth of the unfathomable divine reality that has not even the proper name "God." Hence, in order to endow his egophanic construction of divine-human identity with a semblance of truth, Hegel must abolish the stratification of divine reality in depth; and he does it, as I have said, by referring to the authority of I Corinthians 2:10, where Paul indeed speaks of "the spirit that penetrates (or: searchingly explores, *ereunao*) everything, even the depths of God." But

[6] Hegel, *Phaenomenologie,* 528ff.

what are these "depths of God (*ta bathe tou theou*)?" The immediately preceding sentence (2:9–10) gives the answer:

> But as it is written,
>   "What no eye has seen, nor ear has heard,
>   nor arose as thought from the heart of man,
>   what God has prepared for those who love him,"
> God has revealed to us through the spirit.

The "depths" revealed are not a "divine nature" but the divine plan of redemption through the victory of the Son of God over the hostile forces of
the cosmos, as attested by God himself (*to martyrion tou theou*, 2:1) in the
vision of the Resurrected. In using this passage for this purpose, Hegel pretends the revealed depths of Paul to mean the unrevealed depth of divine
reality that now will be revealed in his speculative system. In Hegel's language,
in his *Philosophie der Religion,* the depth when revealed looks like this: "God
is self-consciousness; he knows himself in a consciousness different from his
own, which is *in itself* (*an sich*) the consciousness of God, but also *for itself*
(*fuer sich*), inasmuch as it knows its identity with God, an identity that however is mediated by the negation of finiteness."[7]

Extraordinary, but not unique. There is the story of the fundamentalist
minister who worried when the women of his congregation began arranging
their hair in attractive topknots. On Sunday he castigated this wave of vanity
and, finally, issued the command "Topknot go down." So it was ordered, he
told them, by Scripture in Mark 13:15. When the women came home, they
looked up the passage quoted, and this is what they found: "And let him that
is on the house top not go down into the house, neither enter therein, to take
anything out of his house."

To sum the matter up, the debate about the "historicity of Christ" is not
concerned with a problem in reality; it rather is a symptom of the modern
state of deculturation. If Hegel's treatment of the issues be considered representative for the class of egophanic thinkers and their epigones, the "debate"
is characterized by a curious medley of motivations and derailments. As the
fundamental motivation, there can be discerned the legitimate discontent with
a doctrinaire metaphysics and theology that has cut loose from the originating
experiences and an earnest desire to return to the reality experienced. The desire, however, did not reach its goal either of reconstructing and re-enacting

---

[7] Hegel, *Vorlesungen ueber die Philosophie der Religion* (Stuttgart, 1965), Vol. 2 (Jubilaeumsausgabe, ed. Hermann Glockner, Vol. 16), 191.

the original experiences, or of advancing beyond them to mysticism; the task of the return was deflected by the outburst of egophany, carried by the momentum of several centuries of growth. The outburst was personally possible, and socially effective, because by the eighteenth century the gulf between symbols and experiences had become so wide that the standards of control by reason and reality were lost. The atrophied dogma, metaphysical and theological, was so badly discredited that it could no longer function as a controlling authority, while the originating experiences, noetic and pneumatic, were so deeply buried under the millennial accretions of doctrine that their recovery proved considerably more difficult than anybody anticipated at the time. As a matter of fact, by now it has taken two centuries of work by historians and philosophers to gain a moderately adequate understanding of Greek philosophical culture as well as of the New Testament period; and even these gains have not yet noticeably expanded beyond the sphere of personal efforts into broader social effectiveness. These characteristics of a deculturation period, it is true, must be taken into account in any judgment on the oddities one encounters in the works of the new Christs as well as their followers to this day. But a proper regard for the extenuating circumstances in the situation must not obscure the clear perception of egophanic self-aggrandizement as the motive power behind the grotesque mixture of brilliant speculation and mischievous semantic games, of vast historical knowledge and arbitrary distortions of facts, of profound insight into problems of the spirit and an almost blasphemous misuse of Biblical texts, of serious concern about the disease of the age and the tactics of deceptive manipulation, of perceptive common sense and the dream of accomplishing a salvation of mankind which the Resurrected of the Pauline vision had not been able to deliver.

2. The Constancy of Transfiguration

Egophanic deformation notwithstanding, the Hegelian speculative revelation is an equivalent to the Pauline vision. Both symbolisms express experiences of the movement in reality beyond its structure. The experience of transfiguration, thus, emerges from the confrontation between Hegel and Paul as one of the great constants in history, spanning the period from the Ecumenic Age to Western modernity. This constant requires a few analytical remarks, in conclusion of the present chapter.

The constant is in need of analysis, because its successive manifestations cannot be brought on a line of compactness and differentiation. The Hegelian system is neither a differentiating advance beyond the Pauline vision, nor is it a regression to a pre-Pauline state of compactness. The two symbolisms are related rather through such phenomena as scotosis by secondary, derivative symbols and deformation by the egophanic outburst. Moreover, the increasing obscurity is not caused by an inexplicable deviation from analytical purity but, on the contrary, is inherent to the constant from its origin in Paul's analytically defective interpretation of his vision. If the exemplification of the process be restricted to the stages that have become topical in the preceding reflections on the "historicity of Christ," one would have to describe it briefly as follows:

(1) There is the original discrepancy in Paul's interpretation between the hard core of truth, as I have called it, and the not-so-hard fringe of ambiguities and metastatic expectations.

(2) The Christ in Paul's myth of the struggle among the cosmic forces, then, was submitted to interpretation by the christological dogma, couched in the philosophically secondary, semihypostatic language of "natures." The doctrinization by means of derivative symbols was necessary under the conditions of philosophical debate in the fourth and fifth centuries A.D., but, as should be noted, it inverted the Platonic procedure of introducing the "true" or "likely" myth when the philosopher's analysis of noetic consciousness had reached its limit. In the christological case, the Pauline myth of the "Son of God" was not superseded by a differentiating analysis of consciousness but rather obscured by a reinterpretation in pseudo-philosophical terms.

(3) On these historical accretions of symbols, finally, there were superimposed the egophanic constructions, as represented by the Hegelian system.

The sequence of symbolizations just adumbrated did little, if anything, to dissolve the initial defect, but rather inflated it to monstrous proportions. The result is the grotesque intellectual mess which today has become the principal obstacle to a rational study of history and its theophanic structure. This many-storied edifice of interpretations, with one derivative symbolism piled on top of the other through almost two thousand years, must be considered beyond repair. There is no longer any sense in discussing the problem of transfiguration within the premises set by the contemporary intellectual disorder. It rather has become the philosopher's task to clarify, as far as that is possible, the problem in reality that has been experienced as existentially important enough to inspire the erection of the building in continuity through the millennia, and still inspires our ideological dogmatomachy, however zealotic, doctrinaire, aberrant, and dilettantic its efforts may be.

The troublesome constant is the experience of transfiguration as symbolized by Paul. As far as Paul is concerned, the vision of the Resurrected assured him that the transfiguration of reality had actually begun and would soon be completed by the Second Coming. The meaning *of* history now was known, and the end was near. This double-pronged assurance, however, ran into the empirical difficulty that the Parousia did not occur; and the variegated responses to the fact of non-occurrence have formed the field of self-understanding for the Western Christianitas right up to the egophanic outburst and the ideological "philosophies of history" which expect the goal of perfection, the *teleion,* to be reached in the near future. The main Church had accepted Augustine's symbolization of the present, post-Christ period as the *saeculum senescens,* as the time of waiting for the Parousia and the eschatological events, while the more fervent expectations were pushed to the sectarian fringe of apocalyptic and Gnostic movements. By the twelfth century A.D., this inconclusive arrangement had experientially outlived itself. The Western empire of the crusades, of the new religious orders, and the cathedral schools, of cities in growth and national kingdoms in formation, could hardly leave the witnesses of the age unaware that a "meaning" beyond a mere waiting was being constituted in history. The spiritual ferment became manifest in such representative reinterpretations of history as the *Chronica* of Otto of Freising (*ca.* 1114–1158) and the writings of Joachim of Flora (*ca.* 1145–1202). Both Otto and Joachim interpreted the flowering of the monastic life as the event that indicated a meaningful advance in the process of transfiguration. Joachim, in particular, apprehended in it the approach of a Third Age of the Spirit, following the ages of the Father and the Son, a symbolism closely resembling in structure and motivation the three theophanic ages of Deutero-Isaiah and Plato. Though Otto's and Joachim's metastatic expectations were no more fulfilled than Paul's, their symbolisms marked a decisive step in the self-interpretation of Western society, because they created a new pattern of expectations: The age of perfection, the *teleion,* would be an age of the Spirit beyond the age of Christ; it would bring the free association of spiritualists, of men of the new monastic type, unencumbered by institutions; and it would be an age, therefore, beyond the establishment of church and empire. The potentialities of the new type of expectations became apparent in the fourteenth century, when Petrarca (1304–1374) symbolized the age that began with Christ as the *tenebrae,* as the dark age, that now would be followed by a renewal of the *lux* of pagan antiquity. The monk as the figure promising a new age was succeeded by the humanist intellectual. Hegel, finally, brought the potential to fruition by identifying revelation with a dialectical process of consciousness in history, a process that reached its *teleion* in his own "system of science." The

Logos of Christ had achieved its full incarnation in the Logos of Hegel's "absolute knowledge." The transfiguration that had begun with the theophany in Paul's vision of the Resurrected was now completed in the egophany of the speculative thinker. The Parousia, at last, had occurred.

The survey of representative manifestations leaves no doubt about the constancy of the constant. Transfiguration is indeed in continuity the problem at issue from Paul to the new Christs. We have not moved so far away from Christianity as the conflict between the Church and modernity would suggest. On the contrary, the modern revolt is so intimately a development of the "Christianity" against which it is in revolt that it would be unintelligible if it could not be understood as the deformation of the theophanic events in which the dynamics of transfiguration was revealed to Jesus and the Apostles. Moreover, there is no doubt about the origin of the constant in the Pauline myth of the struggle among the cosmic forces from which the Son of God emerges victorious. The variations on the theme of transfiguration still move in the differentiated form of the eschatological myth that Paul has created. This is an insight of considerable importance, because it permits one to classify the ideological "philosophies of history" as variations of the Pauline myth in the mode of deformation. The symbols developed by the egophanic thinkers in the self-interpretation of their work, such as *"Wissenschaftslehre,"* "system of science," "philosophy of history," *"philosophie positive,"* or *"wissenschaftlicher Sozialismus,"* cannot be taken at their face value; they are not engendered by bona fide analytical efforts in the noetic and pneumatic fields; they rather must be recognized as mythical symbols in a mode of degradation. The "history" of the egophanic thinkers does not unfold in the Metaxy, *i.e.,* in the flux of divine presence, but in the Pauline Time of the Tale that has a beginning and an end.

The constant has been traced back to its Pauline source. The discrepancy in this source between the hard core of truth and the metastatic expectations must now be examined, with special regard to the reasons why the discrepancy should have resisted analytical dissolution through the millennia.

The experiential cause of the difficulties is the Paradox of Reality, or the Exodus within Reality, as I have called it. Reality is experienced as moving beyond its own structure toward a state of transfiguration. In Paul's language, reality is in transition from the Anaximandrian state of *genesis* and *phthora* to the state of *aphtharsia.* At this point the troublesome complications begin, for the insights as well as the symbols found for their expression are inseparable from the theophanic events in which they reach the luminosity of consciousness. The insights belong, in the Anaximandrian case, to the field of noetic revelation; in the Pauline case, to the field of pneumatic revelation. They occur in the Metaxy, *i.e.,* in the concrete psyche of concrete human beings in their encounters with divine presence. There are no Greek insights into the structure of reality apart from those of the philosophers in whose psyches the noetic theophany occurred; nor are there Israelite, Jewish, and Christian insights into the dynamics of transfiguration apart from the prophets, apostles, and above all Jesus, in whose psyche the pneumatic revelations occurred. The noetic and pneumatic luminosity of consciousness is not an "object" on which somebody stumbles by accident, but a concrete historical event in the Ecumenic Age; and its carriers are the human beings who by virtue of their function as carriers become the historical types of "philosophers" and "prophets." Moreover, the event is experienced as an intelligible advance beyond the more compact experiences and symbolizations of reality in the form of the myth whose principal carriers in the civilizations of the ancient Near East were the royal unifiers of the cosmological empires and the priesthoods who developed the imperial symbolism. Structure and transfiguration do not begin when they become conscious through the theophanic events of the Ecumenic Age; they are experienced as the problems of reality both before and after their differentiation. Transfiguring incarnation, in particular, does not begin with Christ, as Paul assumed, but becomes conscious through Christ and Paul's vision as the eschatological *telos* of the transfiguring process that goes on in history before and after Christ and constitutes its meaning.

The cause of the discrepancy in Paul's interpretation can now be more exactly determined as an inclination to abolish the tension between the eschatological *telos* of reality and the mystery of the transfiguration that is actually going on within historical reality. The Pauline myth of the struggle among the cosmic forces validly expresses the *telos* of the movement that is experienced in reality, but it becomes invalid when it is used to anticipate the concrete process of transfiguration within history. This leaves us with the question why Paul should have indulged this inclination and why it should have remained a millennial constant resisting dissolution by analysis. Regarding an answer to this question I can only make two suggestions, both to be considered tentative:

(1) In the first place, the movement of transfiguration in history requires a human carrier; and in the historical situation of Paul the carriers had become rare. The ecumenic empires had been cast out as possible carriers by the Apocalyptic movement that had become formidably articulate with the Book of Daniel (165 B.C.), while Paul apparently was unable to respond to the intra-

Jewish reinterpretation of history that began to crystallize in his lifetime in the movement of the Tannaim.[8] The radical want of any institutionalized society as a convincingly representative carrier of transfiguring divine presence in history must be considered at least one important factor in Paul's assurance that history had come to its end and the transfiguring incarnation in Christ was the beginning of the end.

(2) There is, second, a fundamental characteristic attaching to all "experience of reality" that makes the "end" more resistant to analytical treatment than the "beginning." At least, the philosophers have no difficulty in coping with the symbolisms of "creation," of a *creatio ex nihilo,*" or of "time" as a dimension internal to reality. Augustine, following Plato on this point, states flatly that there is no Creation in time, because there is no time before the temporality in the structure of created reality. Regarding the "end," however, the matter appears to be less simple. One could imagine a philosopher to create the symbol of a *perditio in nihilo* as the countersymbol to the *creatio ex nihilo.* But philosophers hesitate to let the *nihil* of the beginning become the *nihil* of the end, though there are exceptions. The obvious reason is the fact that we have an "experience of reality" but no experience of the *nihil* other than the creative divine ground of reality or the fall into non-being as the sanction on non-participation in the divinely grounded and ordered reality. The movement that draws man into existential participation is a movement toward a more eminent degree of reality, not toward perdition; it is experienced as the *athanatizein* of the philosophers or the *aphtharsia* of Paul. The experience of reality, one might say, has a built-in bias toward more reality; the symbolism of a cessation of reality would be in conflict with the experience of the movement as an exodus within reality.

While the first of these suggestions is apt to explain the metastatic fervor of Paul, the second will explain why an intense experience of the movement will tend to diminish, and perhaps blot out, the distance between existence under the law of *genesis* and *phthora* and the life toward which we experience ourselves as moving through death. When the contemporary extravaganza of achieving *aphtharsia* in the world of *phthora* has run its course, perhaps the balance of consciousness will be regained in which the participation in the transfiguring movement, without achieving its consummation in this world, will again become bearable as the lot of man.

[8] On the Tannaite conception of history, cf. Nahum Norbert Glatzer, *Untersuchungen zur Geschichtslehre der Tannaiten* (Berlin, 1933).

CHAPTER 6

The Chinese Ecumene

Parallel in time with the rise of ecumenic empires in the Near East and the Mediterranean, the Chinese area of tribal societies transforms itself into an imperially organized civilization which understands itself as the empire of the *t'ien-hsia,* of the ecumene. As far as we know, the two processes are not connected by cultural diffusion or stimulation. Apparently there are two ecumenes.

A plurality of ecumenes presents formidable problems to a philosophy of history. As a first step toward disentangling them it will be appropriate to ascertain the various meanings of the Western symbol *oikoumene,* in order to determine in what sense they apply to the Far Eastern phenomenon.

In the Western course of the Ecumenic Age, the word *oikoumene* changes its meaning. The *oikoumene-okeanos* symbolism of the Homeric period still expresses man's experience of his foothold on the land that rises from the waters and of the horizon at which this habitat of the mortals borders on the mystery of the gods. The compact experience, however, disintegrates under the impact of the imperial drives, of expanding geographical knowledge, and of exploratory passions. As a consequence, the cosmological *oikoumene* suffers the literalist deformation into the *oikoumene* that is a potential object of imperial conquest.

If the term is used in the literalist sense, the ecumene can exist only in the singular; the language of a Chinese ecumene, with its implication of ecumenes in the plural, would be contradictory. If, however, the term is used in its cosmological sense, there may exist an indefinite number of societies in which the experience of a fundamental structure in reality will be equivalently symbolized. In the earlier discussion of the Greek symbolism, in fact, I had occasion to refer to its equivalents in the context of the Sumerian and Egyptian cosmological empires. It would appear obvious, therefore, that the term will have to be used in its earlier, cosmological sense when now we have to analyze the equivalent Chinese experience and its symbolization through the *t'ien-hsia,* the "all-under-heaven."

Unfortunately, however, the matter is more complicated. It cannot be reduced to a simple choice betwen alternatives, because the two meanings are not truly alternative; they are intimately joined to each other as expressions of two phases in the one historical process in which the consciousness of reality differentiates from the truth of the cosmos to the truth of existence. In the cosmological experience, man's habitat on earth has an horizon, and beyond the horizon there lies the mystery of death and the gods. This fundamental experience of man's existence within the horizon of mystery is expressed by the integral symbolism of *oikoumene-okeanos*. When the primary experience of existence in the cosmos disintegrates through the concupiscential unrest of conquest and exploration, the result is not an equivalent, differentiated experience of the same structure in reality, but a fragmentation of reality corresponding to the deformation of existence through the concupiscential drive. The knowledge of the geographical horizon, it is true, has expanded; and the concupiscential drive has been discovered as the motive force of the expansion. The consciousness of reality, thus, has advanced beyond its former state, so that a return to the limited horizon would mean the deliberate adoption of a quietist attitude—a possibility that we find realized, in the Chinese case, in exemplary form by the *Tao Te Ching*. Still, the structure of reality has been fragmented, for the abolition of the mythical horizon has destroyed the divine mystery that lies beyond it. The *oikoumene* that has become a territory, conquerable together with its population, is no longer the habitat of man surrounded by the mystery, but an unmysterious geographical expanse whose conquerors soon enough discover that their conquest requires a new horizon of mystery, if it is to be a habitat of man on earth. The literalist ecumene of the pragmatic conquest is transitory because it conflicts with the strucure of existence; man no more exists in a literalist ecumene than today he exists in a physical universe; forced by the structural necessity of reality, the imperial conquest is in search of the divine horizon that no longer can be symbolized cosmologically. Hence, as a unit of meaning, the Ecumenic Age can come to its internal conclusion only by regaining the horizon of mystery on the level of differentiation set by the new truth of existence. Only when the concupiscential associates with a spiritual exodus, when the empire associates with a spiritual movement, has the structure of existence been equivalently restored to the integrity which it had in the *oikoumene-okeanos* experience.

The two meanings of the term *ecumene,* thus, represent two phases in an historical process which extends from the disintegration of the *oikoumene-okeanos* symbolism, through the differentiation of both the concupiscential and

[handwritten marginalia]

the spiritual exodus, to an equivalent restructuring of existential order in the light of the new truth. If, however, this superior unit of meaning which cuts across ethnic cultures, subcultures, civilizations, empires, migrations, deportations, and such phenomena as the Hellenic and Jewish diaspora, is brought into focus as the issue, we are faced with the fact that the process analyzed in the preceding chapters as the "Ecumenic Age" is paralleled in China by an equivalent process. The problem is not the plurality of societies in which the ecumenic symbolism appears—Sumerian, Egyptian, Persian, Greek, Roman, Chinese—but the plurality of Ecumenic Ages. Inevitably certain questions will impose themselves: Are there two mankinds who independently go through the same process? If not, what justifies the language of the one mankind in whose history both the Western and Eastern Ecumenic Ages occur—assuming that the term Western can legitimately be used for a unit of meaning which comprises the societies of the Ancient Near East? And how is the unit of meaning to be characterized in which the parallel Ecumenic Ages occur, supposing that such a unit can be found at all?

The questions are rather complicated and certainly the larger issue of one or two mankinds cannot be analyzed before the facts concerning the Chinese *t'ien-hsia* are established. Hence, I shall subdivide the discussion of the problem. The present chapter on "The Chinese Ecumene" will deal with the self-interpretation of the imperial society which grew in the Far Eastern area from the earlier tribal societies as the organization of the *t'ien-hsia*. The following chapter on "Universal Humanity," then, will deal with the philosophical problems which arise from this growth of a second ecumene.

§ 1. The Historiographic Form

Chinese culture is distinguished by the development of a magnificent historiography. Its first great work, setting the type for the successors, is the *Shih-chi* of Ssu-ma Ch'ien (145–86 b.c.), which unfolds the course of Chinese history from its mythical beginnings down to the writer's own time.[1] From these sources emerges the picture of early Chinese history that has remained authoritative in the West from the eighteenth century, when the first transla-

---

[1] The *Shih-chi* is available in the French translation of Edouard Chavannes: Se-Ma T'ien, *Les Mémoires Historiques* (5 Vols.; Paris, 1895–1905); and in the English translation by Burton Watson, *Records of the Grand Historian of China* (2 Vols.; New York, 1961). A penetrating study of the *Shih-chi* is Burton Watson's *Ssu-ma Ch'ien, Grand Historian of China* (New York, 1958).

tions were published, well into the twentieth century.[2] Today, however, its authority is shaken. Through the application of critical methods to early literary sources (most of them already at the disposition of Ssu-ma Ch'ien) as well as through the wealth of recent archaeological data, modern scholarship has produced a picture of early China considerably more articulate than the one to be found in the *Shih-chi*.[3] Hence, Western scholars speak today, somewhat condescendingly, of a "traditional history" of China, opposing to it the picture that emerges from their own efforts.[4] And the improvement of critical over traditional history is impressive enough not only to give substance to the opposition, but even to make it necessary. Nevertheless, the distinction is misleading as it tacitly imputes to Ssu-ma Ch'ien the purposes of a modern pragmatic historian, with the implication that the moderns are successful where the ancient historian failed because neither his method nor his critical conscience were too well developed. For Ssu-ma Ch'ien was not altogether a pragmatic historian. Though it definitely was among his purposes to present a reliable record of events by selecting and transmitting to posterity the best sources available, the pragmatic part of his work is preceded by an historio-genetic account of the legends which traces the history of the ecumene back to its divine-cosmic origins. The mytho-speculative part is not as elaborate as that of the Sumerian King List or as majestically profound as that of the Israelite Genesis; the mood in which the legends are reported rather resembles the pious skepticism of a Livy in his report of the legends surrounding the founda-

[2] The first major translation from the *T'ung-chien kang-mu* is the *Histoire Générale de la Chine* by the Père de Mailla (Paris, 1777–1789). The section on "Chinese Origins," in the article on "China" in the *Encyclopaedia Britannica* (11th ed.; 1910–11) is still an abstract of traditional history. It is written by Frederick Hirth, then Professor of Chinese at Columbia University.

[3] In order to appreciate the progress made in the understanding of early Chinese history one should compare the section on China in Hegel's *Philosophie der Geschichte*, which roughly was still valid at the end of the nineteenth century, with such modern works as Henri Maspero's *La Chine Antique* (1927; new ed., Paris, 1955), H. G. Creel's *The Birth of China* (New York, 1935), or Wolfram Eberhard's *Chinas Geschichte* (Bern, 1948).

The understanding of the Chou period, as well as of the transition to the empire, has been substantially advanced by Peter Weber-Schaefer, *Oikumene und Imperium. Studien zur Zivilthe-ologie des chinesischen Kaiserreichs* (Munich, 1968), and Peter-Joachim Opitz, *Lao-tzu. Die Ordnungsspekulation im Tao-tê-ching* (Munich, 1967). These two studies, undertaken at my suggestion at the Institute of Political Science in Munich, should be understood as furnishing the background to the analysis of the narrower problem of the *t'ien-hsia* in the present chapter.

A new dimension has been added to Chinese history, expanding it into the neolithic tribal cultures of the Far East, by the archaeologists. Cf. Chêng Tê-K'un, *Archaeology in China* (3 vols.; Cambridge 1959, 1960, 1963), with the *Supplement to Volume I. New Light on Prehistoric China* (Cambridge, 1966), and Kwang-Chih Chang, *The Archeology of Ancient China* (Revised and enlarged edition; Yale University Press, 1968).

[4] Marcel Granet, *Chinese Civilization* (London, 1930). The exposition of "Traditional History" (9–51) is followed by the critical account of "The Chief Data of Ancient History" (53–137).

tion of Rome; but the historiogenetic opening is definitely there and radiates its cosmological form into the historical account proper. By virtue of its integration into the historiogenetic form, the "traditional history" is more than a mere record of events to be improved by superior modern methods; it rather is an integral part of the order of society itself. The development of an historiographic form, overlaid with historiogenetic characteristics, indicates that the China of the imperial ecumene had achieved something like existence in historical form, even though the cosmological form was not radically broken.

The "traditional history" is constructed in retrospect from the empire. I shall briefly state some data and dates to which the following analysis must frequently refer. China was unified and received its imperial form through Duke Cheng of Ch'in in 221 B.C. After his victory over the last of the six rival lordships, the new ruler assumed the style of Ch'in Shih-huang-ti, that is, of the First Emperor of the house of Ch'in. The short-lived dynasty was followed in 206 by the Former Han. It was in the reign of Wu-ti (140–87) that China received its historiographic form through the work of the Grand Astrologers of the Han court. The *Shih-chi*, the Record of the Grand Astrologer (or Historian), was conceived and initiated by Ssu-ma T'an (*fung*. 130–110), to be executed by his son Ssu-ma Ch'ien (*fung*. 110–86). The historiographic form, thus, followed the imperial form at a distance of roughly a century. The first section of the *Shih-chi* consists of the *pen-chi*, the Basic Annals; they contain the records of the rulers of China. Working backward from the historian's time, the Han dynasty is preceded by the Ch'in; the Ch'in by the *San Wang*, the Three Dynasties; the *San Wang* by the *Wu Ti*, the Five Emperors. The Three Dynasties are the Hsia (1989–1558), the Shang (or Yin, 1557–1050), and the Chou (1049–256).

The first principle of construction becomes apparent if we consider that the history of China gains in age the later the historian writes. The *Shu-ching*, a collection of early documents which existed by the time of Confucius (551–479 B.C.), speaks only of the two emperors Yao and Shun as preceding the Three Dynasties. The Confucian schools of the fourth and third centuries B.C., then, elaborated a pattern of Five Emperors to correspond to the Five Influences of wood, fire, earth, metal, and water. As a result of their labor, we find in the *Shin-chi* the Five Emperors Huang-ti, Chuan-Hsü, Kao-hsin, Yao, and Shun. Later historians, finally, let the *Wu Ti* be preceded by the *San Huang*, the Three August Ones, a group which for the first time appears in the Former Han (206-0-9). They are, according to varying lists, Fu-hsi, Shen-nung,

Nü-kua, or Fu-hsi, Shen-nung, Huang-ti. The chronology for the *Wu Ti* is carried well up into the third millennium B.C.

The motive for extending history into remote ages becomes tangible in the second principle of "traditional history," *i.e.,* in the construction of genealogies for the later ruling houses. The founders of the Three Dynasties are descendants of the ministers of Shun, the last and wisest of the *Wu Ti*. The founder of the Hsia dynasty was Yü, the minister of public works under Shun; the founder of the Shang dynasty, T'ang, descended from Hsieh, the controller of the people; Wen and Wu, the founders of the Chou dynasty from Ch'i, the minister of agriculture. The three ministers of Shun, in their turn, descended from Huang-ti in the fifth generation, that is, in the generation in which new genealogies begin: they furthermore were authentic Sons of Heaven inasmuch as they had virgin mothers who conceived them miraculously, so that the Three Dynasties ultimately descended from Heaven itself.

The third principle is the construction of history in terms of the *tê,* usually translated as virtue or power. The *tê* is the sacral substance of order which can be accumulated in a family through the merits of distinguished ancestors. When the charge has reached a certain intensity, the family is fit to exert the functions of a ruler over society. The *tê* of a ruling family will be exhausted in the end, though in the course of a dynasty recoveries through virtuous rulers are possible before the final relapse. Hence, the great incisions of history are marked by the exhaustion of a family's *tê,* culminating in the replacement of the ruling house by a family whose *tê* at the time has achieved a charge of sufficient strength. This is the pattern followed in the construction of the history of the Three Dynasties.

In the case of the Chou dynasty (1049–256) the pattern is disturbed inasmuch as a new family with sufficient *tê* did not appear when the *tê* of the dynasty was visibly exhausted. The peculiar structure of the Chou period, therefore, required additional categories for its description. The first symptoms of exhaustion became noticeable under King Li. He was forced to resign in 841. The following interregnum by two ministers, until King Li's death in 828, is called the Kung-ho. The final exhaustion became tangible in 771, when the homeland of the Chou in the West was overrun by barbarians so that the capital had to be moved to Lo-yang in the East. The Eastern Chou, though without effective power, survived until 256. The power history during the Eastern Chou is subdivided into the period of the hegemons or leaders (770–479) and the period of the Chan-kuo, the Warring States (479–221), which ended with the unification of China by the Ch'in. In the period of the leaders (*po*), the institution of a protector of the kingdom developed, comparable to the Japanese Shogunate in the situation of a similar eclipse of the imperial house. During the Chan-kuo, the rivalries among the rulers of the several great powers became openly a struggle for supremacy over the whole of Chinese society, culminating in the victory of the Duke of Ch'in. The disintegration of the old kingdom can be gauged by the fact that in the course of the fourth century the major states assumed the title of *wang*—Ch'in in 325. A foretaste of things to come was the treaty of 288, whereby the Ch'in and Ch'i, the western and the eastern great powers, accorded one another the title of *ti*, emperor, for their respective spheres of influence. At the time, however, the two emperors of the Occident and Orient had to abandon their style in the face of the indignation they aroused among the lesser kings.

The principal dates of traditional history can be arranged as follows:

San Huang	no dates
Wu Ti	no dates for the first three Ti
Yao	2145–2043 B.C.
Shun	2042–1990
Hsia Dynasty	1989–1558
Yin (Shang) Dynasty	1557–1050
Chou Dynasty	1049– 256
Western Chou	1049– 771
Eastern Chou	770– 256
Kung-ho (Interregnum)	841– 822
Period of the Hegemons	770– 479
Ch'un-ch'iu	722– 481
Confucius	551– 479
Chan-kuo (The Warring States)	479– 221
Assumption of the *wang* title by Ch'in	325
Assumption of the *ti* title by Ch'in and Ch'i	288
Foundation of the empire by Ch'in Shih-huang-ti	221

Since traditional history is a genealogical construction, with the purpose of pressing the pragmatic events into the pattern of accumulation and exhaustion of the *tê* by the ruling families, questions must be raised with regard to the reliability of both its content and chronology.

With regard to content and the actual beginnings of Chinese history, the pendulum of credence given in the West has swung in a wide arc. Hegel accepted the tradition at its face value; he let the history of China begin about 3000 B.C., though he cautioned the reader that the Chinese distinguished not too carefully between legend and history.[5] At the turn of the century, at the high tide of positivism, when tradition was treated with skepticism, a critical history founded on reliable sources was assumed to begin only with the Spring and Autumn Annals, the *Ch'un-ch'iu,* which covered the period from 722 to 481 B.C. At this time of skepticism, however, began the archaeological discoveries. When the oracle bones of the Yin dynasty, found in Ho-nan province around 1900, were deciphered, the inscriptions rendered a king list which confirmed the traditional list. The effect of the discovery expressed itself in the compromise struck by Maspero in his *Chine Antique* of 1927: He was willing to accept as well attested both the Yin and Chou dynasties, but denied historical value to anything which "the Chinese historians tell us about the origins of the empire, the first emperors, and the first dynasties."[6] By a coincidence, in the year 1927 excavations began at the site of An-yang, the last capital of the Yin dynasty.[7] The rich finds of architecture, plastic art, and artifacts proved of such a nature "that it is necessary to presuppose a long period, at least several centuries, of development. No evidence of the immediate precursors of the Shang culture as revealed at An-yang has, however, as yet been found. It seems clear that the Shang, who dominated a loose, tribute-collecting state, moved from another capital to the An-yang site around the middle of the second millennium B.C. and brought their writing, their religion, their arts, and all the diverse elements of their culture with them."[8] The excavations have given splendid reality to a period of Chinese culture of which a generation earlier the very existence had been doubted. And if the foundation of An-yang must indeed be dated at the middle of the second millennium B.C., and if centuries of development have preceded the maturity of its character, we are getting substantially nearer to the age claimed by tradition for Chinese civilization. Moreover, the excavations of An-yang have chastened the skeptics. Some, though they now must admit the Yin dynasty, still will doubt the Hsia. But on the whole, the climate has become favorable to admitting as historical the

[5] Hegel, *Vorlesungen ueber die Philosophie der Geschichte,* ed. F. Brunstaed, (Leipzig, no date), 169ff.
[6] Maspero, *La Chine Antique* (new edition, Paris, 1955), 29.
[7] Creel, *The Birth of China.*
[8] Laurence Sickman, in Sickman and Soper, *The Art and Architecture of China,* Pelican History of Art (Baltimore, 1956), 1.

Hsia dynasty as well, and even to assuming some reality behind the legends of the mythical emperors. Perhaps Yao, Shun, and Yü were indeed historical figures. This is the present state of assumptions, as cautiously formulated by Eberhard.[9]

The second question to be raised concerns the reliability of traditional chronology. Ssu-ma Ch'ien himself considers 841, *i.e.,* the beginning of the Kung-ho, the first certain date. With more caution one would have to say that no dates are certain before the Imperial Annals, that is before 221. For the time between 722 and 221 B.C. we possess only the relative chronology of such annals of the single *kuo* as are extant; and from their comparison only approximate dates can be constructed. Upward of 722 the dates become ever more uncertain the farther back we go. A vast shadow, however, is cast over the whole of traditional chronology by the penchant of Chinese thinkers to fit their history into periods of approximately five hundred years. The implications and motives will become apparent from a passage of Mencius (VII B 38): "From Yao and Shun to T'ang were over five hundred years. . . . From T'ang to King Wen were over five hundred years. . . . From King Wen to Master K'ung were over five hundred years. . . . From Master K'ung to this day are a little over one hundred years. So near are we still to the time of the Sage, and so close to the place where he lived. And yet we should own nothing to him, really nothing to him?" The five-hundred-year period is considered a cycle of order, with each of the Three Dynasties representing such a cycle. Even the Chou dynasty has run its course—the epoch is marked by the appearance of Confucius, though the Chou still reigned, if they did not rule. Within the cycle, the pattern of exhaustion of the *tê,* with its rally and relapse, prevails. Only a hundred years of the cycle that begins with Confucius have passed, and his substance seems to be spent. What shall one do in such a time of disorder?

With this question, there emerges the function of the cycle as a means of orientation for the thinker. He estimates the historical situation by relating it to the cycle and finds his own role by placing himself in the schema of rally and relapse. A second passage from Mencius will illuminate the role of the thinker (II B 13). Mencius is discontented on leaving the state of Ch'i; and his disciple Ch'ung Yü reminds him that formerly he had said: "The gentleman neither murmurs against Heaven nor is he angry with men." The Master sets him right:

[9] Wolfram Eberhard, *"Geschichte Chinas bis zum Ende der Han-Zeit,"* in *Historia Mundi,* II, (Bern, 1953), 566–69.

That was then; today is different. Every five hundred years there must be a king (*wang*); and in between there must at least be men who create order within their generation. Since the Chou, more than seven hundred years have passed. Hence, the number has been exceeded already. If we examine the situation of the time, the possibility is there. But heaven does not yet want the ecumene pacified and ordered. If it wanted the ecumene pacified and ordered in the present generation, who is there but myself? How should I not be discontented?

The burden of reordering the ecumene that formerly was incumbent on the king is now incumbent on the sage; and the burden does not make Mencius happy. Moreover, the consciousness of the duty incumbent on him had apparently to mature. "Formerly" he was satisfied to act as a gentleman who does not grumble against God or man when times are bad. But "that was then"; today, though reluctantly, he is ready to accept his fate as the sage in the course of the cycle.

The problems of Mencius reappear with Ssu-ma Ch'ien. In his autobiography at the end of the *Shih-chi* (130) he tells the following story:

My father used to say to me: "Five hundred years after the Duke of Chou died Confucius appeared. It has now been five hundred years since the death of Confucius. There must be someone who can succeed to the enlightened generations, who can set right the transmission of the *Book of Changes,* continue the *Spring and Autumn Annals,* and search into the world of the *Odes* and *Documents,* the rites and music." Was this not his ambition? Was this not his ambition? How can I, his son, dare to neglect his will.[10]

The historiographic work of Ssu-ma T'an and his son, thus, is consciously an attempt at restoring the order of Chinese society after the five-hundred-year cycle beginning with Confucius had run its course.[11]

For the question of chronology, which is our present concern, it follows that the symbolism of the five-hundred-year cycle favored by the Confucian thinkers and historians makes the traditional dates for the Hsia, Shang, and Chou dynasties, as well as the lifetime of Confucius—marking periods which indeed approximate five hundred years—highly suspect, though at the present

[10] Translated by Burton Watson, *Records of the Grand Historian of China,* 50 and 87.

[11] The five-hundred-year cycle has an interesting later development in Japanese history. When the Buddhist-Confucian political culture of the T'ang dynasty was introduced in Japan, in the time of Prince Shōtoku, the admonitions of the so-called Kempō Constitution of 604 A.D. contained in Article XIV the advice to the officials not to be envious of talented men as they are rare enough: "Though you may encounter an intelligent man every five hundred years, you will find a real sage hardly in a thousand years." Hermann Bohner, *Shōtoku Taishi* (Tokyo, 1940), 222.

state of science we have no means of correcting them with any certainty. At the most one can say that the disintegration of the Chou power, which beyond a doubt sets in with 771 (assuming this date to be approximately correct), must have been preceded by a period long enough to allow for its establishment by conquest, its stabilization, and gradual decline, bringing us up to the traditionally assumed middle of the eleventh century B.C. for the Chou conquest. But if the Shang culture of An-yang, counting backward from this date by the king list, was flourishing so splendidly in the middle of the second millennium that several centuries must be assumed for its development, the beginnings of the Shang dynasty would have to be placed substantially earlier than the traditional 1557 B.C. And if we assume a higher date, perhaps 1800, then the Hsia dynasty, presuming it existed, would carry us far beyond the traditional 1989 B.C. into the third millennium B.C.[12]

§ 2. The Self-designation of the Ecumene

The traditional history is the history of something, though we do not yet know of what. In a preliminary fashion, we have spoken of the subject as "China," or "Chinese society," or "Chinese civilization," or "Chinese civilizational society," as the context required. But it must be understood that none of these terms occur in the self-interpretation of China, that none of them are part of the Chinese symbols of order. The question of the subject of order must be approached through the self-designations.

In the *Shih-ching*, the Book of Songs, China is on occasion designated by the name of its first dynasty as "the land of Hsia." In general, however, the self-designations are based on relations immanent to the order of Chinese society. At the beginning of the Ch'un-ch'iu period (722–481), China was politically organized as a confederation of states, the *kuo*, which called itself the *chung-kuo*, the central states or lordships, with the cosmological meaning of being the organization of mankind at the center of the world. As Chinese society in the civilizational sense was steadily expanding through Sinification of formerly barbarian tribes, the term *chung-kuo* acquired geopolitical and civilizational connotations in addition to its cosmological meaning. Since the lordships of the center, in relation to the surrounding barbarians, or to lordships which had entered the orbit of Chinese civilization more recently, were

---

[12] These chronological reflections agree with the results of the archaeologists. Cf. Glyn Daniel, *The First Civilizations: The Archaeology of their Origins* (New York, 1968), 131.

of older standing in the Chinese world, the *chung-kuo* were also called the *shang-kuo,* the superior lordships. Equivalent with the term *shang* as an expression of superiority were used the terms *hsia,* civilized, and *hua,* flower or flowering. The term *chung-hua,* central flower, has ultimately become the self-designation of China used to this day: The Chinese Republic (Taiwan) styles itself the *Chung-Hua Min-Kuo* (Central Flower Republic); Communist China has expanded the style to *Chung-Hua-Jen-Min Kung-Ho Kuo* (Central Flower People's Republic).[13]

Of particular importance for our study is, finally, the designation of Chinese society as the *t'ien-hsia,* literally "below heaven." The various translations as "all below heaven," or as the "world," however, are not exact enough. In Chinese, the "world" in the sense of the cosmos is called *t'ien-ti,* "heaven and earth." The *t'ien-hsia,* though, is neither the cosmos nor the earth as a territorial expanse under heaven, but the earth as the carrier of human society. As far as I can see, it is the exact equivalent of the Greek *oikoumene* in the cultural sense. I shall render it, therefore, whenever it occurs, as "ecumene."

The explicit self-designations do not exhaust the range of Chinese self-understanding. There must be added a factor which sharply distinguishes Chinese order from the imperial orders of the ancient Near East.

That an early society understands itself as the one mankind occupying the center of the one cosmos, and accordingly symbolizes its order as a cosmic analogue, is characteristic also of the civilizations of the Near East. In the Mesopotamian and Egyptian cases, however, the infoldedness of societies in cosmological form was under constant pressure from the consciousness that the world-filling empires existed in the plural. In the fifteenth and fourteenth centuries B.C., in the Amarna Age, Egypt entertained marriage and commercial relations with Babylonia, Assyria, the Hittites and Mitanni, with Cyprus and the Minoan civilization, while the diplomatic correspondence reveals the precarious suzerainty exerted over the Phenician city-states and Jerusalem. Under the circumstances, it had to be considered rather surprising that the cosmological form was not visibly affected by the intense "international relations" for so long. But a tentative break occurred at last, though it required the extraordinary personality of Akhenaton (1377–1358) to expand the domain of the sun-god, for the first time, beyond Egypt to embrace mankind, in the great Aton Hymn:[14]

---

[13] For the sources in the *Shih-chi* and the *Tso-chuan,* cf. Granet, *Chinese Civilization,* 76.
[14] *Order and History,* I, 108.

The countries of Syria and Nubia, the land of Egypt,
Thou settest every man in his place.
. . . .
Their tongues are divers in speech,
And their forms as well;
Their skins are distinguished,
As thou distinguishest the foreign peoples.

The radical break, however, did not take place in Egypt itself but on its borders, through Moses and the foundation of Israel. The richly diversified field of societies in the Near East, forming the silent but persistent background of contradiction to the cosmological form of order, became the ferment of experience which brought forth the Israelite conception of mankind and metamorphosed the multiple cosmological orders into imperial organizations, each reaching out for possession of the one ecumene.

The Chinese situation is an entirely different one. At the time of An-yang which, according to the presumed chronology, was contemporary with the Amarna Age, China was neither surrounded by a field of societies of comparable civilizational rank, nor were there any traceable contacts with India or the Near East. China was never one society among others; from its beginnings the history of Chinese society was for its members, to the best of their knowledge, the history of mankind. The structure of Chinese consciousness of order differs profoundly, therefore, from the Near Eastern, inasmuch as the experiential ferment provided by the manifold of societies is missing. If the conception of an ecumene and its organization developed in China nevertheless, it could not do so in the wake of cultural contacts with other societies, or in the process of organizing multicivilizational empires, but had to rise endogenously. Chinese ecumenism received its peculiar coloration from the unbroken consciousness of the identity of China with mankind. This factor must be taken into account above all in an analysis of "Chinese historiography." For, strictly speaking, there exists no such thing. What, from the Western position, is called the "traditional history" of China is, from the Chinese position, the history of civilized mankind of which Chinese society is the sole carrier. In this respect Chinese traditional history may be compared with the Israelite construction of a world-history in which Israel, as the Chosen People, representatively carries the generically human burden of existence in the present under God—with the difference, however, that the divine choice sets Israel apart from the surrounding civilizations in cosmological form, while Chinese ecumenism grows from the matrix of Chinese cosmological order itself without ever completely separating from it.

§ 3. THE INCOMPLETE BREAKTHROUGH

The last reflection has touched upon a characteristic of Chinese order which presents almost insuperable obstacles to analysis, that is, the emergence of institutions and symbolic forms which recognizably belong to the same general type as the Western but have, in China, a habit of never emerging completely. The proposition may, at first hearing, sound ill-considered in view of the fact that incomplete differentiation of experiences and symbols is a phenomenon common to all societies under observation. Only in the cases of Israel and Hellas was the cosmological form so radically broken by the leap in being, *i.e.*, by the pneumatic and noetic theophanies, that it gave way to the new symbolisms of revelation and philosophy. Around the islands of Israel and Hellas extends the sea of other societies with their rich manifold of approximations and intermediate forms, of tentative breakthroughs and compromises. Why, then, should China be singled out as having this characteristic? The reason is that no other civilization is distinguished by such a galaxy of original, forceful personalities, engaging in spiritual and intellectual adventures which *might* have culminated in a radical break with cosmological order, but invariably got bogged down and had to succumb to the prevailing form. In its pre-imperial phase, China is characterized by the immense pressure of an early established order on all movements of the soul that occur within it; in its imperial phase, by the incredible strength of the Confucian style of orthodoxy, which overcomes all rivals in the end.

The bewildering phenomenon of a dynamic and sensitive civilization which in its expression is muted by an unbreakable form has caused a corresponding bewilderment among Western scholars. The more immediate cause becomes manifest in Max Weber's comparison between Chinese and Western culture. Speaking of Confucian bureaucracy he suggests that here an officialdom expressed its attitude toward life "without competition of rational science, rational practice of arts, rational theology, jurisprudence, natural science, and technics, without the rivalry of divine or equally ranking human authority." In the vacuum described, the officials "could expand their peculiar practical rationalism and create a corresponding ethics, limited only by respect for the power of tradition possessed by the clans and the belief in spirits."[15] The comparison receives its weight from the qualifying attribute "rational." For the enumerated phenomena are all present in China, too, though in that

[15] Max Weber, "Konfuzianismus und Taoismus," in *Gesammelte Aufsaetze zur Religionssoziologie* (Tuebingen, 1920), I, 440.

undifferentiated mode that was interpreted by Max Weber as a lack of "rationalism." The absence of "rationalism," which is supposed to explain the ascendancy of Confucian bureaucracy, is, however, itself in need of an explanation. For the bureaucracy of the empire, though it could stifle whatever forces tended to fill the vacuum, had not created it. In search of causes, Max Weber again argues the lack of competitive forces in comparison with the West: China developed no logic, either rhetorical or dialectical, because society did not have the competitive character of the Hellenic polis which required these instruments for political and forensic success; it developed no rational jurisprudence, either of formal procedure or material justice, because there were neither business interests of the Western type, pressing for procedural calculability, nor was there an absolute state, with an effective central administration, that would have been interested in uniformity and codification of the law.[16] The argument, thus, moves backward from the absence of certain phenomena to the absence of motive forces which could have produced them. At this point it breaks off—wisely, we may add; for a further regress, along the line of negatives (supposing it could be pursued at all), could hardly do more than circumscribe a puzzling situation more closely, without contributing much to the positive analysis of the forms that we wish to understand. As the valuable result there remains, nevertheless, an excellent summary, in negative terms, of the aspects of Chinese order that will baffle the Western student. The difficulties express themselves in a variety of conflicting opinions among scholars. On the one hand, for instance, there are the voluminous histories of Chinese philosophy and science; on the other hand, competent authorities assure us that China had developed neither philosophy (only a kind of wisdom) nor logic and mathematics, and consequently no science. On special problems we meet with such flat contradictions as: China's early religion was polytheistic, and China had no polytheism; or Confucianism was a religion, and it was not a religion, and so forth. Obviously the problem is fraught with complexities that will not give way to simple answers.[17]

As so many negatives have been mentioned, it will be appropriate to stress once more that the problems of Chinese order are not caused by the *absence* of differentiations but precisely by their *presence*. If China were merely want-

[16] *Ibid.,* 416, 437f.

[17] The incomplete breakthrough in what is commonly called "Chinese philosophy" has been thoroughly treated in Peter Weber-Schaefer, *Oikumene und Imperium* (Munich, 1968) 24f. A good analysis of the muted mode of Chinese thinking in A. C. Graham, "The Place of Reason in the Chinese Philosophical Tradition," in Raymond Dawson (ed.), *The Legacy of China* (Oxford, 1964), 28–56.

ing in dynamics of order, it would have remained if not primitive, at least no more than a society in cosmological form. But it has, on the contrary, the marks of a classic culture of the Hellenic type; and even more, it has developed an ecumenism peculiarly its own. It is the rather subdued, muted mode of differentiation that causes the difficulties of analysis. This general thesis must now be applied to the special problems and, first of all, to the subdued mode of the great incisions in Chinese institutional history.

§ 4. SYMBOLS OF POLITICAL ORDER

In the Near Eastern and Mediterranean area, the drama of mankind is enacted by a society of societies; in China, due to its geographical isolation, it is enacted within the compass of a single society. In the West, the great incisions are clearly recognizable by the power conflicts between societies, by the rise and fall of empire; in the Far East, they melt down to periods within Chinese history. As a consequence, it is considerably more difficult to ascertain the full meaning of Chinese pragmatic events than of the corresponding Western. That is especially true for the great epoch in Chinese history marked by the foundation of the empire. In the West, there can be no doubt that an age comes to its end, and something new begins: when the Iranians break forth from their highlands, conquer the older societies in cosmological form, and organize an empire that extends from the Punjab to Egypt and Asia Minor; when the Iranian creation is followed by the Macedonian and Roman empires; and when the momentum of assembling empires carries over into India and inspires the founder of the Maurya dynasty. The older type of order breaks down; multicivilizational empires force into their organization masses of humanity which never before had formed one society; and these masses, having lost the shelter of their former order, recover the meaning of their existence in spiritual movements which, in their turn, become powers on the world scene. In the Far East, in the Chinese seclusion, events of the same type occur at about the same time, but they are barely recognizable under such innocuous sounding titles as the disintegration of the Chou empire, the period of the Warring States, the unification of China through the Ch'in, the introduction of Confucianism under the Han, and so forth. Especially misleading is the subordination of the violently moving course of history to the pattern of dynastic succession. In the traditional history of the *Shih-chi,* the three royal dynasties of the Hsia, Shang, and Chou are followed by the imperial dynasties of the Ch'in and Han. China is conceived as having been an empire of some sort from its beginnings. But was there really an empire before the empire was founded by Ch'in Shih-huang-ti, so that the royal and imperial dynasties can rightly be called successive dynasties of substantially the same society? Was the institutional structure, as well as the symbolism of order, the same in 100 B.C. as it had been in 1000 B.C.? Though none of these questions can be answered flatly in the negative, considering that the events occurred within the medium of one continuous society, they nevertheless would have to be qualified so extensively as to come very near to a negative. In order to gain some firm ground for the further analysis of phenomena of this class, it is necessary to scan the principal symbols of the Chou period which pertain to the meaning of empire.

The organization of the Kingdom of Chou had come into existence through the conquest of the Kingdom of Shang, with probably a similar organization, by an alliance of Western clans under the leadership of the Duke of Chou. In the wake of the conquest, Chou society displayed three levels of political and social hierarchy: the king, the ruling society, and the common people. The supreme rank, distinguished by the title *wang,* was accorded the leader of the enterprise and the dynasty descending from him. Next ranked the participants in the raid who became the ruling nobility of the kingdom; their distinguished members were established as lords of territories, of the *kuo,* with lesser families as subvassals. They were collectively called "the Hundred Clans," though there probably were not many more than the thirty whose names are preserved. At least some members of the Shang ruling class must have been absorbed into the Chou nobility. For the dukes of Sung, under the Chou, were descendants of the Shang royal house; and the question is debated whether several literati of the Chou period, among them Confucius, were descendants of the personnel in charge of rites at the Shang court. At the bottom of the social scale were the common people, the *nung,* peasants. These differences of rank have found linguistic expression. In pre-Confucian usage the word "man," *jen,* denotes only members of the clan society, while the commoners are simply called "people," *min.* A blessing of the *Shih-ching,* 249, says:

> All happiness to our lord!
> Illustrious is his good power (*tê*);
> He orders the people (*min*), he orders the men (*jen*);
> He receives blessings from Heaven:
>   Help, support, and appointment
> From Heaven are extended to him.

Above the *min* and *jen* there rises the king, distinguished as the *i jen,* the One Man. The documents of the *Shu-ching* accord the style of the One Man not only to the Chou kings but also to their predecessors of the Shang and Hsia, up to the mythical emperors.

The king ruled over all "below Heaven," *t'ien-hsia.* A comprehensive formula of proverbial character, expressing this relation, is embedded in *Shih-ching,* 205:

> All below Heaven
> None but the king's land;
> All on the land,
> None but the king's men.

The king, besides being ruler of the ecumene, furthermore was the ruler of a territorial state, of a *kuo,* like the other lords. He was, finally, member of a numerous clan whose other members also might hold lordships. Among the members of the Ssu clan were the founder of the Hsia dynasty as well as the lords of Hu, Chen, Hsun, etc.; among the members of the Tzu clan were the founder of the Shang dynasty as well as the lords of Wei, Chi, Sung, etc.; among the members of the Chi clan, the founder of the Chou dynasty as well as the lords of Lu, Wei, etc. The union of the three positions—a ruler of the ecumene, a lord of a *kuo,* and a clan member—in the person of the king raised delicate questions of rank and appellation which still intrigued the scholars of the Han dynasty, at a time when the *kuo* and the pre-imperial clans had disappeared.

The *Po-hu-t'ung,* the official report of the discussions on the classics, held under imperial auspices in A.D. 79, contains some illuminating reflections on the meaning of pre-imperial kingship.[18] The king is the Son of Heaven, *t'ien-tzu,* because Heaven is his father and Earth is his mother; he in his turn is father and mother of the people; and in that capacity he rules over "all under Heaven."[19] The parental ruler over all below Heaven is not the king of a specific state with a name; in the nature of the case, the ecumene is nameless. From this situation arises the problem of an "appellation" of the dynasty. The founder of a new dynasty cannot continue his clan name as it is shared by "high and low," that is, by other clan members who are lords of *kuo* of various rank; nor can he style himself the king of his own territory, which now be-

---

[18] Tjan Tjoe Som, *Po Hu T'ung. The Comprehensive Discussion in the White Tiger Hall* (*Sinica Leidensia,* Volume VI). Volume I (Leiden, 1949), Volume II (Leiden, 1952).

[19] *Ibid.,* 1, a.b. Tjan, *op. cit.,* 218.

comes the royal domain, as kingship is equivalent with ecumenic rule. "The
Feudal Lords, as rulers of the Hundred Clans, are each designated by the
name of one state. The Son of Heaven, as the most exalted, now assumes an
appellation (expressing) the possession of all under Heaven and the union of
the ten thousand states."[20] The founder of a new dynasty can, furthermore,
not continue the name of the preceding one, because then the manner of
appellation would not be different from the case of a lord who succeeds to
another family in the rule of a *kuo*. If the Duke of Chou after the overthrow
of the Shang dynasty, for instance, would continue the name of Shang, the
ecumene would be degraded to a Kingdom of Shang, now ruled by a family
of the Chi clan. A family acquires kingship by a mandate, *ming,* of Heaven; if
the new king did not manifest the exalted favor by the creation of a new
name, he would act "against Heaven's intention." Hence, a new Son of Heaven
"must create a beautiful appellation (expressing his possession) of all under
Heaven, in order thereby to express his achievements and make himself illus-
trious."[21] The *Po-hu-t'ung* then proceeds to interpret the names chosen by the
founders of the Three Dynasties as meaning "great," "harmonious," and
"perfect." These conjectures, however, are in conflict with archaeological facts,
for the oracle bones of the Shang dynasty know about Chou as a territory of
the realm.[22] The name of the Chou dynasty was not "chosen" after the conquest, but attached to the territory. The dynastic names, we may assume, were
all of them the names of territories over which the dynasties ruled before their
accession to kingship.

From the *Po-hu-t'ung* emerges a picture of early China as a group of small
territorial states under chieftains—though the exogamous clans themselves
were ritual units and never occupied definite territories. If one of the states
became strong enough, its chieftain could subject neighboring territories to
his rule under the title of *wang.* Once such a kingdom was established, it could
be conquered by one of the member states, perhaps only recently drawn into
the orbit of civilization, as seems to have been the case in the conquest of the
Shang kingdom by the Chou and their barbarian allies on the western border.
As far back as the historical memory of China reaches, however, both conquerors and conquered belonged to the ritual community of the Hundred
Clans. A chieftain who became king was the ritual head of the community
which understood itself as the ecumene. And though, for reasons of state, the

[20] *Ibid.,* 15, m. Tjan, 235.
[21] *Ibid.,* 15, 1. Tjan, 234f.
[22] Maspero, *Le Chine Antique,* 41.

conquered were liberally massacred, the survivors of the former regime had their respected, if insignificant, status among the lords of the new kingdom.

§ 5. T'IEN-HSIA AND KUO

We know nothing about the origins of either the ecumenic kingdom or the first *kuo*. The oldest literary documents, those of the *Shu-ching,* take their existence for granted: The *t'ien-hsia* is organized as a manifold of *kuo,* while the *kuo* recognize themselves as parts of the ecumene. Moreover, we learn of no act of conquest by which kingship was established as an institution uniting several pre-existent *kuo.* China has no Memphite Theology like Egypt which interprets and celebrates the foundation of the empire by a drama of the gods;[23] nor an *Enuma elish* like the Mesopotamian empires which suggests the crisis character of the erection of kingship over the single city-states.[24] We hear no more of competitive kingdoms than of a founding conquest. There are new *kuo* emerging on the borders of the ecumene, through Sinification and territorial organization of formerly primitive tribes; there are more recent *kuo* whose civilizational status is viewed with condescension by the older members of the club; there is, besides the primary center of Chinese civilization in the Hoang-ho bend, a secondary center (as yet insufficiently explored) in the southern Kingdom of Ch'u; there are *kuo* which try to overthrow and replace the dynasty; but there are no *kuo* which pretend to form a rival ecumene. The Chinese kingship over "all below Heaven," though it is definitely a position of power, acquired and held by force, is singularly devoid of associations with imperial conquest. The extant documents let *t'ien-hsia* and *kuo* exist in a pre-established harmony.

The peaceable, primordial correlation between *t'ien-hsia* and *kuo* forms the nucleus for layers of meaning, partly articulated in language symbols, which stress the ritual and cultural aspects of ecumenic rule in opposition to force as represented by the *kuo.* The *t'ien-hsia,* the ecumene in the cultural sense, is associated with *wen.* The symbol *wen* has originally the meaning of markings, or a pattern; it acquires the further meanings of character, ideogram, decoration, and generally of the ornamental aspects of human life; and finally, of the arts of peace, such as dancing, music, and literature, as opposed to those of war, *wu.*[25] *Wen* and *wu,* peaceful culture and war, furthermore,

---

[23] *Order and History,* I, 88ff.
[24] *Ibid.,* 41ff.
[25] Arthur Waley, *The Analects of Confucius* (London, 1956), 39.

have operational powers: *wen* operates through the attraction of its prestige (*tê*), *wu* operates through the force (*li*). The *Analects* (XVI, 1) reports a saying of Confucius: "If the people of far-off lands do not submit, then the ruler must attract them by enhancing the prestige (*tê*) of his culture (*wen*); and when they have been duly attracted, he contents them."[26] Since the advice was rendered to a *kuo* rather than to the kingdom, the passage is of special interest, because it shows that the meaning of the principle can separate from the institutions—a question to which I shall return presently. On the institutional level, then, we find further ramifications of meaning with regard to the ruling types of *wang* and *po*. The *wang* is the ruler of the ecumene who operates, on principle, through the *tê* of culture. Mencius (I, B, 11) records the exploits of King T'ang: "When he turned his face toward the East to subjugate it, the barbarians of the West were dissatisfied; when he turned his face toward the South to subjugate it, the barbarians of the North were dissatisfied, saying: 'why should we be the last?' The people yearned for him, as in a great drought men yearn for clouds and a rainbow. . . . In the *Shu-ching* it says: 'We wait for our lord; when our lord comes, we shall live again'." The method of expanding the kingdom sounds a bit idyllic; we may suspect that the presence of the king's army was a strong incentive for barbarians to find culture attractive. Anyway, the necessity of holding the kingdom together by *wu* and *li* becomes tangible in the institution of the *po*, of a regional protector of the realm at times when the king's own force proved insufficient to maintain the peace. Originally, in the early Chou period, *po* was the title of the senior lord of the king's clan; in the later Chou period, when the power of the king declined, the *po* was a lord invested by the king with the charge of establishing order within the realm as well as of defending it against barbarians. The *po* operated through *li*, rather than through *tê*, the prestige of culture.[27] In the aggregate, there have developed two sets of symbols: To the series *t'ien-hsia, wen, tê, wang*, there corresponds the series *kuo, wu, li, po*.

The passage from *Analects* (XVI, 1) shows the tendency of a compact symbolism to let a principle separate from the institution to which it originally attached. The differentiated meaning of the principles can best be studied in the context of the late empire, of the Manchu period, when the *kuo* had disappeared long ago and the *chung-kuo* denoted the imperial organization at the center of the *t'ien-hsia*. In the seventeenth century A.D., anti-Manchu scholars criticized the recent conquerors because they operated under the

---

[26] Ibid., 203.
[27] Granet, *Chinese Civilization*, 24–30. Waley, the section on "Wang and Po" in *Analects*, 49f.

principle of *kuo* rather than *t'ien-hsia*. Huang Tsung-hsi developed a law of three phases for the purpose. In a first phase, "at the beginning of life," each man acted for himself. "If there was public well-being in the *t'ien-hsia*, he did not try to extend it; if there was public injury, he did not try to expunge it." In a second phase, the "princely man" appeared. He did not consider well-being or injury his private affair, but tried to bestow well-being on the whole *t'ien-hsia* and to remove injury from it. In the third phase, there appeared the "monarchs." They conceived the idea that "well-being in the *t'ien-hsia* devolved wholly upon them and injury in the *t'ien-hsia* devolved wholly upon others." In ancient times the *t'ien-hsia* came first and the ruler second; now the order was reversed. The implied theory is made more explicit by Ku Yen-wu when he says: "Those who defend the *kuo* are its monarch and its ministers; this is the design of the wealthy . . . but as for defending the *t'ien-hsia*, the mean common man shares responsibility." The *kuo* as the power organization of Chinese society, thus, is distinguished from the cultural substance which it is supposed to shelter. And, finally, Ku Yen-wu finds a formula which comes very close to the Platonic-Aristotelian distinction of good and bad regimes: "When the superior man attains station, he desires to work out the *tao*, the Way; when the small man attains station, he desires to serve his own interests. The desire to work out the Way (*tao*) manifests itself in making *t'ien-hsia* of *kuo-chia;* the desire to serve one's own interest manifests itself in wounding men and destroying things." The passage receives its pungency from the use of *t'ien-hsia* as a verb: "To *t'ien-hsia* the *kuo-chia*" means to transform the empire, which is nothing but a power organization, into a carrier of ecumenic civilization in the Confucian sense.[28]

With the late-Confucian meanings in mind, the classic texts from which they have developed will be better understood. A passage rich with implications is Mencius, VII, B, 13: "There have been men without goodness (*jen*) who have attained a *kuo;* but no man without goodness has ever attained the *t'ien-hsia.*" Mencius introduces the Confucian goodness (*jen*) as a principle which is of the essence in the rule of the *t'ien-hsia* but can be spared in the *kuo*, though it is desirable even there. Moreover, while the passage is cast in the form of an empirical observation, it must be understood as a warning to contemporary princes that their striving for the position of the *wang*, in view of their

---

[28] This paragraph summarizes the argument of Joseph R. Levenson, *Confucian China and Its Modern Fate* (London, 1958), 100–103. All quotations and translations are taken from these pages. The works of Huang Tsung-hsi and Ku Yen-wu were published, respectively, in 1662 and 1670.

lack of qualification, is futile. The attempt can be judged futile, however, only if it is against the nature of things in the cosmological sense; hence, the warning that the rule of the man without goodness will not come to pass, endows the essential goodness of ecumenic rule with unalterable status in the cosmic order. Still, the form of an empirical observation into which the argument is cast leaves it open to the counter-question: But what if it happens? We must say, therefore, that in the passage there lives a premonition of the catastrophe as which the victory of Ch'in Shih-huang-ti must have been experienced by Confucians, when the impossible happened and the man without goodness became the ruler of China.

From the principle that goodness is essentially inherent in the *t'ien-hsia* but not in the *kuo,* there follow certain consequences for the order of the realm. In VII, B, 2, Mencius reflects on the quality of the wars among the *kuo* as related in the *Ch'un-ch'iu.* The wars among the *kuo* were not just wars, though some may have been better than others, because castigation can be ordered only by the royal ruler against a subject *kuo;* the *kuo* of equal rank cannot castigate one another. Nevertheless, such mutual castigations were constantly undertaken in the Ch'un-ch'iu period, and even more so in the times of Mencius. From this observation, in conjunction with the previously asserted principles, emerges something like a philosophy of history in terms of the decay of royal substance. In VII, A, 30, Mencius considers three phases of decay: The mythical emperors Yao and Shun possessed the substance (which is not named, but presumably is the Confucian *jen*) by nature; the founders of the dynasty acquired it; and the hegemons of the Ch'un-ch'iu period borrowed it. The passage closes with the reflection: "But when somebody borrows something and does not return it for a long time, who will still be aware that it is not his property?" The touch of a traitorous usurpation is further elaborated in VI, B, 7, where Mencius counts four phases: "The Five Hegemons (*pa*) were traitors to the Three Royal Dynasties (*san-wang*); the lords (*chu-hou*) of the present time are traitors to the Five Hegemons; the nobles (*ta-fu*) of the present time are traitors to the lords of the present time." The criterion of decay is, in this case, institutionally defined by the methods of maintaining order in the kingdom: (i) Under the dynasties, a recalcitrant lord who made not his due appearances at court, was removed from his *kuo,* on royal order, by the other princes; (ii) in the time of the hegemons, the *po* would attack in person accompanied by other princes for the purpose of a federal execution, but at least a code of law for the conduct of princes was established and the execution did no go beyond its enforcement; (iii) today the princes trespass the five laws of the code in taking violent action; and (iv) their manner of evil action has spread to the powerful families within the *kuo* inasmuch as they do not merely tolerate the evil of the princes but even stimulate it. This picture of a decay which corrodes the whole kingdom is, finally, relieved by the suggestion of a restoration of order, in IV, B, 21: "When the vestiges of the kings (*wang*) disappeared, the songs were lost. After the songs were lost, the *Ch'un-ch'iu* was created. . . . Master K'ung said: 'It is their meaning (i) that I permitted myself to establish'." While the disorder through exhaustion of goodness manifests itself in the institution of the kingdom, the restoration of substance moves on the line from the kings to Confucius.

I should like to stress that there is something amoebic about the manner in which a Chinese universe of meanings changes shape, contracts, and expands. From empirical observations we move to essences, from institutions to principles, from principles to manners of operation, from the *tê* of a dynasty to the *tê* of culture and the *jen* of ecumenic rule, from the *jen* back to methods of federal execution, and finally we arrive at a philosophy of history which pictures the course of a civilization as the exhaustion of its substance, not so very different on principle from Giambattista Vico's *corso*. The differentiated meanings, though present, never become articulate with any precision; and the symbols created for their expression never achieve the status of analytical concepts. As a consequence, at every turn the symbolization may slide back from a theoretical level apparently reached to expressions of extreme compactness and, then, advance to theoretical insights.

An example or two will illustrate this problem for the case of the "historical course." In a tract of the Han period, the phases of spiritual decay are symbolized by their cosmic effects: "When the (sovereign's) spiritual power was abundant and his way perfect the sun and moon (seemed to) go slowly; the more anxious (he became to attend) to the daily affairs the more sun and moon (seemed to) hurry; and when in his diligence he could not stop his thoughts (of his duties) the sun and moon (seemed to) gallop."[29] The text is supposed to serve as commentary to a passage of the *Po-hu-t'ung*: "The Three August Ones (*san huang*) walked leisurely, the Five Emperors (*wu ti*) walked hurriedly, the Three Kings (*san wang*) ran, the Five Hegemons (*wu pa*) galloped."[30] From the foreshortened cosmological language which drastically describes "progress," however, we go back to a clear expression of principles

[29] Sung Chung in his commentary on the *Kou ming chüeh*, quoted in Tjan, *Po Hu T'ung*, note 188, Vol. I, 300.
[30] *Po Hu T'ung*, 12e; Tjan, 231.

governing the phases: "Anciently the Five Emperors esteemed virtue (*tê*), the Three Kings used righteousness (*i*), the Five Hegemons employed force (*li*)."[31] And an even more carefully considered passage of the *Po-hu-t'ung* describes the transition from *ti* to *wang* as a sequence of cosmological and anthropological order, with a precision that leaves nothing to be desired even in modern critical terms: The *tê* of the emperor harmoniously combines "heaven and earth," that is, the cosmos; the *té* of the king harmoniously combines goodness (*jen*) and righteousness (*i*).[32] The method is as charming as it is exasperating. Nevertheless, there can be no doubt that China has, like Hellas, developed the symbolism of an historical course in retrospect.

§ 6. Cycles

The exploration of the amoebic universe is in danger of becoming amoebic itself. It will be time to put some shape on the results that have emerged so far, that is, on the series of cycle symbols by which Chinese thinkers articulate their experiences of the vicissitudes of order in the historical process. Three types can be distinguished: (1) The dynastic cycle; (2) the five-hundred-year cycle; and (3) the cycle of ecumenic decay. The three interrelated cycles, together with their motivating experience, must now be examined.

The substance of the dynastic cycle is the *tê* of a family, accumulated by meritorious ancestors, to be exhausted, with a rhythm of rally and relapse, by the members of the ruling dynasty. Though the component meanings of the complex symbol were never developed in coherent theoretical form, they can well be discerned in the utterances of Chinese thinkers. There is, first of all, to be distinguished the personal from the collective *tê*. The personal *tê* is proper to individuals who, in the role of an "ancestor," contribute to the *tê*-charge of the family, or, in the role of a "virtuous" ruler, recover the fortunes of the dynasty for awhile; the collective *tê* is proper to a family which, by virtue of the accumulated charge, can aspire to royal rank. The family which has acquired the necessary *tê*-charge, then, may ascend to the rule of the ecumene, if it receives the decree or appointment, *ming,* of Heaven. By virtue of the *ming,* the meritorious family becomes a dynasty, to be overthrown when the *ming* has run its course with the empirically manifest exhaustion of the collective *tê*-charge. For the time of its Heavenly appointment, though not before or after, finally, the dynastic family is conceived as a unit of ecumenic order with

[31] Quoted, from *Huai-nan-tzu,* in Tjan, 301.
[32] *Po Hu T'ung,* 12b; Tjan, 230.

regard to time, space, and substance. This character of an ecumenic unit constituted by the *ming* is emphasized through the rule that the Great Happiness
(*ta-fu*) will not descend twice on the same family. Hence, a Chinese dynasty
does not have a "blood charisma" in the Western sense—there are no restorations or legitimist movements in China. With regard to the experiences which
motivate the conception of a dynastic cycle there can be little doubt, for the
dynasties rise and fall indeed: By the time the cycle symbol becomes tangible,
i.e., in the Chou period, China had already had, according to its traditional
history, the experiences of three dynasties. Nevertheless, there is something odd
about the dynastic cycle inasmuch as the symbol, though it suggests itself in
every cosmological civilization, is not applied to dynasties eleswhere. There is
no symbolism of dynastic cycles in Egypt or Mesopotamia.

The dynastic cycle is supposed to be, at the same time, a cycle of five hundred years. That the assumption of this time-span for the rule of a dynasty had
a basis in empirical observation is not probable; as a matter of fact, whenever
the data of traditional history approach the prescribed period too closely, one
is justified to suspect their manipulation in the interest of the symbolism. The
assumed figure originates rather in the symbolism of the number Five. Even
more, the true importance of this second cycle must not be sought in its application to the dynasties at all, but on the contrary in the fact that it can separate
from them. The dynasties, as we just have seen, were units of ecumenic order;
and this sector of meaning differentiates from the complex of the dynastic
cycle when the five-hundred-year cycle is applied to units other than the dynasties, as is done by Mencius when he applies it to the succession of the sages. The
ecumenic order, thus, is articulated by five-hundred-year cycles, whether the
tê-charge is provided by dynasties or by "uncrowned kings." The motive for
creating the symbol can hardly be found elsewhere but in the convincing experience of the ordering *tê* in persons who are not kings.

This second type of cycle, though it obviously belongs to the class of cosmological symbols, again is without parallel in the Near Eastern civilizations.
The appearance of the "sages" in China—as we shall call these persons, following Chinese usage—is rather comparable to that of the "philosophers" in Hellas.
But it is comparable only in some respects; it is by no means the same phenomenon, for the appearance and recognition of the ordering force in a human
soul, regardless of its institutional rank in the cosmologically ordered society,
in China does not flower into philososphy in the Platonic-Aristotelian sense. It
rather manifests itself in the two types of existence represented respectively by
the Confucian and Taoist movements—that is, of the sage who wants to func-

tion as a counselor to the institutional ruler, thereby establishing something
like an ecumenic theocracy, and of the sage who withdraws from the order of
the world into the isolation of the mystical hermit. But one must beware of
drawing the contrast too sharply, for the possibilities of the Chinese development can be discerned also in Hellas, with regard both to the symbol of the
ecumenic cycle and to the two types of sages. As far as the cycle is concerned,
Aristotle was so strongly impressed by the epochal epiphany of Plato that he
conceived a cycle of sages in which the last preceding epoch had been marked
by the appearance of Zoroaster. The ecumenic intention is even more distinct
in the Aristotelian than in the Chinese symbol, inasmuch as the two epiphanies
are distributed over two societies with entirely different institutional orders. As
far as the types of sages are concerned, there is recognizable in the life of Plato,
as well as in the foundation of the Academy, the purpose of forming sages who
will be able to advise rulers; and in the Stoic bureaucracy of the Roman Empire
this purpose has assumed institutional forms which resemble the function of
the Confucian bureaucracy in the Chinese Empire. To the type of the Taoist
sage, finally, Hellas has developed the remarkable parallel of the Pyrrhonic
withdrawal from the philosophies of conduct into the ataraxy of dogma and
the existence of the mystical skeptic.

While it would be hazardous to fix a date for the origin of the dynastic
cycle in its compact form, the differentiated five-hundred-year cycle cannot
have arisen before the appearance and recognition of the sages as a source of
ecumenic order independent of the royal institution. Moreover, an independent
authority of this type can hardly have asserted itself, before the royal institution
had weakened to such a degree that the ecumenic order it was supposed to
represent had manifestly given way to the disorder of a power struggle among
the *kuo*. Hence, the five-hundred-year cycle and the third type, the cycle of
ecumenic order and the decay of its *té*, are experientially connected. The ecumenic institution of kingship continued to exist, but its ordering power had
disintegrated into the force of the *kuo* and the *té* of the sages. The experience
of this triangle could express itself in the symbolism of an ecumenic *té*, of its
decay and restoration.

In the light of these reflections we can develop a view of the Chinese historical course. The early order of China was not an empire in the Near Eastern
sense, but the organization of a clan society which understood itself as the
ecumene of civilized mankind. By the middle of the eighth century, when the
ritual kingship of the ecumene lost its power, something happened that, by

Near Eastern standards, was extraordinary. For neither did the kingdom of the ecumene disappear under the impact of power politics, to be replaced by a newly organized society; nor was the dynasty overthrown and replaced by a new one; nor was, after an interregnum, the old order restored. Instead the compact cosmological order dissociated into power and spirit, as attested by the appearance, on the one hand, of the power politicians and their legalist advisers in the *kuo,* and on the other hand, of the two types of Confucian and Taoist sages. To be sure, it could be argued that none of the contenders for the kingship proved strong enough to acquire it against the will of the others; but the argument would render no more than the possibility that the events of 221 B.C. might have occurred a century or two earlier; it does not touch the fact that Chinese society had moved toward an anthropological conception of order through a leap in being, even though it was not radical enough to break the cosmological order completely. In the wake of the leap in being, the organizers of effective power and the representatives of spirtual order had replaced the compact institution of the *wang.* And once the differentiation had occurred, a return to the compact royal institution was hardly to be expected—none of the contenders could, at any time, have restored the ecumenic kingship because his success on the pragmatic level would have been a victory of power without legitimation by ecumenic spirit. Hence, the conventional interpretation of the late Chou disorders as a weakening of royal power through the growth of the feudal states, though correct in terms of institutional description, is insufficient, because it overlooks the fact that the spirit of the early order had disintegrated. When the wars among the contenders had ended with the victory of Ch'in, the ecumenic kingdom of the clan society was not restored, for the clans were all but exterminated, while the territorial lordships had disappeared; the principle of force, represented by the *kuo,* had swallowed up the ecumene and its order. The foundation of the empire can be defined, therefore, in Chinese terms, as the victory of the *kuo* over the *t'ien-hsia*: The empire was an inflated *kuo* without spiritual legitimacy. With the Han dynasty, as a consequence, there began the struggle among the movements and schools for providing the spiritual substance of which the power colossus was so embarrassingly devoid. But the new synthesis of spirit and power that was found and variously changed, until it became stabilized in the Neo-Confucian orthodoxy, could never restore the order of the early kingdom before it had dissociated into *t'ien-hsia* and *kuo.*

CHAPTER 7

Universal Humanity

There are indeed two ecumenic ages, a Western and a Far Eastern, both unfolding parallel in time. From the fact that ecumenic ages occur in the plural, there arises the question whether there are two mankinds, each having a history of its own and each developing an Ecumenic Age. If we decide that there is only one mankind, there arises the question in what sense the two parallel processes are part of one Ecumenic Age. These questions must now be explored. I shall begin the analysis with a restatement of the ecumenic problem as it has emerged in the West.

§ 1. The Western Ecumenic Age

In the Western Ecumenic Age, the truth of existence differentiates from the truth of the cosmos. The process has turned out to be a sequence of frustrations and catastrophes. I shall recapitulate the principal characteristics of the historical configuration which engendered the Pauline radical despair of finding any sense in the continuation of the process and, at the same time, the radical hope of its meaningful conclusion by the eschatological events:

(1) The cosmological empires are not internally transformed by the emergent consciousness of universal humanity, but broken from the outside through the rise of the ecumenic empires.

(2) The new empires are burdened with the conflict between concupiscential and spiritual exodus. Imperial expansion destroys the societies it conquers; and ecumenic power cannot become existentially authoritative, unless it legitimates itself through association with a spiritual movement.

(3) The concupiscential drives—the Persian, the Macedonian, the Roman—are all ecumenic; a plurality of ecumenic drives competes for the one ecumene. Following the cosmological empires, the ecumenic empires follow each other, producing the historical configuration of a succession of empires that is experienced by the victims as senseless misery.

(4) The ecumenic drives indiscriminately engulf large and populous ter-

ritories of highly developed ethnic cultures, so that the resulting empires are multicivilizational. Regarding this point, already Plato had been skeptical about the ecumenic enterprise, because the plurality of the ethnic cultures incorporated would prove an obstacle to unifying the empire by the consciousness of common humanity; in Plato's immediate experience, even the Hellenic ethnos was apparently unable to overcome the fratricidal sub-ethnicity of the single poleis in a peaceful federation.

(5) Justifying the Platonic skepticism, the ecumenic empires not only destroy one another, but tend to break up along the lines of former ethnic cultures; and this tendency can be aggravated by migratory invasions from tribal cultures beyond the imperial borders.

(6) The disruptions and breaks, however, when they occur do not restore the pre-imperial ethnic cultures to their former state—no more than in our time the withdrawal of Western powers from their colonial empires does restore the former tribal societies. The societies that emerge from an imperial breakup bear the imprint of ecumenic-imperial consciousness; we have noted the movement of expansion and contraction that results in a plurality of ecumenically conscious organizations coexisting in the one pragmatic ecumene.

(7) The truth of existence, finally, does not emerge from one single spiritual event. It does not penetrate a mankind engulfed by imperial drives from one definite point of origin, but assumes the historical form of a plurality of movements springing up in Persia and India, in Israel and Hellas. The differentiation of the one truth of existence, thus, is broken in a spectrum of spiritual eruptions each bearing the mark of the ethnic culture in which it occurs. Moreover, none of the several eruptions expands the exegesis of the theophanic event into a fully balanced symbolization of order that would cover the whole area of man's existence in society and history. The human responses to the divine irruptions rather tend to accentuate different aspects of the one truth of man's existence under God, such as the Greek noetic or the Israelite-Jewish pneumatic revelations of divine reality.

This is "history" as it was experienced by the more sensitive participants in the process down to the time of Paul. Measured by the criterion of meaningful order in society, the performance was a disappointment; for the succession of empires in pragmatic history all too obviously did not realize the truth of existence revealed by the theophanic events. If "history" consisted of nothing but a sequence of imperial dominations, it was not the field in which the true order of personal existence could expand into the order of society. As the Jewish apocalyptics ever since Daniel had seen, the realization of the humanly true order under God in society would require the apocalyptic transfiguration of the "historical" reality in which the truth of order had emerged as insight.

In apocalyptic consciousness, the experience of the movement within reality beyond its own structure has split into the conviction that history is a field of disorder beyond repair by human action and into the metastatic faith in a divine intervention that will establish the perfect order of the realm to come. The tension between order and disorder in the one reality dissociates in the phantasy of two realities following each other in time. This is the disruption of consciousness that was to be healed, through the epiphany of Christ and Paul's vision of the Resurrected, by the assurance that there is indeed more to history than empire: The emergence of the truth is the historical event that constitutes meaning in history; the transfiguration is in progress in untransfigured history. Through the Pauline vision, man's search for order in the time of history becomes luminous as the transfiguring incarnation of divine reality, of the *theotes* of Colossians 2:9, in the reality of this world. The experience of the movement in reality, thus, is not deceptive; the movement is real enough in man's trusting response to the moving presence of divine reality in his soul. The transfiguring exodus within reality achieves the full consciousness of itself when it becomes historically conscious as the Incarnation of God in Man.

In view of the intellectual confusion in our contemporary "climate of opinion," it will not be superfluous to state again that I am not dealing with problems of theology. The present study is concerned with man's consciousness of his humanity as it differentiates historically. The phantasy of two successive realities is a deformation of consciousness that can be caused by exposure to prolonged periods of senseless disturbance of existential order. In the case of the Jewish apocalyptic thinkers, it was caused by the trauma of the empires, but we meet with an equivalent deformation in certain Chinese thinkers, caused by the traumatic period of the Warring States.[1] The healing process, furthermore, is difficult and uncertain, because the disorder in reality

---

[1] The apocalyptic speculation on the two realities has its equivalent in the reflections of Chuang Chou (369–286 B.C.) on dream and reality. The reality of the Warring States becomes a dream, and the dream of true order in personal and social existence acquires the characteristic of true reality. On this equivalent problem of dream and reality cf. the analysis in Weber-Schaefer, *Oikumene und Imperium*, in the chapter on "Chung-tzu: Traum und Wirklichkeit," 89–102. For the equivalent split in Hinduism, cf. *ibid.*, 93f. The same problem of the split arises also in the fourth century B.C. in Greece. Plato deals with it, in the *Republic*, under the title of *doxa-aletheia*, appearance-reality. With Plato, however, the split does not occur in his own consciousness, but is analyzed as the split in the consciousness of the *homo politicus* of his time. On the Platonic treatment of the problem, cf. my own analysis in *Order and History*, III, 78ff.

does not disappear even when the theophany in the person of Christ re-stabilizes the order of existence and becomes socially effective through the organization of the Church. Though the faith that responds to the theophany immunizes the soul to a high degree against the trauma of continuing disorder, the breaking point is never too far off. The phantasy of two realities has remained constant in Western history from antiquity to the present. From sectarian fringe movements it can expand at any time, under the prolonged pressure of surrounding senselessness, into the correspondingly senseless disruption of social order through the outburst of apocalyptic expectations. Truth emerging in history does not abolish the uneasiness of existence on the edge of stability and disruption. Even in the case of Paul we had to note his wavering between acceptance of the one reality in which the Incarnation occurs and indulgence in the metastatic expectation of a second reality to come in the time of the living.

Though disorder continues and the uneasiness of the existence cannot be abolished, the truth of order emerges in history nevertheless. The waverings of Paul do not invalidate the insight he gained through his vision of the Resurrected: Meaning in history is constituted through man's response to the immortalizing movement of the divine pneuma in his soul. Plato and Aristotle, it is true, had already gained the same insight as far as the noetic luminosity of consciousness would allow it to be gained. But their immortalizing response to the theophany of the Nous did not unfold into a full response to the "father-god" whom Plato sensed as the God behind the gods; the stratification of the divine reality in depth remained surrounded by the "deliberate uncertainties" which I have previously analyzed. Hence, the philosophers could unfold the dimensions of order only within the limits of the noetic theophany. They did indeed proceed from the personal order of the immortalizing response to the paradigm of immortalizing order in social existence, and ultimately to the historical symbolism of the Nous as the Third God; the three dimensions of order—personal, social, historical—were fully differentiated. But they conducted their analysis within the limits set by the fundamentally intracosmic character of the theophany to which they responded; the Platonic Third God never became the Pauline one and only God who creates the world and reveals himself in history. The classic analysis reached the divine *aition* as the source of order in reality; it differentiated the structure of existence in the Metaxy, but it did not extend to the structure of divine reality in its pneumatic depth of creation and salvation. Only through Paul's response to his vision did the philosophers' *athanatizein* expand into the pneumatic *aphtharsia;* the paradigmatic polis, into the organization of man's spiritual as distinguished from his temporal order; and the Third Age of the Nous, into the eschatological structure of history under the one God of all ages.

From the Western Ecumenic Age, with its climax of meaning in the differentiations of noetic and pneumatic consciousness, there emerge certain insights into the structure of history which are generally valid:

(1) Through the differentiations of consciousness, history becomes visible as the process in which the differentiations occur.

(2) Since the differentiations advance man's insight into the constitution of his humanity, history becomes visible as a dimension of humanity beyond man's personal existence in society.

(3) Since the differentiating events are experienced as immortalizing movements, history is discovered as the process in which reality becomes luminous for the movement beyond its own structure; the structure of history is eschatological.

(4) Since the events are experienced as movements of human response to a movement of divine presence, history is not a merely human but a divine-human process. Though historical events are founded in the external world and have calendar dates, they also partake of the divine lasting out-of-time. The historical dimension of humanity is neither world-time nor eternity but the flux of presence in the Metaxy.

(5) The mankind whose humanity unfolds in the flux of presence is universal mankind. The universality of mankind is constituted by the divine presence in the Metaxy.

§ 2. Eschatology and Earthly Existence

The conflict between a plurality of ecumenic ages and the universality of mankind originates in the In-Between structure of existence.

Historical events are founded in the biophysical existence of man in society on earth, in the time of external world; they become historical through the experience of participation in the movement of divine presence. The type concept of the "Ecumenic Age" had to be constructed on the level of societies in worldly existence who were involved in the pragmatic process, limited in time and space, from which the consciousness of universal humanity emerged. There was nothing wrong with the procedure; the Western Ecumenic Age is indeed a distinct unit of meaning in history. Still, something seemed to be wrong because of the odd tension between the universality of meaning and the pragmatic limitation of the process: Were the societies not involved in the process—the non-Mediterranean Africa and Europe, the Far East, and the Americas—excluded from its universality? The oddity, then, was further aggravated by the chronologically parallel second Ecumenic Age, as far as we know without cultural diffusion or stimulation, in China: Are there several mankinds who go through the disintegration of cosmological consciousness, independent of one another? Obviously, the question of the subject of history, previously discussed within the context of the Western Ecumenic Age, now imposes itself again on the level of a global mankind.

In the light of the preceding analysis, the problem can now be succinctly resolved. The divine-human flux of presence is a given only as far as it is founded in man's biophysical existence on earth; the divine presence itself, though experienced by man who exists in time and space, is not a spatio-temporal given. The historical dimension of humanity, thus, is no more a given than the reality of man's personal existence in the Metaxy. Universal mankind is not a society existing in the world, but a symbol which indicates man's consciousness of participating, in his earthly existence, in the mystery of a reality that moves toward its transfiguration. Universal mankind is an eschatological index.

The recognition of universal mankind as an eschatological index penetrates to the center of the problem presented by history as a dimension of humanity. Without universality, there would be no mankind other than the aggregate of members of a biological species; there would be no more a history of mankind than there is a history of catkind or horsekind. If mankind is to have history, its members must be able to respond to the movement of divine presence in their souls. But if that is the condition, then the mankind who has history is constituted by the God to whom man responds. A scattering of societies, belonging to the same biological type, thus, is discovered to be one mankind with one history, by virtue of participation in the same flux of divine presence.

If this insight were a constant structure of consciousness, the problems of history would be comparatively simple. What happens on the spatio-temporal level of existence would be of little relevance. An historian could not do much more than register the societies which exist on earth, and perhaps add a few data concerning their size and duration. The matter becomes complicated, because consciousness is not a constant but a process advancing from compactness to differentiation. Even worse, these advances do not occur across the whole field of human societies in the same manner at the same time—some are "chosen," some are not. And still worse, as already Plato had observed, the differentiations have something to do with the material advance of society from stone-age primitivity, through agricultural settlement and the discovery of metals, to the foundation of cities and the development of urban civilization. The great noetic and pneumatic differentiations do not occur among paleolithic hunters and fishers, but in ages of cities and empires; some social and cultural situations appear to be more favorable to differentiating responses than others. The structure of man's earthly existence in society, thus, is somehow involved in the process of differentiating consciousness.

Such observations must not be misunderstood as inchoate constructions of a causal relation between civilization and unconsciousness. The thinkers of the Ecumenic Age who observe these configurations do not intend to determine a Marxian Consciousness by a Marxian Being. They are not immanentist speculators who degrade their consciousness into the epiphenomenon of technical discoveries; on the contrary, they are quite aware of their consciousness as the primary instance which transforms the discoveries into historical events. When the theophanic events make history visible as the transfiguring process in which man participates with his spatio-temporal existence, this process becomes an absorbing human concern to the full extent of its knowability, because it partakes of the sacredness that emanates from the divine presence in the flux. Plato's reflections on the sequence of stone age and metal ages are not an isolated instance. They are preceded by Hesiod's observation on the iron age that follows the Mycenaean bronze age, with its accent on the decline of existential order marked by the advance of metallurgy. And they are paralleled, in the China of the Warring States, by an observation with similar implications, attributed to Feng Hu Tzu:[2]

> In the Age of Hsüan Yüan, Shen Nung, and Ho Hsü, weapons were made of stones for cutting trees and building houses, and were buried with the dead...;

> In the Age of Huang Ti, weapons were made of jade, for cutting trees, building houses, and digging the ground, and were buried with the dead...;

> In the Age of Yü, weapons were made of bronze, for building canals ... and houses...;

> At the present time, weapons are made of iron.

[2] Quoted from Kwang-Chi Chang, *The Archaeology of Ancient China* (Rev. ed.; Yale University Press, 1968), 2.

Returning to the West, in the first century B.C., Lucretius develops in Book V of *De Rerum Natura* his great design of evolution from plant life through animals to man, and of civilizational growth from the stone age through the metal age to the highest perfection (*ad summum cacumen,* V, 1457) in the present. The account of the ages (V, 1283–96) resembles the statements of Feng Hu Tzu:

> The oldest weapons were hands, nails, and teeth,
> and stones and branches broken in the forest,
> and flame and fire as soon as they were known.
> Later then was discovered the power of iron and bronze.
> The use of bronze was earlier known than of iron,
> because it is more easily worked and more of it to be found.
> With bronze men tilled the soil, and with bronze they stirred up
> the waves of war, and dealt horrible wounds,
> and seized cattle and lands; for readily gave way
> all that was nude and unarmed to those who were armed.
> Then very slowly the sword of iron advanced,
> and the sickle of bronze fell into contempt.
> With iron they began to break the soil of the earth,
> and more equal became the struggles of uncertain war.

In the Lucretian case there remains no doubt about the wars of the Ecumenic Age as the context in which the story of the ages is to be read, for the passage just quoted is immediately followed by a long and vivid account of the improvements in slaughtering people made in the Punic Wars (V, 1297–1349).

> Thus Dreary Discord (*discordia tristis*) bred one thing after the other
> that would be frightful to the tribes of men in arms,
> and day by day augmented the terrors of war (V, 1305–1307).

Still, the dreariness of human discord is not the ultimate determinant in the history of mankind. One should note, in both Feng Hu Tzu and Lucretius, the ambivalence of instruments as weapons of war and tools for the works of peace; and behind the instruments, one must not forget, there is the mind that invents them (V, 1449–57):

> Going to sea and tilling the land, walls for the cities and laws,
> arms, roads, clothing, and what else of this kind,
> the prizes and luxuries that lie at the heart of all life,
> poetry, painting, and the smoothing of artful figures,
> were slowly learned, through practice and experience,
> by the restless mind (*mens*) as it advances step by step.
> So by steps the flux of time (*aetas*) brings everything forth
> to attention, to be raised by reason (*ratio*) into the zone of light.

Like Plato before him, Lucretius can admire the restlessly inventive mind of man and the history of civilizational growth without losing his sensitiveness for the questionable character of a process which culminates, in his own experience, both in the philosopher's meditation on the *natura rerum* and in the concupiscential atrocities of the imperial wars. His analysis of existence in the Metaxy, it is true, does not reach the Platonic insight into the tension between apeirontic depth and noetic height, but the more compact symbolization through the darkness of *discordia tristis,* and the light of reason does not impair his spiritualist's understanding of this condition as the universally human in history. Nor is the sacredness of history impaired, when Lucretius expresses the experience of divine presence compactly by his appeal to *alma Venus,* the mother of Aeneas and Rome.

The experience of *oikoumene-okeanos,* once it has disintegrated, cannot be restored to its pristine compactness. The habitat of man has become the open field of the imperial drive; and the divine mystery that had surrounded the limited territory and its people has become luminous as the divine presence in a transfiguring process in which all men at all times and all places participate. When the primary experience of man's existence in the cosmos has dissociated into the opacity of concupiscential expansion and the luminosity of spiritual consciousness, the bond that prevents the two pieces of reality from falling apart into the two realities of apocalyptic and Gnostic thinkers is found in history. On the level of the truth of existence, the transfiguring process takes the place of the *okeanos* as the horizon of the universally divine mystery for a mankind that has become ecumenic through the concupiscential exodus. Hence, only the triad of ecumenic empire, spiritual outburst, and historiography expresses equivalently the structure in reality that had been compactly expressed by the *oikoumene-okeanos* symbolism.

§ 3. Absolute Epoch and Axis-Time

The triad—Ecumenic Empire, Spiritual Outburst, Historiography—and the *oikoumene-okeanos* symbolism are equivalents. The implications of the statement for the central issue of a philosophy of history are not immediately visible; they require unfolding: The statement reduces to experiential analysis, and thereby resolves, the problem that has been raised by Hegel under the title of "the absolute epoch" and further developed by Jaspers under the title of the "axis-time" of world-history.

Hegel's "absolute epoch" is marked by the epiphany of Christ. The appearance of the Son of God is "the hinge around which the history of the world turns," because through the Incarnation God has revealed himself as the Spirit (*Geist*). "And that means: Self-consciousness (*das Selbstbewusstsein*) had raised itself to the moments which belong to the concept of the Spirit, as well as to the need of grasping these moments absolutely." The plan of Providence in world-history becomes knowable when God has revealed his nature as the *Geist* to the thinking *Geist* in man, that is "to the proper organ, in which God is present to man." "The Christians have been initiated (*eingeweiht*) into the mysteries of God, and thus is given to us the key to world-history." Since "history unfolds the nature of God," and the nature of God has become known to us through Christ, it is now incumbent on Hegel as a Christian thinker to penetrate conceptually "this rich production of creative Reason that is world-history." Since the triune God has revealed himself as *Geist* through Christ, the Christian religion as distinguished from all others continues the "speculative element" that "enables philosophy to find in it also the idea of Reason." The reflections on world-history which start from the insight into this absolute epoch will, therefore, be "a theodicy, a justification of God," more effective than the theodicy which Leibniz has attempted in "abstract, indeterminate categories."[3]

The "absolute epoch," understood as the events in which reality becomes luminous to itself as a process of transfiguration, is indeed the central issue in a philosophy of history. For without the noetic and pneumatic differentiations, there would not be a history in which man's humanity achieves its rational and spiritual consciousness, nor would there be a philosopher's intellect to be concerned with this intelligible structure in history. One does not have to accept Hegel's System, if one accepts his problem of the "absolute epoch" as valid. There remains, however, the question whether this epoch must be identified with the epiphany of Christ, or whether it should not be identified with some other event.

Jaspers accepts Hegel's problem, but refuses to identify the absolute epoch with Christ, because Christianity is one faith among others; "it is not the faith of mankind." The Christian "view of universal history can be valid only for believing Christians"; and even the Christians have not tied "their empirical view of history to their faith," but distinguish between sacred and profane history and explore "the Christian tradition itself just like other empirical objects of investigation." "An axis of world-history, if there is one, would have

---

[3] Hegel, *Philosophie der Geschichte*, 440; Hoffmeister (ed.), *Die Vernunft in der Geschichte* (Hamburg, 1965), 45–48.

to be found *empirically* as an event (*Tatbestand*) that can be valid for all human beings, including the Christians." This axis would have to be the time when "the formation of humanity (*Menschsein*)" happened with "such overwhelming fertility" that the result would be empirically convincing both for the West and Asia, and for all men at large, regardless of this or that faith, and thus could become "for all peoples the common basis of historical self-understanding." This axis is indeed to be empirically found in "the spiritual process" that extends from *ca.* 800 to 200 B.C., with a concentration about 500 when Confucius, the Buddha, and Heraclitus were contemporaries. "This age brought forth the fundamental categories in which we think to this day; it laid the foundations of the world-religions in which men live to this day; in every sense the step into the Universal was taken."[4]

The two conceptions of the epoch complement each other and illuminate the problem they try to resolve. Hegel concentrates the epoch in Christ because he believes his construction of the System to complete a revelation that has been only incompletely revealed through the Incarnation of the Logos. In order to make this phantasy plausible, he first projects the noetic differentiation into the pneumatic consciousness of Paul, by letting the concept of *Geist* oscillate between the meanings of Nous and pneuma, and then extracts his own Reason from the Pauline Spirit. Hence, his concentration on Christ as "the hinge around which the history of the world turns" is only apparent; actually Hegel included, by means of his semantic games, the noetic differentiation of the Hellenic philosophers in the "absolute epoch." Jaspers would have been on solid ground if he had dissolved the Hegelian merger and expanded the epoch so as to include not only the epiphany of Christ but all the events that empirically have entered in the constitution of historical consciousness. Instead of carrying out this analysis, however, he forms an oddly doctrinal conception of "Christian faith" that will permit him to remove Christ from his epochal status together with a "religion" in which the majority of mankind does not believe anyway. As a consequence, he can transfer the "axis-time" from Christ to a spiritual process which extends, between 800 and 200 B.C., from the Graeco-Roman West and the prophets of Israel, through the Iranian and Indian civilizations, to China. What induces Jaspers to take this step does not become fully clear from the immediate context in *Vom Ursprung und Ziel der Geschichte,* because on this occasion he leaves his conception of "Christian faith" standing as an insufficiently analyzed block.

---

[4] Karl Jaspers, *Vom Ursprung und Ziel der Geschichte* (Zurich, 1949), 18f. cf. the whole Chapter on the "Achsenzeit," 18–43.

✓ Jesus lived at the beginning of a new world age —and he
certainly lived an exemplary divine —human life to the extent that,
then men killed him for it! Socrates + Jesus are still so radical people

UNIVERSAL HUMANITY *not grasped yet!* 311

Before going into this puzzle further, however, I must state the part of his motivation about which there is no doubt, because Jaspers is explicit on the point: It is his philosopher's concern to re-establish the "absolute epoch" as the center of a philosophy of history against Spengler's and Toynbee's dissection of history into "civilizations" with autonomous internal courses. One must, furthermore, acknowledge his categorization of the "spiritual process," that had on and off attracted attention as an historical epoch, as the axis-times, as a feat of philosophical insight.

On the insufficiently analyzed block of "Christian faith" there falls some light from certain reflections of Jaspers in his debate with Bultmann about *Die Frage der Entmythologisierung*. On this occasion, Jaspers distinguishes between the reality of the existential tension in Jesus toward God and the theological construction of the reality, after the death of Jesus, by the early Christians. To the theological addition (*theologische Zutat*) he declares himself to be existentially not responsive, while about the reality he has to say: "Jesus confronts us only with the moral question of deciding for a life in the faith of God (*im Gottesglauben*). This is truly a critical question in the practice of life. A philosophizing man does hear it in Jesus with a more than ordinary intenseness, but he does not hear it in him alone, but also in the prophets of the Old Testament and in philosophers of high rank."[5] Though he recognizes in Jesus an extraordinary intenseness of existence in faith, Jaspers does not recognize, either in Jesus or in Paul, the differentiation of eschatological consciousness which Bultmann, in his answer, stresses as the specific difference of "Christian faith": "This is the paradox of Christian faith that the eschatological happening in which the world comes to its end has become real as an event within the history of the world, and becomes a real event again in every Christian sermon if it is a genuine sermon."[6]

The overt reason for the exclusion of Christ has become clear. But it is the overt reason only. Jaspers was quite familiar with the eschatological problems in "Christian faith." If he did not acknowledge them as an important step in the differentiation of consciousness, the ulterior reason must be sought in the unsatisfactory state of experiential analysis at the time. Jaspers was repelled by the fusion of the eschatological structure of reality with a semifundamentalist orthodoxy. The character of this fusion becomes manifest in Bultmann's formulation, just quoted, of the Christian "paradox." For "the eschatological happening in which the world comes to its end" has of course not become "real

[5] Karl Jaspers and Rudolf Bultmann, *Die Frage der Entmythologisierung* (Munich, 1954), 103.
[6] *Ibid.*, 72.

as an event within the history of the world." On the contrary, the fact that the world has not come to its end as promised is precisely the effective motive in the apocalyptic movements, with their metastatic expectations, that have sprung up ever since. As if it were not enough that the eschatological structure of reality, and man as the site of transfiguration, have become conscious, Bultmann concentrates the symbols engendered by the experience into a superfluous "paradox of Christian faith" and thereby eclipses the reality experienced. Jaspers in his turn was disturbed by the language of orthodoxy, because he sensed in it the transformation of existential truth into doctrine of which he recognized the murderous consequences in the practice of Communism and National Socialism. The debate had to remain inconclusive, because neither of the two thinkers engaged in the analysis of the eschatological differentiation that would have been necessary to dissolve their disagreement.

The unsatisfactory state of analysis had its repercussions for the understanding of "history." The structure of "history" certainly is smudged when Bultmann describes the theophanic event as happening *in* the very history which it constitutes and makes visible as universal. And the same semiconscious smudging of "history" into a stream of world-time in which the "spiritual process" happens, causes the problems in Jaspers' construction of the "axis-time." There simply is no spiritual outburst marking an "epoch," be it that of Jaspers or that of Hegel, without a consciousness that is formed by the differentiating event and thereby enabled to recognize it as "epochal." The structure of human consciousness as it becomes luminous for its own historicity is obscured if not destroyed, if one isolates the events of the spiritual exodus from the events of historiography that arise in its wake, and if one ignores the fact that the historians deal with the disturbance of order through the concupiscential exodus in the light of the insight gained by the spiritual outburst—be it Herodotus and Thucydides, or Polybius and Livy, or the Israelite historians from the author of the David Memoirs to the Chronicler, or the Chinese historian Sse-ma Ch'ien.

At the present state of experiential analysis, I conclude, the concept of an epoch or axis-time marked by the great spiritual outbursts alone is no longer tenable. Something "epochal" has occurred indeed; there is no reason why the adjective should be denied to the disintegration of the compact experience of the cosmos and the differentiation of the truth of existence. But the "epoch" involves, besides the spiritual outbursts, the ecumenic empires from the Atlantic to the Pacific and engenders the consciousness of history as the new horizon that surrounds with its divine mystery the existence of man in the habitat that has been opened by the concupiscence of power and knowledge.

§ 4. The Epoch and the Structure of Consciousness

The triad is a unit of experience in process of differentiation and symbolization. This process in its personal, social, and historical dimensions, is the period which I have called the Ecumenic Age.

Once the issue is stated in experiential terms, the temptations to misconstrue the problem of the epoch become intelligible as rooted in the structure of consciousness. On the one hand, neither the ecumenic empires nor the spiritual outbursts alone can mark the "absolute epoch," because there is no epoch without historical consciousness. On the other hand, history as the horizon of divine mystery that surrounds the spatially open ecumene can hardly emerge unless the ecumene actually opens under the impact of concupiscential expansion, and the expansion is no more than a senseless rise and fall of peoples and their rulers unless the consciousness of the historians can relate the events to the truth of existence that emerges in the spiritual outbursts. There is no consciousness of epoch unless something that can be experienced as epochal is happening indeed in the process of reality. The experiential complex, though it is an integral unit, thus, suggests by its structure a split into subject and object of knowledge. If one yields to the temptation, empires and outbursts are liable to move into the position of events that happen in history, while the historiographer tends to become the recorder of a history that is structured by the events; and between the hypostatized subject and object of historical consciousness, the reality that has become luminous as a process of transfiguration will evaporate.

This split cannot be healed by a super- or meta-consciousness that will add up the hypostatized components of the experiential complex. If a history of the empires and the "spiritual process," representing the object-pole, were to be supplemented by a history of historiography, representing the subject-pole, the phenotype of the epoch certainly would be improved, but the newly differentiated horizon of mystery would still disappear. Historical consciousness presents the same problem as the philosopher's noetic consciousness. When the luminosity of noetic consciousness is deformed into an "anthropology" of intramundane man and a "theology" of a transmundane God, the theophanic event will be destroyed, and with it will be destroyed man's tension toward the divine ground of his existence and the experience of participation. In the same manner, when the symbolisms engendered in the Ecumenic Age, including historiography, are deformed into events in a "history" other than the history whose experience they articulate, the process with its eschatological tension will be lost. The impasse of such derailments can be avoided only if one acknowledges the process of differentiation itself as the exclusive source of our knowledge concerning the unit of experience that understands itself as historically epochal when it differentiates.

To accept the process of differentiation as the exclusive source of knowledge means, negatively, to renounce all pretense to an observer's position outside the process. Positively, it means to enter the process and to participate both in its formal structure and the concrete tasks imposed on the thinker by his situation in it.

First, regarding the formal structure: What differentiates is the consciousness of a structure in reality. The statement implies that the structure has been present before, and will be present after, it has been experienced and articulated. So far the problem can be couched in the language of a subject and object of consciousness. The matter becomes complicated, because the structure in question happens to be the movement of reality beyond its structure. The insights gained by the triadic unit of experience are part of the reality itself as it becomes luminous for its movement toward transfiguration. The insight gained is not merely a man's knowledge about a structural oddity in which he may be interested or not, for the gaining of the insight is itself an eschatological event that illuminates the transfigurative structure in man's humanity. History, thus, reveals itself as the horizon of divine mystery when the process of differentiation is discovered to be the process of transfiguration. Nevertheless, the event of the process becoming luminous for its movement toward eschatological fulfillment does not abolish the cognitive tension between man the knower and the structure that now becomes known as pre-existent and post-existent to the event of its discovery. Hence, if the structure differentiated happens to be the movement of reality beyond its structure, the event opens the vista into the past and future of a process in which the event itself marks an epoch: the epoch of the process becoming luminous for its structure. In the light of the new discovery, the earlier symbolizations of the order experienced in reality, be it the *oikoumene-okeanos* symbolism, or mytho-speculations of the historiogenetic type, will move into the position of phases in the same process of transfiguration that now can be symbolized as a humanly universal process, open toward its past and its future. As the ecumene opens spatially, the surrounding horizon of mystery opens temporally into

[handwritten margin note, top: "√ + they all know the "sky is changed" / a new age is coming — so they / move to get into position for the "ruling of / the / "world ""]

universal history. This result of the analysis can be expressed in the proposition: In the Ecumenic Age, the process of reality is discovered as a spatially and temporally open field, with man's existence in eschatological tension as its center of consciousness.

The formal structure, though it can be analytically isolated, is only one stratum in the process. Precisely when the formal stratum differentiates, the process comes into view in its concreteness as the process of history in which all men past, present, and future participate. As seen from the new center of consciousness, this process moves through mankind in its earthly concrete existence with its dimensions, no longer limited, of space and time; and inversely, this process is enacted by mankind in its personally and socially concrete diversification. Moreover, the "new center of consciousness" itself is not that of a disembodied mind either, but the consciousness of a great number of human beings, widely dispersed in space and time over a socially and culturally diversified mankind, in whom the epochal event becomes reality in a wide spectrum of degrees of differentation, of degrees of disengagement from the primary experience of the cosmos and specifically from the mythospeculative, historiogenetic experiences, of accents on specific problems and omissions of others, of differences in the actual extent of the ecumenic horizon as it opens for a concrete thinker in his concrete situation, and of his actual knowledge of the past of a mankind that has become for him universal.

Once the stratification and diversification of consciousness is recognized as the structure through which the history of universal mankind moves, the debate about specific marks of the "absolute epoch" will dissolve into the general inquiry concerning the modes of universal participation as well as the configuration of these modes in space and time. Under the debate about the characteristics there lurks the misconstruction of the epoch as an object in the external world whose nature has to be conceptualized by an observer, while in fact it is a phase in the process of differentiation to be described from a participatory position within the process. The conspicuous events which attract attention to the phenomenon of the epoch, to be sure, will stand as the great manifestations of the transition from the truth of the cosmos to the truth of existence, but what is most remarkable about the manifestations is the transiion which they manifest. The transition to the truth of existence is an epoch, because the men in whose psyche the differentiations occur experience them as epochal in the sense of constituting an irreversible Before and After of meaning in history; the Ecumenic Age is the time in which the symbolisms of the "eras" and "periods" were created. When history comes into view as univers-

ally human, it is discovered to be characterized by epochal advances of insight
into its structure.

§ 5. Question and Mystery

The discovery of the epochal structure inevitably raises the disturbing
questions concerning the mystery of history: *the world ages reveal something new each Time*

(1) Why should there be epochs of advancing insight at all? why is the
structure of reality not known in differentiated form at all times?

(2) Why must the insights be discovered by such rare individuals as
prophets, philosophers, and saints? why is not every man the recipient of the
insights?

Why not everyone? aston in the first place?

(3) Why when the insights are gained, are they not generally accepted?
why must the epochal truth go through the historical torment of imperfect
articulation, evasion, skepticism, disbelief, rejection, deformation, and of
renaissances, renovations, rediscoveries, rearticulations, and further differentiations?

In the course of the present study, these questions have obtruded themselves on and off. Their status and function in the process of differentiation
though has not yet been fully developed, because their relation to the problem
of epoch, which must be included in the analysis, has become thematic only
now. The questions are not meant to be answered; on the contrary, they
symbolize the mystery in the structure of history by their unanswerability.
Hence, the Question as a symbolism *sui generis* becomes the problem to be
clarified.

An elementary misunderstanding must be removed first. Since the questions cannot be answered by propositions referring to events in the external
world, an epistemologist of the positivist persuasion will dismiss them as
pseudo-questions, as *Scheinprobleme,* devoid of meaning. Within the limits
of the positivist horizon, the argument is valid; the questions can indeed not
be answered by reference to the world of sense perception. The argument
becomes invalid, however, when it goes on to declare the questions, for this
reason, to be meaningless; for the men who have asked them through several
thousand years of history to this day do not consider them meaningless at all,
even if they find the adequate articulation of their meaning sometimes a baf-
fling task. The denial of meaning runs counter to the empirical fact that they
rise again and again as meaningful from the experience of reality. Hence the
act of denial, especially when it appears in the context of a philosophical

"well attunances"
X occurred shutting by 3000 (in the records) + the temples +
whether the Old age would return or not?! the religious life
_____ 1st UNIVERSAL HUMANITY of men before?
317 why?
to ponder

school or movement, must be characterized as the sectarian idiosyncrasy of
men who have lost contact with reality and whose intellectual and spiritual
growth has been so badly stunted that the meaning escapes them.

The Question capitalized is not a question concerning the nature of this
or that object in the external world, but a structure inherent to the experience
of reality. As a consequence, it does not appear in the same form at all times,
but shares by its varying modes the advance of experience from compactness
to differentiation. The meaning of the Question can be ascertained, therefore,
only by tracing the modes from the setting in the primary experience of the
cosmos, through transitional forms, to their setting in the context of noetic
and pneumatic differentiations.

In the setting of the primary experience, the Question appears as the
motivating force in the act of symbolizing the origin of things through the
myth, *i.e.,* by a story which relates one thing, or complex of things, to another
intracosmic thing as the ground of its existence; the myth is the answer to a
question concerning the ground, even if the question itself, or the problem
of the Question capitalized, is not spelled out. Still moving within the context
of the primary experience, the dynamics of the Question, then, makes itself
felt in the creation of transitional forms such as the aetiological chains which
extrapolate the shorter type of myth toward a cause that is believed to be
the highest one in the cosmos and, therefore, to be eminently qualified to make
the whole chain expressive of the non-existent ground of the cosmos. These
are the chains that, in the chapter on "Historiogenesis," I have analyzed under
the head of "mytho-speculation." The function of the Question becomes
apparent, furthermore, when the creators of the myth reflect on the adequacy
of the myth as an expression of the questioning they are experiencing. On
occasion of the Memphite Theology I have stressed the "footnotes" in which
the creators of the drama explain why the myth of their choice is a more
suitable answer to their quest of the ground than other possible variants.
Though documentations of this kind are rare before the Ecumenic Age, the
manifestations of skepticism and alienation in the First Intermediate Period of
Egypt, or the Akhenaton episode, leave no doubt about a live critical consciousness in the mythopoetic act. A myth is not a final truth; it is supposed
to furnish the answer to a question; and the test of its truth lies with the
changing modes of the Question as experienced. There must be remembered,
finally, the mythopoetic freedom and the insouciance about conflicts between
successive extrapolations to the ground within the same society, or between
simultaneous extrapolations in well-known neighboring societies. In the suc-

cessive Sumerian and Babylonian cosmogonies, one high-god can replace the other without impairing the truth of the myth; and nobody is seriously disturbed when neighboring Egyptian and Mesopotamian empires both claim to represent the order of the cosmos on earth. This insouciance is intelligible only if the richly diversified field of the myth is understood, not as a collection of conflicting statements, but as a realm of equivalent answers to the same structure in reality experienced, that is to the Question. Their weight of meaning again would lie with the Question rather than with the symbolic answer. One might even say that this insouciance, with its weight on the Question, is the compact equivalent of the later differentiated understanding of universal humanity.

The weight on the Question does not make the answer irrelevant. On the contrary, setting aside the stirrings of a critical consciousness that will consider one symbolism preferable to another, the myth has the full relevance of a true insight concerning the aetiological order of the cosmos in response to the Question concerning the divine ground. The creation of a myth, or of a mytho-speculative construction, is always motivated by the experience of a thing and the question its existence raises; but neither the experiential motivation nor the process of creation and construction need be in the foreground of consciousness. If anything is characteristic of stable cosmological societies, it is the lack of concern about the motivating experiences or about conflicts; the finished symbolism which tells the story of a genesis from the highest cause down to the existent thing is accepted without further questions. What is meant by this unquestioned acceptance of the myth in the cosmological style of truth will become clear from the humble but eminently practical instance of a Babylonian incantation against toothache. The ache was supposed to be caused by a worm who had found his habitat in the diseased area. As in the New Year festivals the priest accompanies the ritual with the recitation of the cosmogony, the priest-physician accompanies his healing action with the story of how the worm came to be:

> After Anu had created heaven,
> Heaven had created earth,
> Earth had created rivers,
> Rivers had created canals,
> Canals had created marsh,
> Marsh had created worm—
> The worm came weeping before Shamash,
> His tears flowing before Ea:
> "What will you give me to eat?
> What will you give me to drink?"

I think this is —
humorous — and
takes a manner
unquestion!

The gods offer him ripe figs and apricots as a habitat. But a worm of such ancestry is choosy; he insists on a place between the teeth and the gum; and that he is accorded by Shamash and Ea.[7] In the case of this incantation, the cosmological style can be observed in its compactness. Clearly the genesis of the worm is an answer to the diagnostic question concerning the cause of the toothache. But the process which endows the worm with this impressive aetiological chain does not become thematic. One can only surmise the incantation to be a sub-myth in a comprehensive mythical conception of reality, with "systematic" features formed under the influence of mytho-speculative cosmogonies and theogonies.

When the process becomes thematic, however, it is no longer quite the process that has resulted in the myth of unquestioned acceptance. The process cannot be raised into consciousness without injecting questioning consciousness as a critic. The compact story of a genesis from the highest cause down, it is true, can be reversed, so that the aetiological chain will be transformed into a series of questions from the existent thing up. But when the reversal occurs, the quest of the ground, the Question itself, differentiates as a structure in the experience of reality; and the Question will not rest until the ground beyond the intracosmic grounds offered by the compact myth is found. The Question will not abide by the intracosmic answers but presses toward the answer that is inherent to its own structure. Both the reversal and its critical consequence characterize the procedure of numerous dialogues in the Upanishads. A typical case of competitive questioning by which the wisdom of the Brahmana Yajnavalkya is tested, is the following passage from the *Brihadaranyaka Upanishad* (III.6):[8]

> Then Gargi Vachaknavi asked.
> "Yajnavalkya" she said, "everything here is woven,
> like warp and woof, in water. What then is that in
> which water is woven, like warp and woof?"
> "In air, O Gargi," he replied.
> "In what then is air woven, like warp and woof?"
> "In the worlds of the sky, O Gargi," he replied.

The questioning lady then drives the Brahmana through the following links in the aetiological chain: The world of the Gandharvas (demigods), of Aditya (the sun), of Chandra (the moon), of the Nakshatras (the stars), of the Devas (the gods), of Indra, of Prajapati, and finally the worlds of Brahman. The questioning concludes:

[7] Samuel Noah Kramer, *Mythologies of the Ancient World* (New York, 1961), 123f.
[8] Max Mueller's translation. Quoted from *Hindu Scriptures* (Everyman, 1938).

*which our ancestors
had the good sense not to
describe that which is undescribable. —*

"In what then are the worlds of Brahman woven, like
warp and woof?"
Yajnavalkya said: "O Gargi, do not ask too much, lest thy
head should fall off. Thou askest too much about a deity
about which we are not to ask too much. Do not ask too much,
O Gargi."
After that Gargi Vachaknavi held her peace.

The Indian dialogue goes through a chain of intracosmic causes of the same
type as the Babylonian incantation. And yet, the reversal of the chain is more
than the exploitation of a formal possibility. For the descent from the highest
cause down comes to rest on the thing to be explained; its emphasis lies on
the objective order among things in the cosmos, while the ascent from the
existent thing up, from the "everything here" (closely related to the Heraclitean
"this cosmos here"), moves the tension of existence with its unrest of the quest
to the fore. The Question is not just any question but the quest concerning
the mysterious ground of all Being. The hierarchical fabric of things in the
cosmos is taken for granted, but the knowledge of this order as symbolized
through the myth will not assuage the unrest of the questioner. The Question
urges on, beyond the reality covered by the myth, toward the border where
the realm of symbols is exhausted and the questioner's head is threatened to
fall off, if he persists after the goal has been reached. The dialogue reveals
the questioning ascent as a process of participation by which man's humanity
becomes luminous as that of the Self in its questioning tension toward the
ground, of the *atman* in its relation to the *brahman* in the language of the
Upanishads.

*but there are
"lots"*

The dialogues of the Upanishadic type enact the Question that leads toward
the ground, but in their self-interpretation this differentiating act is a commentary within the Vedic tradition. They establish the questioning consciousness as an ordering force of existence, but they understand this movement
beyond the myth not as a break with the myth. Neither the Upanishadic
differentiations nor their later elaborations in the Vedanta systems are experienced as a breakthrough that constitutes an epoch in history; all have
their status within the comprehensive culture of Hinduism as one possibility
of man's understanding of his relation to the world and the divine forces
among others. Yajnavalkya's Brahmanic mode of the Question is not the
philosopher's mode that engenders the symbolism of the Nous as the Third
God in a sequence of divine ages, nor is it the pneumatic mode of the prophet
who demotes all other gods to the status of false gods, or even no-gods. There

a theophanic event = The divine (light) appears to a man

is no doctrine in Hinduism that attaches itself to an historic theophany like the Christian dogma to the epiphany of Christ. The culture of Hinduism accommodates equally the devotees of Vishnu or Shiva, and the Brahmanic mystics; it has room for polytheism, monotheism, and atheism; for orgiastic cults and ascetic discipline; for a personal God and for an impersonal ground of being. Hinduism as a religion has no historical founder. It is the *sanatana-dharma,* the eternal religion that has no end, as all the things have that have a beginning; it is the archetype of religion that has appeared, and will reappear, in the worlds as in succession they are created, destroyed, and re-created. In the culture of Hinduism, historical consciousness is muted by the dominance of late-cosmological speculations on the cosmos as a "thing" with a beginning and an end, as a "thing" that is born and reborn in infinite sequence. The hypostasis of the cosmos, and the fallacious infinite of cosmological speculation, can be identified as the stratum in the Hinduist experience of reality that has not been broken by epochal events comparable to the noetic and pneumatic theophanies in Hellas and Israel. As a consequence, the Brahmanic experience of reality does not develop the self-consciousness of the Platonic-Aristotelian philosophy as a noetic science; in its self-understanding it is a *darshana,* a way of looking at reality from this particular thinker's position.[9]

The characterization of Brahmanic consciousness had to be chiefly negative, because it presents the case of a breakthrough which, by noetic and pneumatic standards, does not reach its goal. This incompleteness, however, must not obscure the fact that an incipient breakthrough has occurred indeed. The truth of existence has been differentiated up to a point, and the point lies high enough to allow the grandiose flowering of Brahmanic consciousness into the mysticism of Shankara (*ca.* A.D. 800). Still, the dominance of the cosmological fallacies seriously impairs the experience of reality and its exploration. The masterful comparative study of Shankara and Eckhart by Rudolf Otto in his *Mysticism East and West* (1932) shows both the acumen of Shankara, which sometimes is analytically more articulate than Eckhart's, and the fundamental difference between the two thinkers: To the Hindu thinker, the world is a delusion; to Eckhart it is the one and only world in which the God who has created it has become incarnate. The Brahmanic "breakthrough which does not quite reach its goal" can now be more adequately characterized as a truth of existence which, in its differentiation, stops short of the theophanic event which constitutes epochal consciousness. As a consequence, the historical di-

[9] For the characterization of Hinduism I have drawn on Helmuth von Glasenapp, *Der Stufen-weg zum Goettlichen. Shankaras Philosophie der All-Einheit* (Baden-Baden, 1948), 11–23.

mension of humanity cannot become articulate. The most striking manifestation of this phenomenon is the non-appearance of historiography in Hindu
culture.

The incompleteness of the breakthrough does not diminish the importance
of the dialogic ascent in the Upanishads. The ascent through the aetiological
chain, the *via negativa,* remains the analytical instrument in the articulation
of existential truth even when the breakthrough has been achieved. The intimate connection between Brahmanic consciousness and pneumatic truth will
become apparent in a passage from the Apocalypse of Abraham (Chs. 7–8),
an Essene document, to be dated probably in the first century A.D.:[10]

very
late

> More venerable indeed than all things is fire
> for many things subject to no one will fall to it. . . .
> More venerable even is water,
> for it overcomes fire. . . .
> Still I do not call it God,
> for it is subject to earth. . . .
> Earth do I call more venerable,
> for it overcomes the nature of water.
> Still I do not call it God,
> as it is dried up by the sun. . . .
> More venerable than the earth I call the sun;
> the universe he makes light by his rays.
> Even him I do not call God,
> as his course is obscured by night and the clouds.
> Yet the moon and stars I do not call God,
> because they, in their time, dim their light by night. . . .
> Hear this, Terah, my father,
> that I announce to you the God, the creator of all,
> not those that we deem gods!
>
> But where is He?
> And what is He?
> —who reddens the sky,
> who goldens the sun,
> and makes light the moon and the stars?
> —who dries up the earth, in the midst of many waters,

[10] I have translated the following text from the "Apokalypse des Abraham" in Paul Riessler, *Altjuedisches Schriſttum ausserhalb der Bibel* (Augsburg, 1928). Cf. also the translation in G. H. Box, *The Apocalypse of Abraham* (New York, 1919). On the *Apocalypse of Abraham* in the con- text of Jewish Apocalyptic, cf. Paul Volz, *Die Eschatologie der juedischen Gemeinde im neutesta- mentlichen Zeitalter* (2nd ed.; Tuebingen, 1934), 48f, and D. S. Russell, *The Method and Message of Jewish Apocalyptic* (Philadelphia, 1964), 60.

who put yourself in the world?
—who sought me out in the confusion of my mind?

May God reveal Himself through Himself!

When thus I spoke to Terah, my father,
    in the court of my house,
The voice of a mighty-one fell from heaven
    in a cloudburst of fire and called:
Abraham! Abraham!

I said: Here am I!
And He said:
    You seek the God of gods,
    the Creator,
    in the mind of your heart.
    I am He!

The apocalyptic passage is carefully organized. There is a first part, closely resembling the dialogue of the Upanishad with its series of questions. When the aetiological chain is exhausted, however, there does not follow an evasive closure of the quest but the flat announcement of the God beyond the intra-cosmic divinities of the chain as the object of the search. When this point is reached, furthermore, the quest is not discontinued because otherwise the head might fall off, but a further search is recognized as useless because knowledge beyond this point is possible only through a theophany. And the quest is consistently climaxed, finally, by the revelatory confrontation of God and man, couched in the symbolism of the Thornbush Episode.

A well-organized text of this kind, with considerable literary ancestry, is not a primitive document. It is a sophisticated analysis of the transition from cosmological truth to the truth of order in existence through the divine-human encounter. It deserves more attention than, as far as I know, it has hitherto received.

The aetiological chain, it would seem at first sight, is introduced only with the intention of rejecting the symbolisms of a strongly cosmological environment. But there is more to it than the explicit denial of a series of divine presences, of "those that we deem gods." For the chain of the cosmological type is, by virtue of the denial of divinity to the elemental and celestial ranks in the hierarchy of being, already in fact transformed into the *via negativa* of the mystic who, ranging through the immanent realms of being, cannot find God until, after their exhaustion, the search comes to its rest in transcendental reality, in the Beyond (*epekeina*) in the Platonic sense. This transformation, however, is possible only because the chain, especially when it assumes the form of the Question enacted as in the Upanishadic dialogues, is already a *via negativa* on which the wanderer presses toward the ultimate ground. Cosmological chain and post-cosmological *via negativa* must be acknowledged to be equivalents.

But why should the chain, whatever its form, not be discarded once the ground is reached through a pneumatic experience, as obviously it was by the author of the Apocalypse before he sat down to write it? The answer is given by the announcement of the creator-god inasmuch as it restores to an otherwise superfluous chain its function by recognizing it as the order of things existent from the creative ground. Hence, the discovery of the ground does not condemn the field of existent things to irrelevance but, on the contrary, establishes it as the reality that derives the meaning of its existence from the ground; and inversely, the *via negativa,* as it ascends over the hierarchy of being, leads toward the ground because the ground is the origin of the hierarchy. The transformation of the chain is a further step of disengagement from the cosmological style of truth: The Babylonian incantation accepted the finished chain as the objective order of intracosmic things; the Brahmanic dialogue moved the Question into the center and made the border of transcendence visible, without however doubting the order of the intracosmic chain; the Essene Apocalypse abolishes the intracosmic order and replaces it by an order of creation that leads to the creator-god.

Still, the order of creation does not lead by itself to the creator, but does so only if in creation there is a "heart" in search of God. The "mind of the heart," in the Apocalypse, is the Aramaic equivalent to the Platonic-Aristotelian *psyche* and the Augustinian *anima animi* as the term designating the site of the search. It is the site where immanence and transcendence meet, but that is itself neither immanent nor transcendent. The text makes the In-Between character of the tension and its site admirably clear: the tension of God seeking man, and man seeking God—the mutuality of seeking and finding one another—the meeting between man and the Beyond of his heart. Since God is present even in the confusion of the heart, preceding and motivating the search itself, the divine Beyond is at the same time a divine Within. Subtly the unknown author traces the movement from Within to Beyond as it passes from the confusion of the mind, to the search of the unknown that is present in the search as it was in the confusion, and further on to the call from Beyond—until what in the beginning was a vague disturbance in that part of reality called the heart has become a clear confrontation in the "Here am I" and "I am He." The Apocalypse is an analytical masterpiece, comparable in rank to the Platonic ascent to the *kalon* in the *Symposion*.

The Apocalypse of Abraham displays a vivid consciousness of epoch. In the story preceding the passage quoted, Terah produces images of gods and Abraham is his helper (1–6). In this function, Abraham witnesses the deterioration of the images through breakage and fire and is moved to reflections by an obsolescence which is the sound basis of the business. He is particularly impressed when in transport a statue's head falls off (1:7–8); that is what happens to the gods whose creator-god is man (3:3; 4:3). The story ominously preludes the spiritual outburst of Chapters 7–8; and the theophany is immediately followed by God's warning to Abraham to leave his father's house, if he wants to avoid death in its sins (8:5). As soon as Abraham has left, Terah and his house are destroyed by fire that falls from heaven (8:6–7). The spiritual is at the same time a physical exodus; and the epoch is convincingly marked by the destruction of the past. To Abraham who now is the father of the future Israel, then, the course of history is revealed, with its perishable aeon of the pagans, and the aeon to come of the just, with the end of times and the judgment (Chs. 9–32).

One should note the brutality of tribal reaction against the brutality of imperial conquest. Even when consciousness becomes epochal and the horizon of history begins to open, the implications of universal humanity will not be readily realized, because the thinker's concrete position in the process, in which he is engaged with his passions, will limit the perspective sometimes severely. This apocalyptic brutality can still be discerned in the New Testament in the blood-dripping avenger-Christ of the Revelation of John (19:11–16). On a less blood-thirsty level, the deformation of historical perspective under the impact of the concrete position became a major concern for the Apostle to the Gentiles. Apparently his Gentile converts were inclined to feel superior to Jews who rejected the gospel though it was originally addressed to them. Paul had to admonish them: "But if some of the branches were broken off, and you, a wild olive shoot, were grafted in their place to share the rich root of the olive tree, do not boast over the branches" (Rom. 11:17–18). Such feelings of superiority are out of order: "Remember that it is not you who sustain the root; the root sustains you" (11:18). The apocalyptic deformation of epochal consciousness observed by Paul has remained a constant in Western civilization. In the eighteenth century, Kant recognized it in the progressivist intellectuals who believed the meaning of history to be fulfilled in their own existence and degraded all past humanity to the status of "contributors" to the glory of the present. In the twentieth century, we are still plagued with the same deformation in the sect of apocalyptic sociologists who have invented the dichotomy of "traditional" and "modern" societies, and still pursue Condorcet's policy of destroying "traditional" societies by "modernizing" them. And we find the apocalyptic deformation in such surprising places as Rudolf Bultmann's thesis that the Old Testament is of no concern to the Christian theologian. The Pauline admonition, "Remember, the root sustains you," cannot be repeated often enough.

Conventionally historians, philosophers, and theologians are concerned with the answers to the Question. What I am trying to do here is to analyze the Question as a constant structure in the experience of reality and, since the experience is part of reality, in the structure of reality itself. A few results can now be formulated:

(1) In the three cases analyzed, the Question is recognizably the constant in various modes of experience.

(2) The cases, furthermore, are not random manifestations of the constant but reveal, in their succession, a definite pattern of meaning, inasmuch as the Question itself emerges from the compact mode of cosmological truth into the differentiated truth of existence: (a) In the Babylonian incantation, the aetiological chain is the compact symbol that has been engendered as an answer to the yet-undifferentiated Question; (b) in the Upanishadic dialogue, the Question itself is enacted but stops short of noetic or pneumatic differentiations; (c) in the Apocalypse, the pneumatic differentiation is enacted, accompanied by the consciousness of epoch. The field of history opens, but the differentiation of its Mystery is cut short by the apocalyptically predictive answer.

(3) The cases, finally, reveal the structures in reality that are experienced not as givens beyond question, but as raising the questions in search of answers. They are: (a) The existence of the cosmos; (b) the hierarchy and diversification of being; (c) the experience of questioning as the constituent of humanity; (d) the leap in existential truth through noetic and pneumatic illuminations of consciousness; (e) the process of history in which the differentiations of questioning consciousness and the leaps in truth occur; and (f) the eschatological movement in the process beyond its structure.

The results, once they are formulated in this manner, will shed light on further problems. The structures enumerated under (3) are not coordinate, but variously related to one another in the process of the Question as it differentiates. The questions concerning the existence of the cosmos and the essence of its order (3a and 3b) differentiate earlier than the questions concerning the process of consciousness (3e and 3f), and the two groups are linked historically by the differentiation of questioning consciousness and its noetic and pneumatic illumination (3c and 3d). In the nineteenth century, in the climate of a doxography which had separated the symbols from the experiences which engendered them, an interpretation of this sequence could hardly go beyond such clichés as "static-dynamic." Even today one still can read of the ancients who had a "static" conception and philosophy of the cosmos, while the moderns have overcome such backwardness by a "dynamic" conception of reality that comprehends the astro- and geophysical process, the evolution of plant and animal life, and the evolution and history of man. Such categorizations on the doctrinal level transform the process of differentiation and its phases into a true-false game played with propositions by an hypostatized history. They ignore the empirical fact that man's questioning experience of reality is structurally always complete as far back as our historical sources go. The existence and essential order of the cosmos, it is true, predominate in the primary experience, but the cosmos is far from being conceived as a static entity that always had, and always will have, its present structure. The mytho-speculative constructions concerning the origin of the cosmos and its contents, as well as the rituals of cosmogonic renewal, symbolize the experience of a process in which the structure came to be what it is at present and in which it also may disintegrate again. The cosmos, and its order, is experienced not as "static," but as precariously stabilized in a Now that may be engulfed by the process from which it emerged. What keeps the order in being is man's participation in the cosmic-divine process through rituals of renewal. All of the structures enumerated under (3), thus, are present in the questioning experience even in its compact cosmological modes.

The Question is complete even in the cosmological style of truth. Nevertheless, the differentiation of noetic and pneumatic insights, of the historical dimension of human consciousness, and the eschatological movement in reality, affect the experience of a precariously stable cosmos by shifting the accents from stability to precariousness. Nothing, of course, has changed in the cosmos at large, setting aside such natural catastrophes as great floods, prolonged droughts, earthquakes, volcanic eruptions, and the observation of the equinoctial precession, which always serve as reminders that the cosmos is not altogether stable. The sharper awareness of precariousness is caused by disturbing changes in the process not of nature but of history. Since society is part of cosmic reality, a major breakdown of social order as it occurs in the

First Intermediate Period of Egypt can impair the general trust in cosmic order, as well as the faith in its symbolization through the hitherto accepted myth. When the process of history represents the process of reality pre-eminently, the events of history rather than of nature become crucial as criteria of order and disorder in the cosmos.

The responses to the differentiated awareness vary widely. One response, the disintegration of trust in the cosmic order, becomes manifest in the litera-ture of skepticism and alienation in Egypt, in the late third millennium B.C. The same period, however, also witnesses the rise of the historiogenetic speculation which extrapolates the imperial order to its divine-cosmic origin, endowing the historically concrete order with an eschatological index. The most elaborate construction of this type, related to its Sumerian-Babylonian predecessors, is the Israelite historiogenesis *ab creatione mundi.* The general erosion of faith emanating from historical events, thus, is countered by the mytho-speculative symbolization of specific faith in a concrete social order as ultimate; and this feat is accomplished by blending compactly the trust in a not-yet-differentiated truth of existential order into the contingent order of society. When this attempt to save the stability of cosmic order by stopping history is exposed to the further vicissitudes of history, the compact symbolism dissociates into the two realities of apocalyptic consciousness, *i.e.,* a senseless present history to be followed, in metastatic expectation, by a divinely ordered, perfect state of existence. Moreover, problems comparable to those of the imperial Near East can arise on the pre-imperial level of social order. From the archaeological side it has recently been suggested that the spiritual out-burst of the Buddha (*ca.* 500 B.C.) is a response to the expansion of "kingdoms," with their creation of a court and urban center of culture, from the West of India to the Ganges valley. The disturbance of social order on the village and tribal level, accompanied by the glaring discrepancy between the life-style of a luxurious court and the misery of the surrounding countryside, are supposed to have been motivating experiences in the Buddha's search for salvation through escape from the suffering of this world into the divine void of the Nirvana.[11] The Buddha's response to the tension in reality resembles the apocalyptic split of consciousness, but the Buddha could be more consistently radical because in his situation he did not have to contend with a millennial representation of man's order of existence in this world by the cosmological empires, or with an historiogenetic symbolism that raised imperial to the rank

[11] Walter A. Fairservis, Jr., *The Roots of Ancient India. The Archaeology of Early Indian Civilization* (London, 1971), 379 ff. See especially "Table 9. The Movement of Urbanization from West to East in Northern India," p. 379.

of cosmic order, or with noetic and pneumatic revelations that endowed the structure of this world with divine sanction. Once the intracosmic divinities of an agricultural society had been rejected, there was no differentiated experience that would have prevented him from taking the shortcut to the divine void behind the world.

No more in Buddhist consciousness than in Upanishadic does the Question concerning the mystery of the process fully differentiate in India. History obtrudes itself, it is true, but its problems are deformed by the fallacious infinity of a cosmic process that has split off from the void. In the Near Eastern and Mediterranean area, where the differentiation does occur, the historical events cast a shadow so dark that history must be stopped, either historiogenetically or apocalyptically, if the order of the cosmos is to be saved. The "balance of consciousness" achieved by the classic philosophers who could face the Mystery is a rare event indeed, carefully to be preserved as a strand in Western civilization where it has to contend with the unbalanced strand of the "stop-history" movement that has also remained a constant into our present. I have previously quoted the passage from Hegel in which he commends his construction of history as a theodicy superior to that of Leibniz because it is concretely linked to the "absolute epoch" marked by Christ. The full import of the passage can now be better understood. What Hegel found in Christ, or rather in Paul, was a differentiation of the Question so comprehensive that it included the historical dimension of humanity. This completeness of differentiation is the criterion of the "absolute epoch." But in Paul he also found the apocalyptic "stop-history" movement; and since the metastatic expectation of the Second Coming had not been fulfilled, Hegel was going to stop history now by his System in which the self-reflective *Geist* comes to its fulfillment and thereby history to its end. The self-interpretation of the attempt as a "theodicy" leaves no doubt about its motive: It is the same anxiety that motivates the older historiogenetic and apocalyptic symbolisms; and it is induced by the same type of imperial events, in Hegel's case by the French Revolution and the Napoleonic Empire. Such disorder cannot be admitted to be the misery it is; the God who permits it must, in this devious way, pursue an ulterior purpose of order; and the order to come cannot be admitted to be just as contingent as the one that is now being shattered, but must be an ultimate order in the eschatological sense. The construction is meant to assuage the anxiety of a man who cannot face the Mystery of Reality.

To face the Mystery of Reality means to live in the faith that is the substance of things hoped for and the proof of things unseen (Heb. 11:1). When the eschatological "things," hoped for but unseen, are metastatically deformed into an eschatological index bestowed on things to be expected and seen in "history"; and when the "faith" that is the substance and proof of things eschatological is correspondingly deformed into an Hegelian, or Marxian, or Comtean "System of Science" whose evocative magic is meant to realize the expectations "historically;" the Question can be more fully differentiated than it has been ever before in the history of mankind, and yet the Mystery will be destroyed. The destruction of the Mystery becomes manifest in the contemporary dogmatomachy of "answers."

§ 6. The Process of History and the Process of the Whole

The Question as a structure in experience is part of, and pertains to, the In-Between stratum of reality, the Metaxy. There is no answer to the Question other than the Mystery as it becomes luminous in the acts of questioning. Any attempt to find an answer by developing a doctrine concerning spatio-temporal events will destroy the In-Between structure of man's humanity. The "stop-history" Systems which dominate the contemporary scene can maintain the appearance of truth only by an act of violence, i.e., by prohibiting questions concerning the premises and by making the prohibition a formal part of the System. This interdict on the Question is the symptom of a self-contraction which makes the existentially open participation in the process of reality impossible. *peace fully, creatively*

Though the tension between openness toward reality and contraction of the self is a human problem at all times, it will assume the specific forms just adumbrated only when the historical dimension of humanity has differentiated. In the Ecumenic Age, the differentiation had proceeded so far that it engendered the symbolic form of historiography, but not so far that the implications of history as the process of universal humanity could fully unfold: It takes time, to be measured in centuries and millennia, to acquire the empirical knowledge that inevitably lies at the basis of an understanding of the historical process, and still more time to penetrate the accumulated materials analytically. The ecumenic empires, it is true, had enlarged the knowledge of both the human habitat and the mankind inhabiting it, so that at a relatively early date a work like the Herodotean Periegesis had become possible; but this larger horizon was still so limited that a second ecumene could develop in China at the same time, without the two ecumenes knowing of each other. By the time of Augustine, eight centuries after Herodotus, the regions of differentiation were still so far apart in knowledge that the saint's empirical picture of history, though it had expanded by the Israelite-Christian dimension, has today a distinctly provincial flavor, because it is tied to the ecumenic horizon of the Roman Empire. And today, fifteen centuries after Augustine, even though the ecumenic horizon has become global and the temporal horizon has expanded into unexpected depths, the empirical knowledge of the process is still so incomplete that every day brings surprises in the form of new archaeological discoveries, while the experiential penetration of the materials is badly lagging behind. As a matter of fact, empirical knowledge increases so rapidly that the historical constructions which reflect a deformed existence crumble through the obsolescence of their materials rather than through the analysis of deformed existence. The "stop-history" Systems, for instance, though barely 150 years old, and still dominating the "climate of opinion," have become hopelessly incompatible with the present state of the historical sciences; or, in an even briefer time, the developments in archaeology, pre-history, and radio-carbon dating have completely upset the idea that "high-civilizations" have their origin in the conquest of agricultural settlements by nomadic tribes, an idea which still prevailed when I was a student in the 1920s.

These remarks are meant to bring into focus the meaning of existentially open participation in the process of history. History, it appears, has a long breath. If one realizes that we are still grappling today, and still inconclusively, with the problems set by the differentiations of consciousness in the Ecumenic Age, one may feel that nothing much has happened during the last 2,500 years. While it would be wrong to translate this sentiment into the doctrinaire conclusion that there is nothing new under the sun, the feeling has its importance as a safeguard against the human weakness of elevating one's own present into the purpose of history. It will always be a wholesome exercise to reflect that 2,500 years from now our own time will belong to as remote a past as that of Heraclitus, the Buddha, and Confucius in relation to our present. The further reflection on what will be worth remembering about our present, and why, will establish the perspective in which it must be placed: Our present, like any present, is a phase in the flux of divine presence in which we, as all men before and after us, participate. The horizon of the Mystery in time that opens with the ecumenic expansion in space is still the Question that presents itself to the presently living; and what will be worth remembering about the present, will be the mode of consciousness in our response to the Question.

The Question remains the same, but the modes of asking the Question change. Things happen in history indeed. This last sentence, however, is loosely formulated. More precisely one would have to say: What happens "in" history is the very process of differentiating consciousness that constitutes history. This structure of the process creates the peculiar problem that the empirical knowledge of the process has to be included in the mode of response, once man's existence has become luminous for its historical dimension. The obligation has its strange aspects inasmuch as history is not a finite collection of events given once for all, but a process that continues to produce itself through the men who participate in it. Setting aside for the moment all other variables that affect the issue, the "empirical knowledge" of history in A.D. 500 will comprise one thousand years more of the process than in 500 B.C. and one thousand years less than in A.D. 1500. The observation of this structure is commonplace ever since the Ecumenic Age, but the responses vary widely. At the lowest level there is the view of the "present" as a kind of machinery that grinds out an ever lengthening "past." I call it the "sausage view" of history. It induces the frequently heard complaint that the writing of history is breaking down under the burden of steadily accumulating materials. But that would be too much to be hoped for. More interesting is the contest between pagan and Judaeo-Christian historians that I have described under the title of historiomachy in the chapter on "Historiogenesis." Jewish and Christian thinkers consider their history to be of a quality superior to that of the pagans, because it goes much farther back in time and is more reliably documented; the longer history is the better one. In spite of its comic aspects, with Moses accorded temporal priority before Apollo, the contest makes sense, because the greater length of the past is meant to support the greater truth of the God from whom the present ultimately derives. The historiomachy marks the transition from mytho-speculation to the open horizon of history proper; the "empirical knowledge" of history has to enter the response to the Question because history has been discovered as the horizon of the divine Mystery. A third possibility is presented by the thinkers of the "stop-history" movement. Both Hegel and Comte were of the opinion that history must run its course for a certain length of time before it has supplied the material past on which a thinker can base "scientific" propositions concerning the order that governs the process. By now, *i.e.,* about A.D. 1800, the course has run long enough to reveal its meaning and to make the enterprise of the System possible. Marx understands Hegel quite well when he infers that the time has come for man to take matters in his own hand: The older variety of history, now coming to its end, has produced the Marxian superman who takes God back into himself; from now on the metastatic superman will realize himself and produce true history through revolutionary action.

In the cases quoted, the respective thinkers try to resolve problems which belong to the In-Between reality of divine-human participation by projecting them into the time of the external world. Inevitably the structure of the process is distorted, if not destroyed, when the flux of presence is reduced to immanent time. No further criticism is necessary. Nevertheless, the cases cannot simply be dismissed as fallacious constructions, for they show that at critical junctures the "length of time" intrudes itself as a problem. Apparently there is something to it; if it is not treated properly, it will make itself felt in misconstructions. Especially the third case, that of the Systems which declare history to have run long enough to reveal its mystery, is of immediate concern to the present analysis, which tries to explore the Mystery that has no end in time. The Systems, with their ramifications into secondary and tertiary epigonic debates, dominate the contemporary scene; it is not enough to show that they are vitiated by grotesque misconstructions of reality; one must also show what the structure is that obviously imposes itself but has been misconstrued. The crucial point is the interdict on the Question. The thinkers prohibit questioning, using the argument that enough historical time has lapsed to differentiate the Question so fully that now it can be answered definitely by the System; they do not deny, however, that considerable time, to be counted in millennia, has been required to let the revelation of truth reach its present state of fulfillment. What, then, is the relation of the process of differentiation to the lapse of immanent time?

To formulate the problem means practically to resolve it. The divine-human In-Between of historically differentiating experience is founded in the consciousness of concrete human beings in concrete bodies on the concrete earth in the concrete universe. Resuming the earlier reflections on the variety of time-dimensions: There is no "length of time" in which things happen; there is only the reality of things which has a time-dimension. The various strata of reality with their specific time-dimensions, furthermore, are not autonomous entities but form, through the relations of foundation and organization, the hierarchy of being which extends from the inorganic stratum, through the vegetative and animal realms, to the existence of man in his tension toward the divine ground of being. There is a process of the Whole of which the In-Between reality with its process of history is no more than a part, though the very important part in which the process of the Whole becomes luminous for the eschatological movement beyond its own structure. Within this process of the Whole, then, some things, as for instance the earth, outlast other things, as for instance the individual human beings who inhabit the earth; and what we call "time" without further qualifications is the mode of lastingness peculiar to the astrophysical universe which permits its dimension of time to be measured by its movements in space. But even this ultimate mode of lastingness to which as a measure we refer the lasting of all other things, is not a "time" in which things happen, but the time-dimension of a thing within the Whole that also comprises the divine reality whose mode of lastingness we express by such symbols as "eternity." Things do not happen in the astrophysical universe; the universe, together with all things founded in it, happens in God.

The conception of a "length of time" in which history happens, thus, is burdened with a double fallacy. In the first place, the time-dimension of the astrophysical universe which serves as the measure for the lasting of all things in the cosmos is hypostatized into an independent entity. And second, the lasting of the universe is mistakenly supposed to be the lasting of the Whole. Because of this burden, the conception obscures the very structure of reality it tries to clarify.

(1) Concerning the first fallacy: Though there is no "time" in which "history" happens, there are the strata in the hierarchy of being in which the process of consciousness is founded. There is no flux of presence in the Metaxy without its foundation in the biophysical existence of man on earth in the universe. By virtue of their founding character, the lower strata reach into the stratum of human consciousness, not as its cause but as its condition. Only because the strata of reality participate in one another, through the relations of foundation and organization, in the order of the cosmos, can and must the time-dimensions of the strata be related to one another, with the time-dimension of the universe furnishing the ultimately founding measure. The primary relation among the strata of reality is obscured by the diversion of attention to the secondary relation of the time-dimensions. This primary relation, however, is of fundamental importance in the present context, because it reveals the process of history to extend structurally, through participation, into the other strata of reality, including the physical universe.

(2) The insight into the mutual participation of the strata will now help to dissolve the second fallacy. The physical universe as the ultimate foundation for the higher strata in the hierarchy of being cannot be identified as the ultimate reality of the Whole, because in the stratum of consciousness we experience the presence of divine reality as the constituent of humanity. In man's consciousness, the foundational movement within reality from the physical depth becomes luminous for the creative constitution of all reality from the

height of the divine ground. As far as the modes of lasting are concerned we
have to state therefore: In the order of foundation from the depth, the time-
dimension of the universe comprehends the time-dimensions of the other
strata in the hierarchy of being; in the order of creation from the height, the
divine mode of lasting that we symbolize as eternity comprehends the time-
dimensions of the other strata of reality, including the universe.

Once the fallacies are removed, the hierarchy of being comes into view,
not as a number of strata one piled on top of the other, but as movement of
reality from the apeirontic depth up to man, through as many levels of the
hierarchy as can be discerned empirically, and as the countermovement of
creative organization from the divine height down, with the Metaxy of man's
consciousness as the site where the movement of the Whole becomes luminous
for its eschatological direction. When the historical dimension of humanity
has differentiated, the Question thus turns back to the process of the Whole as
it becomes luminous for its directional movement in the process of history.
The Mystery of the historical process is inseparable from the Mystery of a
reality which brings forth the universe and the earth, plant and animal life on
earth, and ultimately man and his consciousness. Such reflections are definitely
not new, but they express, in differentiated form, the experience of divine-
cosmic order that has motivated the oldest cosmogonic symbolisms; and that
is precisely what they should do, if universal humanity in history is real and
not an illusion. More explicitly, they are the mode of questioning engendered
in the contemporary situation by a philosopher's resistance to the distortion
and destruction of humanity committed by the "stop-history" Systems. They
are an act of open participation in the process of both history and the Whole.

Index

Abel-Remusat, J.-P., 3ff.
Abraham, 14ff., 99, 257
Abraham, Apocalypse of, 322ff.
Aemilius Paullus, 125, 131ff., 206
Aeschylus, 104, 180, 252
Agesilaus, 121
Akhenaton, 96, 147ff., 283
Al-Bairuni, 138
Alexander, 31, 35, 41, 67, 109, 116–17, 119ff., 132, 146, 153ff., 205ff., 212
Altaner, Berthold, 259
Amasis, 180
Amenhemet I, 94
Amon Hymns, 9, 147ff.
Anaxagoras, 189
Anaxarchus, 159
Anaximander, 40ff., 174ff., 185, 188ff., 194, 201, 215ff., 226, 241ff., 269
Anaximenes, 42
Antalcidas, 119
Antiochus IV Epiphanes, 93, 168, 206
Apollodorus, 110
Apollodotus, 168ff.
Aristotle, 11ff., 38, 75, 80, 125, 127ff., 146, 155, 161ff., 177, 187ff., 196, 216ff., 232, 236ff., 246, 251ff., 258, 298
Arrian, 153, 156
Arberry, Arthur J., 143
Ardashir, 138, 140
Aristarchus of Samos, 43
Aristobulos, 34
Arnim, Hans von, 43
Artabanus, 180
Artembares, 181
Asoka, 166ff.
Astyages, 118, 181
Athenagoras, 259
Attalus II of Pergamon, 110
Augustine, 47, 88, 108ff., 138, 146, 172ff., 178, 180, 195, 268, 324, 330

Basilides, 21
Barker, Ernest, 157

Baur, F. Chr., 138
Bayet, Jean, 63
Bayle, Pierre, 25
Behistun Inscription, 69, 149ff.
Bergson, Henri, 75
Berossus, 67, 91ff., 109
Bianchi, U., 25
Boeckh, A., 133
Boehme, Robert, 203
Bohner, Hermann, 281
Book of the Torah, the Prophets, and the Writings, 49ff.
Bornkamm, Guenther, 240
Box, G. H., 322
Bright, John, 49
Brihadaranyaka Upanishad, 319ff.
Buddha, 139, 141, 328
Bultmann, Rudolf, 311ff., 326
Burckhardt, Jacob, 192ff., 215, 219, 224
Burkitt, F. C., 138

Callisthenes, 159ff.
Cambyses, 118, 150
Caquot, André, 204
Cassander, 159
Cato, 131
Chandragupta, 165ff.
Chang, Kwang-Chih, 275
Chares of Mitylene, 159
Chavannes, Edouard, 274
Chêng, Tê-K'un, 275
Ch'in Shih-huang-ti, 207, 276
Chrysippus, 40
Chuang Chou, 302
Cicero, 40ff., 44ff., 53, 128
Cleanthes, 40ff., 46ff.
Cleisthenes, 118
Clement of Alexandria, 67, 80, 112ff.
Commodus, 113
Comte, Auguste, 64, 68, 192, 254, 260, 330
Condorcet, 199, 260
Confucius, 281, 292
Creel, H. G., 275

Croesus, 118, 178ff.
Crouzel, Henri, 30
Curtius, 160
Cusanus, Nicolaus, 210
Cyrus, 118, 149ff., 178ff., 212ff.

Daniel, Book of, 24, 26, 71, 115, 146, 183, 239, 270, 301
Daniel, Glyn, 282
Daniélou, Jean, 30
Darius I, 118, 150, 212
Darius Codomannus, 146, 154, 158
David, 95, 151, 212
Dawson, Raymond, 286
Dechend, Hertha von, 81
Declaration of Independence, 47
Demetrius of Phalerum, 131
Demetrius (Bactria), 166
Democritus, 189
Deutero-Isaiah, 26, 116, 212ff., 234
Dicaearchus, 127
Diodorus, 91, 107ff., 110, 164
Diodotus, 167
Diogenes (the Cynic), 30
Diogenes Laertius, 30
Dionysius of Halicarnassus, 110ff.
Dittenberger, W., 133
Driver, G. R., 204

Eberhard, Wolfram, 275, 280
Eckhart, Meister, 321
Eggermont, P. H. L., 166
Ehrenzweig, Victor, 165
Eliade, Mircea, 73, 254
Empedocles, 189–90
Engels, Friedrich, 4
Ennius, 108ff.
Enuma elish, 61, 291
Eratosthenes, 102, 156
Eucratides, 159
Euhemerus, 67, 101ff., 107ff.
Eunus, 131
Eusebius of Caesarea, 92
Euthydemus of Magnesia, 166ff.
Evangelium Veritatis, 20
Ezra, 49

Fairservis, Walter A., 328
Feng Hu Tzu, 306ff.
Festugière, A.-J., 199
Feuerbach, Ludwig, 259ff.
Ficht, Johann Gottlieb, 261
Foerster, Werner, 25
Fontenelle, Bernard, 81
Frend, W. H. C., 263

Freud, Sigmund, 5
Fritz, Kurt von, 121
Furley, D. J., 199

Galilei, Galileo, 203
Gilgamesh Epic, 203–204
Gilson, Etienne, 15
Glasenapp, Helmuth von, 321
Glatzer, N. N., 271
Goez, Werner, 183
Graham, A. E., 286
Granet, Marcel, 275, 283, 292

Haardt, Robert, 25
Hatshepsut, 69ff.
Hecataeus of Abdera, 108
Hegel, 7, 21, 57, 64, 66ff., 74ff., 173, 192, 195, 214, 223ff., 254ff., 260ff., 262ff., 279, 308ff., 329
Heidegger, Martin, 74ff., 175ff.
Hengel, Martin, 30, 52, 183
Henningsen, Manfred, 183
Hephaestion, 159
Heraclitus, 174ff., 228
Herodotus, 103ff., 150, 175, 178ff., 183, 194, 197, 205, 261, 312, 330
Hesiod, 36, 42, 61, 89, 103ff., 191, 306
Heurgon, Jacques, 63
Herzfeld, Ernst, 149
Heuss, Andreas, 63
Hinz, Walther, 25
Hippias, 118
Hitler, Adolf, 254
Homer, 36, 42, 191, 201ff.
Hooke, S. H., 49
Hyde, Thomas, 25
Hymn of the Pearl, 24ff.

Isaiah, 26ff., 115
Isocrates, 119ff.

Jacobsen, Thorkild, 65ff.
Jacoby, F., 108, 160
Jason of Cyrene, 51
Jaspers, Karl, 2ff., 309ff.
Jeremiah, 90
Joachim of Flora, 268
John, Gospel of, 13ff., 47, 53
John, Revelation of, 10, 325
Jonas, Hans, 24ff.
Josephus, Flavius, 85, 102, 111ff.
Jung, C. G., 211
Justin, 165
Justinian, 29

Kant, Immanuel, 77, 176, 224, 325
Kortilya, 166
Koenig, F. W., 149
Kramer, Samuel Noah, 319

Lactantius, 108
Lao-tzu, 275
Leibniz, 73ff., 329
Lesky, Albin, 202ff.
Levenson, Joseph R., 293
Livy, 275, 312
Lubac, Henri de, 30
L. Mummius, 125
Lucretius, 307ff.
Luther, Martin, 88ff.
Lycortas, 125

Manetho, 67, 91ff., 109
Mani, 138ff., 143
Marcus Aurelius, 80, 133
Marx, Karl, 4, 68, 192, 253ff., 261, 306, 330
Maspero, Henri, 275, 279, 290
Matthew, Gospel of, 99, 134
Megasthenes, 168, 207
Memphite Theology, 49, 68, 291, 317
Menander, 168ff.
Mencius, 280ff.
Menes, 93
Mishnah, 55
Mithridates, 169
Mohammed, 142ff.
Momigliano, Arnaldo, 210
More, Thomas, 107, 210
Moses, 5, 12, 14ff., 147ff., 229, 284, 323
Mycerinus, 180ff.

Nabonidus, 118
Naqsh-i-Rustam Inscription, 150ff.
Nehemia, 49
Nietzsche, Friedrich, 176, 231, 255, 261
Noah, 99

Oesterley, W. O. E., 49
Opitz, Peter-Joachim, 275
Oppenheim, A. Leo, 83, 93
Origen, 30, 259ff.
Otto, Rudolf, 321
Otto of Freising, 268

Palermo Stone, 92ff.
Parmenides, 60, 148, 228
Parmenio, 154
Paul, 34, 134ff., 140, 212, 239ff., 301ff., 310, 325, 329
Persepolis daiva Inscription, 150ff.

Petrarca, 268
Philip II of Macedon, 116, 119ff., 154
Philip V of Macedon, 121
Philo, 29ff., 41
Pindar, 112
Pirke Aboth, 54ff.
Plato, 9, 11ff., 27, 31, 36ff., 74ff., 87ff., 116, 125, 127ff., 162, 175, 177, 183ff., 187ff., 195ff., 199, 216ff., 239, 242ff., 249ff., 259, 301ff., 306, 323
Plotinus, 9, 231, 234
Plutarch, 25, 34, 155ff., 163ff., 165
Poimandres, 19
Polotsky, H. J., 138ff.
Polybius, 115, 117ff., 136, 141, 146, 155, 207ff., 222
Polycrates, 180
Pritchard, James B., 69
Nefer-rohu, Prophecy of, 94, 100
Proverbs, 51ff.
Psalm 139, p. 100
Pseudo-Aristotelian De Mundo, 198ff.
Ptolemy VI Philometor, 34
Puech, Henri-Charles, 138
Pushyamitra Sunga, 166, 168
Pyrrho, 298
Pythagoras, 40, 87

Quispel, Gilles, 24ff.

Rad, Gerhard von, 49ff., 52, 84ff., 88ff., 96ff.
Riessler, Paul, 322
Rodwell, J. M., 143
Royal Psalms, 49
Russell, D. S., 25, 322

Sade (Marquis de), 261
Santillana, Giorgio de, 81
Sartre, Jean-Paul, 228
Schachermeyr, Fritz, 157ff., 165
Schelling, F. W. J., 21, 74
Schiller, Friedrich, 4
Schmidt, C., 138ff.
Schnabel, Paul, 85
Schneider, Carl, 38, 45
Scipio Aemilianus, 125, 132
Seleucus I Nicator, 166, 206
Seleucus II, 167
Shankara, 321
Ssu-ma Ch'ien, 274ff.
Ssu-ma T'an, 276
Sumerian King List, 7, 65ff., 68, 73, 83ff., 95, 101, 275
Suppiluliumas, 69
Stalin, 128, 254

Sznycer, Maurice, 204

Table of the Nations, 97ff.
Tarn, W. W., 154ff., 164ff., 167
Tertullian, 46ff., 259
Thackeray, H. St. J., 85
Thales, 40
Theagenes of Rhegium, 36
Theophilus, 259
Thomas, Acts of, 24ff.
Thomas Aquinas, 15, 233
Thomas, F. W., 166
Thucydides, 181ff., 261
Thutmose III, 147, 203
Timaeus, 106
Tiridates, 167
Tjan Tjoe Som, 289ff.
Torah, 30ff., 33ff., 49ff., 53ff.
Toynbee, Arnold J., 3ff., 173ff., 311
Turin Papyrus, 91ff.
Tusratta, 69

Ussher (Bishop), 223

Valentinus, 20ff., 24

Volz, Paul, 322
Varro, 130
Vergil, 111
Vico, Giambattista, 5, 295

Walbank, F. W., 121
Watson, Burton, 274
Weber, Max, 285ff.
Weber-Schaefer, Peter, 275, 286, 302
Weissbach, F. H., 149
Whitehead, Alfred N., 176
Wildung, Dietrich, 203ff.
Wilson, John A., 69, 94, 203ff.
Wolfson, Harry Austryn, 29ff.
Woodcock, George, 167
Wu-ti, 276

Xenophanes, 228
Xenophon, 119, 121, 160
Xerxes, 150ff., 179ff., 205

Zaehner, R. C., 25
Zeno, 40, 46ff., 155ff.
Zoroaster, 138ff., 141, 149, 231, 298